GOD AND PROGRESS

OXFORD HISTORICAL MONOGRAPHS

The *Oxford Historical Monographs* series publishes some of the best
Oxford University doctoral theses on historical topics, especially
those likely to engage the interest of a broad academic readership.

Editors

God and Progress

Religion and History in British Intellectual Culture, 1845–1914

JOSHUA BENNETT

OXFORD
UNIVERSITY PRESS

OXFORD

UNIVERSITY PRESS

Great Clarendon Street, Oxford, OX2 6DP,
United Kingdom

Oxford University Press is a department of the University of Oxford.
It furthers the University's objective of excellence in research, scholarship,
and education by publishing worldwide. Oxford is a registered trade mark of
Oxford University Press in the UK and in certain other countries

First Edition published in 2019

Impression: 1

Published in the United States of America by Oxford University Press
198 Madison Avenue, New York, NY 10016, United States of America

British Library Cataloguing in Publication Data

Data available

Library of Congress Control Number: 2018956928

ISBN 978-0-19-883772-5

Printed and bound in Great Britain by
Clays Ltd, Elcograf S.p.A.

In memory of Rory Allan
(1991–2016)

Acknowledgements

The support of many different institutions and individuals over the space of a decade has enabled me to write this book. The Arts and Humanities Research Council funded the 2015 doctoral thesis upon which it is based, and before that the Master of Studies degree from which it grew, on the recommendation of the Oxford History Faculty. The Deutscher Akademischer Austauschdienst awarded me a stipend which facilitated a period of research in Germany in 2013. A Scouloudi Fellowship at the Institute of Historical Research in London, and additional support from the Oxford University Vice-Chancellors' Fund and the Andrew Smith Memorial Foundation, furnished me with ideal conditions in which to complete the dissertation. By appointing me to a one-year lectureship in History at a crucial moment, the President and Fellows of St John's College, Oxford, allowed me to begin the work of revising the text for publication. By electing me to a Junior Research Fellowship in 2016, the Dean, Chapter, and Students of Christ Church, Oxford, gave me the opportunity to complete it. Christ Church, of which I was also a member during my undergraduate and graduate studies, has proved an intellectually serious and convivial society in which to work over the years.

Institutions are made by the people who inhabit them, and I have been very fortunate in those I have known at Oxford and elsewhere who have helped to shape this project at several stages. My greatest intellectual debt is to Jane Garnett, my doctoral supervisor, and latterly advising editor. I have benefited deeply from her warm encouragement, bracing criticisms, and unfailing good sense, as have so many of her pupils before me. At Christ Church, Brian Young has been consistently generous with ideas formed from his remarkable breadth of reading. Antonia Fitzpatrick, William Whyte, and Hannah Skoda were exemplary in helping me to find my way through a year of undergraduate teaching at St John's. William was furthermore an astute reader of my doctoral research at an early stage of its formation, as was Matthew Grimley; Michael Bentley also offered helpful perspectives as I started out. At a later point, Jeremy Morris and Pietro Corsi were engaging DPhil examiners, whose perceptive criticisms I have taken into account in revising the manuscript. The anonymous reader's report for the Oxford Historical Monographs series has been an invaluable aid to the same end. John Watts and David Parrott, as chairs of the Oxford Historical Monographs committee, and Cathryn Steele at Oxford University Press, have all helped to steer the book into production.

I am also very appreciative of having been given opportunities to discuss aspects of the research for this book with audiences at the Director's and Modern Religious History Seminars at the Institute of Historical Research; the Modern British History Seminars in Oxford and Cambridge; the Oxford Historiography Seminar; the twentieth transatlantic doctoral seminar at the German Historical Institute in Washington DC; and, in the closing stages, the notably rewarding 2017 Summer History Institute at Dartmouth College, New Hampshire. I am very grateful to the convenors and chairs of those meetings for invitations which enabled me to refine the argument and its presentation in more ways than I can summarily enumerate. In this regard I should particularly mention Lawrence Goldman; John Wolffe; Simon Skinner; Jonathan Parry; Renaud Morieux; Richard F. Wetzell; Anna von der Goltz; Udi Greenberg; and Darrin McMahon, in addition to those I have already named. If no historical research can take place without conversation, still less can it proceed without the work of archivists and librarians. I am grateful to many in Britain and Germany, and above all to those of the Bodleian and Christ Church Libraries. The Christ Church librarians have been especially patient in retrieving seemingly innumerable works by Victorian clergymen from the spatial recesses to which twentieth-century intellectual change removed them.

The time I have spent writing this book and its several antecedents has been enriched by discussions with a number of other students of nineteenth-century subjects, and with scholars working in other fields: I hope they will accept my apologies for not naming them all. Paul and Joyce Cullen in Edinburgh, and Paul Cavill in Cambridge, generously offered hospitality during research trips to those cities. Judith Loades has been a steadfast source of helpful advice and encouragement. I owe much to other friends in many places, and a great deal to my parents, Max and Kim, and my sisters, Poppy and Lily. I dedicate the book to the memory of a friend and fellow-appreciator of Victorian historiography who did not live to read it, but who I hope would have found something worthwhile in its pages.

Joshua Bennett

Christ Church, Oxford
September, 2018

Contents

List of Abbreviations

BC	*British Critic*
BEM	*Blackwood's Edinburgh Magazine*
BQR	*British Quarterly Review*
CGHH	*The Century Guild Hobby Horse*
CHR	*Christian Remembrancer*
CM	*The Churchman*
CR	*Contemporary Review*
DR	*Dublin Review*
DUM	*Dublin University Magazine*
ECR	*Eclectic Review*
ENR	*English Review*
ER	*Edinburgh Review*
FM	*Fraser's Magazine*
FR	*Fortnightly Review*
GW	*Good Words*
HCE	H. T. Buckle, *History of civilization in England* (2 vols, London, 1857–1861)
HEM	W. E. H. Lecky, *History of European morals from Augustus to Charlemagne* (2 vols, London, 1869)
HLC	H. H. Milman, *History of Latin Christianity: including that of the popes to the pontificate of Nicolas V* (6 vols, London, 1854–1855)
HRE	W. E. H. Lecky, *History of the rise and influence of the spirit of rationalism in Europe* (2 vols, London, 1865)
JSL	*Journal of Sacred Literature*
LEC	A. P. Stanley, *Lectures on the history of the Eastern Church: with an introduction on the study of ecclesiastical history*, 2nd edn (London, 1862) [first edition 1861]
LQR	*London Quarterly Review*
MM	*Macmillan's Magazine*
NBR	*North British Review*
NC	*Nineteenth Century*
NQR	*New Quarterly Review*
NR	*National Review*
ODNB	H. C. G. Matthew, B. Harrison, L. Goldman, and D. Cannadine (eds), *Oxford Dictionary of National Biography* (2004–) [online edition; last accessed 20 September, 2018]
OED	*Oxford English Dictionary* [online edition, last accessed 20 September, 2018]
PR	*Prospective Review*
QR	*Quarterly Review*

SR   *Saturday Review*
TR   *Theological Review: a journal of religious thought and life*
WR   *Westminster Review*

For information concerning periodicals' editorial sympathies, and (unless otherwise stated) for the identification of anonymous contributors, I have relied on the
online edition of W. E. Houghton (ed.), *The Wellesley Index to Victorian Periodicals, 1824–1900* (5 vols, Toronto and London, 1966–1989) [http://ezproxy-prd.
bodleian.ox.ac.uk:3520/home.do; last accessed 20 September, 2018]. Periodical
contributors thus identified are entered in square brackets.

1

Religion and History
in Nineteenth-Century Britain

THE ARGUMENT

The churches have always proclaimed God's sovereignty over history. Only during the nineteenth century, however, did their critics begin extensively and contentiously to declare that history was, in fact, sovereign over God. As a result, it was in this period that religious and secular moralists in the western world started to ask themselves, more generally and publicly than ever before, whether the movements of human time confirmed and strengthened, or else challenged and undermined, Christianity's claims to intellectual authority and cultural leadership. History, understood both as the past's own space and as the intellectual attempt to narrate and explain its significance, became recognizable to religious apologists as a mediator between mankind and divine purposes. For others, it came to record humanity's supersession of its imagined dependence on a supramundane sphere, and the opening up of new realms of possibility for its untrammelled spirit. At a period of heightened religious activity, the question of religion's place in the modern age became central to wider divisions over the deeper foundations and ultimate tendencies of the new era. This book considers how, in such a climate, the intensifying interaction between religious awakening and historical consciousness gave shape to contemporary debates about the meaning of progress in nineteenth-century Britain.

In particular, this account focuses on the evolving patterns and wider ramifications of Victorian conceptions of the history of Christianity. It reconstructs the ways in which Victorian historians explored and reappraised the different layers of religious history in their attempts to critique and modify their audiences' beliefs and practices. As students of the nineteenth century are aware, one such layer was biblical history.[1]

---

[1] On nineteenth-century biblical criticism, see M. Bauspiess, C. Landmesser, and D. Lincicum (eds), *Ferdinand Christian Baur und die Geschichte des frühen Christentums*

Less well known to posterity, however, is the equal importance which Victorians attached to the post-apostolic history of the church, and the different phases which constituted it.[2] Those epochs, nineteenth-century commentators generally believed, had left legacies deeply embedded in the religious life, social customs, and cultural divisions of the present day, which it was the province of historical criticism to identify and remould. The book explores the twofold and reciprocal process by which progressive and developmental understandings of the history of Christianity came to acquire intellectual authority in religious debate, and by which religious categories came to permeate Victorian understandings of historical progress more generally. As static understandings of Christian history gave way to dynamic ones, the normative assumptions underlying nineteenth-century religious culture changed fundamentally. In a simultaneous and connected transition, the emergence of new ways of thinking about Christian time came also to structure wider understandings of the general movement of history, and hence the role of God in progress. Focusing on the history of historical thought across a culture, rather than the history of historiography in a more limited sense, and recovering the lines of dialogue connecting the Protestant mainstream of Victorian thought to secular criticism, the study offers a new assessment of the significant transformations at work in nineteenth-century British intellectual life.

This book seeks to understand the remarkable process by which religious history shed its internal or narrowly ecclesiastical character in Victorian conditions, to become foundational to wider cultural critique. Church history, read in the light of the Bible in different senses, offered Victorians located at the conventional centre of British intellectual activity a framework within which to situate the ultimate significance of history as a whole. Precisely on this account, it also furnished an authoritative

---

(Tübingen, 2014); H. Harris, *The Tübingen School: an historical and theological investigation of the school of F.C. Baur*, new edn (Leicester, 1990); J.W. Rogerson, *Old Testament criticism in the nineteenth century: England and Germany* (London, 1984). On the wider cultural impact of the Bible in nineteenth-century Britain, see T. Larsen, *A people of one book: the Bible and the Victorians* (Oxford, 2011); M. Wheeler, *St John and the Victorians* (Cambridge, 2012); D. Gange and M. Ledger-Lomas (eds), *Cities of God: the Bible and archaeology in nineteenth-century Britain* (Cambridge, 2013).

[2] Existing explorations of religious themes in nineteenth-century historical writing include: J. Garnett, 'Protestant histories: James Anthony Froude, partisanship and national identity', in P. Ghosh and L. Goldman (eds), *Politics and culture in Victorian Britain: essays in memory of Colin Matthew* (Oxford, 2006), pp. [171]–191; J. Kirby, *Historians and the Church of England: religion and historical scholarship, 1870–1920* (Oxford, 2016); T. Lang, *The Victorians and the Stuart heritage: interpretations of a discordant past* (Cambridge, 1995); J. Bennett, *The Victorian high church and the era of the Great Rebellion* (Oxford, 2011); M. Nixon, *Samuel Rawson Gardiner and the idea of history* (London, 2011); A.G. Dickens and J. Tonkin, *The Reformation in historical thought* (Oxford, 1985), pp. 150–97.

resource through which nineteenth-century actors could appraise their own religious culture, and the large spheres of human experience which it affected. In this way, historical study itself became an active medium through which believers could arrive at their own responses to biblical investigation, religious diversity, changing ethical sensibilities, and the claims of science, whilst influencing those of others. Historians came to embody truth in tales of progressive movement, dissonantly told, in which religion was the major protagonist. Nineteenth-century arguments over democracy, evolutionary naturalism, political economy, and empire have proved more legible than these debates to historians socialized amidst what Colin Matthew once described as the 'profound secularity' of two or three lifetimes later.[3] But the narration and explication of the history of religion, in which two peculiarly pervasive Victorian phenomena came into relationship with one another, was at least an equally vital means by which contemporaries made sense of the world around them, and sought to sway its unfolding directions.[4]

Just as this study is concerned with the depth of religion's penetration into wider areas of historical life and thought from the Victorian point of view, so too does it emphasize the breadth of perspective in which the subject enabled nineteenth-century Britons to situate their culture's leading features. The history of Christianity afforded Victorians the most readily available framework they possessed for understanding universal history, allowing them to see their own society and churches in the light of

---

[3] Important studies of these topics include J.W. Burrow, *Evolution and society: a study in Victorian social theory* (London, 1966); S. Collini, *Public moralists: political thought and intellectual life in Britain 1850–1930* (Oxford, 1991); F.M. Turner, *Between science and religion: the reaction to scientific naturalism in late Victorian England* (New Haven, CT, and London, 1974); D. Winch, *Wealth and life: essays on the intellectual history of political economy in Britain, 1848–1914* (Cambridge, 2009); D. Bell, *The idea of greater Britain: empire and the future of world order, 1860–1900* (Princeton, NJ, 2007). I quote from H.C.G. Matthew, 'Introduction: the United Kingdom and the Victorian century, 1815–1901', in Matthew (ed.), *The nineteenth century: the British Isles: 1815–1901* (Oxford, 2000), p. 36.

[4] Religious subjects are becoming more integrated into the study of nineteenth-century intellectual history than they once were: J.D.S. Rasmussen, J. Wolffe, and J. Zachhuber (eds), *The Oxford handbook of nineteenth-century Christian thought* (Oxford, 2017); B. Hilton, *The age of atonement: the influence of evangelicalism on social and economic thought, 1795–1865* (Oxford, 1988); C. Kidd, *The world of Mr Casaubon: Britain's wars of mythography, 1700–1870* (Cambridge, 2016). The waymarks laid down in Maurice Cowling's *Religion and public doctrine in modern England* (3 vols, Cambridge, 1980–2001) have, as yet, found few followers: for an interpretation of the historiographical significance of this text, see S.J.D. Green, 'As if religion mattered: an alternative reading of English intellectual history since *c.* 1840', in R. Cowcroft, S.J.D. Green and R. Whiting (eds), *The philosophy, politics and religion of British democracy: Maurice Cowling and conservatism* (London, 2010), pp. 189–222.

the history of civilization.[5] Victorians typically treated universal history as though it were practically synonymous with, or spearheaded by, the history of Christendom. The centre of that history lay in Europe and its Near Eastern and North African hinterlands, extending more recently to encompass polities of European, especially British, descent elsewhere. These assumptions now appear less compelling to western intellectuals than they once did. In the period of their ascendancy, they nevertheless prevented large provinces of Victorian historical writing from acquiring the insular or nationalist character which many scholars take, in too unqualified a sense, to have been a general hallmark of nineteenth-century historiography.[6] This book shows that Victorians were in fact constantly concerned critically to evaluate their own beliefs and customs in the light of the world-historical patterns and norms which the history of Christianity, more than any other dimension of historical experience, made visible. The pursuit of universal ideas of history demanded commensurate tools of analysis. The following chapters draw particular attention to the role of different kinds of German Idealist philosophy in renovating British intellectual life, by enabling Britons to integrate spiritual history and religious tradition with abiding moral reason.[7] The subsequent analysis therefore reflects the way in which many nineteenth-century British writers understood their own culture and history in cosmopolitan terms.

The reciprocal interactions between religious ideas of history and historical ideas of religion, and between general historical models and specific cultural problems, were quintessentially expressed in the liberal Anglican and future archbishop of Canterbury Frederick Temple's offering to the radical 1860 collection, *Essays and Reviews*. The work was itself largely dedicated to the implications of historical criticism for conventional Christianity. 'The human heart refuses to believe in a universe without a purpose', Temple declared, in a contribution arguing that the

---

[5] On the 'civilisational perspective' in Victorian historiography, see P. Mandler, '"Race" and 'nation' in mid-Victorian thought', in S. Collini, R. Whatmore, and B. Young (eds), *History, religion, and culture: British intellectual history 1750–1950* (Cambridge, 2000), pp. 224–44.

[6] For example, S. Berger and C. Lorenz, *Nationalizing the past: historians as nation builders in modern Europe* (Basingstoke, 2010). Classic studies of the 'Whig' tradition have naturally centred on British understandings of British history: J.W. Burrow, *A liberal descent: Victorian historians and the English past* (Cambridge, 1981); P.B.M. Blaas, *Continuity and anachronism: parliamentary and constitutional development in Whig historiography and in the anti-Whig reaction between 1890 and 1930* (The Hague, Boston, MA, and London, 1978).

[7] I alternate between an upper and a lower case 'i' in 'idealist' and 'idealism', in order to make a category distinction. In reference to German or British Idealism as specific movements, I use a capital letter; in reference to the broader diffusion of the assumption that reality was primarily to be approached through the active faculties of the mind, and their historical fruits, I do not.

history of religion should be understood, in progressive terms, as 'the education of the world'.[8] 'The power, whereby the present ever gathers into itself the results of the past', he continued, 'transforms the human race into a colossal man', growing in knowledge and judgment over time. 'The creed and doctrines, the opinions and principles of the successive ages, are his thoughts', which were never stationary.[9] In this way, Temple ascribed a providential meaning and authority to the movements of human time. He particularly turned those dynamics to confer legitimacy upon modern departures from the classically Protestant belief in the Bible's verbal inerrancy. Such a conviction could no longer serve as the absolute religious norm into which many of his contemporaries sought to elevate it. For it belonged to a particular phase in the developing history of religious opinion. 'We are now men', Temple concluded his essay by remarking, 'and cannot rely any longer on the impulses of youth and the discipline of childhood'.[10] Historical criticism thereby offered Temple a route to redefining Protestantism, by creating greater space within it for the advances in biblical understanding which dogmatism was currently stymying. Efforts at altering historical perceptions, in this sense, were not secondary or incidental consequences of Victorian intellectual change, but belonged to the chief modes through which it came about.

By integrating religion into the history of Victorian historical consciousness and its implications, the book offers a fresh interpretation of the wider dynamics of British intellectual culture in that period of redefinition between the evangelical revival and 'the passing of Protestant England', if not quite 'the death of Christian Britain'.[11] By illustrating how sequestered dons and comfortable clergy inhabited a discursive continuum with popular preachers and jobbing journalists, it demonstrates that higher-level intellectual and scholarly developments drew energy from and galvanized wider attitudinal changes among more middlebrow Victorians. Considered in this holistic framework, the consequences of the mutual permeation of religious and historical thought ran in two main directions. First, as developmental ideas of history acquired intellectual authority in religious controversy, the arena of the latter

---

[8] F. Temple, 'The education of the world', in V. Shea and W. Whitla (eds), *Essays and reviews: the 1860 text and its reading* (Charlottesville, VA, and London, 2000), pp. [137]–64, here at [137].

[9] Ibid., p. 138.   [10] Ibid., p. 164.

[11] For alternative characterizations of religious history in modern Britain: C.G. Brown, *The death of Christian Britain: understanding secularisation 1800–2000*, 2nd edn (London and New York, 2009), first edition 2001; J. Garnett et al. (eds), *Redefining Christian Britain: post-1945 perspectives* (London, 2007); S.J.D. Green, *The Passing of Protestant England: secularisation and social change, c. 1920–1960* (Cambridge, 2011).

gradually and controversially shifted from a textual and scholastic basis to one grounded much more broadly in the perceived relationship between divinity, the historical subject, and human temporal experience.

The decision to found religious apology upon history informed and implied a second, and in some ways more fundamental intellectual manoeuvre. This was history's elevation into what Thomas Carlyle, within an unusually heterodox frame of reference, called 'the true Epic Poem, and universal Divine Scripture'.[12] Religious belief, brought into active relationship with rising awareness of history as an autonomous sphere of human experience, now integrated the diversity of history into a providentially purposeful whole. Scientific developments and changing moral sensibilities came to sap the power of Enlightenment-era natural theology.[13] But history's gathering witness to the expansion and practical force of human moral consciousness enabled it to offer a dynamic evidential alternative: a new space within which divine intentions might be discerned and vindicated. Protestants in the mainstream of Victorian intellectual culture accordingly began to locate present and future progress within a spiritual framework stretching across time. In 1845, the fact of religious pluralism in Britain and Europe; the consolidation of natural and social science; the rise of biblical criticism; and the growth of that human ethical autonomy capable of asserting itself against inherited religious prescriptions had been deeply disturbing phenomena. By 1914, they had very widely acquired a spiritual rationale, by virtue of having been synthesized with religiously originating conceptions of progress. Religious conservatism underwent its own kind of historically mediated renewal, while secular images of the past pressed in ominously at the edges of Victorian culture. Neither can be understood, however, if treated in isolation from the larger process by which theological ideas of history worked their way to the heart of the nineteenth-century liberal imagination. The religious dimensions of history became integral to how Victorians imagined the origins, texture, and prospects of the world they inhabited. They structured what it meant for Victorians to come out of the past, and to enter their own, ultimately fleeting kind of modernity.

---

[12] T. Carlyle, 'On history again', in Carlyle, *Critical and miscellaneous essays* (4 vols, London, 1893), ii [pt. 2], 220 (repr. from *FM* for 1833).

[13] On the problems encountered by natural theology during the nineteenth century, see R.M. Young, *Darwin's metaphor: nature's place in Victorian culture* (Cambridge, 1985); P. Corsi, *Science and religion: Baden Powell and the Anglican debate, 1800–1860* (Cambridge, 1988); J.H. Brooke, *Science and religion: some historical perspectives* (Cambridge, 1991), esp. pp. 192–225. It was a tradition possessed of considerable powers of adaptation, however: P.J. Bowler, *Reconciling science and religion: the debate in early-twentieth-century Britain* (Chicago, IL, and London, 2001).

REVIVAL AND LIBERAL HISTORICISM
IN PROTESTANT INTELLECTUAL CULTURE

By pursuing these overlooked lines of development through nineteenth-century British history, the following chapters set several of its more familiar themes in a new and newly interconnected perspective. The book does not take the form of a disciplinary history of history or theology, but rather considers the transformative effects of historical thought, in its diverse manifestations, on religious traditions across Protestant culture. The subject is ordered into three themes. First, by identifying the religious influences that fed Victorian 'historicism', a richer and more complex understanding emerges of what it meant for Victorian actors to think historically. One route to historicism lay through religious revival and 'revivalism': the intellectual strategies of which constitute the second subject of the following chapters. In the earlier part of the period, promoters of different kinds of religious revival became reliant upon static images of the religious past, which they deemed worthy of resuscitation in the present day. Critics who wished to challenge traditionalists' understanding of religion accordingly began, from around the mid-century, to interpret religious tradition in newly developmental and progressive ways, making religion's improvement or indeed its supersession central to civilizational progress in past and present. In this way, religious history became central to the articulation and reception of Victorian 'liberalism' in its ambition to depart from what were seen as outdated beliefs and practices. A deeper exploration of the religious and historical dimensions of Victorian liberalism furnishes the book's third theme. By recognizing the porous boundaries between scholarly and more popular discourse, and the importance of dialogues crossing denominational lines, it becomes possible to draw out the interrelationship between revivalism, liberalism, and historicism in driving general intellectual-historical transformations in Victorian Britain.

Victorian 'historicism' was something larger than existing scholarly frameworks allow for. Not a term greatly used by the Victorians themselves, historicism is often associated with the belief, especially as held by Leopold von Ranke, that history, unlike nature, is composed of unique and unrepeatable individualities.[14] Whilst this book certainly takes

---

[14] G.G. Iggers, *The German conception of history: the national tradition of historical thought from Herder to the present*, rev. edn (Middletown, CT, 1983), pp. 4–5; Iggers, 'Historicism: the history and meaning of the term', *Journal of the History of Ideas*, 56:1 (1995), pp. 129–52; M. Bevir, 'Historicism and the human sciences in Victorian Britain',

historicism to have included this meaning, it conceives it much more amply, as a composite of different frameworks within which the past became significant in different ways, to different groups, at different times. Historical consciousness, in the sense of an awareness that the institutions and norms of the past had changed at some date prior to the present in potentially problematic ways, was not invented in the nineteenth century.[15] But it acquired greater intellectual scope and conceptual richness in these years, as different notions of progress and development subsumed mere 'change'—by itself, an atomized sequence of events—into a larger, more meaningful, and steadily evolving whole. The authority of older, more stationary conceptions of the past accordingly began to weaken. Where faith in 'progress' often boldly and optimistically synthesized the past and prophesied the future, interest in 'development' tended to possess a more limited, and sometimes ambivalently retrospective character, involving the assumption that the true nature of a phenomenon might be realized, or corrupted, in human time.[16] Whilst contemporaries invested these categories with multiple kinds of significance, both ideas overlapped in presuming that past experience amounted to more than a datum for disinterested analysis or a register of the crimes, follies, and misfortunes of mankind. Their accelerating tendency to blend with, or even originate within, religious beliefs encouraged Victorians to assume that evolving history pointed beyond itself, to a world of ultimate realities towards which the study of the past might beckon.

These changing argumentative contours intersected only partially with the development of history as a professional and 'scientific' discipline in the reformed universities after 1870.[17] This book surveys a larger landscape.

in Bevir (ed.), *Historicism and the human sciences in Victorian Britain* (Cambridge, 2017), pp. 1–20.

[15] J.G.A. Pocock, 'The origins of study of the past: a comparative approach', in his *Political thought and history: essays on theory and method* (Cambridge, 2009), pp. 145–86.

[16] Here I allude to J.B. Bury's definition of the idea of progress: *The idea of progress: an inquiry into its origin and growth* (London, 1920), p. 5. More recent studies of the idea have given more prominence to its theological contexts than the Cambridge rationalist allowed: R. Nisbet, *History of the idea of progress* (London, 1980); B. Loewenstein, *Der Fortschrittsglaube: europäisches Geschichtsdenken zwischen Utopie und Ideologie*, 2nd edn (Darmstadt, 2015).

[17] On these subjects, see M. Bentley, *Modernizing England's past: English historiography in the age of modernism, 1870–1970* (Cambridge, 2005); P.R.H. Slee, *Learning and a liberal education: the study of modern history in the universities of Oxford, Cambridge and Manchester, 1800–1914* (Manchester, 1986); D.S. Goldstein, 'The professionalization of history in Britain in the late nineteenth and early twentieth centuries', *Storia della storiografia*, 3 (1983), pp. 3–27; J.P. Kenyon, *The history men: the historical profession in England since the Renaissance* (London, 1983); I. Hesketh, *The science of history in Victorian Britain: making the past speak* (London, 2011).

It considers how diverse progressive and developmental forms of historicism, reworking the interpretative resources which had passed into Victorian intellectual culture from earlier ages, acted as solvents and catalysts within different religious traditions.[18] Biblicism, patristic textualism, classicism, an English literary heritage, and Enlightenment-era conjectural history continued to invigorate early Victorian intellectual culture, moulding contemporary ideas of the religious past amidst the new disruptions of the period. Among religiously apologetic historians, different emanations of German Idealist historical philosophy crucially intersected with those conceptions, and injected a new and often transformative dynamism into them.[19] The notably smaller number of radically anti-theological critics, by contrast, looked to the resources of Comtean sociology and the philosophy of John Stuart Mill in constructing their own, avowedly secular visions of the religious past and future.[20] In a culture relatively slow to experience the professionalization of history and theology, moralists throughout the century persistently drew on a complex body of intellectual resources as they developed richly conflicting understandings of what it meant to think historically about religion.[21]

In order to understand the emergence and effects of the multiple varieties of Victorian historicism thus conceived, and to differentiate between them, it is important to situate them in the context of British

---

[18] The distinction between 'historiography' and 'historical thought' is important to J.G.A. Pocock: 'Working on ideas in time', in his *Political thought and history*, pp. 20–32.

[19] On Idealism and *Historismus*, see for example A. Wittkau-Horgby, *Historismus: zur Geschichte des Begriffs und des Problems* (Göttingen, 1992); J. Rüsen, *Konfigurationen des Historismus: Studien zur deutschen Wissenschaftskultur* (Frankfurt am Main, 1993); F.C. Beiser, *The German historicist tradition* (Oxford, 2011). For comparisons and connections between nineteenth-century British and German historiography, see B. Stuchtey and P. Wende (eds), *British and German historiography, 1750–1950: traditions, perceptions, and transfers* (Oxford, 2000); K. Dockhorn, *Der deutsche Historismus in England: ein Beitrag zur englischen Geistesgeschichte des 19. Jahrhunderts* (Göttingen, 1950). On Anglo-German cultural transfer in the nineteenth century in general, see for example R. Ashton, *The German idea: four English writers and the reception of German thought 1800–1860* (Cambridge, 1980); M. Ledger-Lomas, '*Lyra Germanica*: German sacred music in mid-Victorian England', *German Historical Institute London Bulletin*, 29:2 (2007), pp. 8–42; J.R. Davis, *The Victorians and Germany* (Oxford and Bern, 2007); H. Ellis and U. Kirchberger (eds), *Anglo-German scholarly networks in the long nineteenth century* (Leiden and Boston, MA, 2014). On the influence of German theology in nineteenth-century America, a story with significant parallels to that presented here, see A.G. Aubert, *The German roots of nineteenth-century American theology* (Oxford, 2013).

[20] See chapter five of this volume.

[21] On the rise of the discipline of theology in nineteenth-century Britain, see D. Inman, *The making of modern English theology: God and the academy at Oxford, 1833–1945* (Minneapolis, MN, 2014). For German parallels, see T.A. Howard, *Protestant theology and the making of the modern German university* (Oxford, 2006); J. Zachhuber, *Theology as science in nineteenth-century Germany: from F. C. Baur to Ernst Troeltsch* (Oxford, 2013); Z. Purvis, *Theology and the university in nineteenth-century Germany* (Oxford, 2016).

Protestant intellectual culture as a whole. By positing that this culture
was at once richly diverse, yet sufficiently unified to justify treating its
different manifestations in relation to one another, the book challenges a
number of current readings of Victorian religious and intellectual history. Its subjects include both English and Scottish writers, as well a
small number of Irish Protestants and representatives of the Church of
Wales. They are located on a wide spectrum, encompassing high church
Anglicans (including the Catholic convert, John Henry Newman), evangelical Protestants, liberal Anglicans, nonconformists, conservative and
liberal Presbyterians, Positivists, agnostics, and Idealists. There are several reasons why these groups tend not to be considered together.
Students of nineteenth-century religious politics have naturally centred
their attention on disputes between church and dissent, in ways that
emphasize the points of conflict between them.[22] Demarcations between
denominations, or between established and dissenting churches, tend
still to be privileged as organizing principles.[23] There was, of course, an
axis of difference between England and Scotland, as well as between
church and chapel. Scholars sceptical of the argument that common
Protestantism helped to forge a British national identity in the eighteenth and nineteenth centuries have accordingly emphasized the periodically centrifugal tendencies of Britain's ecclesiastical settlements.[24]
This book does not seek to deny that fundamental differences existed
between and within denominations and ecclesiastical polities in the
nineteenth-century British Isles. It focuses, however, on the less acknowledged parallels, overlaps, and affinities that linked these churches and

---

[22] For example, R. Brent, *Liberal Anglican politics: whiggery, religion, and reform 1830–41*
(Oxford, 1987); J.P. Parry, 'Nonconformity, clericalism and "Englishness": the United
Kingdom', in C. Clark and W. Kaiser (eds), *Culture wars: secular-Catholic conflict in
nineteenth-century Europe* (Cambridge, 2003), pp. 152–80; D.W. Bebbington, *The
nonconformist conscience: chapel and politics, 1870–1914* (London, 1982); J.P. Ellens, *Religious
routes to Gladstonian Liberalism: the church rate conflict in England and Wales, 1832–1868*
(University Park, PA, 1994); T. Larsen, *Friends of religious equality: nonconformist politics in
mid-Victorian England* (Woodbridge, 1999).

[23] See most recently T. Larsen and M. Ledger-Lomas (eds), *The Oxford history of
Protestant dissenting traditions: volume III: the nineteenth century* (Oxford, 2017);
R. Strong (ed.), *The Oxford history of Anglicanism: volume III: partisan Anglicanism and its
global expansion, 1829–c.1914* (Oxford, 2017).

[24] For the integrationist case, see L. Colley, *Britons: forging the nation, 1707–1837* (New
Haven, CT, and London, 1992); J. Wolffe, *God and greater Britain: religion and national
life in Britain and Ireland 1843–1945* (London, 1994). For countervailing arguments, see
S.J. Brown, *The national churches of England, Ireland, and Scotland 1801–1846* (Oxford,
2001); 'in many ways Protestant religion was the grit in the Union, not its glue': C. Kidd,
Union and unionisms: political thought in Scotland, 1500–2000 (Cambridge, 2008), p. 211.

nations together, by recognizing that they belonged, as they often recognized themselves as belonging, to a shared intellectual space.[25]

The British churches, and those who drifted away from them into what were often religiously inflected kinds of agnosticism or secularism, shared lines of descent from the verbal, personal, and biblical genus of religion fostered by the Reformation. This was also true of the sizeable proportion of high Anglicans who rejected the 'Protestant' appellation, taking 'ultra-Protestantism' or 'popular Protestantism' to involve separation from the Catholic Church,[26] as it was of the freethinkers who had avowedly left dogmatic Protestantism behind. For both groups tended to think of themselves as dissidents from what they assumed to be the predominantly Protestant culture in which they had been nurtured, and continued to protest against Roman Catholicism.[27] Rancorously divided Anglicans still shared universities, and a history, with one another. In the broader public sphere, dogmatists and unbelievers, English and Scottish writers, establishmentarians and dissenters were not discursively separated from their critics. The spread of public lectures, periodicals, affordable books, and a strikingly widespread appetite for serious argument made it difficult for religious or irreligious moralists to remain unexposed or unrelievedly hostile to those who thought differently from themselves. Amidst the ruptures that marked the Victorian religious landscape, shared points of reference—the preconditions of dialogue—also existed. 'Contrast is a kind of relation',[28] and different thinkers who are not often treated together are here brought into conversation with one another as part of a common argumentative field. Protestantism, both as a formative influence and as the object of approbatory or more disapproving commentary, cast long shadows from its place at the centre of Victorian intellectual life.

This point of departure posits that religious debate functioned as a backdrop to Victorian culture as a whole, rather than as the more sectional

---

[25] T. Larsen, *Contested Christianity: the political and social context of Victorian theology* (Waco, TX, 2004), attends to points of intellectual contact between Anglicans and nonconformists.

[26] I distinguish between 'Catholic', as among Protestants conventionally referring to the body of religious doctrine, structure, and practice that had matured during the Middle Ages, and 'catholic', which was understood in a more positive sense as referring to original, universal Christianity. High Anglicans often identified with the former variant, and always with the latter.

[27] On the anti-Protestant thrust of the Oxford Movement, see F.M. Turner, *John Henry Newman: the challenge to evangelical religion* (New Haven, CT, and London, 2002); on the religious contexts for Victorian unbelief, see T. Larsen, *Crisis of doubt: honest faith in nineteenth-century England* (Oxford, 2006); B. Lightman, *The origins of agnosticism: Victorian unbelief and the limits of knowledge* (Baltimore, MD, and London, 1987).

[28] [A. Hare and J.C. Hare], *Guesses at truth by two brothers*, new edn (London and New York, 1871), p. 156 (first edition 1827).

activity it later became. It is on this basis that the protagonists in this study have so far been described as 'thinkers', 'commentators', 'historians', 'apologists', 'moralists', and 'critics'. Those such as the liberal Anglican Henry Hart Milman and the liberal Church of Scotland divine John Tulloch were also clerics and theologians. But in common with their secularizing opponents, they aspired to exercise intellectual leadership within a society that shared their assumptions as to the centrality of religion to historical and social experience. The protagonists in this book should accordingly be regarded as historically minded 'public moralists', for whom religion was a more fundamental theme than Stefan Collini's original account of that subject conveys.[29] They addressed themselves to a common culture, the holistic character of which they hoped to conserve, improve, or restore through religious analysis and historical retrospect and prophecy.

The historical imagination of this culture, for all its rich variety, developed in common phases. The earliest nineteenth-century impetus tending to cast religious positions into historical forms came from the experience of religious revival. In the post-revolutionary west, evangelicals mobilised for new kinds of reconstructive religious, political, and social activism across the Protestant world, spurred on not least by the parallel spectre of the devotional resurgence and Ultramontane reconstruction of European Catholicism.[30] In Britain, Catholic regeneration, commonly animated by the wish to restore the supposedly stable religious and social hierarchies destroyed by industrial and political upheaval, won high-society converts and, to their less receptive countrymen, risked entrenching priestcraft's hold over much of Europe and Ireland.[31] Voluntary religion, in the forms of 'old' and 'new' dissent, grew strongly in the later eighteenth and early nineteenth centuries as the established churches struggled to keep pace with urbanization, old social hierarchies buckled, and the bewildering events of the French Revolution inflamed millennial or anti-Jacobin feeling.[32] In addition to external hostility, the British

[29] Collini, *Public moralists*; see also J. Holloway, *The Victorian sage: studies in argument* (London, 1953).
[30] General surveys of this theme include H. McLeod, *Religion and the people of Western Europe 1789–1989*, 2nd edn (Oxford, 1997), of which the 1981 first edition was seminal; C.A. Bayly, *The birth of the modern world 1780–1914: global connections and comparisons* (Oxford, 2004), pp. 325–65; M. Heimann, 'Catholic revivalism in worship and devotion', in S. Gilley and B. Stanley (eds), *The Cambridge History of Christianity: volume 8: world Christianities c. 1815–c. 1914* (Cambridge, 2006), pp. 70–83.
[31] J. Wolffe, *The Protestant crusade in Great Britain 1829–1860* (Oxford, 1991); D.G. Paz, *Popular anti-Catholicism in mid-Victorian England* (Stanford, CA, 1992); D. Newsome, *The parting of friends: the Wilberforces and Henry Manning* (London, 1966).
[32] D.W. Bebbington, 'The growth of voluntary religion', in Gilley and Stanley, *World Christianities*, pp. 53–69.

established churches faced internal dissension from insurgent groups who insisted upon their denominations' spiritual independence from the interference or doctrinal laxity of state authorities. After 1833 the Church of England was thrown into turmoil by Oxford Movement 'Tractarians', who radicalized older Anglican high churchmanship and sometimes disconcerted its adherents by stressing their church's apostolic authority and Catholic heritage.[33] The Movement swiftly inflamed latent divisions within the Church of England between high churchmen, 'low church' evangelicals, and 'broad church' figures committed to doctrinal comprehension.[34] In what was in certain respects a comparable development, one third of the ministers of the Church of Scotland left for the anti-Erastian and rigorously Calvinist Free Church at the Disruption in 1843.[35]

These events had intellectual implications, which were worked out in an increasingly historicist climate. Religious revivalists, whether Protestant evangelicals or anti-Protestant Tractarians, were also 'revivalist' in a specifically historical sense. Although evangelicals fundamentally rejected the inherent authority of ecclesiastical tradition upon which Tractarians laid stress, both groups were alike traditionalist, in that they called for the nation to return to unsullied religious 'types'. In a sense partly redolent of post-Reformation notions of ecclesiastical history, traditionalists presumed that pure witness to scriptural or primitive orthodoxy had existed, with a kind of normative fixity, at certain idealized moments in the past. The latter deserved to be defended and, if possible, restored.[36] Where evangelicals exalted the Reformation, Tractarians held up the early church

---

[33] The best synoptic study of Tractarianism remains P.B. Nockles, *The Oxford Movement in context: Anglican high churchmanship 1760–1857* (Cambridge, 1994); see more recently J. Pereiro, S.J. Brown, and P.B. Nockles (eds), *The Oxford handbook of the Oxford Movement* (Oxford, 2017); S.J. Brown and P.B. Nockles (eds), *The Oxford Movement: Europe and the wider world 1830–1930* (Cambridge, 2012). On the later impact of Anglo-Catholicism in English intellectual culture and ecclesiastical politics, see J. Bentley, *Ritualism and politics in Victorian Britain: the attempt to legislate for belief* (Oxford, 1978); M. Wellings, *Evangelicals embattled: responses of evangelicals in the Church of England to ritualism, Darwinism and theological liberalism 1890–1930* (Carlisle, 2003).

[34] On evangelical Anglican theology in the period, see P. Toon, *Evangelical theology 1833–1856: a response to Tractarianism* (London, 1979). Church-party labels, though helpful for purposes of summary description, are liable to mislead when reified: for a discussion, see A. Burns (ed.), 'W. J. Conybeare: "church parties"', in S. Taylor (ed.), *From Cranmer to Davidson: a Church of England miscellany* (Woodbridge, 1999), pp. [215]–385.

[35] The contexts, course, and afterlives of the Disruption are studied most exhaustively in A.L. Drummond and J. Bulloch, *The Scottish church 1688–1843: the age of the moderates* (Edinburgh, 1973); Drummond and Bulloch, *The church in Victorian Scotland, 1843–1874* (Edinburgh, 1975); Drummond and Bulloch, *The church in late Victorian Scotland, 1874–1900* (Edinburgh, 1978). For a comparative study of the Oxford Movement and the events leading up to the Disruption, see Brown, *National churches*.

[36] E.K. Cameron, *Interpreting Christian history: the challenge of the churches' past* (Malden, MA, and Oxford, 2005), pp. 122–44.

and the Middle Ages to the reproach of the present day: positions expressing different kinds of reaction against the religious laxity they discovered in the world around them. Both manoeuvres derived from, and helped to corroborate, a dualistic view of the relationship between mankind and divinity, which stressed the fallen nature of the one and the absolute transcendence of the other. Religious traditionalists, who in Britain as in other settings were the products of the modern volatility that left them 'stranded in the present', thus developed a restabilizing preoccupation with history that was at once innovative and reactionary.[37]

In this environment, liberal Protestant critics—such as Temple—found that in order to wean their readers off religious reaction, they had to offer an appeal to history of their own. Rather than jettisoning the religious traditions in which they found themselves, religiously liberal critics sought to understand them in a different way. From around the mid-century, they began self-consciously to explain that tradition was in fact historically dynamic. Where revivalists tended to stress the distance between the human and the divine, religious liberals treated the histories of the church, its doctrines, and their sociopolitical and philosophical contexts as a progressive point of contact between them. Proceeding from a different understanding of history itself, liberal historicism could thus prise religious tradition away from traditionalism. Its practitioners elucidated how tradition in fact contained space for future progress and development, beyond the limits established by historic precedent.

Religious liberalism, quite as much as religious revivalism, thereby became integrally reliant upon certain images of the human past and future. Like 'historicism' and 'historicist', 'liberalism' and 'liberal' are here used more operationally than ontologically, to convey certain affinities between otherwise divergent, progressively minded critics concerning the place of religion in the modern age. First entering widespread theological parlance in the 1860s, 'liberalism' was as much a term of abuse as it was one of self-description.[38] It was less a freestanding intellectual entity than a contentious yet increasingly pervasive category in relation to which

---

[37] P. Fritzsche, *Stranded in the present: modern time and the melancholy of history* (Cambridge, MA, and London, 2004); S. Hellemans, 'How modern is religion in modernity?', in J. Frishman, W. Otten, and G. Rouwhorst (eds), *Religious identity and the problem of historical foundation: the foundational character of authoritative sources in the history of Christianity and Judaism* (Leiden and Boston, MA, 2004), pp. [76]–94.

[38] Where John Henry Newman denounced liberalism in his 1864 *Apologia* as 'the anti-dogmatic principle and its developments', liberalism's Anglican sympathiser, William Page Roberts, somewhat later affirmed the commitment of 'liberal Protestantism, liberal Christianity' to dogma and doctrine, whilst insisting that they encouraged 'mind and soul to seek out more and more knowledge' of theological questions: W. Page Roberts, *Liberalism in religion and other sermons* (London, 1886), pp. 56–7; cf. J.H. Newman, *Apologia pro vita*

contemporaries defined themselves; a self-conscious anti-liberal such as John Henry Newman could in many respects think in liberal ways. Although its admirers and detractors placed different value judgements upon it, both could agree that liberalism elevated individual human reason and affirmed its freedom from persecution and external or ecclesiastically authoritative constraints. It also involved the belief that religious forms should be open to progressive development in the light of intellectual and ethical advance, and not forever tied to a specific historical mode of belief or expression.[39]

These were capacious starting points, however, and they could extend in multiple directions. The uses made of them by religiously committed liberal historians came to constitute a crucial part of the conventional imaginative landscape of Victorian liberalism. The importance of progressive understandings of English constitutional history to Victorian political liberalism is well known.[40] But beyond what one poet called 'the democratic whirl and hum' of constitutional debate, religiously liberal moralists frequently sought to attribute the historical growth of the free individual subject, and the progress of civilization, primarily to the working of spiritual forces on universal and normative planes, and only secondarily to political activity.[41] Religious liberalism of this kind was not without political implications, which could be explored further in future research into the intellectual and religious contexts of Victorian politics.[42] But it exerted a striking power of its own. Historians of the period tend no longer to assume the inherent tension between liberal progressivism and religion once posited by the Jesuit historian Jeffrey Paul von Arx.[43] They should nevertheless recognize more distinctly the ways in which Victorian liberals conceived of Christian history as a temporal realm that was both relatively autonomous from national politics, and yet whose providential energies swayed the forms of individual, religious, and cultural life by which society and politics were ultimately moved.

---

sua: being a reply to a pamphlet entitled 'What, then, does Dr. Newman mean?' (London, 1864), p. 120.

[39] Here I echo the helpful discussion of J. Morris, 'Liberalism Protestant and Catholic', in Brown, Nockles, and Pereiro (eds), *Oxford Movement*, pp. [585]–604.

[40] Burrow, *A liberal descent*.

[41] A. Gurney, *King Charles the First: a dramatic poem*, 2nd edn (London, 1852), xi–xii.

[42] Several historians have mapped the religious mentalities of individual Victorian statesmen: H.C.G. Matthew, *Gladstone 1809–1898* (Oxford, 1997); D.W. Bebbington, *The mind of Gladstone: religion, Homer, and politics* (Oxford, 2004); M. Bentley, *Lord Salisbury's world: Conservative environments in late-Victorian Britain* (Cambridge, 2001).

[43] J.P. von Arx, *Progress and pessimism: religion, politics, and history in late nineteenth century Britain* (Cambridge, MA, 1985); cf. J.P. Parry, *The rise and fall of liberal government in Victorian Britain* (New Haven, CT, and London, 1993), pp. 134–41.

Although the advocates of religiously apologetic forms of liberal historicism afforded a powerful challenge to Victorian revivalism, they did not secure a universal acceptance of the tenets of theological liberalism. Instead they provoked intense debate. Developmental historicism generated not so much a linear swing as a tripartite branching effect, through which religious liberals called out a creative response from theologically conservative historians, and both evolved in reply to the avowedly secular understandings of progress and progressive knowledge gaining in self-confidence in the second half of the century. Evangelical Protestantism was not assimilated to a liberal movement—which should not be lazily equated with the denial of the supernatural aspects of Christianity in any case—but adapted elements of liberal historicism in order to reinvigorate evangelical witness.[44] Second- and third-generation Tractarians comparably maintained their confidence in the apostolic character of ecclesiastical tradition, but began to define its authority in a way that made a virtue of its newly apprehended historical dynamism.

These writers, who were conservative in the relative sense that they sought to defend historic doctrines which religious liberals typically sought to marginalize or reinterpret in a bolder way, joined the latter in coming under pressure from an avant-garde of secular liberals. The latter were animated by a radically different understanding of history, which was related to a non-metaphysical conception of knowledge. Whereas many of the churches' Enlightenment-era critics had still outwardly defended rational Christianity, or at least natural religion, their nineteenth-century successors frequently sought more completely and overtly to expunge metaphysics from modern thought. For the latter, the historical emancipation of the human mind demanded the progressive euthanasia of theology. In a period when they were unable to assume—as had become possible by the later part of the twentieth century—that secularity represented the neutral or commonly accepted basis of public discussion, the determination of religion's past and future direction became integral to radical as well as to apologetic critique.[45] The desirable telos of religious development lay in the replacement of theological religion by scientific

---

[44] I follow the definition of evangelical Protestantism offered by D.W. Bebbington, *The dominance of evangelicalism: the age of Spurgeon and Moody* (Leicester, 2005), pp. [19]–47. On evangelicalism's contact with 'liberalism', see M. Hopkins, *Nonconformity's romantic generation: evangelical and liberal theologies in Victorian England* (Carlisle, 2003).

[45] Important studies of 'secularisation' in Britain and Europe include H. McLeod, *Secularisation in western Europe, 1848–1914* (Basingstoke and London, 2000); Clark and Kaiser, *Culture wars*. For illuminating remarks on the relationship between secular and religious thought in the period, see L. Schwartz, *Infidel feminism: secularism, religion and women's emancipation, England 1830–1914* (Manchester and New York, 2013), pp. 1–29.

induction, to which many hoped that a religion of humanity would give emotional clothing. This book seeks to hold the respective development of religiously liberal, theologically conservative, and pointedly secular ideas of history in dynamic relation to one another, so as to recapture something of the sense of open-ended possibility for the future which contemporaries once took them to possess.

NETWORKS AND GENERATIONS

In the twentieth century, it came to appear as though tough-minded Darwinians, social scientists, and the popularizers of biblical criticism had carried the nineteenth century into the modern age. Yet the kinds of intellectual activity studied here followed a different course of evolution. They drew in networks of historians, essayists, and divines typically omitted from the canon which seemed obvious to the first historians of Victorian thought, who imbibed their points of reference from the Victorian period's more secular successor culture.[46] The connections between the book's main protagonists, chosen in order to exemplify the evolving relationship between conservative, religiously liberal, and secular visions of religious history, were multiple and complex. Often they belonged to the same universities, or to networks united by friendship and ties of tutelage. All held in common a commitment to history, variously understood, as an authoritative medium for religious argument. In addressing themselves to common historical issues, they drew on persistent philosophical, theological, and literary frames of reference which they shared with their critics and with British educated society more generally. Newer influences, however, worked to rearrange the different parts of the bricolage as generation succeeded generation. In a moment symbolized by the 1845 publication of John Henry Newman's *Essay on the Development of Christian Doctrine*, the centrality of exclusive confessionalism to early-Victorian understandings of the religious past began to give way, across denominations, to an increasing concern with the spiritual dimensions of mind and history as a whole.[47] German intellectual currents commonly lay behind that transition, and were themselves richly diverse. Sometimes intersecting with a rising fashion for supposedly 'scientific' modes of historical

---

[46] N. Annan et al., *Ideas and beliefs of the Victorians: an historic revaluation of the Victorian age* (London, 1949); G.M. Young, *Victorian England: portrait of an age* (London, 1936); W.E. Houghton, *The Victorian frame of mind, 1830–1870* (New Haven, CT, and London, 1957). Lytton Strachey naughtily included Mandell Creighton in his *Portraits in miniature and other essays* (London, 1931), pp. 207–[218].

[47] J.H. Newman, *An essay on the development of Christian doctrine* (London, 1845).

appraisal, successive waves of German historical criticism ultimately ran in conflicting directions. In the final third of the century, the by-then widely diffused influence of idealist metaphysics over British historical typologies came into fundamental conflict with boldly anti-metaphysical conceptions of mind and its history. The reinvigoration of spiritual modes of understanding humanity's past and prospects could not prevent the consolidation of secular anticipations of its future.

From the early decades of the nineteenth century, and with accelerating insistency in the 1830s and 1840s, church history became a crucial polemical and rhetorical resource for the first generations of nineteenth-century revivalists. History mirrored a certain kind of theology. Protestant and Catholicizing writers used ecclesiastical history as a proxy onto which to project acute denominational divisions, and a dualistic separation between God and fallen humanity, which militated against the idealisation of religious, political, or social progressivism. A central text of the evangelical revival, for instance, was Joseph Milner's *History of the Church of Christ*, completed after his death by his brother, Isaac.[48] It offered a compendious record of biographical examples of past effusions of grace, showing the abiding presence of the Protestant conception of the Holy Spirit through history.[49] The evangelical Anglican leader, Edward Bickersteth, hailed Milner as 'an eminent instrument' of that revival of religion which had once more encouraged Christians to think of their purpose in earthly life as being to prepare for the next.[50] Milner conveyed his sense of the role of historical writing in articulating the true church's struggle against the world, and in inspiring its continued perseverance in the good fight, by quoting Christ's declaration in the Gospel of Matthew that 'the gates of hell shall never prevail against' his church.[51] Though from the point of view of one hotly suspicious of Milner's enthusiasm, the Cambridge-educated high churchman and cautious Tractarian sympathizer, Hugh James Rose, repeatedly returned to the same severe image in a lecture on the purposes of church-historical study which he delivered to the newly founded University of Durham in 1834. There was no better mode of study than history, he argued, for establishing 'fixed, calm, and

---

[48] I use the 1847 edition here: J. Milner, *The History of the Church of Christ*, ed. I. Milner and T. Grantham (4 vols, London, 1847), first edition 1794–1809.

[49] On Milner, see J.D. Walsh, 'Joseph Milner's evangelical church history', *Journal of Ecclesiastical History*, 10:2 (1959), pp. 174–87.

[50] E. Bickersteth, *The Christian student designed to assist Christians in general in acquiring religious knowledge: with lists of books, adapted to the various classes of society*, 3rd edn (London, 1832), [v]–xi, pp. [1], 347.

[51] Milner, *History*, i, [xvii]; cf. Matthew 16:18.

Christian views of divinity' against 'the gates of hell' in the shape of contemporary infidels and sectaries.[52]

Milner's and Rose's common deployment of a combative biblical metaphor for interpreting ecclesiastical history and its significance illustrated an important affinity. Despite the radical differences between the Protestant and more Catholic manifestations of religious revival, it is possible to point to views of the nature of religious truth, and its relation or lack of relation to history, which they held in common. Although the evangelical revival's inherent opposition to the Enlightenment should not be overstated, its early-Victorian literary apostles reanimated what may be described as pre-Enlightenment readings of church history in order to reverse what they often understood to be the eighteenth century's religious indifference and scepticism.[53] When they looked to the past experience of the church, evangelical Protestants and awakened high churchmen were not primarily interested in its connections with civil or social history, as the profaner historians of the eighteenth century—especially Gibbon—had so often been.[54] Instead they posited an immutable core of faith, and centred their attention on tracking its fortunes. The inspired apostles and holy fathers of the first Christian centuries communicated that core in its fullness to succeeding generations, to be defended or restored by great systematic theologians or zealous sixteenth-century Reformers. Evangelicals treated religious truth as an historically continuous experience, and high churchmen more as though it were a sacred deposit. Both were nevertheless comfortable to define its content in the form of scholastic doctrinal propositions. They were not yet troubled by the notion that these might have more of a 'subjective' than an 'objective' character. In such treatments, orthodoxy was radically separable from heresy, which arose from poor textual logic driven by moral rebellion, rather than from historical situation. Not yet touched by developmental historicism, traditionalists of different kinds tended to fasten on particular periods—the early church, the Middle Ages, the Reformation—as canvases onto which they could project good and evil as discerned by the inferences they made from scriptural or patristic writings. It was an approach that led them to think of history as a sequence of golden pasts and dramatic ruptures,

[52] H.J. Rose, *The study of church history recommended* (London, 1834), pp. 10–11, 20, 26–7, 41–2; P.B. Nockles, 'Rose, Hugh James (1795–1838)', *ODNB*.

[53] Cf. D.W. Bebbington, 'Revival and Enlightenment in eighteenth-century England', in A. Walker and K. Anne (eds), *On revival: a critical examination* (Carlisle, 2003), pp. [71]–85.

[54] Rose, *Study of church history*, p. 57; Bickersteth, *Christian student*, p. 354.

where later liberals—who typically adopted a more immanent view of providence—saw progressive continuities.

The first major British intervention which made historical reflection not merely a proxy for scholastic theology, but inherent to determining ultimate value, did not come from a straightforwardly progressive thinker. It was instead the mystical and quintessentially Romantic convert to Catholicism, John Henry Newman, who pushed the issue of religious development to the centre of British intellectual debate with his *Essay on the Development of Christian Doctrine.*[55] Its publication in 1845 provides an appropriate starting date for this book. Newman's early evangelicalism, taking a liberal turn following his election to a fellowship at Oriel College, Oxford, in 1822, gradually changed into a high church position guided by his intensive reading of the church fathers after 1828. The vicar of Oxford's University Church from that year, and thereafter a leader of the Oxford Movement, Newman's growing conviction that development was inherent to religion, and that the dynamics of past development might legitimize future change, led him steadily closer to Roman Catholicism, his ultimate conversion to which he justified in his *Essay.*[56] In his movement towards a developmental understanding of religion, if less so in the conclusions to which he pressed it, Newman was no isolated figure.[57] However widely its author was reviled by his former co-religionists, the *Essay* was in fact an early and seminal instance of a significant change in the conventional framework of Victorian religious discussion.

Newman's decision to make a particular mode of reading ecclesiastical history his preferred medium of religious criticism brought him intellectually (though not personally) near to an influential grouping of liberal Anglican historians. Reaching intellectual maturity between the end of the Napoleonic wars and the intensification of Tractarian agitation, their voices were to resound powerfully with an early- and mid-Victorian public. Arthur Penrhyn Stanley, Henry Hart Milman, Julius Hare, and Connop Thirlwall, who privileged church history as a medium for replying to evangelical and high church self-assertion, formed less a close circle than a network loosely connected through friendship, institutions, and patronage. Thirlwall and Hare edited *The Philological Museum* together at Trinity College, Cambridge between 1831 and 1833. Thirlwall became the bishop of St David's in Wales in 1840, retiring shortly before his death in 1875, while Hare accepted the family living of Hurstmonceaux in Sussex in 1832, from where he occasionally journeyed to Cambridge to

[55] Newman, *Essay*.   [56] I. Ker, 'Newman, John Henry (1801–90)', *ODNB*.
[57] See chapter two of this volume.

sermonize on the results of his prodigious German reading.[58] Stanley and
Milman were both products of Oxford, though Milman had left his
Brasenose College fellowship for a clerical living at St Mary's, Reading,
sixteen years before Stanley arrived as an undergraduate at Balliol in
1834.[59] Their acquaintance developed later. Milman, who left Reading
to serve as the incumbent of St Margaret's, Westminster, from 1835 until
his appointment to the deanery of St Paul's Cathedral in 1849, warmly
endorsed Stanley's appointment as Regius Professor of Ecclesiastical History at Oxford in 1856.[60] They met often after Stanley's instalment as dean
of Westminster Abbey in 1864 until Milman's death in 1868, consulting
one another on points of mutual historical and literary interest.[61] Stanley
wrote the standard biography of Thomas Arnold, his former headmaster
and an early Victorian advocate of ecclesiastical comprehension. Stanley also
wrote a respectful obituary for Hare, and edited Thirlwall's letters.[62]

Linked to this grouping, though not a part of it, was Frederick Denison
Maurice. Maurice came from Unitarian stock, but decided to seek ordination in the Church of England while studying at Cambridge in the
1820s. A pupil and, later, friend and brother-in-law of Hare, Maurice
also looked for God's purposes in the past. But he understood history, as
he approached religion, in an idiosyncratically mystical way that was in
some respects closer to Newman's sensibility than to that of the liberal
Anglican historians. Maurice advocated an eschatology that controversially
rejected a conception of God as the dispenser of rewards and punishments,
in the belief that mankind's unity with Christ was the starting point
of ethical association.[63] Unlike Arnold or Stanley, for whom history

[58] J.W. Clark, rev. H.C.G. Matthew, 'Thirlwall, Connop (Newell) (1797–1875)',
ODNB; N. Merrill Distad, *Guessing at truth: the life of Julius Charles Hare (1795–1855)*
(Shepherdstown, WV, 1979).

[59] P.C. Hammond, 'Stanley, Arthur Penrhyn (1815–1881)', *ODNB*; H.C.G. Matthew,
'Milman, Henry Hart (1791–1868)', *ODNB*. When George Eliot, depicting pre-Reform
Middlemarch, made Mr Casaubon fear for the reception of his *Key to all mythologies* among
'the leading minds of Brasenose', she may have had Milman in mind: G. Eliot, *Middlemarch*, ed. D. Carroll (Oxford, 1997), p. 263 (first edition 1871–1872).

[60] G.G. Bradley, *Recollections of Arthur Penrhyn Stanley, late Dean of Westminster: three
lectures delivered in Edinburgh in November, 1882* (London, 1883), pp. 78–9.

[61] A. Milman, *Henry Hart Milman, D.D. Dean of St. Paul's: a biographical sketch*
(London, 1900), pp. 262–3; H.H. Milman, 'Preface to the third edition', in his *History
of Latin Christianity; including that of the popes to the Pontificate of Nicolas V*, 4th edn (9 vols,
London, 1867), i, [iii].

[62] C. Thirlwall, *Letters to a friend*, ed. A.P. Stanley (London, 1881); [A.P. Stanley],
'Archdeacon Hare', *QR*, 97:193 (1855), pp. [1]–28; Stanley, *The life and correspondence of
Thomas Arnold* (2 vols, London, 1844).

[63] J. Morris, 'A social doctrine of the Trinity? A reappraisal of F. D. Maurice on eternal
life', *Anglican and Episcopal History*, 69:1 (2000), pp. 73–100. Morris stresses that
Maurice's past and present reputation for universalism has little basis in his own writings.

showed the marginality of the variable 'opinions' expressed in creeds and formularies to the moral life of nations, Maurice took the ideas they preserved to express the immutable voice of God in past and present.[64] A remarkable number of Victorian thinkers were touched by his intellectual sensibility, which signified wider divisions within Victorian religious liberals' ways of understanding the importance of history for modern religion.

The network extended beyond England. John Tulloch, who also combined the roles of religious historian and public figure, represented a similar reforming tendency within the Church of Scotland, of whose General Assembly he served as Moderator in 1878. As the principal and primarius professor of theology in St Mary's College, St Andrews, from 1854 until his death in 1886, he was physically distant from these English clerics, save perhaps for when he was at the Athenaeum in London.[65] But he wrote warmly of them in periodicals and in his *Movements of Religious Thought*, a review of Victorian intellectual history published in 1885.[66] Lord Palmerston, then Home Secretary, had appointed Tulloch to his chair partly on the advice of the Prussian historian and diplomat Christian Karl Josias Bunsen.[67] A student of Niebuhr, minister of the Prussian crown in London from 1842 to 1854, and transmitter of German historical philosophy into British intellectual life, Bunsen became something of a guru to liberal theologians while in his host country.[68] He had energetically befriended a significant portion of British literary society during his time as a diplomat in Rome from 1816 to 1838, where he entertained visitors including Hare, Thirlwall, and Stanley. It was in part the strength of his English connections that led Frederick William IV to send him to London in 1841 to negotiate the creation of the controversial Anglo-German bishopric at Jerusalem.[69] The king rewarded Bunsen's

---

[64] B.M.G. Reardon, 'Maurice, [John] Frederick Denison (1805–1872)', *ODNB*; J. Morris, *F. D. Maurice and the crisis of Christian authority* (Oxford, 2005); J. Tulloch, *Movements of religious thought in Britain during the nineteenth century* (Leicester, 1971), pp. 53–65, [254]–286 (first edition 1885).

[65] M. Oliphant, *A memoir of the life of John Tulloch, D.D., LL.D.*, 3rd edn (Edinburgh and London, 1889), p. 238.

[66] J. Tulloch, 'Dean Stanley as a spiritual teacher and theologian', *NC*, 10:58 (1881), pp. 869–85; Tulloch, *Movements of religious thought*; T.W. Bayne, rev. H.C.G. Matthew, 'Tulloch, John (1823–1886)', *ODNB*.

[67] Oliphant, *Memoir*, pp. 98–105.

[68] F. Bunsen, *A memoir of Baron Bunsen* (2 vols, London, 1868), i, 315, 593–635, ii, 18–19; W. Höcker, *Der Gesandte Bunsen als Vermittler zwischen Deutschland und England* (Göttingen, 1951); F. Foerster, *Christian Carl Josias Bunsen: Diplomat, Mäzen und Vordenker in Wissenschaft, Kirche und Politik* (Bad Arolsen, 2001).

[69] R. Preyer, 'Bunsen and the Anglo-American community in Rome', in E. Geldbach (ed.), *Der Gelehrte Diplomat: zum Wirken Christian Carl Josias Bunsens* (Leiden, 1980), pp. 35–44.

success by appointing him to the ambassadorship in the succeeding year. The Jerusalem initiative also led to the profound alienation from him of another of his guests at Rome, and a rather different student of doctrinal development, John Henry Newman.[70]

The religious liberals of this period were distinguished by effusive mutual admiration, and more substantially by their belief that history amounted to more than an aggregate of atomized human events. History was instead the sphere in which the religious life of mankind was gathered up and cast into its denominational, national, and intellectual forms. To align oneself with the larger movements of history, grounded in providence, was a surer guide to truth than the private or sectarian opinions of individuals who resisted the purposive sweep of time. In his *The Liberal Anglican Idea of History*, Duncan Forbes brilliantly recaptured how liberal Anglican historians thought of national history in this way.[71] Yet there was another crucial side to liberal Anglican historical interest, distinct if never apart from their preoccupation with the nation, which Forbes left relatively unremarked. This was the history of the church: the plane at which the history of nations flowed into a universal history, where the ends and destiny of mankind were made most visible. In this context, Anglican and many other British historians of religion applied themselves to the philosophical, doctrinal, and sociopolitical histories of Christianity, in ways that led them beyond national or denominational questions. For these scholars, the history of civilization was driven by the churches whose role was to elevate the individual souls in which societies and polities took root. The histories of races, nations, and denominations could only be rightly interpreted when placed in the universal perspective which ecclesiastical history alone afforded.

Stanley's inaugural lectures as Regius Professor of Ecclesiastical History, delivered in 1857, exemplify the importance which he and a whole generation of British religious liberals ascribed to his subject. The spirit in which church history was to be written, he assumed, was pre-eminently a religious, not a secular one. For Stanley, ecclesiastical history was not a study of institutional, dogmatic, and liturgical forms for their own sake— the faults, as he saw them, of older approaches to the subject—but the moral and spiritual side of general history, analytically distinct whilst conceptually inseparable from civil history, which gave world history its

---

[70] 'We have been much pleased with Mr Bunsen': J.H. Newman to Henry Jenkyns, 7 April 1833, in J.H. Newman, *The letters and diaries of John Henry Newman*, ed. I. Ker et al. (32 vols, Oxford, 1978–2008), iii, 280; 'I distrust Bunsen indefinitely': J.H. Newman to J.R. Hope, 11 November 1841, in Newman, *Letters and diaries*, viii, 325; C.C.J. Bunsen to F. Bunsen, 24 January 1839, in Bunsen, *Memoir*, i, 498.
[71] D. Forbes, *The Liberal Anglican idea of history* (Cambridge, 1952).

progressive unity.[72] The subject fulfilled specifiable cultural functions. Just as the peaks and valleys of a mountain range only came into visual relation when the traveller turned back to gaze upon them from a distant point, Stanley argued, the leading truths of the Bible could only be grasped after the long passage of time.[73] The enlarging effects of ecclesiastical-historical study served to reduce divisions between the churches. 'The distinguishing characteristic of the Christian Church', Stanley argued, 'has been, that it has assumed different forms, and yet not perished in the process; that the gulf, however wide, which separates Greek from Latin, and both from Protestant, has yet not been wide enough to swallow up the common Christianity which has been transmitted from one to the other.'[74]

Connected to Stanley's admiration for the historic mutability of Christianity was his belief, volubly shared by more and more, that the history of the church and its relation to the world was itself a form of Christian evidence: 'nothing less than one of the prime agencies of the world could be so interwoven with the progress of great events.' He continued by asking, 'what is the history of the church but a long commentary on the sacred records of its first beginnings?'[75] Stanley cited one of Thirlwall's charges, given in 1857, in which the bishop remarked of church history that 'the fullness of the stream is the glory of the fountain; and it is because the Ganges is not lost among its native hills, but deepens and widens until it reaches the ocean, that so many pilgrimages are made to its springs.'[76] Such sentiments implied confidence in the future, as well as faith in the past. Reviewing the history of the nineteenth century in a sermon on 'War and Peace' which he delivered in St Paul's Cathedral in the aftermath of the Crimean War, Milman posed a significant prognostication to his congregation as to the future of civilization. 'Will there be a more close, intimate alliance between Christian doctrine and Christian morals; emancipation from sectarianism in all its forms; honest, fearless, single-minded reverence for truth, truth sought in love, maintained in love?', he asked.[77] Where revivalist historians often liked to dwell on scriptural evocations of the church militant, more peaceable verses tended to resonate with the historical dispositions of their liberal challengers. The text of Milman's sermon was taken from the prophet Isaiah:

Lord, thou wilt ordain peace for us. Thou also hast wrought all our works in us.[78]

---

[72] *LEC*, xxxii–xxxvii. [73] Ibid., lxxv–lxxvi. [74] Ibid., lxxii–lxxiii.
[75] Ibid., lxxii–lxxiv. [76] Quoted at ibid., lxxiv n. 1.
[77] H.H. Milman, *War and peace: a sermon* (London, 1856), p. 12.
[78] Ibid., p. [5]; cf. Isaiah 26:12.

The pacifying and moralizing possibilities of history, for these historians, derived not solely from its providential witness, but also from its character as empathetic literature. Stanley was devoted to the writings of Walter Scott, for him 'one of the greatest religious teachers of Scottish Christendom', whose historical novels wove themes of religious reconciliation into the interplay of characters embodying contrasting theological and social types. The two authors shared not only an easy facility for revivifying past scenes and characters, but also, in the words of Stanley's biographers, a deep sympathy with 'conflicting schools of opinion and feeling, and both held the balance evenly between contending parties'.[79] His friend, Milman, had taken his first historical inspiration not so much from Scott's novels as from his and Byron's verse dramas. Milman's own variable essays in the genre, often on historical themes, helped to win him early celebrity as a poet and, in 1821, Oxford's professorship of poetry, an honour in which he was to be succeeded by the Tractarian leader, John Keble. Though his interests changed from drama to history after the publication of *Anne Boleyn* in 1826, he was bold enough to republish such ephemerally successful meditations on sacred history as *The Fall of Jerusalem* (1820), *The Martyr of Antioch* (1822), and *Balshazzar* (1822) in 1840. He reflected in his preface to *Balshazzar* that his 'latitudinarian love for poetry' had enabled him to enlarge his 'sphere of blameless enjoyment' across Hebrew, Greek, Latin, and modern vernacular literature.[80] The poet's catholicity was to linger into Milman's turn of mind as an historian of the Hebrew, Greek, Latin, and Teutonic phases of religion.[81] He was far from being the only nineteenth-century historian to see a natural affinity between poetry and history. In their remarkable aphoristic collection of 1827, *Guesses at Truth*, Julius Hare and his brother, Augustus, declared that one of historians' chief defects was that 'they have seldom enough of the poet in them.' Not through imitating Scott's 'pantomime of life', but by straining after Shakespeare's perception of 'the powers which have striven and struggled' in the human soul, historians should be able to 'find many more characters in history to admire and love, and fewer to hate and despise'.[82]

Despite the liberal Anglican historians' shared confidence in the spiritually instructive and religiously ameliorative facets of the historical enterprise, the Hares' implicit deprecation of Scott's local colour, so beloved of Stanley, in favour of historical-poetical evocations of inward

---

[79] R.E. Prothero and G.G. Bradley (eds), *The life and correspondence of Arthur Penrhyn Stanley, D.D.* (2 vols, London, 1893), ii, 384–5.
[80] H.H. Milman, 'Balshazzar', in his *The poetical works* (3 vols, London, 1840), i, 245–6; Matthew, 'Milman'. On Victorian religious poetry, see K. Blair, *Form and faith in Victorian poetry and religion* (Oxford, 2012).
[81] See chapter three of this volume. [82] [Hare and Hare], *Guesses*, pp. 283–5.

conflict was one clue to larger variations of emphasis amongst religious liberals in these years. The difference can be summarized as a divergence over whether the right way for historicism to bolster Christianity was to redirect attention away from its doctrinal content onto the religion's social and political benefits, or instead to renew doctrine by redefining it as the organic outcome of the reflectively faithful mind, a view which enabled doctrine to be invested with new meanings. Iterations of this basic distinction formed and reformed throughout the century. They derived in no small measure from differing responses to the successive waves of German historical philosophy that began to enter Britain with Coleridge, a point of European contact that was deeply formative for successive generations of Victorian religio-historical thinkers.[83]

Well before Britons came to see new kinds of apologetic potential in historical dynamism, an extraordinary transition had reshaped the normative analytical assumptions of German academic church historians between the late eighteenth and the early nineteenth centuries. It would ultimately lead British historians, nurtured in very different academic settings, towards a comparable epiphany. Eighteenth-century German ecclesiastical historiography had been dominated by the so-called 'pragmatism' of historians such as Johann Salomo Semler, Johann Lorenz von Mosheim, and Christian Walch. These writers had cast church history as a series of atomized events, separate from revelation, upon which the historian could pronounce edifying judgement from the point of view of superior, universal reason.[84] Kant's post-Humean subversion of the classical forms of rationalism and empiricism heralded a fundamental change in how such history was conceived. By arguing that the objects of experience were only knowable in the forms in which the active faculties of the mind intuited and ordered them, Kant provoked the Idealist turn to history as the sphere in which the world of sense might be reunited with that which lay beyond it.[85] The concomitant blending of the knower and

---

[83] When Forbes wrote of the 'German Movement' behind liberal Anglican thought, he primarily meant the attraction of Barthold Georg Niebuhr's conception of national life-courses, above all to Thomas Arnold: Forbes, *Liberal Anglican idea*, pp. 1, 12–62. The lines of German influence were far more differentiated than this, however.

[84] On eighteenth-century German church-historical study, see D. Fleischer, *Zwischen Tradition und Fortschritt: der Strukturwandel der protestantischen Kirchengeschichtsschreibung im deutschsprachigen Diskurs der Aufklärung* (2 pts, Waltrop, 2006); F.C. Baur, *Die Epochen der kirchlichen Geschichtschreibung* (Tübingen, 1852), pp. 108–97; M. Mulsow et al. (eds), *Johann Lorenz Mosheim (1693–1755): Theologie im Spannungsfeld von Philosophie, Philologie und Geschichte* (Wiesbaden, 1997).

[85] For a summary of this epochal shift, see J. Rasmussen, 'The transformation of metaphysics', in Rasmussen, Wolffe, and Zachhuber, *Nineteenth-century Christian thought*, pp. [11]–34.

the object of knowledge in time soon manifested itself in church history and historical theology.[86] Building on Kant in thinking about subjectivity and self-consciousness, Friedrich Wilhelm Joseph Schelling posited a divine Absolute that realized itself in history. The study of theology, accordingly, properly involved the integration of the historical dimension of Christianity with its speculative element.[87]

The pietistic Friedrich Schleiermacher, a leading force behind the 1810 foundation of the University of Berlin, pioneered the more systematic absorption of the anti-pragmatic organicism Schelling had expounded into church history.[88] The latter, which mainly interested Schleiermacher in the form of historical theology, was to him no longer the sealed-off ecclesiastical structure studied by the pragmatic historians, but an element of world history, and a moving whole in which advancement could be nothing other than a greater affinity and more complete unification with the laws of Christ.[89] Schleiermacher posited, however, a fundamental distinction between a religious feeling of absolute dependence and the dogmatic systems which bore an historically specific relation to it. It was that subjective feeling, an 'intuition of the universe', upon which religion rested.[90] Outward religious forms took their meaning solely from the way in which they gave voice to the religious consciousness, a necessarily social activity which arose from feeling and took shape in time.[91] Historical theology and church history thus became essential components of Schleiermacher's wider intellectual endeavour to give 'philosophical' theology status as a positive *Wissenschaft* in the modern university, by making history integral to theological critique.[92] Schleiermacher's views exerted a major influence on university research in Germany and critical attitudes further afield.[93]

---

[86] J. Zachhuber, 'The historical turn', in ibid., pp. [53]–71.

[87] F.W.J. Schelling, *System des transcendentalen Idealismus* (Tübingen, 1800), pp. 438–41; Schelling, *Vorlesungen über die Methode des akademischen Studium* (Tübingen, 1803), pp. 189–210.

[88] G.A. Benrath, 'Evangelische und katholische Kirchenhistorie im Zeichen der Aufklärung und der Romantik', *Zeitschrift für Kirchengeschichte*, 82 (1971), pp. 203–17; Howard, *Protestant theology*, pp. [130]–211.

[89] Benrath, 'Evangelische und katholische Kirchenhistorie', p. 211.

[90] F.D.E. Schleiermacher, 'Über die Religion: Reden an die Gebildeten unter ihren Verächtern', in his *Werke: Auswahl in vier Bänden*, ed. O. Braun and J. Bauer (4 vols, Leipzig, 1910–1913), iv, [211]-399, at 243 (first edition 1799); B.A. Gerrish, 'Friedrich Schleiermacher', in N. Smart et al. (eds), *Nineteenth-century religious thought in the west* (3 vols, Cambridge, 1985), i, 123–56.

[91] F.D.E. Schleiermacher, 'Der christliche Glaube nach den Grundsätzen der evangelischen Kirche im Zusammenhang dargestellt', in his *Werke*, iii, [633]–729 (first edition 1821–2).

[92] M. Rössler, *Schleiermachers Programm der philosophischen Theologie* (Berlin and New York, 1994).

[93] Howard, *Protestant theology*, pp. 310–11.

A British educated public became acquainted with Schleiermacher's positions less from his own writings, than through the work of German church historians who drew inspiration from his abstract and programmatic dicta for their more concrete and particular researches. Johann Adam Möhler was one such author. A member of the Catholic theological faculty at Tübingen, Möhler's 1825 *Einheit in der Kirche* had portrayed the church as an organism, moved by the Holy Spirit, in which interior faith was the root of exterior faith, or assent to dogmas.[94] He would later change his position to demarcate himself more clearly from his more radical Tübingen colleagues; but the fact that he had adopted it revealed his close intellectual relationship with Johann Sebastian Drey, the Schleiermacher-inspired leader of the early Catholic Tübingen School.[95] Newman's *Essay* showed significant traces of contact with this way of thinking.[96]

A broader channel connecting Schleiermacher's innovations to British audiences lay in the Protestant *Vermittlungstheologie*, or mediating theology, which became a powerful German academic fashion in the earlier decades of the century. The term described a form of theology, practised by a wide spectrum of divines touched by Schleiermacher, which attempted to 'mediate' between subjective or speculative intellectual tendencies and orthodoxy.[97] One of its foremost representatives was the church historian Johann August Wilhelm Neander, who acquired a wide following during and immediately after his lifetime in the English-speaking world.[98] Though largely forgotten today, in his time Neander was widely thought to have made an epoch in the writing of church history. Born in 1789, Neander converted to Lutheranism from his ancestral Judaism under the influence of Schleiermacher and especially Plato; in 1813, at Schleiermacher's instigation, he joined the Berlin theology faculty. His great work was to be a *General History of the Christian Religion and Church*, published in successive volumes between

---

[94] J.A. Möhler, *Die Einheit in der Kirche oder das Prinzip des Katholicismus dargestellt im Geiste der Kirchenväter der drei ersten Jahrhunderte* (Mainz and Wiesbaden, 1925), first edition 1825; O. Chadwick, *From Bossuet to Newman*, 2nd edn (Cambridge, 1987) pp. 108–10.

[95] Ibid., pp. 104–105; J.R. Geiselmann, *Lebendiger Glaube aus geheiligter Überlieferung: der Grundgedanke der Theologie Johann Adam Möhlers und der katholischen Tübinger Schule*, 2nd edn (Freiburg im Breisgau, 1966), pp. [17]–53, 167–8.

[96] See chapter two of this volume at pp. 68–9.

[97] For a definitional discussion, see Aubert, *German roots*, pp. 71–3.

[98] [S.D. Worthington], 'Neander's Werke', *BQR*, 96 (1868), pp. [305]–350. On Neander, see K.-V. Selge, 'August Neander—ein getaufter Hamburger Jude der Emanzipations- und Restaurationszeit als erster Berlin Kirchenhistoriker', in G. Beiser and C. Gestrich (eds), *450 Jahre evangelische Theologie in Berlin* (Göttingen, 1989), pp. [233]–76.

1825 and 1852.[99] His other projects included a reply to David Friedrich Strauss's radical *Leben Jesu*, which reduced the gospel narratives to the status of mythic consciousness.[100]

As an historian, Neander married a deep reverence for Schleiermacher's pietistic and psychological approach to religion with an explicit affirmation that the Christian revelation descended on mankind from without. He sought to move beyond Schleiermacher's subjectivism by studying concrete historical personalities rather than abstract ideas.[101] But his seminal contribution was generally taken by his admirers to have been the abolition of the division between speculative and empirical history, by integrating a depiction of the unrepeatable individuality of each Christian life with a broader picture of church history as the slow upwards movement of the footsteps of Christ on earth. He was not, like the more familiar Leopold von Ranke, particularly interested in the interaction of the church with international politics. Neander preferred to bring forward the life of the church insofar as it flowed from the life of Christ, and especially as it was expressed in the psychological and intellectual lives of its great members.[102] His conviction that Christianity's historical progressiveness witnessed to the truth of its claims was expressed in his favourite historical metaphor, drawn from one of Christ's parables in Matthew's Gospel. 'The kingdom of God is like a leaven', he held, growing with the wider and deeper knowledge of Jesus Christ's reconciliation of sinners to God.[103] It was a passage of which Newman was also fond.[104]

Classical precursors and indigenous analogues to the German Idealist tradition helped to predispose many British readers towards it and the histories it shaped. British students of Idealist philosophy, in common with its German progenitors, were heirs to successive attempts, stretching back to Paul and Justin Martyr, to bring classical philosophy to the aid of a

[99] J.A.W. Neander, *Allgemeine Geschichte der christlichen Religion und Kirche* (6 vols, Hamburg, 1825–52). The work began to be translated into English soon after it started to appear: Neander, *The history of the Christian religion and church during the first three centuries*, trans. H.J. Rose (2 vols, London, 1831–1841); more substantially, J.A.W. Neander, *General history of the Christian religion and church*, trans. J. Torrey (9 vols, Edinburgh, 1847–1855).
[100] D.F. Strauss, *Das Leben Jesu, kritisch bearbeitet* (2 vols, Tübingen, 1835-1836); J.A.W. Neander, *Das Leben Jesu in seinem geschichtlichen Zusammenhange und seiner geschichtlichen Entwickelung* (Hamburg, 1837).
[101] O. Krabbe, *August Neander: ein Beitrag zu seiner Charakteristik* (Hamburg, 1852), pp. 26–8.
[102] Ibid., p. 100.
[103] Neander, *Allgemeine Geschichte*, vol. i, pt. 2, frontispiece; cf. Matthew 13:33.
[104] Newman, *Essay*, p. 113.

religion that offered a radical affront to 'philosophy and vain deceit'.[105] Platonism, especially, offered anti-materialist resources to Christian apologists educated within the classical tradition dominant in English, and influential in Scottish, universities.[106] This philosophical approach was characterized less by a close allegiance to Plato himself, than by a flexible openness to his and subsequent Neoplatonists' characteristic positions: the eternity of truth, the reality of ideas, the reconciliation of opposites in a higher spiritual principle. A major nineteenth-century representative of the English Platonist tradition, Samuel Taylor Coleridge, placed great emphasis in his 1825 *Aids to Reflection* and elsewhere on the capacity of the Reason to penetrate to a world of permanent truth which lay beyond the scope of the sensuous Understanding.[107] For Coleridge, Reason disclosed that the Bible was no mere text, but a symbolic clothing for divine truth. History connected the experience of the inspired writers to that of the Bible's later readers, thereby verifying biblical testimony: an argument that reflected Coleridge's own contact with Kant and Schelling.[108] Coleridge met the normal fate of genius, and became more esteemed in death than in life, living on as a constant reference point for Victorian theologians and philosophers. Maurice would adapt Coleridgean epistemology to locate the apprehension of religious verities in the universal experience of mankind, rather than in individual deduction.[109] Julius Hare, whose lectures on Plato Maurice had keenly attended at Cambridge, was also among Coleridge's apostles, lobbying Trinity College to establish a prize essay in his memory which would take the 'philosophy of Christianity' as its theme.[110]

Thus prepared by Coleridge and a certain kind of classicism, early- and mid-Victorian religious liberals actively promoted the results of German historical philosophy and mediating theology, eclectically arranged and distinctively interpreted, to British audiences. In Hare's view, the prime contribution of German philosophy was to have established the principle

[105] On literary explorations of this theme, see S. Goldhill, *Victorian culture and classical antiquity: art, opera, fiction, and the proclamation of modernity* (Princeton, NJ, 2011), pp. [193]–244; on its role in ecclesiastical historiography, see J.G.A. Pocock, *Barbarism and religion* (6 vols, Cambridge, 1999–2016), v, 21–45; Colossians 2:8.

[106] D. Newsome, *Two classes of men: Platonism and English romantic thought* (London, 1972); W.R. Inge, *The Platonic tradition in English religious thought: the Hulsean lectures at Cambridge, 1925–1926* (London, 1926).

[107] S.T. Coleridge, *Aids to reflection and the confessions of an inquiring spirit* (London, 1893), pp. 20 and n. 143–56.

[108] M.J. Lloyd, 'The historical thought of S. T. Coleridge: the later prose works' (Oxford Univ. DPhil, 1998), pp. 27–63, 212-4.

[109] Morris, *Maurice*, pp. 38–41.

[110] Trinity College, Cambridge, Add. MS a206/165-6: J.C. Hare to W. Whewell, 12 October 1834; Newsome, *Two classes*, pp. 41–56.

that the worth of any religious system could only be judged in relation to its place in the progressive history of human opinion. Maurice, not himself a great reader of German, relied on Hare to translate intriguing passages of Schelling and Schleiermacher for him.[111] In common with his Trinity friend and co-translator of Niebuhr's *Roman History*, Thirlwall, Hare regarded Schleiermacher as one of the greatest Christian philosophers, though both resisted attempts to read Christian history as pantheistically or logically determined.[112] Bunsen regarded himself as particularly instrumental in connecting British leaders of opinion to the world of Schleiermacherian mediating theology.[113] He evoked Friedrich Schelling's philosophical and theological promise in his letters, at a time when Schelling—now proclaiming a 'philosophy of revelation' rooted in concrete historical existence—was becoming the intellectual figurehead of the German reaction against the 'atheism' of young Hegelians such as David Friedrich Strauss, Bruno Bauer, and Ludwig Feuerbach after 1840.[114] August Neander's writings, giving Schleiermacher's mesmerizing insights a tangible basis in historical science, were still more important in effecting the transmission after which Bunsen strove. Hare judged him to have exquisitely combined faith and knowledge to fulfil the ideal of the historian of Christianity: 'the setting forth of this twofold manifestation of Christianity, in its constancy and in its progressiveness'.[115] John Tulloch agreed, describing Neander as 'in some respects the highest expression of the Christian reason in this century'.[116]

Not every early- or mid-Victorian religious liberal thought about history within discernibly germanized or Coleridgean terms of reference. Those who did so tended to privilege intellectual and doctrinal history, read as the growth of mind or conscience. History, theology, and philosophy tended to

---

[111] F. Maurice (ed.), *The life of Frederick Denison Maurice chiefly told in his own letters* (2 vols, London, 1884), i, 289, 453–4, 468.

[112] [Hare and Hare], *Guesses*, pp. 312–3, 470. Thirlwall had been Schleiermacher's first English translator: F.D.E. Schleiermacher, *A critical essay on the Gospel of St Luke*, [trans. C. Thirlwall] (London, 1825). Thirlwall called Hegel 'one of the most impudent of all literary quacks': Trinity College, Cambridge, Add. MS a 213/180: C. Thirlwall to W. Whewell, 31 October 1849.

[113] C.C.J. Bunsen, *Hippolytus and his age; or, the doctrine and practice of the church of Rome under Commodus and Alexander Severus: and ancient and modern Christianity and divinity compared* (4 vols, London, 1852), i, 86–8, ii, 27–8; Foerster, Bunsen, pp. 55–67.

[114] C.C.J. Bunsen to T. Arnold, 1 August 1838, in Bunsen, *Memoir*, i, 463–4; C.C.J. Bunsen to G.C.F. Lücke, 25 April 1849, ibid., ii, 219–24. On the work of Schelling and Bunsen in supposedly preserving religion and nation, see J.E. Toews, *Becoming historical: cultural Reformation and public memory in early nineteenth-century Berlin* (Cambridge, 2004), pp. 1–114.

[115] [Hare and Hare], *Guesses*, p. 313.

[116] J. Tulloch, 'Rationalism', *CR*, 1 (1866), pp. [361]–84, at 369.

bind and blend themselves together in attempts to make Christianity—and often in an orthodox form—credible. John Stuart Mill, whose utilitarian hostility to doctrines of innate ideas made his philosophy a useful resource to secular critics, but whose humanely eclectic turn of mind made him interested in religious debate and sympathetic to religion's social function, observed half-approvingly that 'the Germano-Coleridgean school' applied itself to finding life and meaning in the opinions of earlier ages.[117] A second broad approach to religious history, however, followed a notably different line of analysis. It was promoted by historians who, though still deeply interested in the historical effects of religion, deliberately tried to separate historical from theological categories. They construed historical development more as a matter of the interaction between Christianity and 'external' circumstances than as a growth of 'internal' spirit in religious history. Historians who thought in this way generally turned to ecclesiastical history not in order to vindicate the spiritual wellsprings of religious thought, but so as to nudge doctrinal formulations to the margins of ecclesiastical life.

Among the earlier liberal Anglicans, and before the later form of British Idealism gained momentum, Milman and Stanley had been notably distant from Hare's attempts to invigorate established theology by portraying it as the fruit of Coleridgean Reason and, from one aspect, subjective consciousness. They belonged more identifiably to an indigenous, latitudinarian tradition. Their brand of historically projected liberalism did not centre on an attempt to revitalize orthodoxy by making it the outcome of a reconceived process of reasoning. They instead emphasized the relative unimportance of doctrine, when compared to the variety of social forms and ecclesiastical polities in which moralizing religion flourished. Such an emphasis was, in Milman's and Stanley's case, connected to their desire to establish a comprehensive Church of England on the basis that there were essentials and non-essentials in orthodox religion. Stanley was more stridently Arnoldian than Milman on this point; his historical writings were in some ways the narrative counterpart to Arnold's *Principles of Church Reform*.[118] Hare, by contrast, preferred to set about the work of instructing in what orthodoxy meant, and was relatively unmoved by political questions.[119] The difference between them, partly expressed in

---

[117] J.S. Mill, 'Coleridge', in his *Essays on ethics, religion and society*, ed. J.M. Robson (Toronto, 1969), pp. [119], 138–9 (repr. from the *WR* for 1840); J. Harris, 'Mill, John Stuart (1806–1873)', *ODNB*.

[118] J. Witheridge, *Excellent Dr Stanley: the life of Dean Stanley of Westminster* (Norwich, 2013), pp. [25]–67, 83–4, 272–3; Milman, *Milman*, pp. 244–5; T. Arnold, *Principles of church reform* (London, 1833).

[119] Cf. J. Morris, 'The spirit of comprehension: examining the Broad Church synthesis in England', *Anglican and Episcopal History*, 75:3 (2006), pp. 423–43.

Hare's preference for Shakespeare over Scott, also reflected the greater intensity of his engagement with German Idealism. Liberal critics of Milman and Stanley were to remark on their unhelpfully unspeculative casts of mind. In the eyes of John Tulloch, for example, who combined impatience with dogmatism with a growing interest in the development of thought as the expression of Christian mind and character, this disposition did not make enough of the epistemological promise of religious history in the face of new conceptual dangers. Idealism, more often than simple unsectarianism, was increasingly to meet that need among religious liberals of the later Victorian period.

Milman and Stanley were intellectually distant from the arguments over how to conceptualize the role of divinity and spirit in historical time that followed in the wake of the British Idealist movement. Gathering pace from the 1860s, British Idealism represented a newly systematic and academically influential successor, founded upon Plato, Kant, and Hegel, to the idealist tremors of the earlier part of the century. Tulloch and Hare had complained, in counterpoint to their fondness for Neander, about the hard and abstract historical logic of the Hegelians; and, from Bunsen's point of view, the extremism of some of Hegel's followers contaminated his philosophy. But for some, historical logic was the only way to overcome the inherent subjectivism of trying to locate a sustainable foundation for religious commitment in personalities or particular theological approaches.[120] The later British Idealists, reflecting their more unapologetically Hegelian roots, included philosophers who were also historians of religious ideas, and who took a keen interest in identifying a more thoroughgoing logic in the course of church history.[121] The brothers John and Edward Caird were influential figures in this context. John, the elder of the Caird brothers, was consecutively professor of divinity at Glasgow and then the university's principal from 1862 to his death in 1898.[122] Edward, after a period as Snell Exhibitioner at Balliol College, Oxford, where he came under the influence of T. H. Green, became professor of moral philosophy at Glasgow in 1866 before returning to Balliol as master of the college following the death of Benjamin Jowett in 1893; unlike his brother, he did not take holy orders.[123] Although these Idealists seldom described themselves as Hegelians, and wrote fondly of Coleridge and Carlyle, they were intellectually and physically distant from Stanley, or even from Thirlwall and Tulloch. The latter

[120] Cf. F.C. Baur on Neander: Baur, *Epochen*, pp. 202–32.
[121] W. Mander, *British Idealism: a history* (Oxford, 2011), pp. [137]–180.
[122] Stewart J. Brown, 'Caird, John (1820–1898)', *ODNB*.
[123] S.M. den Otter, 'Caird, Edward (1835–1908)', *ODNB*.

generation were coming to the ends of their lives just as Idealists were entering intellectual maturity who assumed very different points of intellectual reference.

Idealists tended not to make the interventions in denominational disputes periodically undertaken by the earlier liberals, having left such alleged trivialities much further behind. Nor did they make the same separation between religion and reflection which their predecessors or Schleiermacher tended to do. 'Faith is *just undeveloped knowledge*', said Edward Caird in a lecture to Glasgow students. Caird's maxim reflected his and other later-nineteenth-century Idealists' fundamental desire to resolve the growing Victorian conflict they perceived between faith and reason, by showing how such strife rested upon a false antithesis.[124] All knowledge, they held, was ultimately rational. Thought moved from implicit to self-conscious recognition of this truth in history. The end of philosophy, therefore, was to explain the rationality of the universe and the reality of an underlying spirit upon which such rationality necessarily depended. For Idealists, Christianity became a stage or a central means of the working of absolute spirit, which was the ground and end of the universe, as part of which all other things were intelligible. Christ became the earthly impress of a greater idea, rather than intrinsically the ground and end of all theologico-historical development, as he was with Tulloch or the earlier liberal Anglicans. That idea was divine–human unity, which could only be realized in time, as it was being realized in the mutually completing stages of the history of the church—which was also the history of the world. Where earlier religious liberals had typically made church history the engine of general history, Idealists dissolved the distinction between the two more systematically: the world, in the end, was the church. Edward Caird regarded attempts to go beyond the progressive self-realization of spirit in time, and to lay hold of an 'eternal something' at the heart of Christianity, as absurd.[125]

Idealism, whether in the absolute form represented by the Cairds or in the shape of the personal Idealism that broke with Hegel's identification of thought and reality in favour of a greater emphasis upon the autonomy of experience, came unsystematically to suffuse many parts of British intellectual life from the 1880s onwards. It was typical of the delayed

[124] Glasgow University Archive, DC 379/1/1 31,355: J.L. Steven, 'Notes of lectures on moral philosophy delivered by Professor Edward Caird in the Glasgow University session 1875–6', vol. ii, 81–3.

[125] Edward Caird to Mary Talbot, 14 January 1906, in H. Jones and J.H. Muirhead (eds), *The life and philosophy of Edward Caird LL.D., D.C.L., F.B.A.* (Glasgow, 1921), pp. 241–2.

reaction which characterized British assimilation of German intellectual innovations that Hegelianism should have acquired its greatest British popularity after it had become outmoded in Germany itself. Yet British authors also proved attentive to the new intellectual formations yielded by the ebb tide, especially the growth of Ritschlian theology. Taking shape in the 1860s and 1870s as part of the wider Kantian revival, Ritschlianism tended to give a more secular appearance to church history than mediating theology or absolute Idealism had encouraged. Albrecht Ritschl, professor of theology at Bonn from 1852 to 1864 and thereafter at Göttingen until his death in 1889, sought to free Christianity from metaphysics by returning it to its sources in the New Testament.[126] He proposed that the essence of Christianity lay in the direct moral impression produced by Christ on the disciples. The kingdom of God was not to be obtained through mysticism or dogmatism; rather, it was to be worked out socially, in secular time. Theological science, in Ritschl's view, had to start from this position, which church history tended to confirm. But the study of church history, which he construed as the study of a phenomenon radically different from the normative expression of positive religion in the historical Christ, could not be guided by the Idealist assumption that historical change necessarily belonged to an inherently divine progressive evolution.[127]

Rather as Neander had proceeded from Schleiermacher's principles, Adolf von Harnack gave Ritschl's theological assumptions extensive application to church-historical scholarship. Harnack, who became professor of theology at Berlin in 1888, reacted against dogmatic Lutheranism, vague mediation-theology, and speculative Idealism in favour of a heavily ethicized Ritschlian Christology.[128] This total idea of Christianity was, for Harnack, confirmed by imaginative grasp of the sum of doctrinal development understood to consist of the genetic evolution of autonomous historical individualities.[129] As with Ritschl, however, such development was not development in the sense of the logical ascent of an idea or the

---

[126] Rasmussen, 'Transformation of metaphysics', p. 23.

[127] Zachhuber, *Theology as science*, pp. [135]–174.

[128] C. Nottmeier, *Adolf von Harnack und die deutsche Politik 1890–1930: eine biographische Studie zum Verhältnis von Protestantismus, Wissenschaft und Politik* (Tübingen, 2004), pp. 66–8 and 68 n.; M. Basse, *Die dogmengeschichtliche Konzeptionen Adolf von Harnacks und Reinhold Seebergs* (Göttingen, 2001), p. 54; Universitätsbibliothek Marburg, HS 695/371–411: A. Harnack to A. Jülicher, 6 January 1889; A. Harnack, 'August Neander', in his *Reden und Aufsätze* (2 vols, Giessen, 1904), i, [195]–218.

[129] A. Harnack, *Lehrbuch der Dogmengeschichte* (3 vols, Freiburg im Breisgau, 1886–1890); K. Nowak, 'Theologie, Philologie und Geschichte: Adolf von Harnack als Kirchenhistoriker', in K. Nowak and O.G. Oexle (eds), *Adolf von Harnack: Theologe, Historiker, Wissenschaftspolitiker* (Göttingen, 2001), pp. 189–237.

progressive unfolding of divine truth. In place of these older, Idealist, and *vermittlungstheologische* ideas, there came a tension. History continued to be privileged as the means of arriving at theological truth, and procedural specialization coexisted alongside an abiding ideal of higher epistemological unity, founded on God. Yet divinity was substantially removed from historical time; in writing history, it was no longer necessary to be seen to record God's footsteps.[130] For Harnack, the history of dogma recorded not rational progress, but declension from a primitive state, as Christianity expanded into the Hellenistic world and absorbed its intellectual assumptions.

Echoes of this late-Idealist German moment were heard in Britain, especially in the controversies generated by Edwin Hatch, Harnack's admirer and correspondent, and Oxford's reader in ecclesiastical history from 1884 until his death in 1889.[131] Hatch, a self-consciously 'scientific' historian, clothed his professedly impartial examinations of doctrinal history with analytical formulations drawn from the natural sciences. In seeking thus to bolster his scholarly authority, Hatch was not alone among late-Victorian religious historians. But different kinds of scientific metaphor, in common with the differing German typologies to which they were sometimes connected, possessed notably divergent resonances when applied to the movements of religious history. Some critics used scientific motifs to burnish the organic vitality of the religious past by drawing comparisons or philosophical connections between it and natural evolution. But Hatch deployed scientific images to stress that past's deadness, and others its violence.[132]

Whilst the polyphony of liberal historicism originated in liberal circles, it reverberated across a wider intellectual landscape. Classically high church and evangelical understanding of the past did not disappear in the years after 1850, but high churchmen and evangelicals who came to maturity in the second half of the century were increasingly touched by progressive ideas of history. On the whole, the latter acted not so much as the solvent of these traditions, as a reagent that stimulated their remoulding. Within the Church of England, the heirs to the Tractarians often began to suppose that idealism offered a way of linking divine and earthly reason through a process of historical development. The high churchman

---

[130] Peter Ghosh has argued that the Ritschlian relative secularization of religious history, alongside its continuing affirmation of religion's world-historical importance, was a crucial context for Max Weber's disenchanted yet religiously originating vision of modernity: P. Ghosh, *Max Weber and* The Protestant Ethic: *twin histories* (Oxford, 2014), pp. 92–3.

[131] See chapter two of this volume at pp. 94–104.

[132] On the polyvalent nature of scientific metaphors in Victorian literary culture, see G. Beer, *Open fields: science in cultural encounter* (Oxford, 1996).

Mandell Creighton, Cambridge's first Dixie Professor of Ecclesiastical
History from 1884 until his 1891 elevation to the see of Peterborough,
always maintained that the Oxford undergraduate tutor to whom he
owed the most was Edward Caird.[133] 'The Church and the world must
be studied together, in their mutual relations', he said in his 1885
inaugural lecture.[134] Amongst Anglican evangelicals, Henry Wace, professor of ecclesiastical history at, and subsequently principal of, King's
College, London, from 1875 until his 1903 appointment to the deanery
of Canterbury, was more resistant to German Idealism, although he
maintained an estimable library of the biblical and historical scholarship
its several permutations undergirded.[135] He was, however, a student of
Coleridge's *Aids to Reflection*, and used him to evoke the 'large poetry' of
the emphatically Protestant doctrinal settlement yielded by the upheavals
of the English Reformation.[136] In interpreting orthodox doctrine as a
force of spiritual life verified in historical experience, Wace joined a
significant number of late-century evangelicals. In his corresponding
insistence that whilst 'circumstances are an unquestionable element in
human development', 'its most characteristic and important factor is the
influence of personal and spiritual agencies in controlling circumstances',
he gave voice to a position which liberal churchmen also defended.[137]

The notions that doctrine was historically dynamic, and that the
common Christianity at work beneath civilizational and dogmatic forms
might be in greater need of historical delineation and affirmation than it
had once been, also informed evangelical renewal within Britain's dissenting traditions. If an early nineteenth-century generation of evangelical
nonconformists typically placed less emphasis upon doctrinal theology
than Anglican churchmen, the difference became notably less pronounced
over time, as nonconformity's intellectual leaders in common with those
of other churches found the beliefs they professed to be deep in history.[138]
Robert William Dale, whose work on Christ's atonement was studied in

---

[133] L. Creighton, *Life and letters of Mandell Creighton, D.D. Oxon. and Cam., sometime bishop of London* (2 vols, London, 1904), i, 26.

[134] M. Creighton, 'The teaching of ecclesiastical history. Inaugural lecture as Dixie professor of ecclesiastical history', in his *Historical lectures and addresses*, ed. L. Creighton (London, New York, and Bombay, 1903), p. 9.

[135] S. Gregory, 'Wace, Henry (1836–1924)', *ODNB*; [Anon.], *A catalogue of the valuable theological library of the late Very Revd Henry Wace, D.D., Dean of Canterbury* (London, [1924]), pp. 11, 17, 21, 24, 25–6.

[136] H. Wace, *Christianity and morality or the correspondence of the Gospel with the moral nature of man: the Boyle Lectures for 1874 and 1875* (London, 1876), frontispiece; Wace, *The foundations of faith considered in eight sermons preached before the University of Oxford in the year M.DCCC.LXXIX* (London, 1880), pp. 220–1.

[137] Wace, *Christianity and morality*, pp. 151–2.

[138] Hopkins, *Nonconformity's romantic generation*, pp. 2–3.

Anglican seminaries, devoted considerable intellectual labour to doctrinal history whilst serving as a Congregational pastor at Carr's Lane Chapel in Birmingham, where he was sole minister from 1859 until his death in 1895.[139] After shedding his early Calvinist leanings, Dale looked to historical theology to help to preserve the central features of evangelical witness from mechanical traditionalism, on the one hand, and insufficiently scriptural 'modern Evangelicals' on the other.[140] Dale's sensitivity to the moral and pastoral necessity of this balance led him to commend the mediating theologian Isaak Dorner's *History of Protestant Theology* to future preachers, warning them against the temptation to lay it to one side should their attention instead wander onto fashionable novels during the hours they set aside for study.[141]

A fellow, rather older Congregationalist, John Stoughton, who began his pastorate at Windsor in 1833, served as professor of historical theology at the denomination's New College, St John's Wood, from 1872 until his retirement in 1884.[142] Less of a controversialist than Dale, his work as an historian tended over time to soften the astringent tone, though not the evangelical content, of his earlier Protestantism. In 1880, he commended historical theology as a means of disentangling the human from the divine in religious questions; it even offered a 'prelibation of heaven', by awakening spiritual sympathies across time and space.[143] Stoughton's pacific and literary inclinations made him a model dissenter in the eyes of broad church Anglicans. Matthew Arnold proposed him for membership of the Athenaeum; and he acted as a pallbearer at Stanley's funeral in Westminster Abbey in 1881.[144] John Cairns represented a similar tendency within Scottish Presbyterian dissent. He served as principal of the United Presbyterian Church's Divinity Hall in Edinburgh from 1879 until shortly before his death in 1892, using his position as the denomination's leading divine to advocate a more catholic evangelical than traditionally

[139] Ibid., pp. [46]–84; A.W.W. Dale, *The life of R.W. Dale of Birmingham* (London, 1899), p. 132; D.W. Bebbington, *Evangelicalism in modern Britain: a history from the 1730s to the 1980s* (London, 1989), p. 141. On Dale, see C. Binfield (ed.), *The cross and the city: essays in commemoration of Robert William Dale 1829–1895*, supplement to the *Journal of the United Reformed Church History Society*, vol. 6 (Cambridge, 1999).

[140] R.W. Dale, *The evangelical revival and other sermons with an address on the work of the Christian ministry in a period of theological decay and transition* (London, 1880), [iii]–v.

[141] On Dorner, see Aubert, *German roots*, pp. 89–93; R.W. Dale, 'Reading', in his *Nine lectures on preaching: delivered at Yale, New Haven, Connecticut*, 9th edn (London, 1896), pp. 64-65 (first edition 1876).

[142] J.M. Rigg, rev. H.C.G. Matthew, 'Stoughton, John (1807–1897)', *ODNB*.

[143] J. Stoughton, *An introduction to historical theology: being a sketch of doctrinal progress from the apostolic era to the Reformation* (London, 1880), pp. 6–13.

[144] Stoughton, *Recollections of a long life*, 2nd edn (London, 1894), p. 196; Prothero and Bradley, *Arthur Penrhyn Stanley*, ii, 572.

Calvinist theology.[145] A critical hearer of Neander's, Ranke's, and Schelling's lectures while studying at Berlin from 1843 to 1844, Cairns become a correspondent of Bunsen and Milman after his return to Scotland.[146] 'The differences of our common Christianity are after all external and accidental', he told Milman in a letter of 1864.[147]

Such sentiments became increasingly vocal amongst religious moralists of all kinds in the final third of the century. They were evoked not solely by developments within theological culture, but also by the tendency for loss of faith to replace denominational conflict as the chief focus of these historians' anxieties. That anxiety was given a significant historical dimension by the fact that a number of historical thinkers rose to prominence after the mid-century who were united in their sometimes regretful confidence that the nature of sociopolitical and intellectual progress eroded Christianity's claims to rational commitment. These critics did not represent a unified group, so much as occupants of an area of twilight shading from the outer verges of Christian profession to combative unbelief. The Renaissance historian, John Addington Symonds, and the student of the Reformation, James Anthony Froude, represented the former tendency, passing through the clerical atmosphere of the ancient universities into heterodox yet vestigially religious forms of historical moralism. Symonds came to repose upon Hellenistic humanism, rather than Christian Platonism, albeit in ways tinctured by idealist spirituality, whereas Froude developed a disruptive and culturally Protestant authorial voice.[148] Their religious and intellectual trajectories were idiosyncratic; but expressed that strand of Victorian doubt whose reluctance to jettison Christian morality and Protestant feeling was stronger than its willingness expressly to affirm their theological foundations.

For more unambiguously secular historians, the history of progress became more clearly the history of secularization. In their hands, historical analysis was not a means of purifying theology so as to maintain its sway, but rather a way of encouraging its replacement by properly scientific forms of knowledge which might provide the basis of post-Christian social forms.[149] Such secular progressivism consisted of several interacting

---

[145] D.C. Smith, 'Cairns, John (1818–1892)', *ODNB*.

[146] A.R. Macewen, *Life and letters of John Cairns D.D., LL.D.* (London, 1895), pp. 154–6, 422, 486.

[147] Bodleian Library, Oxford, MS Eng. lett. d. 166 (Milman letters 1841–1904)/14–15: J. Cairns to H.H. Milman, 4 April 1864.

[148] See chapter four of this volume.

[149] I refer to 'secularization' in this more ultimate, disenchanted sense, rather than in its more common nineteenth-century signification of religion's privatization or separation from politics: cf. M. Borutta, *Antikatholizismus: Deutschland und Italien im Zeitalter der europäischen Kulturkämpfe* (Göttingen, 2010), pp. [267]–389.

strands. The reverend Mark Pattison, the rebarbative Rector of Lincoln College, Oxford, from 1861, became notably interested in the law-governed historical conditions of intellectual life and scholarship after falling away from his youthful, and seemingly rather forced Tractarianism. Though he professedly found a way out of agnosticism in devotion to the principle of reason itself, inflected by Hegel and Fichte, this pioneering advocate of the research university often targeted religion in his studies of intellectual history.[150] Pattison's work guided Leslie Stephen's interests in the history of thought as a means of validating the origins of the agnosticism into which he had settled as a clerical fellow at Trinity Hall, Cambridge, a position from which he resigned in 1867 after he no longer felt able to take chapel services.[151] An indigenous form of older, Enlightenment rationalism, in which conspicuously unfashionable deist sympathies commingled with the structuring influence of Mill's philosophy, lived on in Henry Thomas Buckle's *History of Civilization in England* (1857–1861).[152] Buckle, a largely home-educated prodigy enabled by a modest inheritance to pursue a London literary life free from correction or contradiction by others, developed a radically secular conception of scientific history which immurement in a college fellowship would have inhibited. His exuberantly anticlerical reading of European history registered contact with Auguste Comte's 'Positivist' sociological system, which prophesied the supersession of theological religion by a non-metaphysical 'religion of humanity'. Buckle's *History* instanced how Comtism exerted a diffusive influence that extended far beyond the small circle of its devoted British acolytes.

What united these historians was their commitment to the idea that law-governed history completely or practically excluded divine involvement; and their assumption that social progress ultimately rested upon intellectual change. Yet once again, aspects of the structure of their thought could find an affinity with those who drew very different conclusions. Their apologetically minded readers returned few objections to the putative orderliness of history, or to the idea that history was led by thought. What religiously committed critics rejected were the anti-metaphysical foundations upon which Buckle and Comte constructed their understandings of historical law and the dynamics of intellectual

[150] D. Nimmo, 'Learning against religion, learning as religion: Mark Pattison and the "Victorian crisis of faith"', in K. Robbins (ed.), *Religion and humanism: papers read at the eighteenth summer meeting and the nineteenth winter meeting of the Ecclesiastical History Society* (Oxford, 1981), pp. 311–24. On Pattison's life and work, see H.S. Jones, *Intellect and character in Victorian England: Mark Pattison and the invention of the don* (Cambridge, 2007).
[151] A. Bell, 'Stephen, Leslie (1832–1904)', *ODNB*.
[152] T.W. Heyck, 'Buckle, Henry Thomas (1821–1862)', *ODNB*.

history. For the most advanced critics, however, scientific induction, not spirit, drove historical progress. At this point, historical argument became enmeshed with epistemological debate. When the Anglo-Irish historian and future Member of Parliament for Dublin University, William Lecky, sought to render a sociological approach to history informed by Comte and Buckle compatible with an intuitive and theistic account of ethics in the 1860s, he anticipated a wider movement on the part of religious apologists. This aimed at expanding the notions of induction and experience so as to make the latter encompass the validity of spiritual witness in time. History thus came to be turned against Positivism, as it was also used to rebut the apparently related challenges of agnosticism and scientific naturalism.[153] In the writings of John Tulloch and the more conservative Church of Scotland divine, Robert Flint, idealist emphases on the active power and divine significance of mind in history began to blend with and even supplant the older tradition of Scottish 'common sense' philosophy as religious bulwarks. The philosophy of history became bound up with a new form of the philosophy of mind. Around the opening of the twentieth century, religious history began noticeably to pass into the psychology of religion in the hands of William Inge, a future dean of St Paul's Cathedral. History remained a vehicle for religious argument into the twentieth century.[154] But Inge's writings recorded how the authority newly ascribed to the reflective historical subject could lead critics beyond history, and into analysis of the subjective consciousness, in ways that were at least potentially independent of reliance upon historical argument. The changing apologetic locus suggested by Inge's explorations of mysticism, together with the wider damage done to progressivist assumptions by the Great War, make 1914 an appropriate end date for this book's examination of British religious historicism and the power it once exercised.

RELIGIOUS HISTORY IN THE VICTORIAN PUBLIC SPHERE

The evolving conceptual paradigms outlined above appealed to real and often rather conventional personalities. As has already been intimated, they spread through personal relations, universities and colleges, journalistic

---

[153] For a definitional discussion of these phenomena, see pp. 200–1of this volume.
[154] J. Garnett, 'Hastings Rashdall and the renewal of Christian social ethics, c. 1890–1920', in Garnett and H.C.G. Matthew (eds), *Revival and religion since 1700: essays for John Walsh* (London and Rio Grande, TX, 1993), pp. 297–316.

ventures, and the activity of the churches. The friendships between liberal Anglican historians forged in common rooms, deaneries, and at the Athenaeum, or the pedagogical relationships fondly recalled by Idealist philosophers and those who sat at their feet, stimulated conversations within a small literary elite; but their voices carried far beyond it. The reform and expansion of Victorian higher education brought ecclesiastical history to the attention of intending ministers and other university-level students. The religious historians who held chairs in these institutions, or wrote and lectured outside them, unembarrassedly belonged to a selective circle. Their consciousness of so doing nevertheless involved a dutiful commitment to public engagement through writing and didacticism. They drew responses from a wide spectrum of educated society in an age when the expansion of the popular and periodical press brought intellectual and religious debate to unprecedentedly large audiences. Religious moralists' senses of authorial voice and cultural leadership should accordingly be seen as an integral part of the expanding public sphere they hoped and expected to shape.

Although many of the works considered in this book were written by independent men of letters and beneficed ecclesiastics, nineteenth-century university reform placed the study of religious history upon a newly extensive and secure institutional basis. Specifically clerical influence in British universities declined during the second half of the nineteenth century; but it would be quite mistaken to suppose that a broader clerisy was swept out of Victorian seats of learning as part of a general 'secularization of thought' in the period.[155] The desire to expand the critical study of religion, so as to enhance its intellectual credentials and improve the quality of clerical graduates, constituted a significant current of reformist sentiment, and informed decisions as to academic preferment. 'These magnificent societies', the biblical critic, church historian, university reformer, and future Bishop of Durham, Brooke Foss Westcott, remarked in a sermon at Trinity College, Cambridge, in 1868, 'which are themselves the monuments of the ancient spiritual power of England, contain within them the elements of a new spiritual power fitted to deal with the problems of our own age.'[156] 'The first work of the University as a spiritual

---

[155] A.G.L. Haig, 'The church, the universities and learning in later Victorian England', *Historical Journal*, 29:1 (1986), pp. 187–201; T.W. Heyck, *The transformation of intellectual life in Victorian England* (London, Sydney, and New York, 1982), pp. 66–7, 82.

[156] B.F. Westcott, *The spiritual office of the Universities: a sermon preached in the chapel of Trinity College, Cambridge, at the Commemoration of Benefactors, 15 December, 1868* (London and Cambridge, 1869), pp. 7–8; G.A. Patrick, 'Westcott, Brooke Foss (1825–1901)', *ODNB*.

power', he continued, was 'to connect its literary teaching both in form and purpose with the whole progress of humanity'.[157]

As part of this wider movement of educational and ecclesiastical renewal, church history obtained new footholds in the older seats of learning. Stanley's chair—Oxford's Regius Professorship of Ecclesiastical History—was founded, alongside a chair in pastoral theology, in 1842, to improve the education of candidates for holy orders. A writer in the non-denominationally Protestant *Eclectic Review* hoped that the new foundations would encourage deeper study of ecclesiastical history, 'the consequences of which cannot be foreseen'.[158] Cambridge's new Dixie Professorship of Ecclesiastical History had its first incumbent from 1884.[159] Mandell Creighton held the position until his elevation to the see of Peterborough in 1891, whereupon he was succeeded by his more Protestant friend, Henry Melvill Gwatkin.[160] The subject extended its reach to undergraduates as new courses of study were established at Oxford and Cambridge. Creighton was involved in the reform of the new historical tripos at Cambridge.[161] At Oxford, church history was a prominent subject in the theology and modern history schools after their foundations in 1869 and 1872 respectively.[162] In theology, especially after the initially Puseyite character of the degree began to change, examination questions inviting consideration of the philosophical implications of history for religion, not restricted to scripture, began to be posed.[163] Related questions grew in importance in English and Scottish university philosophy as Idealism became more influential.[164] In the 1880s it did not seem

---

[157] Westcott, *Spiritual office*, p. 12.

[158] 'Taylor's *Ancient Christianity*', *ECR*, 12 (1842), p. 2 and n.

[159] S. Bendall, C. Brooke, and P. Collinson, *A history of Emmanuel College, Cambridge* (Woodbrige, 1999), pp. 425–6.

[160] P.R.H. Slee, 'Gwatkin, Henry Melvill (1844–1916)', *ODNB*; C.M.D. Crowther, 'Creighton, Mandell (1843–1901)', *ODNB*.

[161] Slee, *Learning and a liberal education*, pp. 76–7.

[162] Inman, *Modern English theology*, pp. 145–50. The following two questions, for example, were put to candidates for the honour school of modern history in 1898: 'General History. Period I. (476–1002.) 8. Estimate the immediate influence of the Mahometan awakening on the Christianity of Europe', and 'General History. Period II. (919–1273.) 10. "The thirteenth century was the golden age of the medieval Church." Discuss this statement.': *Oxford University Examination Papers: Second Public Examination: Honour School of Modern History: Trinity Term, 1898* (Oxford, 1898).

[163] The two following questions, for example, were put to candidates for the honour school of theology in 1895, under 'The evidences of religion: I' section of the paper: '1. To what extent have Oriental influences produced sceptical reactions against Christianity in different ages?'; and '11. Is the modern conception of historical method favourable to dogmatic belief?': *Oxford University Examination Papers: Second Public Examination: Honour School of Theology: Trinity Term, 1895* (Oxford, 1895).

[164] On Scottish philosophy in the period, see G. Graham (ed.), *Scottish philosophy in the nineteenth and twentieth centuries* (Oxford, 2015).

jarring for books surveying the histories of Oxford and Cambridge, from the medieval era down to the present day, to be included in a publishing series entitled '*Epochs of Church History*', edited by Creighton.[165]

Thus even after religious tests and clerical fellowships began to be abolished at Oxford and Cambridge from 1854, England's ancient universities remained closely connected to the Church of England. 'The ruling minds of those ancient seminaries', Mill remarked in his 1867 inaugural address as Rector of St Andrews, 'have at last remembered that to place themselves in hostility to the free use of the understanding, is to abdicate their own best privilege, that of guiding it.'[166] Mill's observation reflected how those 'ruling minds' often understood that new kinds of scholarship were to be welcomed partly on the grounds that they offered surer routes to religious defence. Until 1882, most Oxford and Cambridge fellowships were tenable only by Anglican clergymen or those intending to take orders, and as late as 1912, almost one fifth of Oxford college fellows were still men in holy orders.[167] Scotland's older universities, where theological tests practically restricting divinity chairs to ministers of the Church of Scotland lasted until 1932, also retained strong ecclesiastical connections throughout the period.[168] John Tulloch probably had a hand in Arthur Penrhyn Stanley's election as Rector of St Andrews, news he was pleased to communicate to the dean in November 1874, following the death of the decidedly unclerical Mill.[169]

The reforming universities were not as successful as some of their defenders hoped they would be in saving their graduates from unbelief. George Gordon Coulton, taking deacon's orders in Llandaff in 1883 after leaving St Catharine's College, Cambridge, where he had held a classical scholarship, found himself unable to proceed to the priesthood after his religious doubts grew. His reservations were stimulated by reading such heterodox authors as Buckle, the eighteenth-century German philosopher Gotthold Ephraim Lessing, and the contemporary biologist Thomas Henry Huxley.[170] Turning first to schoolmastering, and ultimately to the medieval researches which secured him literary fame and in 1919 a Cambridge University Lectureship, he reminisced in his 1944 autobiography

[165] J.B. Mullinger, *A history of the University of Cambridge* (London, 1888); G.C. Brodrick, *A history of the University of Oxford* (London, 1886).

[166] J.S. Mill, *Inaugural address delivered to the University of St Andrews Feb. 1st 1867*, 2nd edn (London, 1867), p. 83.

[167] Kirby, *Historians*, pp. [41]–74.

[168] A.W. Curtis, 'The faculty of divinity', in A. Logan Turner (ed.), *A history of the University of Edinburgh 1883–1933* (Edinburgh, 1933), pp. 78–9.

[169] J. Tulloch to A.P. Stanley, 26 November 1874, in Prothero and Bradley, *Arthur Penrhyn Stanley*, ii, 458–9.

[170] G.G. Coulton, *Fourscore years: an autobiography* (Cambridge, 1944), pp. [141]–64.

on the strikingly clerical character of the Cambridge he had known as an undergraduate in the 1870s. It had been 'a world of strange survivals', he wrote, mixing favourable reminiscences of Gwatkin with more derisive recollections of the bibulous antics of J. R. Lumby, the Norrisian Professor of Divinity from 1879 to 1892.[171] In common with the 1891 Oxford graduate and historian of the Tudor Reformation, Albert Frederick Pollard, Coulton preserved a dispositionally Protestant and anti-Catholic sensibility that outlived discernible doctrinal commitment. But such secular-mindedness among British historians of religious movements was still relatively unusual by 1900, and represented something of a counter-culture to a rather less remembered but still vital intellectual establishment. In this context, it was significant that radical critics typically launched their arrows from outside the ancient universities.

The religious forces driving so much of nineteenth-century academic life were quintessentially evident in the expansion of nonconformist colleges. Denominational consolidation and rivalry drove that process, as did the wish of dissenters, often standing proudly apart from traditional elites, to assert their intellectual and cultural respectability. Commonly entering their students for degrees awarded by the new, non-denominational University of London, these colleges often made the promotion of ecclesiastical-historical study a main instrument of securing their objective of a learned ministry.[172] New English colleges opened, such as the Methodists' Westminster College in 1851, of which that church's first ecclesiastical historian of acknowledged distinction, Herbert Brook Workman, became principal in 1903.[173] Others were consolidated and refounded. R. W. Dale was instrumental in relocating the Congregationalists' Spring Hill College in Birmingham to an Oxford newly open to nonconformists, where Mansfield College opened in 1889.[174] The Unitarians moved their itinerant Manchester College to Oxford in the same year.[175] In Scotland, the Free Church energetically busied itself with raising money for ministerial education in the wake of

---

[171] Ibid., pp. 94, 105–6, 118–19; J.D. Pickles, 'Lumby, Joseph Rawson (1831–1895)', *ODNB*.

[172] D.A. Johnson, *The changing shape of English nonconformity, 1825–1925* (Oxford, 1999), pp. 15–32; W. Whyte, *Redbrick: a social and architectural history of Britain's civic universities* (Oxford, 2015), p. 50.

[173] E.G. Rupp, rev. R. Brown, 'Workman, Herbert Brook (1862–1951)', *ODNB*.

[174] E. Kaye, *Mansfield College, Oxford: its origin, history, and significance* (Oxford, 1996), p. 47.

[175] P. Hinchliff, 'Religious issues, 1870–1914', in M.G. Brock and M.C. Curthoys (eds), *The history of the University of Oxford: volume VII: nineteenth-century Oxford, part 2* (Oxford, 2000), pp. [97]–112.

the Disruption, opening Edinburgh's New College in 1843.[176] Thomas Martin Lindsay became professor of church history at the Glasgow Free Church College in 1872, and an authority on the Reformation.[177]

Despite these colleges' origins in interdenominational rivalry, Matthew Arnold's caricatures of dissenting self-absorption and narrowness neither fairly reflected their character nor that of those who studied in them.[178] Lindsay, whose first book was a translation of a German treatise on logic, told an audience of pupils that the Kantian, self-regulative moral freedom guaranteed to the Free Church by its severance from the Establishment gave it the necessary scope for the reverent advance of theology.[179] James Martineau, lecturing in 1868 to an audience at the London incarnation of Manchester College, where he was professor of mental and moral philosophy, defended the 'just primacy' of '*historical theology . . .* in this place' on the grounds that Christianity must be studied in the historical forms in which it has been known to the world, as the result of processes of growth.[180] In common with numerous Unitarian and other nonconformist ministers during the 1830s and 1840s, Martineau had spent time studying in Germany.[181] Such connections were reflected in the acquisitions made over the course of the century by Manchester College library, which included works by Neander, Bunsen, and copies of the archetypal journal of mediating theology, the *Theologische Studien und Kritiken*, together with the writings of liberal Anglicans such as Milman and Stanley.[182]

In a profusely verbal and intensely didactic intellectual culture, churchmen and scholars energetically carried the fruits of their university or collegiate learning to wider audiences of men and women, drawn from all social classes, through lectures and sermons. Milman praised the empathetic possibilities of historical study to working-class listeners at

[176] H. Watt, *New College Edinburgh: a centenary history* (Edinburgh and London, 1946), pp. 10–13.

[177] R.S. Rait, rev. J. Kirk, 'Lindsay, Thomas Martin (1843–1914)', *ODNB*.

[178] Made chiefly in M. Arnold, *Culture and anarchy*, ed. J. Garnett (Oxford, 2006); first book edition 1869.

[179] F. Ueberweg, *System of logic and history of logical doctrines*, trans. T.M. Lindsay (London, 1871); T.M. Lindsay, 'The study of church history', in his *College addresses: and sermons preached on various occasions* (Glasgow, 1915), pp. 85–7.

[180] J. Martineau, *A word for scientific theology in appeal from the men of science and the theologians* (London, 1868), pp. 26–7; R. Waller, 'Martineau, James (1805–1900)', *ODNB*.

[181] J.C. Paget, 'The reception of Baur in Britain', in Bauspiess et al., *Ferdinand Christian Baur*, pp. 339–40; on the transformative effects of German historicism within Unitarian intellectual culture, see A. Kennedy, 'John Kenrick and the transformation of Unitarian thought' (Stirling Univ. PhD, 2006).

[182] 'Manchester College Library chronological catalogue', Harris Manchester College, Oxford, MS Misc 25 xvi–xviii, xvi, 241, 484, 628, 2608, xvii, 6567.

mechanics' institutes.[183] His sermon on 'War and Peace' was one of many instances of the emanation of historical themes from Victorian pulpits. 'The manhood of each generation makes its own tools, and will not carve a truncheon from the exhumed bone of an ancestor', the Congregationalist historian Robert Alfred Vaughan, son of the president of the Lancashire Independent College, Robert Vaughan, told his Birmingham congregation during his ministry there in the 1850s.[184] Reform-minded clergy tried to draw crowds to their churches by arranging historical addresses. During the 1870s, Dean Stanley instituted special lectures to be delivered in the nave of Westminster Abbey by prominent laymen and non-Anglicans; speakers included Stoughton and Tulloch. Stanley donned his black Geneva gown for these semi-liturgical occasions, which included hymns and prayers.[185] Milman worked hard as dean of St Paul's, in cooperation with Tractarian sympathisers, to remodel the cathedral's interior in order to make it more suitable for larger congregations and evening services.[186] One of his successors in the deanery and a continuator of Milman's reforming labours, the critical high churchman Richard William Church, used the opportunities provided by an increasingly active cathedral to lecture within its precincts on problems in ecclesiastical history.[187] Reflecting the Victorian assumption that religious history was a suitable subject for female writers and audiences, Edward White Benson undertook a similar office as archbishop of Canterbury, when he lectured on apostolic church history to an audience of upper-class London ladies in Lambeth Palace's chapel from 1887 to 1892. They were posthumously edited for publication by his daughter, Margaret, with the assistance of Adeline Mary Russell, the Duchess of Bedford. The duchess explained in her introduction to the volume that the addresses had aimed to strengthen the religious fibres of those ladies who were most responsible for 'the tone of society'.[188]

---

[183] H.H. Milman, *Address delivered at the opening of the City of Westminster literary, scientific, and mechanics' institute*, 2nd edn (London, 1837), pp. 21–2; cf. J. Rose, *The intellectual life of the British working classes* (New Haven, CT, and London, 2001).

[184] R. A. Vaughan, *Essays and remains of the Rev. Robert Alfred Vaughan* (2 vols, London, 1858), ed. R. Vaughan, ii, 359.

[185] Prothero and Bradley, *Arthur Penrhyn Stanley*, ii, 295–8.

[186] Bodleian Library, Oxford, MS Phillipps-Robinson, c. 549/200–2: circular letter from H.H. Milman and A.C. Tait, [1858]. On the uses made of Victorian 'sacred space' more generally, see W. Whyte, *Unlocking the church: the lost secrets of Victorian sacred space* (Oxford, 2017).

[187] M.C. Church, *Life and letters of Dean Church* (London, 1894), pp. 209–19; on Church, see chapter three of this volume at pp. 143–4.

[188] A.M. Bedford, 'Introduction', to E.W. Benson, *Addresses on the Acts of the Apostles*, ed. M. Benson (London, 1901), [ix]–x; cf. K. Flint, *The woman reader 1837–1914*

The permeable boundary between sermons and public lectures in the period was reflected in the development and expansion of lecture series endowed to support particular kinds of intellectual and theological discussion. Among older institutions, the Boyle Lectures, given in London churches, were dedicated to the relationship between Christianity and natural philosophy.[189] The Bampton Lectures were specifically Anglican, being preached in St Mary's Church in Oxford, and lecturers were expected to defend Trinitarian orthodoxy.[190] In 1836, Congregationalists established the Congregational Lecture, to emulate the Church of England's equivalent foundations.[191] In Edinburgh, the Cunningham Lectures were founded by the generosity of an Edinburgh surgeon and Free Churchman in his will of 1862, to honour the memory of one of the Disruption's leaders, William Cunningham, and to provide the centrepiece of the New College's academic calendar.[192] In 1878, the Hibbert Trustees established a lectureship for the treatment of philosophy, biblical criticism, and 'comparative theology' in a freer spirit than the Congregational or Bampton lectures supposedly permitted, after receiving a request from liberal worthies including Tulloch, Stanley, and John Caird to do so. The lectures were to be delivered either in London or in one of the main British cities.[193] The Gifford Lectures, endowed by a bequest from a rich judge in 1887 and thereafter delivered in the ancient Scottish universities, were dedicated to natural theology, a specification that proved amenable to Idealist philosophers in the early years of the series.[194] Historical subjects were commonly treated within these avowedly apologetic frameworks. Enlightenment-era natural theology increasingly gave way to historical philosophy in these platform set pieces. The publication

(Oxford, 1993), pp. 80–1; R. Gagnier, *Subjectivities: a history of self-representation in Britain 1832–1920* (New York and Oxford, 1991).

[189] On the earlier history of the Lectures, see J.J. Dahm, 'Science and apologetics in the early Boyle Lectures', *Church History*, 39:2 (1970), pp. 172–86.

[190] 'Extract from the last will and testament of the late Rev. John Bampton, Canon of Salisbury', prefixed to W.D. Conybeare, *An analytical examination into the character, value, and just application of the writings of the Christian Fathers during the ante-Nicene period: being the Bampton Lectures for the year MDCCCXXXIX* (Oxford, 1839).

[191] 'Advertisement', prefixed to J. Stoughton, *Ages of Christendom: before the Reformation* (London, 1857).

[192] 'Extract declaration of trust, etc, 1 March, 1862', prefixed to R.S. Candlish, *The fatherhood of God: being the first course of the Cunningham Lectures delivered before the New College, Edinburgh, in March 1864* (Edinburgh, 1864).

[193] [James Martineau], 'Preface', to F.M. Müller, *Lectures on the origin and growth of religion as illustrated by the religions of India: delivered in the Chapter House, Westminster Abbey, in April, May, and June, 1878* (London, 1878), [vii]–viii; 'Memorial for the foundation of a Hibbert Lecture', prefixed to Müller, *Lectures*; A. Ruston, 'Hibbert, Robert (1769–1849)', *ODNB*.

[194] J. Tait, rev. E. Metcalfe, 'Gifford, Adam, Lord Gifford (1820–1887)', *ODNB*.

of these lectures, which the deeds of trust typically made a condition of the accompanying stipend, often sparked major intellectual controversies.

These were years during which the scale of publishing, not least of historical and theological works, was expanding at an unprecedented rate.[195] Individual publishing houses, which played a more active role in authorial cultivation and book production than that of the passive conduit, often aligned with and reinforced different schools of religious thought. Seeley and Burnside promoted evangelical Anglicans in the earlier Victorian period.[196] John Henry Parker and the Rivingtons had high church connections.[197] T. & T. Clark of Edinburgh, whose proprietors were Free Churchmen, reflected the remarkable intellectual trajectory of that denomination by becoming Britain's chief marketer of cautiously critical theology. Mark Pattison's characteristically vinegarish and rhetorically exaggerated complaint to a German correspondent that there was no English public for German translations was belied by the Clarks' notable industry in supporting series such as the 1832–1844 *Biblical Cabinet* and, from 1846, the *Foreign Theological Library*.[198] At a more popular level, the Religious Tract Society flooded Britain and the wider world with cheap copies of non-denominational evangelical literature.[199] One of Henry Mayhew's clerical collaborators in carrying out the social investigations published as *London Labour and the London Poor*, William Tuckniss, described the Religious Tract Society and the Society for Promoting Christian Knowledge as 'the two great emporiums of religious literature', second only in importance to personal evangelistic effort as 'curative agencies' in leading the populace away from vice. In the year 1860–1861 alone, Tuckniss reported, the Religious Tract Society made grants of tracts, handbills, and periodicals to schools, village libraries,

---

[195] S. Eliot, *Some patterns and trends in British publishing 1800–1919* (London, 1994), pp. 45, 50–1; L. Howsam, *Kegan Paul: a Victorian imprint: publishers, books and cultural history* (London and Toronto, 1998); Howsam, *Past into print: the publishing of history in Britain, 1850–1950* (London, 2009); J. Altholz, *The religious press in Britain, 1760–1900* (New York and London, 1989); M. Ledger-Lomas, 'Mass markets: religion', in D. McKitterick (ed.), *The Cambridge history of the book in Britain: volume VI: 1830–1914* (Cambridge, 2009), pp. 324–58.

[196] For example, E. Bickersteth, *A brief practical view of the Evangelical Alliance; in regard to its character, principles, objects, organization, and Christian spirit* (London, 1846).

[197] S. Rivington, *The publishing house of Rivington* (London, 1894); R. Riddell, 'Parker, John Henry (1806–1884)', *ODNB*.

[198] Universität- und Landesbibliothek Bonn, S.971, 155–66/156: M. Pattison to J. Bernays, 21 July 1856; J.A.H. Dempster, *The T&T Clark story: a Victorian publisher and the new theology with an epilogue covering the twentieth-century history of the firm* (Durham, 1992), pp. 3–11, 16, 26, 43–84.

[199] S.G. Green, *The story of the Religious Tract Society for one hundred years* (London, 1899).

prisons, and hospitals totalling 5,762,241 items.[200] Both evangelistic Societies often produced historical texts; but it was not solely religious publishers who saw a market for ecclesiastical history. Stanley and Milman often published with John Murray, Milman once offering him the revealing and rather bad advice not to become commercially involved with the emerging Thomas Carlyle, on the grounds that his writing was 'strange and fantastic', and too germanized for an English audience.[201] John Tulloch was close to the Blackwoods' firm in Edinburgh.[202] Milman captured something of the spirit of these intellectual and commercial partnerships when he remarked, in the course of characterizing the transition from Catholic and Latin to Protestant and Teutonic Christianity, that books were becoming 'a co-ordinate priesthood'.[203]

Religious debates were not solely disseminated through books, but also through the periodicals, magazines, and newspapers in which readers found platforms for responding to the authors they read. As with book publishing, the growing religious press gave much attention to religious historians' works and the cultural problems to which they were addressed; but so too did general and avowedly secular journals. Josef Altholz estimated that of the twenty to twenty-five thousand Victorian periodicals, three thousand were specifically religious. He located the greatest expansion of Victorian newspapers in the context first of the reduction, then the repeal of the stamp tax, the advertisement duty, and the paper duties— the so-called 'taxes on knowledge'—between 1836 and 1861.[204] Mass-circulation and intellectually weighty religious weeklies grew up, such as the moderately high church *Guardian* newspaper, which Gladstone reportedly praised as the best available news weekly, not merely for ecclesiastical but for general intelligence.[205]

Where newspapers often carried book reviews, the many religious periodicals founded in the period offered platforms for more extended essays, which often represented the fruit of substantial intellectual labour in an age without specialized academic journals. To instance only a few of the most pertinent to this study, the *Prospective Review, National Review,*

[200] W. Tuckniss, 'The agencies at present in operation within the metropolis, for the suppression of vice and crime', in H. Mayhew (ed.), *London labour and the London poor* (4 vols, London, 1861–1862), iv, xxiii.

[201] National Library of Scotland, John Murray archive, MS 40819, 77–8: H.H. Milman to J. Murray, 4 October 1831.

[202] Oliphant, *Memoir*, pp. 350–1.   [203] *HLC*, i, 9.

[204] Altholz, *Religious press*, pp. [1]–13.

[205] A *bon mot* from R. W. Church, one of the *Guardian*'s founders: A.B. Donaldson, *Five great Oxford leaders: Keble, Newman, Pusey, Liddon and Church*, 3rd edn (London, 1902), p. 330.

and *Theological Review*, which succeeded one another between 1845 and 1879, helped Unitarian writers to exercise a liberalizing intellectual influence disproportionate to their church's small numbers.[206] The ultra-liberal Anglican cleric and historian John Hunt made tours of Germany in which he sought eminent professors to contribute to the *Contemporary Review* during and after Dean Henry Alford's editorship of the periodical, which was founded in 1866.[207] Alford was a critical evangelical, but Hunt justifiably characterized the *Review*'s historically minded leanings as liberal Protestant to those German scholars he wished to solicit to write for an English audience.[208] If the religious press was by no means narrowly sectarian in this period, nor were secular journals inattentive to religious debate. The whiggish *Edinburgh Review* under Henry Reeve's editorship, and the radical *Westminster Review* were among the many non-religious journals which published essays offering historical treatments of religion.[209]

The energy driving the exploration of religious history in these institutions and media relied on historically specific ideas of authorial voice and cultural leadership among those who pursued it. These did not obviously attenuate with the increasing professionalization of academic study in the later decades of the century. John Caird, welcoming the greater specialization in Scottish university studies for which he pushed, told Glasgow students in 1885 that 'the science of history' encouraged mankind to be confident of a future of ripened wisdom and self-control. Alluding to Macaulay's metaphor, he declared that no New Zealander would ever come to sketch the ruins from Westminster Bridge provided that Britain resisted insularity, and remained opened to the world as to the past.[210] These assumptions about the power of written and spoken argument to sway attitudes, for better or for worse, were not internal to the self-appointed clerisy. An anonymous reviewer of Stanley's *Lectures on the History of the Eastern Church* in 1861 considered that, in the present state of higher learning,

---

[206] Altholz, *Religious press*, pp. [67]–78.

[207] Staatsbibliothek zu Berlin—Preussischer Kulturbesitz: Slg. Darmstaedter/2 m 1852: John Hunt to Emil Du Bois-Reymond, 13 November 1877.

[208] Universitätsbibliothek München, 4⁰ Cod. ms. 917 m (181)/4: John Hunt to Jakob Frohschammer, 18 June 1870.

[209] T. Lynn Broughton, 'Reeve, Henry (1813–1895)', *ODNB*; on the *Westminster Review*, see R. Ashton, *142 Strand: a radical address in Victorian London* (London, 2006).

[210] J. Caird, 'The science of history', in his *University addresses: being addresses on subjects of academic study delivered at the University of Glasgow* (Glasgow, 1898), pp. 254–77; G.E. Davie, *The democratic intellect: Scotland and her universities in the nineteenth century*, 3rd edn (Edinburgh, 2013).

the Oxford Professor of Ecclesiastical History is entitled to regard himself as the Professor for all England, with a chair only locally situated at Oxford. He speaks to the nation, and for the nation.[211]

By treating ecclesiastical history in a spirit of large-minded comparison and universal fraternity, the writer added, Stanley breathed philosophy into the habitual insularity of English divinity. They were sentiments Stanley certainly shared.

STRUCTURE

The organization of the book's subsequent chapters reflects an important characteristic of Victorian historical argument about religion. Rather than adopting a biographical or prosopographical form, the chapters are instead thematic, each taking an evolving response to a particular problem as its subject matter. In nineteenth-century historical discourse, discussion of particular periods—whose legacies seemed to be embedded in the present—focused attention on particular complexes of intellectual issues. The early church, always foundational to the high church Anglican tradition, acquired new and, in Newman's case, eventually subversive importance for Tractarians in their search for the basis of dogmatic authority. Medieval religion, generally understood to live on in the nineteenth century in the form of Roman Catholicism, invited discussion of the rights and wrongs of that newly re-energized system. The Reformation, and the difficult religious history of post-Reformation Britain and Europe, were understood to have formed the Protestant traditions by which British social and intellectual life were still so deeply coloured. The possibilities and limits of those traditions were reshaped in the Victorian period by engagement with Protestant history. Distinct from these arguments, but increasingly tending to converge with them, was a debate about the intellectual origins of modernity. Sociologically minded accounts of historical progress, which located its crucial motor in the spread of an anti-metaphysical, scientific epistemology, stimulated opposing, theologically apologetic interpretations of how the seventeenth and eighteenth centuries had prepared the ground for nineteenth-century thought. Behind these debates, implicitly or explicitly, stood competing philosophies of history. By examining changing Victorian attitudes to the epochs in which Christian orthodoxy, Catholicism, Protestantism, and

---

[211] [Anon.], 'Lectures on the History of the Eastern Church', *SR*, 11:289 (11 May 1861), p. 482.

modernity were understood to have originated, it becomes possible better to understand how critics viewed the present and future prospects of religion and civilization.

Where traditionalists wished either to reignite or to denounce different elements of the religious past, liberal interpreters of tradition— recognizing their opponents' revivalist instincts—sought to represent the past's internal unity and newly apparent progressive dynamism. The Hares reminded their readers that 'ghosts never work miracles: nor do they ever come to life again'; 'the past is past, and must pass through the present, not hop over it, into the future.'[212] John Caird insisted, echoing Carlyle, that religious and political life could only ever be the spontaneous expression of the age as it was in the present. For men to 'revive what they call primitive customs, re-introduce the cloister-life into a world of railways and stock exchanges' was no saner than for a man 'to speak in baby-talk, or clothe himself in the bibs and tuckers of his childhood'.[213] The metaphor of spiritual progression from childhood to manhood in the history of the race often surfaced in religiously liberal historical argument. John Tulloch encapsulated the liberalizing spirit in a sermon he preached at St Andrews in 1875:

> Faith is a progressive insight, and dogma is a variable factor. No sane man nowadays has the faith of the medievalist. No modern Christian can think in many respects as the Christians of the seventeenth century, or of the twelfth century, or of the fourth century. No primitive Christian would have fully understood Athanasius in his contest against the world. It was very easy at one time to chant the Athanasian hymn – it is easy for some still; but very hard for others. Are the latter worse or better Christians on this account?[214]

The following chapters trace how liberal historians sought to apply analogous insights to the intellectual problems raised by different periods of the religious past, and the effects such attempts had in reshaping a wider religious spectrum. Chapter two considers the supersession of the high church monopoly on early church history by two alternative approaches. Social and political histories of the period emerged which tended to decouple the Christian spirit from formal orthodoxy; whilst, at the same time, new kinds of doctrinal history became available which treated the history of orthodoxy more favourably, as a process driven by Christian experience, the self-realization of an idea, or some combination of the two.

---

[212] Hare and Hare, *Guesses*, p. 184.
[213] J. Caird, 'The study of history', in his *University addresses*, p. 238.
[214] J. Tulloch, *Religion and theology: a sermon for the times*, 2nd edn (Edinburgh and London, 1875), p. 12.

The chapter relates Newman's *Essay* to other understandings of religious development emerging in the years around 1850, contending that these epitomized wider changes in the epistemological significance of history itself in Victorian argument about religion. Chapter three, focusing especially on Milman's *History of Latin Christianity* and its contexts, explores how liberal histories of medieval Catholicism acted to challenge both anti-Catholicism and reactionary eulogies for 'medievalism', as the period came to seem to have played a progressive role in the emergence of modern Europe. Chapter four examines how demands for a reformation of British Protestant culture required a reassessment of the origins and significance of the Reformation and its legacy. Across these several spheres of discussion, the self-consciously confessional nature of religious historiography tended, with some exceptions, to diminish as differing religious positions came to be located within the larger spiritual stream of history. Religious liberalism gained in rhetorical shape and intellectual purpose, whilst more conservative theologies shed their supposedly accidental or temporary features, as developmental historicism became integral to religious debate.

These chapters indicate how, especially after 1870, the rising spectre of open unbelief offered theologians further encouragement to convert history into a new source of religious knowledge. As secularizing intellectuals looked to history to legitimize their own conceptions of progress, and intellectual alternatives to Christianity appeared to gain ground, it became increasingly necessary to construe mankind's moral past as a form of theistic witness. The fifth chapter focuses directly on this strand of debate. Its starting point is the dual recognition that the advocates of secular conceptions of progress typically treated different kinds of anti-metaphysical epistemology as the normative basis of modern thought; and that this involved particular claims about the history of mind. Scientific induction, in such treatments, became both the motor and the outcome of intellectual advance, and thus the key to progress in a more general sense. These writers called out a theological reply itself consisting of two interrelated elements. The first was the argument that modern intellectual history, the period broadly encompassing the seventeenth and eighteenth centuries which anti-metaphysical writers claimed for themselves, bore witness not to progressive secularization, but to the purification of Christianity rooted in the rationalization of theology. The second was the suggestion that true induction, expanded so as to encompass religious experience, itself vindicated a providential philosophy of history as a whole. The power and limits of mind itself thus edged closer to the centre of religious argument. But the ground had been prepared by debates about history. By 1914, the beliefs that Christian doctrine had been shaped and purified by human subjective experience, and that historical progress could not be severed from the spiritual roots of higher human volition, had become reassuring, if somewhat fragile barriers to materialist and secularised understandings of human time. It was only later that post-theological conceptions of historical dynamism acquired their appearance of irresistibility.

2

The Early Church

THE TRANSFORMATION OF CHRISTIAN ANTIQUITY

> The unrest of our time is essentially religious, for political questions depend on social, and social on religious. Thus the reconstruction of society depends on the reconstruction of religion; and that is a work we shall have to do from the foundations, as it was done in the time of Athanasius.[1]

Lecturing to a Church Congress at Bradford in 1898, Henry Melvill Gwatkin, Dixie Professor of Ecclesiastical History at Cambridge, spoke for many of his generation when he identified a close resemblance between the early Christian era and the nineteenth century. In depicting the fourth century as being of foundational importance for his own time, Gwatkin was offering a late-Victorian inflection of a view which to his contemporaries and immediate forebears, clerical, lay, and secular-minded, would have seemed unexceptionable. The importance of the growth of a new religion which had subsumed classical civilization into incipient Christendom, in a process that had entrenched theological dogmatism as the intellectual starting point of the modern West and carried with it the seeds of long-distant revolutions, appeared obvious to them. Victorian critics engaged intensively with this epoch, whose political and intellectual transformations were ultimately constitutive of their own mental worlds. To study it—to narrate and analyse afresh the early doctrinal controversies and their relation to later classical civilization—was, as Gwatkin perceived, also to re-examine and possibly to rework the founding assumptions of national and European religion and, by Victorian extension, the framework of all other experience.

Gwatkin's claim was one product of a transition from the static and textual conception of patristic orthodoxy that characterized early Victorian

---

[1] H.M. Gwatkin, *The unrest of our time: a paper read at the Church Congress, Bradford, September, 1898* (Derby, 1898), p. 2.

discussion of the subject, to the dynamic and contextual one that predominated by the century's end. This chapter explores that change as an intellectual-historical episode. In a parallel to the ways in which the Victorian fashion for depicting the life of Christ created a more human cultural image of Jesus, the distinct and growing interest in the early history of the church he founded led to a more ethicized sense of that history's importance.[2] Historians and historical theologians have generally been drawn towards nineteenth-century treatments of the church fathers in a fragmentary way, by their prior interests in the Oxford Movement, or else in contemporary reconstructions of the textual history of the New Testament.[3] But there has been no attempt at an holistic interpretation of Victorian preoccupation with the history of the early church as an autonomous and creative period in its own right.[4]

Such an account is offered here. Jean-Louis Quantin has shown how, in the seventeenth century, an authoritative conception of patristic witness became essential to the construction of a distinctively Anglican orthodoxy

[2] D.L. Pals, *The Victorian 'lives' of Jesus* (San Antonio, TX, 1982); I. Hesketh, *Victorian Jesus: J.R. Seeley, religion, and the cultural significance of anonymity* (Toronto, Buffalo, NY, and London, 2017).

[3] On the relationship between the Oxford Movement and the study of patristics, see Nockles, *Oxford Movement*, pp. 104–45; L. Frappell, '"Science" in the service of orthodoxy: the early intellectual development of E.B. Pusey', in P. Butler (ed.), *Pusey rediscovered* (London, 1983), pp. 1–33; N. Lossky, 'The Oxford Movement and the revival of patristic theology', in P. Vaiss (ed.), *From Oxford to the people: reconsidering Newman and the Oxford Movement* (Leominster, 1996), pp. 76–82; K.L. Parker, 'Tractarian visions of history', in Brown, Nockles, and Pereiro, *Oxford Movement*, pp. [151]–65. A suggestive foray into the publishing history of the early church fathers in the Victorian period may be found in D.F. Wright, ' "From a quarter so totally unexpected": translation of the Early Church Fathers in Victorian Scotland', *Records of the Scottish Church History Society*, 30 (2000), pp. 124–69. The development of British New Testament criticism has understandably loomed large in scholarly accounts of Victorian interest in early Christianity, though a synoptic history of biblical criticism in nineteenth-century Britain has yet to be written: Paget, 'reception of Baur'; S. Neill and T. Wright, *The interpretation of the New Testament 1861–1986*, 2nd edn (Oxford, 1988), esp. pp. [35]–64; D.M. Thompson, *Cambridge theology in the nineteenth century: enquiry, controversy and truth* (Aldershot, 2008), pp. [95]–121; G.R. Treloar, *Lightfoot the historian: the nature and role of history in the life and thought of J.B. Lightfoot (1828–1889) as churchman and scholar* (Tübingen, 1998); G.A. Patrick, *The miners' bishop: Brooke Foss Westcott*, 2nd edn (Peterborough, 2004), esp. pp. 42–66; G.A. Patrick, *F. J. A. Hort, eminent Victorian* (Sheffield, 1988). On treatment of the early church in Victorian literature, see N. Vance, *The Victorians and ancient Rome* (Oxford and Cambridge, MA, 1997), pp. [197]–221; M. Wheeler, *The old enemies: Catholic and Protestant in nineteenth-century English culture* (Cambridge, 2006), pp. 51–76. On Arianism in the nineteenth century, see M. Wiles, *Archetypal heresy: Arianism through the centuries* (Oxford, 1996), pp. [165]–76.

[4] For essays in this direction, see J. Bennett, 'The age of Athanasius: the Church of England and the Athanasian Creed, 1870–1873', *Church History and Religious Culture*, 97:2 (2017), pp. 220–47; B.J. King, *Newman and the Alexandrian fathers: shaping doctrine in nineteenth-century England* (Oxford, 2009).

in the face of Roman Catholic and dissenting challenges. In the early modern period, exploration of Christian antiquity thus became an important source of doctrinal innovation.[5] The church fathers, and the nature of the 'orthodoxy' they shaped, were no less contentious and historically contingent subjects in very different, nineteenth-century intellectual conditions. Within the Church of England, and more and more in Presbyterian and nonconformist denominations, the story of the initial consolidation of Christian doctrine and civilization became acutely relevant to contemporary religious and philosophical problems. The rising idea that orthodoxy had 'developed' down to its formal definition by the general councils presented interpretative problems and, increasingly, apologetic opportunities both to the relatively liberal and to the relatively conservative divines who alike drew air in an historicist climate. Within its recovery of the texture of the wider Victorian encounter with the early church, the chapter pays particular attention to attempts to historicize the doctrine of the Trinity. In the form laid down under Athanasius' influence at the first general council of Nicaea in 325, this posited the consubstantial relationship between the Father, Son, and Holy Ghost that became enshrined in the Nicene Creed. Together with the Apostles' and Athanasian Creeds, this symbol became one of the three catholic creeds of Christendom. Representing the first moment at which an ecumenical council had issued a credo binding on the faithful, its theology had presented orthodoxy with a problem of philosophical and historical explanation since the Enlightenment.[6]

A discussion of the Victorian response to the early church must begin with the intellectual prehistory and consequences of the Oxford Movement. A vital foundation of Anglican claims for centuries, patristic texts became fundamental to the articulation of a newly dynamic, anti-dissenting and anti-latitudinarian Tractarian ecclesiology in the 1830s. Old-fashioned high churchmen's and Tractarians' intensive search for an essentially static principle of orthodoxy began to terminate, at the Oxford Movement's most radical wing, in the conclusion that there was no such thing: that doctrine had, in fact, developed. John Henry Newman's 1845

[5] J.-L. Quantin, *The Church of England and Christian antiquity: the construction of a confessional identity in the 17th century* (Oxford, 2009).

[6] On Trinitarian disputes in eighteenth-century England, see B. Young, *Religion and Enlightenment in eighteenth-century England: theological debate from Locke to Burke* (Oxford, 1998). On eighteenth-century encounters with early church history, cf. Pocock, *Barbarism and religion*, v; H.R. Trevor-Roper, 'From deism to history: Conyers Middleton', in his *History and the Enlightenment*, ed. J. Robertson (New Haven, CT, and London, 2010), pp. [71]–119.

Essay on the Development of Christian Doctrine, which presented doctrinal development as suggesting and requiring the regulative authority of an infallible church, offered the quintessential statement of that case.

Newman's was in one respect an anti-liberal argument. But his recognition that doctrine had a history—in the sense that orthodoxy was not straightforwardly inferable from a privileged body of primitive texts, but grew in the mind of the church over time—in fact brought him near to less authoritarian strands of criticism. The controversy elicited by the *Essay* encouraged several liberal Anglican critics to agree with him that the early church had progressively developed, but not in the way Newman had supposed. In presenting two alternative characterizations of the development of early Christianity, liberal Anglicans also adopted two distinct modes of idealizing it, which expressed different and ultimately conflicting ideas of how best to come to religion's intellectual defence. Henry Hart Milman located the progressiveness of Christianity in its healthful social and political effects, and treated its complex doctrinal statements as comparatively unimportant. F. D. Maurice and Julius Hare, on the other hand, regarded the study of the history of doctrine as an integral part of apologetics, for to them doctrine distilled the historical growth of the Christian consciousness in the apprehension of eternal truth. The liberal Lutheran Christian Bunsen's 1852 *Hippolytus and his Age*, though the work of a German diplomat, was the first systematic treatise on early doctrinal history, understood in this second sense, to arise within liberal Anglican intellectual circles. Although they differed profoundly in many respects, Bunsen resembled Newman in that both made historical interpretation not merely corroborative of past logical inferences, but inherent to determining what religion ought to be. Both men also blurred the distinction between the knower and the object of religious knowledge by contending that evolving history represented the expansion of the Christian conscience.

The chapter's second half considers the wider percolation of these assumptions amongst growing numbers of British historians of the early church in the years after 1850. One broad strand of criticism saw promise in interpreting the history of doctrine as the outcome, at least in part, of the subjective mind of the church. This approach admitted of a spectrum of interpretations, running from the advanced liberal to the imaginatively conservative. Beginning with Bunsen, Trinitarianism began to wear new aspects. Doctrinal historians of idealist inclination, contemplating the connections between Christianity and Greek thought, started more distinctly to historicize that interaction in order to discuss the relationship between faith and reason. Such scholars tended more and more to cast the interlocked doctrines of the Trinity and the Incarnation no longer as ineffable mysteries, but as reasonable Christian resolutions to problems left unsolved by unaided Greek philosophy.[7] Especially important to that argumentative manoeuvre was the prologue to John's Gospel, expositing the divine Logos or Word which existed from eternity with God, created the world and mankind, and became incarnate in Christ.[8] Late-century evangelicals became more interested than they had once been in the history of orthodoxy, and more comfortable with the suggestion that it involved the history of the human response to revelation: an idea which high churchmen increasingly also shared. But these relatively conservative groups preferred to cast doctrinal history less as a history of reason, which in some forms risked marginalizing revelation, than as a history of Christian experience. At the same time, there emerged a parallel, alternative approach to early church history, nascent in Milman's reply to Newman, which was more critical of formal orthodoxy, and less susceptible to conservative appropriation. A. P. Stanley in a mild and literary way, and Edwin Hatch with a more radical and self-consciously 'scientific' purpose, began to ascribe Christianity's dogmatic forms to factors external to the religion itself. They preferred to emphasize the historical relationship between religious ethics, society, and the state, rather than the wisdom immanent in doctrinal history, as a means of presenting a liberal ecclesiastical ideal. The widespread opposition which Hatch's reductive approach to doctrine encountered, however, expressed a general intellectual realignment that had matured by the end of the century. As older alarms over denominational and political threats to religion receded into the past, Idealist and experiential understandings of orthodoxy often became indispensable bulwarks against the newer dangers of materialist, pantheist, and agnostic conceptions of human value.

THE PATRISTIC REVIVAL
AND RULES OF FAITH

'Sad rubbish': thus Thomas Gaisford, the anachronistically unenthusiastic dean of Christ Church, Oxford, from 1831 to 1855, dismissed the

---

[7] The literature on nineteenth-century reception of Greek antiquity is large; important contributions include D.J. DeLaura, *Hebrew and Hellene in Victorian England* (Austin, TX, 1969); R. Jenkyns, *The Victorians and ancient Greece* (Oxford, 1980); M. Beard, *The invention of Jane Harrison* (Cambridge, MA, and London, 2000); C. Stray (ed.), *Classics in 19th and 20th-century Cambridge: curriculum, culture and community* (Cambridge, 1999); S.-M. Evangelista, *British aestheticism and ancient Greece: Hellenism, reception, Gods in exile* (Basingstoke, 2009); L. Dowling, *Hellenism and homosexuality in Victorian Oxford* (Ithaca, NY, and London, 1994); S. Goldhill, *Who needs Greek? Contests in the cultural history of Hellenism* (Cambridge, 2002). On contemporary literary characterisations of the transformation from antiquity to Christianity, largely absent from these studies, see Goldhill, *Victorian culture*, pp. [153]–244.

[8] John 1:1–14; cf. Wheeler, *St John*.

editions of the church fathers lining the shelves of the college library.[9] Increasing numbers of his contemporaries, not least in Oxford, thought otherwise. Tractarian lamentations that the Enlightenment had ignored or arrogantly scorned patristic writings in favour of cold and abstract reason were rhetorical and depended on a boldly selective reading both of Georgian churchmen and more subversive historians. But if post-revolutionary high churchmen, and their eventual Tractarian wing, did not exactly unearth patristic texts which had lain dormant since 1688, they did seek to invest them with renewed religious authority, often in conscious contradistinction to the cavils of eighteenth-century authors. Amidst the stresses of the 1820s and 1830s, a vision of the first Christian centuries as a period when holy martyrs and almost-inspired exegetes had, under providence, subdued the Greco-Roman world, clearing heretical sophistries from an original deposit of faith as they did so, exerted a powerful sway over the imaginations of embattled high Anglicans, and even began to touch their evangelical Protestant opponents. The energizing of high Anglicans' traditional, textual investigation of primitive orthodoxy—an idea with notably uncertain chronological limits—by a romantic historical imaginary contained latent risks, however, for the traditional supposition that revealed truth, and its historical restatements, existed outside human time.

Contemporary observers, not least critical ones, often wrote of a revival of interest in patristics and its central place in high church argument.[10] The primary reason for this intensification lay in the Oxford Movement's renewed search for the apostolic origins of the Church of England, which could be authoritatively asserted against Roman Catholic, dissenting, and allegedly 'Erastian' Whig opponents. High churchmen looked to the early church as the source of sound answers to controverted questions concerning the faith once delivered to the saints. This prioritization, however, concealed notable differences of emphasis. Peter Nockles has observed that the differences between the traditional high churchmen of the Hanoverian period and a new generation of Tractarians often followed the distinction between those who took a more corroborative, or alternatively a more dynamic view of early Christianity. All agreed that the rule of faith was to be the so-called 'Canon of Vincentius'—the principle that catholic truth was equivalent to what had been taught always, everywhere, and by all ('quod semper, quod ubique, quod ab omnibus')—but this was applied

---

[9] T. Mozley, *Reminiscences chiefly of Oriel College and the Oxford Movement*, 2nd edn (2 vols, London, 1882), i, 356.
[10] J.J. Blunt, *An introduction to a course of lectures on the early fathers, now in delivery in the University of Cambridge* (Cambridge, 1840), p. 11; M. Pattison, *Memoirs of an Oxford don*, ed. V.H.H. Green (London, 1988), p. 95 (first edition 1885).

in distinctive ways. Pre-Tractarian high churchmen tended to value the fathers as interpreters of ambiguous points of scripture, and called them in as witnesses to the truth of the Thirty-Nine Articles and apostolic status of the Church of England. Tractarians, on the other hand, romantically elevated patristic divinity to the status of an absolute judge, which might potentially overrule or imaginatively reinterpret established Anglican tenets and usages on matters such as fasting, celibacy, and prayers for the dead.[11]

One significant divergence was related to another. This concerned when, exactly, primitive and consequently authoritative 'antiquity' had ended. All high churchmen recognized the authority of the three catholic creeds and the first four general councils down to that held at Chalcedon in 451. But the seventeenth-century theologians whom the early-nineteenth-century orthodox treated as their standard divines had given particular weight to the Greek-speaking fathers of the first three centuries.[12] Tractarians, however—searching for patristic precedents for medieval usages, or disturbed by the doctrinal ambiguity of some ante-Nicene fathers—began for argumentative purposes to ascribe a later date to the limits of the catholic consensus. Some writers started to insist that the fifth and sixth general councils were also binding on the consciences of believers.[13] The first of several nineteenth-century patristic translation projects, the *Library of the Fathers* which began to appear under the editorship of Pusey, Newman, and Keble in 1838, privileged fourth-century texts and Latin authorities over their antecedents.[14] The *Library* even featured Gregory the Great's commentary on Job.[15] In time, the respective weight to be accorded to earlier or later fathers, and to Greek or Latin divinity, came to be explained with reference to different theories of doctrinal development. But the Vincentian rule had first to be strained before certain of its adherents began to perceive and theorize upon its limitations. The Anglican search for patristic orthodoxy would eventually generate newly dynamic understandings of how that orthodoxy had arisen.

---

[11] Nockles, *Oxford Movement*, pp. 104–45; E.B. Pusey, *The rule of faith, as maintained by the fathers, and the Church of England* (Oxford, 1851), pp. 2–10.

[12] Quantin, *Church of England*, pp. [1]–21; King, *Newman*, p. 5; W.A. Butler, *Letters on the development of Christian doctrine in reply to Mr. Newman's Essay*, ed. T. Woodward (Dublin, 1850), pp. 225–37.

[13] W. Palmer, *A treatise on the church of Christ: designed chiefly for the use of students in theology*, 3rd edn (2 vols, London, 1842), ii, 128–9; first edition 1838.

[14] E.B. Pusey, J.H. Newman, and J. Keble (eds), *A library of fathers of the Holy Catholic Church anterior to the division of the east and west* (47 vols, Oxford and London, 1838–1881); J. Stoughton, *Religion in England from 1800 to 1850: a history with a postscript on subsequent events* (2 vols, London, 1884), ii, [182]–4.

[15] Gregory I, *Morals on the book of Job*, trans. C. Marriott and J. Bliss (3 vols, Oxford, 1844–1850).

Whilst older and newer high churchmen stressed different aspects of antiquity, the underlying tensions between them lay relatively dormant before they were acutely inflamed by Newman's conversion and the publication of his *Essay on Development*. Around the time of the first appearance of the Tracts, in practice the two kinds of writer shared a highly textual and ahistorical approach to the use of the fathers in argument. They did not think that doctrines had 'developed', but instead assumed that an unchanging deposit of faith had been handed down by the apostles to their post-apostolic successors. The doctrinal definitions offered by councils and fathers were merely restatements of or logical inferences from that shared substance, drawn out by heretical attacks. Thus it was assumed that the fathers' chronologically varied writings, whether composed before Nicaea or afterwards, could be treated as a unity, and quarried for proof-texts that would yield reliable conclusions as to the canon, text, and interpretation of scripture; the doctrine and discipline of the church; the evidences for Christianity; and the nature of infidel objections to religion.[16] John Kaye, an old high church Regius Professor of Divinity at Cambridge, published a series of lectures on the church history of the second and third centuries in 1826 in which he devoted a chapter to deploying Tertullian's writings in support of the Thirty-Nine Articles.[17] Tractarians often adopted a similar procedure even whilst they chafed against, as many of their co-religionists would have thought, the Articles' Protestant sense. Pusey's *Tract 67* arranged 'the general interpretation of the Ancient Church' in defence of the sacramental efficacy of baptism, supportively citing *catenae patrum*, or authoritative quotations, from Augustine, Tertullian, Irenaeus, and Origen as though those writers belonged to one and the same time and place.[18]

This dogmatic and often controversial focus assumed and helped to reinforce an interdependent series of sharp antitheses: between the church and the world; salvific truth and damnable error; the believer and the object of belief. Early Victorian high churchmen adopted a highly internalist view of ecclesiastical history, in which the subject was important for its aid in instructing a divine society in questions of doctrine, discipline, sacraments, and liturgy. The belief that the church, invisible and visible, properly stood apart from and above the sinful world led Edward Burton,

---

[16] Blunt, *introduction*, p. 9; E. Burton, *Testimonies of the ante-Nicene fathers to the divinity of Christ*, 2nd edn (Oxford, 1829), viii.

[17] J. Kaye, *The ecclesiastical history of the second and third centuries: illustrated from the writings of Tertullian* (Cambridge, 1826), pp. [262]–401.

[18] [E.B. Pusey], 'Scriptural views of Holy Baptism, as established by the consent of the Ancient Church, and contrasted with the systems of modern schools', *Tracts for the Times*, vol. 2, 3rd edn (London and Oxford, 1840), no. 67., p. 51 and n. 2.

an anti-dissenting Bampton Lecturer who became Regius Professor of Divinity at Oxford in 1829, to claim in his *History of the Christian Church* that 'the History of the Church is the history of truth'.[19] Because that truth did not have a history in the sense of being the result of development shaped by context, it was clearly separable from heresy, which resulted from moral rebellion rather than historical situation. 'Few things, perhaps, can more remarkably exemplify the tendency of the human heart to evil', wrote the sometime Tractarian sympathizer, William Palmer of Worcester College, Oxford, 'than those subterfuges which it devises in order to avoid obedience to the will of a pure and all-wise God.'[20]

The acute separation these historians posited between God and the fallen world—and so between ecclesiastical and general history—corresponded to the distance they emphasized between the revelation wondrously given to mankind in history, the fortunes of which it was the duty of the church historian to record, and the capacity of the human mind to fathom it. 'If the scheme of Christian redemption was not only revealed by God,' Burton argued in his *History*, 'but every part of it was effected by the agency of God, without man knowing anything concerning it until it was thus effected and revealed, it seems impossible that such a system could be modified or improved by later and successive discoveries.'[21] High churchmen accordingly stressed the transcendent mystery of the Trinity, and tended to regard it in Augustinian terms as an inscrutable set of relations among the divine natures. 'It were vain to try amplification or ornament of such things as these', remarked the professor of moral philosophy at Trinity College, Dublin, William Archer Butler, in a sermon on the Incarnation.[22] An emphasis on the limitations of human knowledge often implied a certain suspicion of ante-Nicene philosophical theologians such as Origen and other Alexandrian fathers of the second and third centuries, whom seventeenth-century advocates of authoritarian orthodoxy had also found problematic.[23] William Conybeare, an old high churchman and geologist, warned in his 1839 Bampton Lectures 'that the Neological speculations of the nineteenth century are to the full as dangerous as

---

[19] E. Burton, *History of the Christian church; from the ascension of Jesus Christ, to the conversion of Constantine* (London, 1836), pp. 4–5.

[20] W. Palmer, *A compendious ecclesiastical history, from the earliest period to the present time* (London, 1840), new edn, pp. 14–15.

[21] Burton, *History*, p. 9.

[22] W.A. Butler, 'The mystery of the Holy Incarnation preached on Christmas Day', in his *Sermons, doctrinal and practical*, ed. T. Woodward, 2nd edn (Dublin, 1852), pp. 16–17; cf. E. Burton, 'Defence of the Athanasian Creed', in his *Sermons, preached before the University of Oxford* (London, 1832), p. 279.

[23] Quantin, *Church of England*, pp. 288, 362–3.

the Alexandrian speculations of the third'.[24] Many later critics came to see the historical explanation of doctrinal development, especially in its Hellenistic aspects, as a means of drawing out that development's essential reasonableness; but the early Victorian orthodox were a long way from that apologetic procedure.

High churchmen's stress on an unchanging and unitary primitive tradition ensured that antiquarianism became a standard charge made against them by scripturally minded critics.[25] The Congregationalist John Stoughton, in a course of critical *Lectures on Tractarian Theology* delivered at his William Street Chapel in Windsor in 1843, repeated John Milton's strongly worded deprecation of patristic tradition as the addition to 'the evangelic manna' of 'the tainted scraps and fragments of an unknown table'.[26] But evangelicals' rejection of the authority of tradition did not exclude the pregnant possibility that the early church might be a source of something more than mere refutations of Oxford's self-appointed 'apostolicals'. One evangelical Anglican stalwart, William Goode, supported his own rejection of Tractarianism with the argument that the early church had itself had the wisdom to recognize the supremacy of scripture.[27] Another, Edward Bickersteth, agreed with Milner that Protestants ought not to neglect the field, even while confessing that he did not know much about it.[28] Invalid though it may have been to confect a catholic consensus out of the fathers, staunch Protestants increasingly argued that the study of the early church had a pragmatic value, as a witness to revealed truth. The founding professor of ecclesiastical history at the Free Church's New College, David Welsh, in keeping with his belief that church history exclusively pertained to the fortunes of Christ's spiritual kingdom, treated the history of early heresies as an opportunity to warn against 'a love of novelty, a spirit of enthusiasm, a passion for notoriety'. This was a rigorist approach to doctrinal orthodoxy similar to that adopted by Edward Burton, whom Welsh admired.[29] In a process that would take further shape in succeeding decades, even Protestants who stressed biblical supremacy, including Stoughton, began to see patristic

---

[24] Conybeare, *Christian fathers*, p. 256; cf. Burton, *History*, pp. 320–1.
[25] I. Taylor, *Ancient Christianity and the doctrines of the Oxford Tracts for the Times* (2 vols, London, 1839–1842), i, vii.
[26] J. Stoughton, *Lectures on Tractarian theology* (London, 1843), p. 30.
[27] W. Goode, *The divine rule of faith and practice* (2 vols, London, 1842), i, xxvi, 569–71, ii, 259–61.
[28] E. Bickersteth, *Christian student*, pp. 214–18.
[29] D. Welsh, *Elements of church history: vol. I: comprising the external history of the church during the first three centuries* (Edinburgh, 1844), pp. [1]–2, 28, 51; G. Stronach, rev. H.C.G. Matthew, 'Welsh, David (1793–1845)', *ODNB*.

researches as a valuable aid to exploring the workings of the divine in temporal experience.

As both high church and Protestant critics looked to the early church to help them to delineate, in different ways, an unchanging essence of faith, the search for that essence through historical study acted subtly to change what it was understood to involve. High churchmen sometimes became Tractarians; and Protestants began to think in new ways about the work of the Holy Spirit in history after the death of the inspired apostles. The consequences of becoming deep in history were at first not obvious, however. Although roused to action by the Erastian and nonconformist dangers of their own time, early-Victorian high churchmen often wrote as though the main intellectual challenge to their patristic researches came from Edward Gibbon, or the Huguenot and Counter-Reformation scholarship of a still earlier period, rather than from newer, French or German threats to the very possibility of religious knowledge.[30] But as it became necessary to protect religious authority from agnostic or pantheist forms of infidelity, it became increasingly attractive to see historical inquiry as more than a matter of making logical inferences from a body of historically atomized if collectively privileged texts. Rather, for high churchmen as for other religious critics, historical study became the exploration of the spiritual depths of a dynamic process which carried a religious authority of its own: a process which, though not confined to the limits of the institutional church or a particular period of its growth, was one in which the fathers played a formative and still-living role. The controversy generated by two authors, in particular, made such a conception of development the subject of self-conscious reflection among students of the early church in a way that it had not been previously.

FROM NEWMAN TO BUNSEN

Published seven years apart from one another, John Henry Newman's *Essay on the Development of Christian Doctrine*, and Christian Karl Josias Bunsen's *Hippolytus and his Age*, were in the most obvious respects radically contrasting texts. Newman, who would claim in his 1864 *Apologia* that his life's work consisted in opposition to liberalism, offered his *Essay* in part as a justification of his 1845 conversion to Roman Catholicism. He had come to see this as the only unbroken communion of

---

[30] J.J. Blunt, *On the right use of the early fathers: two series of lectures, delivered in the University of Cambridge* (London, 1857), pp. 3–24; the lectures were delivered in 1845 and 1846.

believers, holding the infallible ecclesiastical authority for which he had long searched.[31] The liberal Protestant Bunsen, on the other hand, used his own patristic platform to call for a rational Christianity of the future that would be led, not by an ecclesiastical hierarchy, but by free congregations. Part of the reason why these works of church history both created publishing sensations akin to those familiar from the history of contemporary natural science, however, was because they coincided in presenting the notion of doctrinal development to a culture that was already beginning anxiously to entertain it.[32] From opposing points on an emergent spectrum of innovative critics, Newman and Bunsen thereby pushed a shocking idea from the edges of contemporary debate to its centre. For neither figure was religious truth something to be abstracted from a stereotyped patristic consensus. Rather, they both treated it as the fruit of developing conscience, the study of which offered a point of contact between God and history's present-day human interpreter. Old orthodox and evangelical reviewers typically faulted them for making religious truth depend on theories that unduly elevated the subjective faculties. But liberal Anglican writers, more fulsomely in Bunsen's case than in Newman's, began to identify distinctive kinds of apologetic promise in their writings that heralded wider changes in understandings of orthodoxy's history.

Newman's *Essay*, and the historical disposition it expressed, grew out of the interconnections between the intensive patristic investigations which he had begun as an Anglican in the 1820s and his abiding concern with the relationship between faith and reason. Important aspects of his mature historical outlook had solidified by the time he published his *Arians of the Fourth Century* in 1833. Here he explained the Arian heresy, which claimed that Christ was a created being, primarily as a moral failing, for it delved into the irreducible mystery of the Trinity with a disputatious and intellectualizing spirit.[33] Thus Newman projected onto an historical canvas his tendency to blend right belief with right moral disposition. His insistence that the book was no essay in 'controversy or proof', but was instead 'historical and explanatory', showed his preference for grasping at moral principles and their expression in supposedly concrete and indisputable historical facts, rather than relying on the proof-text methods of

---

[31] I. Ker, *John Henry Newman: a biography* (Oxford, 1988), pp. [257]–315.

[32] cf. J.A. Secord, *Victorian sensation: the extraordinary publication, reception, and secret authorship of* Vestiges of the Natural History of Creation (Chicago, IL, and London, 2000).

[33] J.H. Newman, *The Arians of the fourth century, their doctrine, temper, and conduct, chiefly as exhibited in the councils of the church between A.D. 325, & A.D. 381* (London, 1833), pp. [1]–42.

his contemporaries.[34] One of those principles was that of reserve in the transmission of religious truth, manifested in the early church by its reticence in publicly defining its teaching or in referring initiates to the letter of an 'obscure' biblical text.[35] But he initially resisted the suggestion from advanced Tractarians, first made in private correspondence two years after the publication of *Arians*, that the church could propose doctrines for belief that were not explicitly known by the primitive church.[36] Newman's confidence that permissible development could only ever be in the narrowly explicative sense that accorded with the orthodox Anglican understanding of the Vincentian rule, only began to give way around 1840. Now he came to think, contrary to this interpretative tradition, that the ante-Nicene fathers had been uncertain as to the co-equality of the Son with the Father in the Trinity. He began to suppose that the movement from implicit to explicit knowledge in doctrine was the fruit of legitimate development, a case he presented to Oxford's University Church in the last sermon he delivered as its incumbent in 1843, on 'The Theory of Developments'.[37]

Ideas drawn from patristic texts themselves offered one conduit to such a conclusion. Origen's exegetical method enabled Newman to apply non-literal meanings to non-biblical texts. He did so when he imposed a Catholic sense onto the Thirty-Nine Articles in his *Tract 90* of 1841, thereby positing the outwardly uncatholic Articles' continuity of faith from that of an earlier period.[38] Newman's later apprehension, therefore, could become a valid light by which to interpret earlier historical intimation: a stance that would soon enable him to free the ante-Nicene church from its Anglican trammels.[39] Another, more shadowy presence in Newman's intellectual direction was Johann Adam Möhler, who had explored doctrine's subjective and historically dynamic dimensions, before he recanted of having done so.[40] It would be going too far to say that Newman, who could not read German, was influenced by the Catholic Tübingen school; but the circle that closed around him at Littlemore after he withdrew there from the University Church in 1843 were certainly reading Möhler in French translation.[41] Newman's critics—some of

[34] Ibid., p. 151.   [35] Ibid., pp. 63–5, 67–76.

[36] J. Pereiro, 'Tradition and development', in Brown, Nockles, and Pereiro, *Oxford Movement*, pp. [201]–15.

[37] Ker, *Newman*, pp. 266–9; King, *Newman*, pp. 51–2.

[38] See chapter four of this volume at pp. 164–5.

[39] [J.H. Newman], 'Remarks on certain passages in the Thirty-Nine Articles', *Tracts for the Times*, vol. 6 (London, 1841), no. 90; King, *Newman*, pp. 47–8.

[40] Newman, *Essay*, p. 27; on Möhler, see chapter one of this volume at p. 28.

[41] Chadwick, *Bossuet to Newman*, pp. 96–119.

whom also attacked Bunsen along similar lines—were not slow to accuse him of German 'rationalism'.

Newman sent his *Essay on Development* to the printers in September 1845, and the next month he was received into the Roman Church.[42] The treatise integrated his earlier moral philosophy of ecclesiastical history with the radical theory of historical dynamism that had been growing in his mind for some years. Newman had become certain that the Church of Rome was a truer image of primitive Christianity than the Church of England. Such an argument had always been a staple of the Counter-Reformation; but Newman's rendering of it in his *Essay* was new and, to some commentators, subversive. The radicalism lay in his acceptance that the modern Roman Catholic Church did not exactly resemble the church of the first age either, and, crucially, in his claim that its present doctrine and practice were nevertheless explicable and defensible on the basis of a theory of development. The Vincentian rule, in its old Anglican sense, offered no reliable doctrinal authority, he argued, because patristic *catenae* were always selective. Nor could *catenae* mask the fact that ante-Nicene fathers, when taken by themselves, were often ambiguous as to the Trinitarian faith laid down by the councils.[43] The Bible was similarly limited, for the canon of scripture emerged only slowly, and the biblical text contained 'omissions' from the church's subsequent definitions of right belief.[44]

Textual data, therefore, had to be vivified by a theory or principle, rooted in faith, which recognized that doctrinal development did not end with the Bible, or the fathers of the first three centuries, but was a continuing vital sign of the church's life. Building on Joseph Butler, Newman argued on the analogy of organic nature and progressive revelation that there was an antecedent probability of development in religion. If it were part of the counsels of providence that development should occur, then so too was an infallible authority capable of deciding between true and false developments also probable.[45] That probability was converted into actual certainty, Newman felt, by the observable facts of Catholic history. When read in the light of his seven tests of true development, these revealed that an authoritative church and the Marian, purgatorial, and intercessory doctrines and practices it supported were all legitimate outgrowths from primitive Christianity.[46] The true meaning of the hints and enticements of scriptural and patristic sources, therefore, became clear

---

[42] Ker, *Newman*, pp.301, [316]–17.   [43] Newman, *Essay*, pp. 12–13, 397–8.
[44] Ibid., pp. 5, 140–4, 160.   [45] Ibid., pp. [94]–130.
[46] Ibid., pp. [30]–93, 122–3, 269, 316–17, [369]–445.

when they were set in the perspective of their full accomplishment in the Roman system.

Although Newman deployed his theory of development in defence of an infallible ecclesiastical order, several of the features of doctrinal development which he emphasized overlapped with those that liberal Protestant historians would also come to stress. Christianity, he urged, was a 'fact in the world's history'; its nature, accordingly, was known through its actual historical operation.[47] Although Christianity impressed itself on Newman as a 'fact', he was also fond of describing the form in which it was known, in almost Platonist terms, as an 'idea'. Newman, also a philosopher of education, described the development of Christian doctrine as the process by which the human mind assimilated the aspects of that idea, slowly but actively:

> It is the peculiarity of the human mind that it cannot take an object in, which is submitted to it, simply and integrally. It conceives by means of definition or description; whole objects do not create in the intellect whole ideas, but are, to use a mathematical phrase, thrown into series, into a number of statements, strengthening, interpreting, correcting each other, and with more or less exactness approximating, as they accumulate, to a perfect image.[48]

Whilst popes and councils necessarily regulated the form taken by Christian facts and ideas, Newman treated the latter as though they initially grew spontaneously and universally, in the bosom of the church as a whole. 'Doctrine too is percolated, as it were, through many minds, beginning with writers of inferior authority in the Church, and issuing at length in the enunciation of her doctors'; in the worship of Mary, 'the spontaneous or traditional feeling of Christians... in great measure anticipated the formal ecclesiastical decision'.[49] Newman's doctrine of conscience—the centrality he ascribed to his own conscience, blended with a notion of the expansion of the universal Christian conscience in time—thus regulated what kind of external religious authority he was prepared to accept.[50] By arguing for an objectively infallible religious authority on the basis of an historical theory that knowingly privileged moral subjectivity, Newman came into partial alignment with critics who argued from comparable premises to markedly anti-authoritarian conclusions.

Newman's more sophisticated high church and evangelical critics recognized the danger immediately after the *Essay*'s first appearance. For a number of writers, the rights and wrongs of Romanism became a

---

47 Ibid., p. [1].   48 Ibid., p. [94].   49 Ibid., pp. 352, 407.
50 Ibid., p. 124.

second-order question to that of whether it could ever be appropriate to regard a theory, of the human mind's deliberate devising, as an appropriate route of approach to the oracles of God. Whereas the old high churchmen and early evangelicals examined above typically regarded truth as ascertainable by the reverential exercise of logic upon a self-authenticating original deposit, Newman seemed to make truth an outgrowth of the human mind in history. William Palmer accused him of reviving mysticism, for he made conscience the sole judge of religious truth to the exclusion of external evidences.[51] Another high church critic thought it absurd to imagine that a lawgiver would ever shift the grounds of his enactments to 'the subject's own reason'.[52] William Archer Butler, snatching hours from his work at famine relief to dispatch letters on Newman to the *Irish Ecclesiastical Journal* between 1845 and 1847, argued that the 'Development-Hypothesis' was little more than a substitution of 'hightoned and elaborate descriptions of the course of mere *historical eventuation*, or little more than this, for the legitimate *logical connexion* of the disputes with admitted doctrines'.[53] It could accordingly be turned to any use, rationalist or superstitious, according to taste.

Butler likened Newman's theory to that of German neologians who made developing reason overrule revelation. William Cunningham, Welsh's successor as professor of ecclesiastical history at New College, Edinburgh, and subsequently its principal, agreed.[54] Even theologians not reputed for their dogmatic astringency sometimes pursued this line of criticism. Edward Burton's independent-minded successor as Oxford's Regius Professor of Divinity, Renn Dickson Hampden—whose 1836 appointment Newman had sought to overturn on the grounds of his alleged heterodoxy—deployed Vincentius and English standard divinity against the theory of development in a pair of sermons delivered in the city's Christ Church Cathedral in 1846. He insisted that 'true development' consisted not in the issuance of doctrines from the mind of the church, an inherently sceptical idea, but in the building up of the individual Christian in faith and grace. He blamed Möhler's influence for his former persecutor's aberration from that understanding.[55]

---

[51] W. Palmer, *The doctrine of development and conscience considered in relation to the evidences of Christianity and of the Catholic system* (London, 1846), viii.

[52] [Anon.], 'Newman's Essay on Development', *ENR*, 4:8 (1845), pp. 412–13.

[53] Butler, *Letters*, pp. 85–8.

[54] W. Cunningham, 'Romanist theory of development', in his *Discussions on church principles: popish, Erastian and Presbyterian* (Edinburgh, 1863), pp. 41–2, 53–7; the essay was reprinted from the *NBR* for 1846; L.A. Ritchie, 'Cunningham, William (1805–1861)', *ODNB*.

[55] R.D. Hampden, *The work of Christ, and the work of the spirit, considered in two sermons* (London, 1847), pp. 26–32, 42–3, 48, 63–5. Historians have generally taken heated

Whilst Newman's strongest critics attacked him for making Christianity subject to historical development, a cluster of liberal Anglican writers—though still hostile to the inferences he drew from it—greeted this idea notably less frostily. It was not Newman's *Essay* that persuaded them that religion might, in a positive sense, develop. But the controversy attendant upon its publication encouraged liberal critics to set out two alternative modes of understanding development, growing for some time, which signalled wider changes in how Protestant critics came to understand the history of orthodoxy, and Christianity as a whole, in the second half of the century: changes which, in an unusually systematic and doctrinally speculative direction, Bunsen was to pioneer. The differences between the two approaches—the one more doctrinal, and the other more sociopolitical in emphasis—involved disagreements, at first latent rather than explicit, over what kind of historicism best served to uphold religion's cultural authority.

Henry Hart Milman, reviewing Newman's *Essay* in the *Quarterly Review* for 1846, laid the stress on the second of these two accents. Milman assailed its author as strongly as any high church critic for having bent historical evidence to the requirements of his own inner light. The *Essay* represented a 'transfiguration' of Newman's mind; in his insistence on equating Roman Catholic to fundamental Christian claims—by maintaining, for example, that the authority of Purgatory was bound up with that of the Psalms—'the desperate apology is to his own conscience.'[56] Implicit in the distinction Milman here made between religious essentials and non-essentials, however, was his confidence in an ethicized simple gospel that looked back, in some respects, to the reasonable churchmanship of the eighteenth century. Born in 1791, Milman had left Oxford for a clerical living in 1818, and always remained intellectually closer to the age of Gibbon than to that of Newman and Coleridge.[57] Milman agreed with Newman that beneficial development in Christianity had taken place.[58] But when he considered religion as a fact in the world's history, he was not drawn to contemplate 'the dry and barren sands of metaphysical or theologic discussion'.[59]

The question that ought to guide the historian of the religion was rather '*what it was* in the ordinary life and in the bosom of Christian families'.

Tractarian characterizations of this complex philosopher-theologian as 'unorthodox' at face value: Ker, *Newman*, pp. 124–5.

[56] [H.H. Milman], 'Newman *on the Development of Christian Doctrine*', QR, 77:154 (1846), pp. 405, 412.

[57] Matthew, 'Milman'.   [58] [Milman], 'Newman', p. 420.

[59] Ibid., p. 434.

Progress in religion meant not doctrinal expansion, but the development 'of its morality, of its social influence, of its humanity'.[60] In support of his position, Milman quoted the anticlerical French political economist, Charles Dunoyer: 'It is often said that Christianity has civilised us. Perhaps it is not less just or less exact to say that civilisation has purified our Christianity.'[61]

In this way, Milman hinted at a separation between Christianity's doctrinal history, as representing in some ways a distraction from the gospel, and the history of the religion's progressive interactions with Christendom. Milman's historical vision, worked out in his studies of the early and medieval church, thus served to authorize a relatively undogmatic religion of the future, as did that of A. P. Stanley.[62] But it was not one that necessarily answered an anxious younger generation's desire for the established doctrines of Christianity to be brought into constructive relationship with philosophical truth and personal and social experience.

For a very large number of Victorians, Frederick Denison Maurice effected just such an integration, pointing thereby to a second and, in some respects, more popular liberal Anglican approach to early Christianity. This sought to reinterpret or revivify orthodoxy, rather than to lessen its religious centrality. Maurice included a preface on Newman's theory in the published version of his Warburton Lectures on the *Epistle to the Hebrews*, which appeared in 1846. He had been baptised into the Church of England from Unitarianism in 1831, but his abiding interest in Coleridge and Platonist ontology encouraged him to interpret particular forms of polity and doctrine from the point of view of an ideal of Christian catholicity that was at once outside time, and yet presumed in and discovered through history.[63] Although his conception of religiously authoritative tradition thus bore comparison with Newman's, he extended it beyond developing Catholicism to incorporate all of mankind's spiritual past. Maurice agreed with Newman that there was an 'antecedent probability' that God should have placed 'a developing authority in the midst of all'. But that authority was not an infallible pope. If it was true, as Maurice believed, that the manifestation of divine power took place through the conscience of man, that authority instead lay in history and its heroes and crises, which might be studied for signs of higher counsels.

---

[60] Ibid., pp. 434–5, 459.

[61] Ibid., p. 459 and n. On Milman's contact with French liberalism, see chapter three of this volume at pp. 117–20.

[62] On Milman's *HLC*, see chapter three of this volume.

[63] Morris, *Maurice*, pp. [55]–97.

To separate the institutional church from that wider activity, as Newman did, was to commit the prevailing contemporary sin of mechanicalism.[64] Maurice's *Ecclesiastical History of the First and Second Centuries*, published in 1854, accordingly depicted the historical emergence of Trinitarianism in the subjective mind of the church as the necessary expression and guarantee of the transformed consciousness of ethical life, and its basis in the relationship between man and God, wrought by the Christian revelation.[65] Newman had made a similar stress on developing conscience end very differently, in the foreclosure of argument by ecclesiastical authority. Maurice, however, aimed to show that the origins of orthodoxy in moral and spiritual consciousness made orthodoxy, properly understood, the prism through which to view experience and the basis of ethical action.

Julius Hare agreed with his friend Maurice as to the eternity and catholicity of doctrinal truth, in almost a Platonic sense, but combined this with a more distinctly germanized interest in the particular historical dynamics of the human mind's growth in the perception of it.[66] Although Hare commended Maurice's reply to Newman in his preface to *Hebrews*, the two men tellingly clashed in private correspondence over the relative merits of August Neander. Maurice held that Neander did not sufficiently grasp the ideal of the church whose history he sought to relate. Hare, by contrast, believed that such an ideal powerfully emerged from the historical life he painted.[67] Nourished by the works of German mediating theology that lined the shelves of his Sussex rectory, Hare published *The Mission of the Comforter* in 1846. In this series of sermons, mainly preached before the University of Cambridge and dedicated to Coleridge's memory, Hare posited that the Holy Spirit guided the progressive development of Christian thought in a process that had no arbitrary endpoint. He directed his case against the 'mechanical' understandings of the Holy Spirit held by Biblicist evangelicals and Tractarian 'patrolaters'. But in a formidable apparatus of endnotes, he made clear that he also objected to the appropriation of the idea of doctrinal development by English

---

[64] F.D. Maurice, *The Epistle to the Hebrews; being the substance of three lectures delivered in the chapel of the honourable society of Lincoln's Inn, on the foundation of Bishop Warburton* (London, 1846), xxxiv–xliii.

[65] Maurice, *Lectures on the ecclesiastical history of the first and second centuries* (Cambridge, 1854), pp. [289]–308.

[66] J. Hare to F. Hare, 26 December 1837, in A.J.C. Hare, *Memorials of a quiet life*, 12th edn (2 vols, London, 1875), ii, 185–6; [Hare and Hare], *Guesses*, p. 1.

[67] J.C. Hare to F.D. Maurice, 5 March 1838, in Maurice, *Frederick Denison Maurice*, i, 249, F.D. Maurice to J.C. Hare, 8 March 1838, ibid.; cf. F.D. Maurice, *The kingdom of Christ: or hints on the principles, ordinances, and constitution of the Catholic Church* (3 vols, London, [1838]), ii, 284–9.

Roman Catholic writers such as Newman. It was impossible for a church which, in Hare's view, had always aimed to repress the intellect now to deploy in its support a theory which depended on permitting the free growth of mind.[68]

In Hare's assessment, however, that free growth led towards doctrinal orthodoxy, not away from it. In a sermon preached at the consecration as bishop of St David's of his Trinity contemporary, Connop Thirlwall, who shared Hare's understanding of orthodoxy as the fruit of mental development, he advanced the Coleridgean case that there could be no real conflict between the intellect and the religious conscience. For the intellect, he considered, could only operate truthfully in the light of the higher moral reason.[69] The historical development of orthodoxy, on this reading, witnessed to just such an operation. In a course of sermons directed against Newman's views of justification, yet rather as Newman was given to argue, Hare explained that the best way to refute anti-Trinitarian heresy was to explain the animating principles behind the doctrinal controversies preceding the Council of Nicaea.[70] Credal formularies were therefore necessary to lead individuals to faith. 'One cannot spend a fortnight in the care of a parish', he told William Whewell in 1834, 'without finding that to talk about "the full consciousness of freedom" as necessary to religion is totally inapplicable to the present condition of mankind.'[71]

If Hare and Maurice considered that Protestantism might be renewed rather than subverted by reinterpreting orthodoxy as the fruit of morally guided reason, it was their mutual friend Christian Bunsen who first gave the idea a programmatic and, for many, strangely foreign shape in a critical history of the early church written for British readers. Bunsen's four-volume *Hippolytus and his Age* generated considerable if short-lived excitement upon its appearance in 1852. It attracted extensive commentary in contemporary periodicals and book-length replies; William Gladstone and

---

[68] J.C. Hare, *The mission of the comforter and other sermons with notes* (2 vols, London, 1846), i, xi–xii, ii, 413–14, 425–32. Though clearly aware of Möhler, Hare did not name him, instead citing the writings of Anton Günther as an instance of Catholic developmental thought: cf. A. Günther, *Vorschule zur speculativen Theologie des positiven Christenthums: in Briefen*, 2nd edn (2 vols, Vienna, 1846–1848), ii, 278–81.

[69] C. Thirlwall, *The spirit of truth the Holy Spirit: a sermon, preached before the University of Cambridge, on Whitsunday, May 16, 1869* (London, Oxford, and Cambridge, 1869), pp. 9–11, 13–15; J.C. Hare, 'The church the light of the world', in his *Mission of the comforter*, i, 195–212.

[70] Hare, 'Office and province of faith', in his *The victory of faith, and other sermons* (Cambridge, 1840), pp. 62–3.

[71] Trinity College, Cambridge, Add. MS a 206/162: J.C. Hare to W. Whewell, 1 June 1834.

the legal philosopher, John Austin, were among its readers.[72] *Hippolytus* drew the histories of the New Testament, the papacy, liturgy, and doctrine into its massy scope by means of a focus on a third-century Roman presbyter and lesser church father of that name, to whom Bunsen attributed a recently discovered text, known as the *Philosophumena*, which had come to attract European scholarly attention.[73] The work accordingly appealed to the intense contemporary fascination with Christian origins. But it did so in a way quite unlike any ecclesiastical history previously written in English. Identifying himself with 'the German method of inquiry', Bunsen signalled his intention to go beyond the mere narration of primitive ecclesiastical history—a field in which Neander offered the highest model—by integrating it with the wider philosophy of history which he had periodically adumbrated since his youth.[74]

Bunsen's *Hippolytus* offered nothing less than a manifesto for world-historical religious transformation. He argued that no contemporary religious grouping—Protestant, Catholic, or Tractarian—could claim the third-century church as a mirror of itself.[75] For unlike the dogmatic religion of prelatical and conciliar compulsion that had solidified during the fourth century and afterwards, the Christianity of Hippolytus' day was characterized by communal ethical life among substantially independent congregations. The growth of Christianity unlocked freedom, for it 'rested upon the idea of a community freely submitting to a divine order of society which calls mankind to freedom, and makes man free'.[76] A reinvigoration of this ideal in the present day, such as Bunsen had already unsuccessfully sought to press upon Frederick William IV of Prussia, would involve the establishment of joint assemblies of clergy and laity in England and Germany. These would appoint bishops and regulate church affairs, so that the church and the nations would ultimately be united.[77]

Bunsen's case involved more than a classically Protestant call for a return to lost simplicity. For he rooted his argument in a philosophy of history, grounded in the doctrine of the Trinity. Bunsen regarded Trinitarianism as essential to Christianity. But he interpreted the Trinity in a speculative way, insisting—by way of an invocation of Maurice, and a

---

[72] W.E. Gladstone, *The Gladstone Diaries*, ed. M.R.D. Foot and H.C.G. Matthew (14 vols, Oxford, 1968–1994), iv, 463 (24 October 1852); S. Austin to H. H. Milman, 21 January 1853, in Milman, *Milman*, p. 186.

[73] For the story of the discovery of the manuscript, see for example 'Bunsen's *Hippolytus and his Age*', *ER*, 97:197 (1853), pp. [1]–4. Milman may have written this essay: S. Austin to H.H. Milman, 21 January 1853, in Milman, *Milman*, pp. 185–6.

[74] Bunsen, *Hippolytus* (1852), i, vi, xvi–xvii.   [75] Ibid., ii, 121–2, iii, 331–5.

[76] Ibid., iii, pp. 217–18, 225–6.   [77] Ibid., iii, 233–52.

negative allusion to Newman and his followers—that the human mind could not receive Christianity unless it were truly rational.[78] The 'universal conscience', Bunsen wrote, was 'God's highest interpreter'.[79] In common with Newman, he treated the Nicene definition as the result of doctrinal development. Bunsen observed, as Newman had done, that Hippolytus did not conform to that formulation, in that he did not regard the Son's hypostasis, or personality, as eternal with the Logos.[80] Newman, however, had turned the symbolic and suggestive nature of ante-Nicene Trinitarianism to the support of an infallible church. Bunsen instead attributed a positively rational and Hellenistic character to Hippolytus' theology, inhering especially in his high view of the essentially reasonable Logos doctrine. Bunsen regretted how ecclesiastical authority had come to hedge with dogmatic restrictions a doctrine which, rightly understood, guaranteed that human reason existed in a continuum with divine reason. He reinforced the point by making Hippolytus out to have been a friend of the supposedly reasonable Origen, whom Newman had admired more for his mystical principle of economy in conveying divine truth, than for his ratiocination in expounding it.[81] This betokened a difference over the nature of Greek theology in which Victorian Protestant posterity was, on the whole, to lean more towards Bunsen's stance than to Newman's.[82] Because 'development is normal, objectively, so far as it evolves reality', Bunsen argued, Hippolytus' Johannine ideas might be made the subject of further rational development in the present day when excavated and systematized by historical criticism.[83] The fathers' ideas themselves warranted movement beyond antique precedent.

Bunsen rose to the challenge in a series of dense philosophical aphorisms, in gestation since 1816, which sought to reanimate Hippolytus by pressing his theology through the sieve of German speculative philosophy.[84] The apostolic Christianity, to which Hippolytus had given voice, Bunsen argued, recognized the unity of the Father, and the divine Sonship of all believers by virtue of their participation in the Logos, even if only Christ was truly the incarnate Logos. It also posited that the Spirit of God worked through the totality of believers in the church.[85] Yet development was only complete, Bunsen insisted, when the infinite thought of the divine being was given a finite, historical form.[86] The modern recommencement of the stunted progress of early Christianity towards an

---

[78] Ibid., i, 170–1. [79] Ibid., i, 172.
[80] Ibid., i, 293–303; cf. Newman, *Essay*, p. 354. [81] King, *Newman*, pp. 41–2.
[82] Bunsen, *Hippolytus* (1852), i, 177–9, 303–4, ii, 49, iv, 5. [83] Ibid., ii, 68.
[84] Ibid., i, xi. [85] Ibid., ii, 46–8. [86] Ibid., ii, 66–7.

ethical, congregational, and world-transforming religion was thus truly a
philosophical necessity, for the Trinitarian self-manifestation of the divine
mind involved the development of mankind. Here Bunsen found a helpful
support in Hippolytus' conception of the Logos as working itself out in
three stages: as reason in the mind of God, as the act of creation, and as the
Incarnation. Was this not, thought Bunsen, an early recognition of the
operation of the perfectly rational divine spirit in human history?[87] Despite
his Niebuhrian stress on the historical autonomy of the early church, in
practice Bunsen made apostolic Christianity echo Schelling's historical
philosophy, and Schleiermacher's philosophical theology, in his efforts to
commend it to the progressive intelligence of his day.

Bunsen's British reviewers greeted his *Hippolytus* with a mixture of
gratification and perplexity. 'Papal Aggression' was still a heated subject
in 1852, and many eagerly seized upon Bunsen's work because of the
anti-papal imputation which could be laid upon the *Philosophumena*'s
portrayal of Pope Callistus.[88] It also provided reassuring evidence for an
early dating of John's Gospel, against the radical Tübingen critics whose
disturbing views were then becoming more widely known in Britain.[89]
But Bunsen had viewed these issues as essentially subordinate to his
presiding interest in the philosophy of history and its bearing on the
religious consciousness; and on this question his readers were either
uncomprehending or unpersuaded. A reviewer in the *Examiner* found
Bunsen's philosophical aphorisms simply unintelligible.[90] Old orthodox
writers such as Christopher Wordsworth, a canon of Westminster and
future bishop of Lincoln, linked Bunsen's unsound views of development
to Newman's. Bunsen's ascription of supposed doctrinal development to
'the Universal Conscience', Wordsworth argued, was simply a way of
making private opinion infallible: a position Newman also took up, except

---

[87] Bunsen made these points in obscure language in ibid., ii, 32–52. After criticism from
reviewers he attempted to render his arguments more accessible in later editions:
C.C.J. Bunsen, *Hippolytus and his age; or, the beginnings and prospects of Christianity*,
2nd edn (2 vols, London, 1854), i, 78–82; Bunsen, *Christianity and mankind, their
beginnings and prospects* (7 vols, London, 1854), iii, 3–32, iv, 157–65.

[88] On anti-Catholicism and the study of religious history, see chapter three of this
volume.

[89] For Bunsen's refutation of the Tübingen arguments, and appropriations of Bunsen
on this point, see Bunsen, *Hippolytus* (1852), i, 53, 86–8; [J. Tulloch], 'Hippolytus
and his age', *NBR*, 19:37 (1853), pp. 113–15; 'T.', 'Hippolytus and his age', *JSL*,
3:6 (1853), pp. 461–77. For use of the *Philosophumena* against papal presumption, see
Bunsen, *Hippolytus* (1852), i, 125–36; [Anon.], 'Bunsen's Hippolytus', *Times*, 18 May
1853, p. 7; W. Elfe Tayler, *Hippolytus, and the Christian church of the third century*
(London, 1853), pp. 200–8.

[90] [Anon.], 'The literary examiner', *The Examiner*, 30 October 1852, pp. 691–2.

that he made the infallible private opinion reside in the pope.[91] This was not the transformation Bunsen had hoped to inaugurate. He tried in successive editions to make his philosophical claims more intelligible to British audiences, but without much success as the intense interest first generated by his writings faded away.[92]

It was the liberal Anglican historians, particularly those interested in the history of religious thought, who best grasped and sympathized with what Bunsen was trying to achieve. Julius Hare, the advertised addressee of the first volume, told William Whewell that *Hippolytus* 'throws a great deal of new light on the early history of the church' and contained 'some beautiful specimens of Niebuhrian combinations'.[93] Connop Thirlwall, perhaps significantly for a prominent bishop, expressed his admiration privately rather than publicly. Following the publication of Frances Bunsen's *Memoirs* of her husband in 1868, Thirlwall reminisced in a letter to Alexander Ewing, the bishop of Argyll, about his privilege of having known one who gave such comprehensive and timely warnings to the church.[94] He raised *Hippolytus and his Age*, by then generally ignored, in a letter to another correspondent in 1873.[95] Thirlwall continued to insist that metaphysics remained the highest of all intellectual problems; but even the notably unspeculative Arthur Penrhyn Stanley was moved to contribute a preface to a posthumous edition of Bunsen's *God in History*.[96] He acknowledged that 'it relates, in so large a measure, to philosophical and abstract questions on which I do not feel myself competent to enter.' Bunsen's works nevertheless stood as an enduring witness to 'the possibility of the influence of a Christian layman or statesman on the highest questions which can occupy the heart and mind of man'.[97]

Bunsen articulated his ideas in a uniquely systematic way. But by the mid-century, his conviction that religious truth emerged from criticism of the 'real life and action' of history, especially the 'proof of a divine

[91] C. Wordsworth, *St. Hippolytus and the Church of Rome in the earlier part of the third century* (London, 1853), pp. 179–94; cf. R. Hussey, 'The church from the beginning until now', in his *Sermons mostly academical* (Oxford, 1849), pp. [118]–46.

[92] [Anon.], 'Bunsen's Christianity and Mankind', *JSL*, 1:1 (1855), pp. 1–16; [C.W. Russell], 'Pope Callistus on the Trinity', *DR*, 39:78 (1855), p. 384.

[93] Trinity College, Cambridge, Add. MS a206/185: J.C. Hare to W. Whewell, 22 October 1851. Hare appears to have read Bunsen's work before it was published.

[94] C. Thirlwall to A. Ewing, 20 April 1868, in his *Letters literary and theological of Connop Thirlwall, late Lord Bishop of St. David's*, ed. J.J.S. Perowne and L. Stokes (London, 1881), pp. 282–4.

[95] C. Thirlwall to G. Clark, 26 March 1873, ibid., pp. 353–5.

[96] C. Thirlwall to [Elizabeth Johnes], 8 May 1871, in his *Letters to a friend*, pp. 265–6; for the identity of the correspondent, see Clark, 'Thirlwall'.

[97] A.P. Stanley, 'Preface', to C.C.J. Bunsen, *God in history or the progress of man's faith in the moral order of the world* (3 vols, London, 1868–1870), trans. S. Winkworth, i, [v]–viii.

ordinance of human destinies' manifested in church history, was
becoming common to those critics who wished to salvage the patristic
witness by aligning it with the facts of human moral experience.[98] The
dualistic ecclesiasticism positing a clear separation between the facts of
revelation and the temporal human response to them, which Newman had
subverted in order subtly to defend, dissolved in the hands of Bunsen and
his liberal Anglican admirers. Robert Hussey, Oxford's first Regius Professor of Ecclesiastical History and Stanley's old orthodox predecessor in
the chair, recognized the danger in a series of sermons, preached at Christ
Church and the University Church, which he collated and published in
1849. To Newman's and Bunsen's theories, among other threats, Hussey
opposed 'the *one mind and one mouth*' of Christian antiquity. This, he
believed, was to place 'religion on the basis of *objective* truth, rather than of
the *subjective* emotions of the human mind'.[99] Hussey's stationary conception of the patristic witness never completely dissipated in nineteenth-
century Anglican divinity.[100] But for many of his successors, the best route
to vindicating the mind and mouth of antiquity lay precisely in revivifying
its subjective historical life. Insofar as that enterprise ran on to vindicating
orthodox metaphysics on newly interior grounds, it ultimately came into
conflict with a distinct strand of anti-metaphysical liberal historicism that
had more in common with Milman than with Maurice.

HELLENISM, TRINITARIANISM, AND THE
EXPERIENCE OF THE EARLY CHURCH

The public incomprehension and private approval which had met
Bunsen's philosophical claims, in one respect a singular moment, in another
belonged to a wider movement. As scholars became more and more
interested after 1850 in how doctrine had emerged from life and criticism
in Levantine metropolises and Greek philosophical schools, doctrinal history ceased to be primarily a translated German subject and became
naturalized in British academic discussion. The minute critical investigations into the history of the Apostles' and Nicene Creeds which succeeded
the suggestive generalizations of early Victorian liberal Anglicans tended
to be less idiosyncratically speculative than Bunsen's writing. But the

---

[98] Bunsen, *Hippolytus* (1852), i, 177, ii, 23.
[99] Hussey, 'Preface', to his *Sermons*, vii–viii; Hussey, 'The witness of antiquity', ibid.,
pp. 163–4. Hussey was alluding to Romans 15:6.
[100] Cf. C.A. Heurtley, *Wholesome words: sermons on some important points of Christian
doctrine preached before the University of Oxford*, ed. W. Ince (London, 1896).

historians who undertook them increasingly emphasized the subjective and spontaneous over the textual and syllogistic aspects of creedal growth. This came to be a way of making orthodoxy seems the fruit of collective spirit, more than a set of inferences from a body of external data. Brooke Foss Westcott told a public audience in Peterborough in 1880 that the Apostles' Creed was 'the spontaneous expression of the life, of the feeling, of the experience, of the Christian Society'.[101] Fenton Hort, who in 1852 had told a more sceptical Westcott how much he admired Newman, was pleased to conclude in his 1876 *Two Dissertations*, a treatise on creedal history, that what was popularly called the Nicene Creed was in fact no conciliar construction at all, but was instead an ancient and popular creed of Jerusalem.[102] This fashion, in which the voice of Maurice could often be heard, was not solely an Anglican one. John Tulloch, in lectures to his St Andrews students in which he also discussed Coleridge and Schleiermacher, depicted early orthodoxy as the product of free growth, in common with all the religious thought he admired.[103] A new generation of critics came to assume that it was easier to render orthodoxy acceptable to the autonomous individual, if it could be presented as the outcome of, or capable of being clarified by, free subjectivity in response to revelation.

This broad transformation contained distinct and sometimes incompatible analytical trajectories. After Bunsen's early venture into the subject had been drowned out by what had then been louder anxieties over the papal revival and the scriptural canon, the relationship between Christianity and Greek thought steadily became a major focal point of patristic debate. Where Gibbon had used history to emphasize the perennial tension between world-affronting Christianity and the sophisticated reasonableness of classical philosophy, later-nineteenth-century philosophers and theologians, without denying that antithesis, looked to historical narration more and more as one means of overcoming it. Early revivalists had been given to emphasizing the externality of revelation to reason, and

---

[101] B.F. Westcott, *The historic faith: short lectures on the Apostles' Creed* (London and Cambridge, 1883), p. 23.

[102] F.J.A. Hort, *Two dissertations* (Cambridge and London, 1876), pp. 107–8; F.J.A. Hort to B.F. Westcott, 8 and 13 October 1852, in A.F. Hort, *Life and letters of Fenton John Anthony Hort D.D., D.C.L., LL.D., sometime Hulsean Professor and Lady Margaret's Reader in Divinity in the University of Cambridge* (2 vols, London, 1896), i, 231; in 1890, Hort told his wife that the two congratulatory letters he most prized in relation to his *Two Dissertations* came from Stanley and Newman: 24 August 1890, ibid., ii, 423–4; B.F. Westcott to M. Whittard, 4th Sunday after Trinity 1846, and B.F. Westcott to M. Whittard, 7 May 1850, in A. Westcott, *Life and letters of Brooke Foss Westcott D.D., D.C.L., sometime bishop of Durham* (2 vols, London, 1903), i, 71, 163–4.

[103] University of St Andrews spec. coll., James M'Turk Strachan notebooks: MS BT 19. T8 (MS 4357), 51–78r, MS BT 19.T8 (MS 4356), 1–6, MS BT 19.T86 (MS 4358), 11–16. On Tulloch, see chapters four and five of this volume.

the unutterable transcendence and mystery of the scheme of Christian redemption as expressed in the creeds. William Van Mildert, an early-nineteenth-century high churchman, used his Boyle Lectures to describe philosophy as 'the instrument, which of all others, the great Enemy of mankind has most frequently employed in his service' because it gratified 'men's vanity and self-importance'.[104] But to Idealist philosophers, and historians of differing ecclesiastical tendencies who selectively appropriated idealist motifs, it became attractive to present the early history of Christian theology as though it had historically evolved in reasonable dialogue with Greek ideas. Origen and the Alexandrian fathers became newly appealing in this context. The late-Victorian popularity of Incarnationalist thought, familiar to social and economic historians of the period, arose in part for the less-remembered reason that Trinitarian belief appeared to offer a metaphysical solution to the problem of evil, and the relationship between the world and its creator, which Greek philosophy and its late forms had been unable to solve unaided.[105] Modern unbelief, to critics who thought in this way, often resembled a cyclical recurrence of the errors Christianity had dispersed long ago.

Historical explanation thus became a kind of rational justification; and historical succession started to wear the appearance of a logical sequence. In its absolute Idealist form, however, the historical rationalization of Christian doctrine ran on to the argument that Trinitarian belief arose, not from an interventionist revelation, but from philosophical necessity. Evangelicals resisted that conclusion, preferring instead to emphasize that Trinitarian doctrine resulted from Christian experience. So too did more moderate 'Hellenists', who stressed that it was not reason that subsumed revelation, but the other way round. Despite these differences, by 1900 a striking range of theologians and historians of philosophy, including more nonconformist and popular historians than had once been drawn to patristic inquiry, agreed that the authority of orthodoxy was strengthened, rather than weakened, by historicizing the process of its emergence from the mind of Christendom.

Aided by the steady percolation of German and French critical studies, as well as by native contributions, late-Victorian historians were increasingly aware that orthodoxy shared an historical context with Greek, Jewish, and eastern philosophical, religious, and theosophic schools and sects. Identifying a progressive movement amongst the occidental Greeks which they tended to deny to Semitic or oriental cults, later-Victorian

---

[104] W. Van Mildert, *An historical view of the rise and progress of infidelity, with a refutation of its principles and reasonings* (2 vols, London, 1806), i, 300.
[105] Cf. Hilton, *Age of atonement*, pp. [298]–339.

scholars commonly sketched or assumed the existence of a broadly upwards, or even dialectical movement in Greek thought. This ran from Plato and Aristotle, to Stoicism, Epicureanism, and later Pythagoreanism, ultimately ending in the unveiling of Christian truth. After the coming of Christianity, but before the church had formalized its dogmas, this trajectory had terminated or dispersed, it was argued, in two supposed dead ends. The first was Gnosticism. This was an umbrella term describing a diverse array of first- and second-century soteriologies mixing Christian, Platonist, Jewish, and eastern beliefs, chiefly concerned with the origin of evil, the situation of man in the world, and the possibility of redemption.[106] The second was 'Neoplatonism', of which the third-century Alexandrian philosopher, Plotinus, was understood to have been the first systematic exponent. This nineteenth-century coinage denoted a religious philosophy which united Plato's distinction between the eternal world of thought and the transitory world of sense with a mystical belief in the possibility of union with the transcendent One, from whom reality was said to derive.[107] Early Victorian revivalists had generally assumed a radical separation between orthodox belief and these parallel intellectual phenomena, which had once seemed entirely spurious. Early in the century, the evangelical Anglican historian Joseph Milner had dismissed the Gnostic theories as 'scenes of nonsense'.[108] To the Free Churchman William Cunningham, they were 'very like the ravings of madmen'.[109] But as interest in doctrinal development spread, and as new philosophical challenges to religion arose from agnosticism, scientific materialism, and Hegelian pantheism, the relations which Christianity bore to these outworkings of the heathen mind attracted closer scrutiny.

For the late-Victorian revivers of interest in the Hellenistic Christianity which grew out of these encounters, the first argumentative step was to draw out the legitimacy and significance of the questions which earlier Greek philosophies had raised, in order to show that such philosophy alone was incapable of answering them. A former headmaster of Brighton College and, from 1901, Regius Professor of Ecclesiastical History at Oxford, Charles Bigg, published a history of *Neoplatonism* in this vein

---

[106] For a modern summary, see H.R. Drobner, *The fathers of the church: a comprehensive introduction*, trans. S.S. Schatzmann (Peabody, MA, 2007), pp. 105–12.

[107] For a modern summary, see R.M. Berchman, 'Neoplatonism', in E. Ferguson (ed.), *Encylopedia of early Christianity*, 2nd edn (New York and London, 1998), pp. 801–4; 'Neoplatonism, n.', *OED*.

[108] Milner, *History of the church of Christ*, i, 221.

[109] W. Cunningham, *Historical theology: a review of the principal doctrinal discussions in the Christian church since the apostolic age* (2 vols, London, 1960), i, 122; first edition 1862.

with the Society for Promoting Christian Knowledge in 1895.[110] In his work on the New Testament, Bigg treated radical German theories with scepticism; and yet his sympathies as a preacher lay with the typically broad church notion that church and state were in idea one and the same. These independent-minded stances expressed an intellectual catholicity, and distance from the conventional lines of party controversy, which his friend William Inge attributed to his love of Plato.[111] It was Christianity, in Bigg's treatment, which had led Platonist thought out of its cave.

Bigg's *Neoplatonism* presented a conception of the course of ancient philosophy that was fairly characteristic of the late-Victorian theologians who brought Christianity into relation to it. Bigg believed that Plato had introduced a dualism between the unchanging and the eternal, accessible by mind, and the transitory and inferior world of sense, existing only insofar as it participated in the life of thought. Heathen philosophy never escaped from it. The result was to render all subsequent attempts to explain the problem of evil, and the nature of absolute existence manifested in the relationship between God and man, essentially inadequate, despite the nobility of the inquiry. For such attempts were incapable of giving an account of the rational unity which inhered, Bigg assumed, in the universe and man's experience of it. The Stoics failed, because their correct belief that happiness was to be found in the pursuit of moral perfection, in accordance with natural law, could not truly follow from their pantheist assumption that God and the soul were material.[112] The Pythagoreans made the One God who was above all lower gods perfect, but shielded that perfection by making him cold, ineffable, and in need of nothing.[113] The Neoplatonists of the second and third centuries AD preserved what was true in these earlier systems, whilst recognizing that some point of unity between the mind and sense had to be sought in the One.[114] They therefore arrived at a more dynamic and reciprocal sense of divine activity and its relationship with the world: hence the Neoplatonist interest in intermediate beings between God and matter. But God, being the good, necessarily remained passive and cut off from creation in this scheme. Gnostic 'phantasmagoria', vainly seeking to explain how man might be redeemed within such a system, was the most extreme manifestation of a

[110] C. Bigg, *Neoplatonism* (London, 1895); M.D.W. Jones, 'Bigg, Charles (1840–1908)', *ODNB*.

[111] C. Bigg, 'Religion and secular life', in his *The spirit of Christ in common life*, ed. T. Strong (London, 1909), p. 235; Bigg, *A critical and exegetical commentary on the epistles of St. Peter and St. Jude* (Edinburgh, 1901), p. 34; W.R. Inge, 'Charles Bigg', *Journal of Theological Studies*, 10 (1908), pp. [1]–2.

[112] Bigg, *Neoplatonism*, pp. [9]–26.   [113] Ibid., pp. [27]–42.

[114] Ibid., p. 26.

general problem in ancient thought.[115] Thus Bigg drew the incomplete reasonableness of Greek thought into the service of an historical justification of the Christian revelation.[116]

The Idealist philosopher Edward Caird, then master of Balliol College, Oxford, presented a comparable, gently dialectical narrative in his Gifford Lectures—a foundation dedicated to natural theology—for 1900–1902 on *The Evolution of Theology in the Greek Philosophers*. Hegel's was a background voice in this text, as he was in Caird's wider oeuvre. Post-Hegelian historians of philosophy such as Clemens Baeumker and the sometime Tübingen theologian Eduard Zeller, who sought inner connections between historically occurring ideas without equating historical causation with the rigid sequence of a logical dialectic, were more immediate points of contact.[117] In common with many idealizing thinkers of the day, Caird minimized the difference between theology and philosophy by defining theology as 'religion brought to self-consciousness'.[118] Caird then explained the stages in the growth of this self-consciousness, from the earliest spiritualization of rude mythology in the Greek poets and tragedians to the speculation of the Neoplatonists.[119] The Neoplatonists, he argued, had realized that the consciousness of the reflective subject presupposed a unity underlying all things. This was the consciousness of God. But the Neoplatonists, especially Plotinus, held the doctrine in a negative, mystical way, being still detained by an insurmountable dualism which felt the impossibility of positively connecting the material and intelligible worlds.[120] H. M. Gwatkin, who combined staunchly Protestant Anglicanism with Idealist inclinations, made a similar point in his 1904–1905 Gifford Lectures on *The Knowledge of God and its Historical Development*, delivered while he was Dixie Professor.[121] Greek thought

---

[115] Ibid., [119]–27, 146–7.

[116] Cf. C. Bigg, *The origins of Christianity*, ed. T.B. Strong (Oxford, 1909), p. 334.

[117] E. Caird, *The evolution of theology in the Greek philosophers: the Gifford Lectures delivered in the University of Glasgow in sessions 1900–1901 and 1901–1902* (2 vols, Glasgow, 1904), i, vii–ix; cf. C. Baeumker, *Das Problem der Materie in der griechischen Philosophie* (Münster, 1890), [v]–x. Caird did not cite Zeller, but did correspond with him: Tübingen Universitätsbibliothek, Md. 747.100: E. Caird to E. Zeller, 23 October 1877; E. Zeller, *Die Philosophie der Griechen in ihrer geschichtlichen Entwicklung*, 2nd edn (3 vols, Tübingen, 1856–1865), i, [Dedication], [v]–vi; G. Hartung, 'Eine Schatzkammer des Wissens: Leben und Werk des Gelehrten Eduard Zeller', in Hartung (ed.), *Eduard Zeller: Philosophie- und Wissenschaftsgeschichte im 19. Jahrhundert* (Berlin and New York, 2010), pp. [1]–18.

[118] Caird, *Evolution of theology*, i, 31. On the British Idealist philosophy of religion, see Mander, *British Idealism*, pp. [137]–80.

[119] Caird, *Evolution of theology*, i, 31–57.   [120] Ibid., ii, 162–83, 210–31, 282–4.

[121] H.M. Gwatkin, *The knowledge of God and its historical development* (2 vols, Edinburgh, 1906). Gwatkin apparently regarded this as his *magnum opus*: Emmanuel College, Cambridge, H.M. Gwatkin papers, Letters/214: L. Creighton to H.M. Gwatkin,

had come to a stop, he argued, because it could not reconcile divine transcendence with divine activity.[122]

The second stage of the argument, therefore, was to establish that Christianity had shown a reasonable way out of that tension. The Greek theologians, late-Victorian doctrinal historians argued, had been able to overcome it by the Incarnation, a doctrine expressed and rationalized in the Johannine principle of the Logos. Doctrinal historians recognized that the term 'Logos' had had an ancestry in Stoic and Neoplatonist thought, but they regarded its meaning as having been transformed and made wholesome by its usage as part of an historical revelation. The Logos was no mere cosmological principle, Gwatkin argued, but the revealer of God and the teacher of men.[123] Westcott's introduction to his edition of John's gospel, though expressing a critical opinion that the apostle derived the term from a Palestinian rather than an Alexandrian source, nevertheless considered that its meaning was not determined by its origin. No Greek or Jewish thinker, he was confident, would have deduced that the Word became flesh from his own principles.[124] Westcott appreciated the stress which Origen and the Alexandrian theologians laid upon the Logos, because this privileged the relationship between human and divine reason and consecrated man's moral freedom.[125] Bigg argued along the same lines in his 1886 Bampton Lectures on *The Christian Platonists of Alexandria*. According to Clement and Origen, he reported, every person was an image of the divine word.[126] Bigg suggested that in this they had understood true freedom, by joining 'the spontaneity of individualism with unity through the trained and sanctified intelligence'.[127]

The apologetic shift in favour of presenting the incarnate Logos as answering a long-standing problem in ancient thought was allied to attempts to rationalize the Trinity. As Bunsen had once represented it, this doctrine came to appear as the denotation of a distinctly historical process of divine self-realization. John Caird, fellow-Idealist brother of Edward and, unlike Edward, in holy orders, argued the point in the Gifford Lectures on *The Fundamental Ideas of Christianity*, which he

13 September 1906. Peter Slee characterizes Gwatkin's works, rather summarily, as 'solid, if unexciting': P.R.H. Slee, 'Gwatkin, Henry Melvill (1844–1916)', *ODNB*.

[122] Gwatkin, *Knowledge of God*, ii, 74, 91–3.   [123] Ibid., ii, 97.

[124] B.F. Westcott, *The gospel according to St John: the authorized version with introduction and notes* (London, 1882), pp. xv–xviii; cf. Wheeler, *St John*, pp. 63–6.

[125] B.F. Westcott, *Essays in the history of religious thought in the west* (London, 1891), pp. [194]–252.

[126] C. Bigg, *The Christian Platonists of Alexandria: eight lectures preached before the University of Oxford in the year 1886* (Oxford, 1886), p. 297.

[127] Ibid., p. 283.

delivered in 1896 while principal of Glasgow University. One of those ideas was the Trinity, which, he regretted, was generally taken to be unintelligibly mysterious even by those who accepted it. It was not so. Joining other late-century divines who imported biological comparisons in order to represent theological evolution, Caird argued that just as the highest natures in the world were marked by internal differentiations—the living organism was above the stone—so too was the divine nature. By expressing the idea of God's pouring-forth by the Logos, and his reciprocal incorporation of all that was good in the world into himself, the one in three persons was 'the very essence of all intelligence'.[128] His brother, Edward, argued in his own Gifford Lectures that the Trinity was an early and imperfect formulation of the Christian insight into the absolute: the unity between God and the progress of the race.[129] A number of clerical writers responded favourably to these adventures of ideas. Gwatkin appreciated John Caird's interpretation of the Trinity.[130] One liberal Church of Scotland minister argued that Idealist philosophy, by presenting God as a 'Divine Organism', enabled '*Trinitarian thought*' to assert 'itself with keenness and depth unexampled since the age of Arianism'.[131] The essential interrelations of eternal Father, historically manifested Son, and abiding Spirit, on these readings, reflected and sustained evolution in the human and natural worlds.

The growing prominence of intellectual challenges to religious belief after 1870 stimulated the breadth of these inquiries. New forms of unbelief, which increasingly replaced ecclesiological error as the focus of patristic students' anxieties, came to appear as though they were visitations from a vanquished ancient world. By discovering analogies between ancient heresies and modern theories, it became possible to argue, by prolepsis, that the Christianity which had answered earlier unbelief would in the course of time also rationally confute its modern restatements. Bigg compared Plotinus' inert doctrine of matter, radically separate from divinity, to that of modern-day agnosticism.[132] For Westcott, the Gnosticism overborne by his favoured Alexandrians resembled 'the Transcendentalism of the last generation', in that it fixed attention on the great problems of life—such as the relationship between the absolute and the finite—while providing wildly speculative answers to them.[133] Gwatkin

---

[128] J. Caird, *The fundamental ideas of Christianity* (2 vols, Glasgow, 1899), i, [55]–79, here at 79.

[129] Caird, *Evolution of theology*, ii, 358–67.

[130] Gwatkin, *Knowledge of God*, ii, 111 n. 2.

[131] J. Lindsay, *The progressiveness of modern Christian thought* (Edinburgh and London, 1892), pp. 77–80.

[132] Bigg, *Neoplatonism*, p. 199.   [133] Westcott, *Religious thought*, p. 201.

considered that the movement from Arianism to Nicene orthodoxy mirrored the transition from unimaginative, mechanistic deism to the immanent, progressive providence he postulated as an alternative.[134] The Free Church professor, Thomas Martin Lindsay, was by the early 1900s melancholically fond of comparing the present age of the world to the dissipated wane of antiquity. He thought that in the growing Christian Science movement, which equated disease with sin, he could catch a glimpse of the old Gnostic speculations.[135] The occultism that bewitched so many at the outset of the twentieth century could only be met, as its ancient manifestations had been, by an anti-materialist and anti-mechanical Christianity.[136] Some contemporary critics of Christianity were even prompted to give a newly sympathetic hearing to its ancient opponents in this developing argumentative context. Thomas Whittaker, a future associate of the Rationalist Press Association, published a sympathetic history of Neoplatonism in 1901 which argued that it had been crushed, not lifted up, by dogmatic religion.[137] The history of unbelief and revival, it appeared, moved in cycles.

Henry Longueville Mansel had developed this observation in an apologetic direction, although his aversion to philosophical Christianity made him unusual among those who did. Mansel had made his lasting reputation with his 1858 Bampton Lectures on *The Limits of Religious Thought* as Waynflete reader, subsequently professor, in moral and metaphysical philosophy at Oxford.[138] He later enjoyed a brief and less-remembered period as Regius Professor of Ecclesiastical History in the same university, the chief fruits of which were his lectures on *The Gnostic Heresies of the First and Second Centuries*. These were posthumously published, under Joseph Barber Lightfoot's editorship, in 1875.[139] Mansel's Bampton Lectures had made a provocative epistemological argument, derived from Kant, for accepting revelation on the grounds that natural human reason was inherently incapable of deciding in questions of absolute reality. He quietly wove the same argument into his history of Gnosticism.

---

[134] Gwatkin, *Knowledge of God*, ii, 106–11.

[135] T.M. Lindsay, 'Modern religious difficulties' (1907), in his *College addresses*, pp. 20–1.

[136] Lindsay, 'Occultism: ancient and modern' (1908), in his *College addresses*, pp. 34–8.

[137] T. Whittaker, *The Neo-Platonists: a study in the history of Hellenism* (Cambridge, 1901), viii; F.J. Gould, *The pioneers of Johnson's court: a history of the Rationalist Press Association*, rev. edn (London, 1935), p. 54.

[138] H.L. Mansel, *The limits of religious thought examined: in eight lectures, preached before the University of Oxford, in the year M.DCCC.LVIII* (Oxford, 1858); Lightman, *Origins of agnosticism*, pp. 32–67.

[139] H.L. Mansel, *The Gnostic heresies of the first and second centuries*, ed. J.B. Lightfoot (London, 1875).

The rational search for an absolute first principle, he warned, almost inevitably ran on to a denial of the personality of God, and the redefinition of evil not as the product of sin but as the result of finite and relative existence. As it had once proved with fantastical Gnostic constructions of hierarchies of divine beings, so the same law had recently made itself known in Hegel's philosophy of religion.[140]

Among late-Victorian religious conservatives, Mansel's mode of separating the provinces of reason and faith, criticized by Edward Caird and Gwatkin (as by Newman and Maurice) attracted fewer followers than historically grounded ways of bringing them together.[141] This inclination cut across denominational and church party divisions. Mandell Creighton, Gwatkin's high church friend and predecessor as Dixie Professor, warmly praised his 1882 *Studies of Arianism*.[142] A contributor to the 1889 critical and Incarnationalist high church essay collection *Lux Mundi*, J. R. Illingworth, argued that the Trinity guaranteed both divine immanence in man and nature, and the divine transcendence which made Nicene orthodoxy authoritative.[143] He also regarded the fact that the Trinity had been formulated slowly, by fathers who drew terminology from Greek philosophical debate whilst also transforming it, as a testament to its evolutionary resilience. 'In biology we know that the nature of their environment modifies organisms,' Illingworth wrote with notes of Lamarckianism, 'but it only does so by stimulating their internal energies to respond to itself.'[144] Charles Gore, editor of *Lux Mundi* and principal of Oxford's newly established Pusey House, argued that the Trinity corresponded to man's 'upward-soaring' reason in his 1891 Bampton Lectures on the Incarnation; Mansel was one of his targets. The only form of rational theism in a complex universe of relations and processes was not pantheism or deism, he argued, but the recognition of a threefold, personal distinction in the divine nature which preserved a loving God's active, transcendent, and communicative attributes. Gore rounded off his arguments with

---

[140] Ibid., pp. 11–15, 107–9. The old orthodox Christopher Wordsworth endorsed Mansel's *Gnostic Heresies* on this point: *A church history to the Council of Nicaea A.D. 325* (London, 1881), pp. 182 n. 4, 186.

[141] Caird, *Evolution of theology*, i, 10–11; Gwatkin, *Knowledge of God*, i, 151–2.

[142] Emmanuel College, Cambridge, H.M. Gwatkin papers, Letters /203: M. Creighton to H.M. Gwatkin, 3 September 1884; H.M. Gwatkin, *Studies of Arianism, chiefly referring to the character and chronology of the reaction which followed the Council of Nicaea* (Cambridge and London, 1882).

[143] J.R. Illingworth, *Divine transcendence and its reflection in religious authority* (London, 1911), pp. 5–47; C. Gore (ed.), *Lux mundi: a series of studies in the religion of the incarnation* (London, 1889).

[144] J.R. Illingworth, *The doctrine of the Trinity apologetically considered* (London, 1907), pp. 96–7, 124.

allusions to Coleridge, Maurice, and Hermann Lotze, a fashionable guru to late-century personal Idealists.[145]

This broad agreement over the developing rationality of orthodoxy only partially concealed, however, considerable differences over the role of historical revelation in bringing about the transition from Greek philosophy to Christian theology. Doctrinal historians who held that revelation was something imparted to history from without, whilst also affirming that philosophy played a constructive historical role in preparing for and interpreting the truths by which philosophy was transformed, emphasized that the process of doctrinal development was driven by the church's response to a personal saviour. Gore praised the Greek theologians who treated the Incarnation as gathering together all the previous workings of the divine in the human mind; but it was the church's experience of Christ as its resurrected lord and master that led it, through metaphysical reasoning, towards Trinitarian doctrine.[146] Bigg comparably intoned in a sermon at the University Church in Oxford that the early councils, rather than consisting of disputatious philosophers, comprised those concerned to safeguard their intuitions of a great personality.[147] For the absolute Idealists whom late-century clerics often liked to quote, however, the transition from Hellenistic to Christian culture ultimately did not require an explanation that looked beyond the historical process itself. Edward Caird notably declined to stress the role of the miraculous character of the gospel history in pushing the dialectical *Evolution of Theology* into its Christian stage.[148] Such omissions did not pass unnoticed. Bigg appreciated aspects of Hegelianism; in his case, for its recognition of the role of art, knowledge, and discipline in religion. But in *Neoplatonism*, Bigg periphrastically criticized 'the Master of Balliol' and the German Hegelians with whom Bigg associated him for regarding religion 'as the natural evolution of capacities implanted in the soul of man'. 'On this view', he wrote, 'Hellenism is precisely Idealism', and in this sense Christian doctrine 'was the very antipodes of Hellenism'.[149]

The late-century evangelicals who applied themselves to early doctrinal history advanced a similar argument, emphasizing more exclusively than

---

[145] C. Gore, *The Incarnation of the Son of God, being the Bampton Lectures for the year 1891* (London, 1891), pp. 115–37; on Lotze, see Mander, *British Idealism*, pp. 22–4; W.R. Woodward, *Hermann Lotze: an intellectual biography* (Cambridge, 2015); H. Lotze, *Mikrokosmus: Ideen zur Naturgeschichte und Geschichte der Menschheit* (3 vols, Leipzig, 1856–1864).

[146] Gore, *Incarnation*, pp. 22–3, 42–6.

[147] C. Bigg, 'The Good Shepherd', in his *Spirit of Christ*, pp. 140–4.

[148] Caird, *Evolution of theology*, ii, 347–72.

[149] Bigg, *Neoplatonism*, pp. 136, 143; Bigg, *Critical and exegetical commentary*, p. 34.

did the Alexandrians' higher-church admirers the experiential rather than the metaphysical dimensions of the growth of orthodoxy. In his 1879 Bampton Lectures on *The Foundations of Faith*, Henry Wace moved from a philosophical exploration of the nature of faith, through to its historical action in scriptural and subsequently ecclesiastical history. Dedicating one of the later sermons to 'the faith of the early church', Henry Wace insisted that the Nicene Creed was no expression of 'Alexandrian metaphysics', but of 'the whole of Christian life'. When Arianism sought to divide the Son from the Father, 'it was not the Christian intellect, so much as the Christian heart, that revolted'.[150] This claim expressed and reinforced the larger argument of his series that the correct apology for faith in modern conditions did not lie in rationalizing the Bible down to the mere expression of natural reason. Rather, Wace advanced an argument, inflected by Kant and Butler, that the acceptance of revelation was a matter of personal trust extended by the moral subject towards Christ and the inspired writers who recorded his promises: a trust the early Christians had kept to the point of death.[151]

Evangelical nonconformists shared this assessment. 'Philosophical attempts to demonstrate that by an eternal necessity there must be a Trinity in the divine life... do not seem to me to have been successful', R. W. Dale explained in his 1894 study of *Christian Doctrine*, a work based on a series of lectures delivered to his Carr's Lane congregation. 'It was not by any process of philosophical speculation on the nature of God that the Church finally reached the doctrine of the Trinity, but by the path of faith and Christian experience', he continued.[152] Anxious to reject the suggestion that he undervalued the historical role of the church, Dale understood that work in a democratic sense. He insisted that the knowledge which Trinitarian doctrine expressed—of God as transcendent yet immanent, in Christ and perceived by the spirit—was not something limited to a creed framed by conciliar elites. Rather, as Newman had also been given to argue, Dale regarded this faith as the possession of 'the common millions of Christian men in all ages'.[153] Dale's 1887 proposal that the chapel of Oxford's new Mansfield College should feature statues of Augustine, Athanasius, John Chrysostom, and Gregory the Great, nevertheless reflected a newly elevated view of the scriptural character of patristic theology in nonconformist circles.[154]

---

[150] Wace, *Foundations*, pp. 158–60.   [151] Ibid., p. 143–4.

[152] R.W. Dale, *Christian doctrine: a series of discourses* (London, 1894), pp. 152–3.

[153] Ibid., pp. 168–9, 305–8.

[154] R.W. Dale to A.M. Fairbairn, 5 February. 1887, in Dale, *Life of R.W. Dale*, p. 503. The scheme that was finally adopted positioned statues of Athanasius, Augustine, and

In one respect, therefore, evangelicals discussed the development of doctrine in a distinctive register. The fact that they increasingly identified an energizing spirit in that process alongside, if often apart from, liberal and high Anglican theologians betokened, in another, a shared response to a changing climate. The heirs of those who looked indifferently or with suggestive glimmers of interest upon patristics amidst the storms emanating from Oxford in the 1830s and 1840s, became more concerned systematically to explore the continuity of evangelical experience which they found in the figures who had shaped doctrinal orthodoxy. This interest was further stimulated as intellectual forces which challenged orthodoxy's epistemological premises gathered, or renewed, their strength. An older John Stoughton, in a work on early Christianity printed for private circulation in 1891, now argued that Protestants should overcome their aversion to the Tractarians' misuse of the fathers, and see the latter—with Maurice—as agents of providence.[155] Wace insisted that, whereas Athanasius' teaching only restated what the church had 'verified by her own experience', it was Auguste Comte and Herbert Spencer who were guilty of introducing 'metaphysics into religion and moral philosophy' by propagating 'abstractions like Humanity or the Unknowable'.[156] Dale reflected on how Gnosticism and Arianism represented 'the "advanced" thought of the early Christian centuries'. 'The result of intellectual and spiritual tendencies which have appeared and re-appeared time after time', Arianism arose whenever ministers constructed an account of God that did not heed revelation. He gave his cyclical observation local colour by warning that Birmingham nonconformists had made this mistake after 1689, when they had become infatuated with 'Natural Theology'.[157]

The spread of substantive patristic study to denominations beyond the Church of England was accompanied by an expansion of its scholarly accessibility and popular reach. Wace made a point of giving extended quotations from the fathers in English rather than Greek or Latin. From 1886 he co-edited, with the Swiss-American and German-educated Reformed scholar Philip Schaff, a *Library of Nicene and Post-Nicene Fathers*, a series of critical translations by British and American divines

---

Origen around the chapel entrance: Kaye, *Mansfield College*, p. 77; C. Binfield, *So down to prayers: studies in English nonconformity 1780–1920* (London, 1977).

[155] J. Stoughton, *Lights and shadows of primitive Christendom* ([n.p.], 1891), pp. 116–17 and n. 1. Stoughton revised and expanded the essay for general publication after received encouragement from churchmen and nonconformist professors: *Lights and shadows of church life* (London, 1893), [v]–x.

[156] Wace, *Foundations*, pp. 162–3.   [157] Dale, *Christian doctrine*, pp. 94–5.

of Episcopal and Presbyterian allegiances.[158] The project originated as an attempt to provide a critical alternative to the Tractarians' *Library of the Fathers*, and a successor-series to the American edition of T. & T. Clark's *Ante-Nicene Christian Library*.[159] This earlier venture had begun to appear in 1867 under the editorship of Alexander Roberts, a Free Churchman shortly to become professor at St Andrews, and James Donaldson, Tulloch's ultimate successor as vice chancellor of that university, who had once trained for Congregational ministry at New College, London.[160]

At the same time as a widening spectrum of editors sought to make the fathers available to a public without facility in classical languages, popularizing authors sought to embed the religion for which they contended in picturesque personalities. Eliza Hunt, the wife of the decidedly liberal Church of England cleric, John Hunt, made the movement from Neoplatonism to rational Christianity the theme of a three-volume historical novel, *The Wards of Plotinus*.[161] From a more doctrinally conservative point of view, in 1878 the Society for Promoting Christian Knowledge launched its *Fathers for English Readers* series, intended to supply 'the intelligent Churchman with a lively, accurate, and fairly complete view of the most important periods of church history'. The young, incarnationally minded high churchman, Henry Scott Holland, contributing a volume on *The Apostolic Fathers*, accordingly wrapped their '*individual characters*' and 'human heroism' in floridly dramatic prose. Holland simultaneously drew them into a longer-term story of reasonable development, in which the second-century fathers first conserved the original deposit of faith, before subsequent apologists came to its more speculative defence.[162] The early church, it appeared to writers such as Holland, witnessed powerfully to the necessary union and constructive interaction between orthodox theology

---

[158] Wace, *Foundations*, xii; H. Wace and P. Schaff (eds), *A select library of Nicene and post-Nicene fathers of the Christian church*, second series (14 vols, Oxford and Buffalo, NY, 1890–1900). On Schaff, see H.W. Bowden (ed.), *A century of church history: the legacy of Philip Schaff* (Carbondale and Edwardsville, IL, 1988); K. Penzel (ed.), *Philip Schaff: historian and ambassador of the universal church: selected writings* (Macon, GA,1991).

[159] P. Schaff (ed.), *A select library of the Nicene and post-Nicene fathers of the Christian church*, first series (14 vols, Buffalo, NY, and New York, 1886–1890), i, [v–vii].

[160] A. Roberts and J. Donaldson (eds), *Ante-Nicene Christian library: translations of the writings of the Fathers down to A.D. 325* (24 vols, Edinburgh, 1867–1872); E.M. Craik, 'Donaldson, Sir James (1831–1915)', *ODNB*, and J. Hawke, 'Roberts, Alexander (1826–1901)', *ODNB*. On the *Ante-Nicene Christian Library*, see Wright, ' "From a quarter so totally unexpected" '.

[161] [E.M. Hunt], *The wards of Plotinus* (3 vols, London, [1881]). For the attribution, see 'Hunt', *Meyers Grosses Konversations-lexikon*, 6th edn, vol. 9 (Leipzig and Vienna, 1905), pp. 659–60. On John Hunt, see chapter five of this volume at pp. 223—6.

[162] 'Preface to the series', in H.S. Holland, *The Fathers for English readers: the apostolic fathers* (London, 1878), and pp. 3, 115–16; J.H. Heidt, 'Holland, Henry Scott (1847–1918)', *ODNB*.

and religious life. This idea—with which both liberal and conservative theologians could sympathize in different ways—came under pressure from a second, more radical strand of criticism, which saw orthodox formularies as representing not healthy religious development, but distortion.

PROGRESS AND DECAY IN CHURCH AND SOCIETY

Historians of doctrine after 1850 became increasingly inclined to conceive of it, with Newman, as the gathering fruit of Christian experience; as the expansion of absolute reason; or else as some mixture of the two. At the same time, a notably different tendency in the study of the early church began to coalesce among critics who were more inclined to locate the essence of Christianity in an undogmatic simple gospel. These critics sought the progressiveness of Christianity in the new morality it injected into social and political life. Orthodoxy, too, had a history; but this was not so much marvellous as regrettable, and to be accounted for with reference to the external rather than the internal determinants of Christian teaching. This approach generally involved a liberal, anti-dogmatic approach to the early church in a way that the more capacious, affirmatively 'doctrinalist' kind of theological history did not necessarily imply. The fact that its practitioners could regard early doctrinal contro-versies either as inconsequential, or, rather differently, as positively cor-rupting, showed that it nevertheless admitted of different emphases.

Arthur Penrhyn Stanley out of the mid-, and Edwin Hatch among the late-Victorian generation were the two foremost exponents of these respective modes of appraising the earlier history of Christianity. Con-nected by friendship and mutual admiration, the difference between them can be understood as expressing the radicalisation, partly under Ritschlian influence, of an Anglican broad church tradition which supposed that a modernised Christianity would blur the boundaries between church, state, and a religiously plural society. It connectedly insisted that the only constructive purpose to present-day doctrinal debate was to press the point that dogmatism properly belonged to bygone eras. Both men looked to early church history, in part, to stimulate and authorize the Church of England to lessen the doctrinal barriers that stood between itself and reunion with nonconformity. But Hatch was a self-consciously 'scientific' theologian where Stanley had disclaimed such a role, preferring to broaden charity by focusing on the social transformations wrought historically by the gospel. Hence Hatch made explicit a tension between historical analysis and formal orthodoxy which in Stanley had only been latent. It was a stance that left him a revealingly isolated figure in an idealizing and experientialist late-Victorian environment.

The origins of the species of criticism which Hatch would husband lay in the first half of the century, when Stanley began to form his own understanding of the progressiveness of the early church. To some extent, Stanley's formation reflected experiences common to the pioneers of liberal Anglican historicism. As a young fellow of University College, Oxford, he travelled to Germany with Benjamin Jowett in 1844, where Bunsen facilitated an introduction in Berlin to Neander, by whom he was much impressed.[163] In common with his friends Maurice and Hare, Stanley could see redeeming features in Newman's *Essay*, describing its ending as 'one of the most affecting passages ever written by an uninspired pen'.[164] But the concretely sociopolitical way in which he construed the importance of religious development brought him closer to the historical approach Milman had defended in his own assessment of Newman's *Essay* than Hare and Maurice had adopted in theirs. Stanley's pictorial historical imagination and self-contained, stately prose attached themselves less to the 'spiritual city and all her spires', than to a cultural and institutional ideal of ecclesiastical comprehensiveness. He had inherited the commitment from his Whig ancestors, and found it strengthened by his education at Thomas Arnold's Rugby.[165]

Stanley's treatment of the course and contexts of the Council of Nicaea in his *Lectures on the History of the Eastern Church*, delivered while he was Oxford's Regius Professor of Ecclesiastical History, instantiated the historical approach he favoured as his principal mode of contending for that position. Though actively committed to an undogmatic vision of the national church, Stanley drew a large part of its rationale from a universal idea of ecclesiastical history. According to Stanley, nations shaped religious movements, and vice versa, in a series of transformations which showed the breadth of forms under which moralizing Christianity could flourish.[166] As one who insisted that ecclesiastical history should be integrated with the broader history of civilization, his *Lectures* aimed to present the general outlines of the history of what he grouped together as the present-day churches of the eastern peoples, stretching from Russia to Abyssinia. But his general interpretative scheme for those societies,

[163] Prothero and Bradley, *Arthur Penrhyn Stanley*, i, 331.
[164] Quoted in ibid., i, 345.
[165] Witheridge, *Excellent Dr Stanley*, pp. 28–30, [45]–67, 194; Prothero and Bradley, *Arthur Penrhyn Stanley*, i, 94–7.
[166] See chapter one of this volumeat pp. 23—4.

foregrounding his treatment of fourth-century metaphysical debates, was not as inclusive as his rhetoric implied. He began by insisting that, in an important sense, they had no history—or at least, no modern history. 'It is a field rather of space than of time', he declared.[167] 'The nations which it embraces have been, for the most part, so stationary, and their life so monotonous, that they furnish few subjects of continuous narration.'[168] What was true of eastern peoples, extended to their religion. The modern Greek church shared in this general immobility.[169] Western Christendom, first Catholic and Latin, then Protestant and Teutonic, had left it behind in the advance of Christian civilization. The east had an historical, but not a living interest.[170]

It was the Council of Nicaea which, in Stanley's hands, set the tone for the East's subsequent religious history.[171] Although the modern western churches continued to acknowledge the decrees of the early councils, these had arisen, in Stanley's view, in a period of antiquity so remote as to be more picturesque than authoritative. Thus he relegated doctrinal controversy to a deep past, lying far behind the subsequent attainments of the progressive Christian mind. Stanley's history of the Council accordingly paid notably little attention to the conceptual debates which preceded or animated it. Stanley, a lover of Walter Scott, instead delighted in word-painting landscapes and character portraits.[172] The empathy generated by immersing his readers in a past place or occasion would, he hoped, produce indulgent charity towards transitory ancient opinions. Describing the opening of the Council, he called to mind not the Arian agitation, but 'the chestnut woods then as now green with the first burst of summer, the same sloping hills, the same tranquil lake, the same snow-capped Olympus from far brooding over the whole scene' of the Council.[173] He visualized the assembly room itself, full of distinctive characters: the 'bright, serene countenance' of Athanasius; Arius, 'this strange, captivating, moon-struck giant'; 'scholars from the more civilised cities of Syria; wild ascetics from the remoter East'.[174] Stanley regarded what followed as a crucial precedent for his undogmatic vision of the state church. The Council was convoked by a prince, showing that there was no need to fear the involvement of

[167] *LEC*, pp. 1–2. Stanley's case does not support Forbes' generalization that a reaction against Europocentrism was a hallmark of liberal Anglican history: Forbes, *Liberal Anglican idea*, pp. 9–10. On the ambiguities of liberal Protestant approaches to other forms of contemporary Christianity, see chapter three of this volume.

[168] *LEC*, pp. 1–2.   [169] Ibid., pp. 13–16.   [170] Ibid., pp. 42–50.
[171] Ibid., p. 18.
[172] Cf. A.P. Stanley, *Lectures on the history of the Church of Scotland: delivered in Edinburgh in 1872* (London, 1872), pp. 165–6.
[173] *LEC*, p. 83.   [174] Ibid., pp. 97–112.

secular authority in church affairs. Its deliberations were free, giving voice to 'the conscience of the whole Christian community'.[175] But whilst he did not dissent from the Nicene definition of the Trinity, he strongly implied that it was wrong to cut the Arians off from the church.[176] He alluded to subsequent textual variations in the creed decided at Nicaea between churches, to underscore the essential independence of the faith from credal statements of it.[177] The whiggishly anti-clerical Stanley even wished that Constantine had imposed a scheme of comprehension on the church, instead of sanctioning persecution in its name.[178] For Stanley, to resummon the external contingency of politics and character underlying the formation of orthodoxy, within a context of the slow, reciprocal transformations of civilization and religion over the centuries, was the historical legitimation of his assessment of the normative place of religion in national and European life. John Tulloch, reviewing Stanley's life and work after his death, spoke for a more epistemologically embattled generation of religious liberals when he accounted the 'absence of the speculative faculty . . . a certain weakness in his theology'.[179]

Stanley's mild and literary celebrations of changefulness, and implicit contempt for doctrinal controversy, drew the attention of Edwin Hatch, a younger scholar. Hatch had been born into a family of Derby nonconformists in 1835. While being educated in Birmingham he joined the Church of England under the influence of John Cale Miller, an evangelical clergyman committed to philanthropic work alongside Jews and nonconformists.[180] His background therefore predisposed him towards that conception of the church as innately broad, and as a vehicle for social improvement and class conciliation, which he applied to his scholarship and ministerial career. After graduating from Oxford in 1857, he worked first in an East End parish, during which time he was ordained priest, before migrating to teach in Canada. In 1867 he returned to Oxford in the impoverished office of vice principal of St Mary Hall. He was to remain in Oxford for the rest of his life, despite suffering financial and positional insecurity partly on account of his bold and original views. Stanley was an early patron, and stood as godfather to one of his sons.[181] The Dean of Westminster praised Hatch for a paper in which he had stressed the importance of parliamentary government of the church as a means of

---

[175] Ibid., pp. 67–9.   [176] Ibid., p. 142.   [177] Ibid., p. 152.
[178] Ibid., pp. 196–7.   [179] Tulloch, 'Dean Stanley as a spiritual teacher', p. 872.
[180] H.C.G. Matthew, 'Hatch, Edwin (1835–1889)', *ODNB*; A.F. Munden, 'Miller, John Cale (1814–1880)', *ODNB*.
[181] Lambeth Palace Library, Edwin Hatch papers, MS 1467/84–85A: A.P. Stanley to E. Hatch, 12 November 1865.

saving it from introspective clericalism.[182] Their sermons often addressed similar themes. The church, Hatch declared before the University of Oxford in 1881 in words that Stanley himself might have used, was 'human society itself—ultimately the whole, at present a part of it'.[183]

From one point of view, therefore, Hatch belonged to an older, practically minded and relatively unspeculative broad church tradition. But from another, he markedly departed from its characteristic assumptions. Stanley looked indulgently on the results of early Christian political, social, and doctrinal development. The historical novelist in Stanley rendered him distant from absolute commitment to any one form of church polity or doctrinal formulation. But nor was his disposition conducive to radical critique. Stanley thought of providence as leading a slow and shaky but nevertheless unmistakable upwards ascent through successive forms of ecclesiastical and social polity. Hatch instead forensically and very secularly dissected the doctrinal and institutional legacies left by the early church in order to show how the roots of modern religious disorder lay in a set of wrong turnings taken at a very early point. Where writers such as Illingworth would use biological metaphors to convey the organic life still at work within historical doctrines, Hatch preferred to invoke the palaeontologist's notably more inanimate subject matter in his lectures on ecclesiastical-historical methodology. His hope that 'the search for essences' would give way to contemplation of 'the operations of spiritual force', processes which embedded dogmas in certain historical phases just as they locked fossils in strata of rock, assumed that life had departed from the doctrines and institutions of the past.[184]

Hatch's inclinations were strengthened by his respect for scholarship written under the impress of Ritschlianism, especially Adolf von Harnack's studies of church history, though Hatch appears to have formed his views independently of him at first.[185] Harnack, it will be recalled, united a belief in Christianity understood as an autonomous moral system with the view that the growth of dogmatic theology, overturned in

[182] Lambeth Palace Library, Edwin Hatch papers, MS 1467/88–89: A.P. Stanley to E. Hatch, 26 June 1868. Stanley had probably seen a draft of E. Hatch, 'A Free Anglican Church', *MM*, 18 (1868), pp. [449]–60.

[183] E. Hatch, 'Diversity in unity the law of spiritual life', in S. Hatch (ed.), *Memorials of Edwin Hatch, D.D. sometime reader in ecclesiastical history in the University of Oxford, and Rector of Purleigh* (London, 1890), p. 167; cf. A.P. Stanley, *Essays chiefly on questions of church and state from 1850 to 1870* (London, 1870).

[184] Oriel College, Oxford, Edwin Hatch papers, Orielensia H 50, Hatch's 1889 Lee Lecture on 'Modern Methods in Theology', given in St Giles' Cathedral, Edinburgh: press cutting from *The Scotsman*, 27 May 1889 (Unnumbered pages).

[185] On Harnack, see chapter one of this volume at pp. 35–6.

principle at the Reformation, amounted to a secularizing constriction of its essence. Hatch, who not coincidentally had a penchant for writing distinctly gloomy religious poetry, was drawn to the potential this held for making a systematic separation between the moral essence of Christianity and the historical forces that had shaped the religion's melancholy subsequent history.[186] In doing so, he went far beyond what any British clerical predecessor had argued. Although Harnack did not think of physical science as analogous to historical *Wissenschaft* in the way Hatch did, they knew one another personally and appear to have regarded themselves as kindred spirits.[187]

Hatch applied these methodological principles in two seminal works. The first, his 1880 Bampton Lectures on *The Organization of the Early Christian Churches*, concerned the origin of ecclesiastical institutions.[188] Stanley and Milman, rooted in an indigenous latitudinarian tradition, denied that the distinction between bishops, priests, and laity possessed divine authority; but they accepted it on the practical grounds that it had grown out of the needs of the early church.[189] Hatch, however, radicalized the earlier liberal Anglican maxim that church history was part of general history, by arguing that the growth of ecclesiastical hierarchy and authoritative general councils derived from the importation and subsequent petrification of alien forms from the secular world.[190] The church of the New Testament, Hatch supposed, consisted of free congregations whose main function was to collect and disburse charitable gifts.[191] By the fourth century, however, the late-Roman world of heathen associations, homogenizing administration, and financial and judicial exemptions granted by imperial fiat, had remade the visible church in its own hierarchical and authoritative image.[192] Only by returning to the 'brotherhood' and 'democracy' of the primitive ideal in the age of the industrial proletariat, he argued, would the church survive agnosticism, just as it had once outlived Gnosticism.[193]

---

[186] E. Hatch, *Towards fields of light, sacred poems* (London, 1890).

[187] Lambeth Palace Library, Edwin Hatch papers, MS 1467/34: A. Harnack to E. Hatch, 15 February 1885; [S. Hatch], 'Biographical notices', in his (ed.) *Memorials of Edwin Hatch*, xxix–xxx; Nowak, 'Theologie, Philologie und Geschichte', pp. 209–10.

[188] E. Hatch, *The organization of the early Christian churches: eight lectures delivered before the University of Oxford, in the year 1880* (London, Oxford, and Cambridge, 1881). N.F. Josaitis, *Edwin Hatch and early church order* (Gembloux, 1971), offers a primarily theological study of this text.

[189] H.H. Milman, *The history of Christianity, from the birth of Christ to the abolition of paganism in the Roman Empire* (3 vols, London, 1840), ii, 63–79; A.P. Stanley, *Sermons and essays on the apostolical age* (Oxford, 1847), pp. [46]–77.

[190] Hatch, *Organization*, pp. 208–9.   [191] Ibid., pp. [26]–54.

[192] Ibid., pp. [82]–110, [140]–64, 168–70.   [193] Ibid., pp. 208–16.

Hatch applied the same treatment to doctrinal history in his Hibbert Lectures for 1888. These were posthumously published as *The Influence of Greek Ideas and Usages upon the Christian Church*.[194] Where Hatch's idealizing contemporaries liked to portray orthodox Trinitarianism as the fruit of moral reflection, and Stanley's mind was drawn more to the human drama surrounding its definition than to doctrine itself, Hatch's lectures foregrounded doctrinal history, but interpreted it as the process by which external influences had secularized Christianity. The problem, he explained, was to account for how the religion of the Sermon on the Mount could have been transmogrified into the metaphysical and dogmatic statements of the Nicene Creed within the space of three centuries. Whereas he had primarily blamed the development of church institutions on Roman imperial and cultural practices, he attributed the course of doctrinal history to the transference of Christianity from a Semitic to a Hellenic soil.[195]

The result was not the mastery of Greek universality by a Christian idea, but the practical neutralization of the latter by 'the whole mental attitude of that time'.[196] Hatch went on to argue that Christianity, after its first proclamation by Christ, had been corrupted by the social and intellectual culture of the Hellenistic world. It was impossible that, in such a society, a pure religion should have long survived. By the second and third centuries, the spread of Greek education around the eastern Mediterranean had fostered a professionalization of philosophy, where sophists disputed the thoughts of others for money, but offered no positive contribution of their own. The Greeks had grown accustomed to think in terms of artificial categories which compelled them to dispute points of Christianity, rather than to accept it in its simplicity.[197] Christian dogma, itself an originally harmless Greek term for an affirmation of a personal belief, won a victory over Gnosticism, but it was a victory purchased at the price of engaging in religious controversy on philosophical Gnostic terms. 'The absorption was less of speculations than of the tendency to speculate.'[198] This latter argument bore marked similarities to that made by Harnack in his *Dogmengeschichte*, the first volume of which had appeared in 1886, and which Hatch extensively cited.[199] Hatch even used recent studies of religious anthropology provocatively to attribute the growth of sacraments to the practices of Greek and Near

---

[194] E. Hatch, *The influence of Greek ideas and usages upon the Christian church*, ed. A.M. Fairbairn (London, 1890).

[195] Ibid., pp. 1–2.   [196] Ibid., pp. 2–3.   [197] Ibid., pp. 25–49.

[198] Ibid., pp. 116–36, here at 133.

[199] Cited at for example ibid., pp. 130 n. 1, 262 n. 2; cf. Harnack, *Dogmengeschichte*, i, 45, 158–71.

Eastern mystery cults.[200] He ended the work by raising the possibility, to which he did not definitely commit himself, that Christianity might shear itself of its Hellenism and return to the religion of the Beatitudes.[201] The history of doctrinal development, therefore, authorized Christianity's severance from its results.

Hatch's conception of the development of the early church as amounting to incremental secularization found voluble sympathy in certain quarters. His far-reaching plea for the simple gospel, and fundamental criticisms of the Church of England's structures, attracted a notable following among nonconformists. Hatch could not be accused, as earlier liberal Anglicans such as Stanley and Thirlwall sometimes had been, of holding to the personally comfortable but intellectually incoherent position that the early creeds were at once historically relative, and yet should continue to define the Church of England.[202] The editor of Hatch's lectures on *Greek Ideas* was Andrew Martin Fairbairn, the first principal of Mansfield College, Oxford, the foundation of which Hatch had supported and at whose 1889 opening he was an honoured guest.[203] Nonconformist and provincial papers reported on his sermons and were full of approbatory obituary notices after his premature death, apparently from overwork, in the same year.[204] Hatch also attracted favourable notice in Germany, where Harnack translated his Bampton Lectures and contributed a *Nachwort* to the German edition of his *Greek Ideas*.[205] The triangle thus created between Hatch's non-metaphysical theology, dissenting anti-sacerdotalism, and strands of German neo-Kantianism represented one way in which the study of the early church could forge new intellectual alignments across denominational and national divides in a late-Victorian setting.[206]

Hatch, and the wider Ritschlian moment to which he was generally understood to belong, nevertheless encountered a strong reaction from critics located across a spectrum whose breadth indicated how the church

---

[200] Hatch, *Greek ideas*, pp. [283]–309. [201] Ibid., pp. 350–2.

[202] For example, [Anon.], 'The Eastern Church: its past and future', *NR*, 13:25 (1861), pp. 47–8; C. Beard, 'Bishop Thirlwall's Remains', *TR*, 15:61 (1878), p. 226.

[203] [Hatch], 'Biographical notices', xxxiii–xxxv; Kaye, *Mansfield College*, p. 46, 71–3.

[204] The surviving Hatch papers contain approving clippings from, among other publications, the *Sheffield Independent*; the *Methodist Times*; the *Nonconformist*; the *Nottinghamshire Express*; the *Aberdeen Free Press*, and the *Methodist Recorder*. Oriel College, Oxford, Edwin Hatch papers, Orielensia H50 (unnumbered pages).

[205] E. Hatch, *Die Gesellschaftsverfassung der christlichen Kirche im Alterthum: achtVorlesungen*, trans. A. Harnack (Giessen, 1883); A. Harnack, 'Nachwort' to E. Hatch, *Griechentum und Christentum: zwölf Hibbertvorlesungen über den Einfluss griechischer Ideen und Gebräuche auf die christliche Kirche*, trans. E. Preuschen (Freiburg im Breisgau, 1892), pp. 263–8.

[206] Identified by Bigg, *Neoplatonism*, pp. 138–42.

fathers now cast their rays across a far larger terrain, and with quite different effects, than had been the case in the 1830s. R. W. Dale gave voice to a strand of nonconformist unease at Hatch's *Greek Ideas* in his Birmingham lectures. Although the death of his fellow-supporter of Mansfield College represented 'an irreparable loss' to learning, Hatch had been wrong to insist that doctrinal development from the Sermon on the Mount to the Nicene Creed amounted to 'a change in the centre of gravity from conduct to belief'. For had not the preacher of that discourse assumed his own divine authority, a truth 'verified in the life of the commonalty of the Church'?[207]

Hatch faced more traditional opponents, too. His difficulties in Oxford during his lifetime partly reflected the continuing watchfulness of an Anglican establishment in the reforming university over what it perceived to be religious subversion. Mark Pattison, who had long since come to regard early Christian thought as a corruption of Greek philosophy, remarked to Mrs Hatch after being impressed by her husband's Bampton Lectures that they would rule him out of promotion in the university.[208] The philologist Max Müller agreed.[209] Although Hatch was made university reader in ecclesiastical history in 1884, this was an impecunious position which he had to combine with other duties in order to make ends meet, and friends such as Fairbairn and T. H. Green thought the lack of security placed too great a strain upon him.[210]

Hatch's experience of academic marginalization expressed something more, however, than a classically Tractarian reaction against doctrinal novelty. Oxford's high churchmen did not seek to rebut Hatch, as an earlier generation would have done, by citing long *catenae* of early fathers. Their argumentative strategy had changed. In a manner akin to how Newman had blended historical interpretation with moral intuition, the Tractarians' successors now objected to the ways in which Hatch sought to overturn the fruits of the life of the Christian community; he seemed to read church history from the outside, without sympathy for its leading ideas. The high church classical scholar and former fellow of Merton College, Oxford, Charles Thomas Cruttwell, rejected Hatch's claim that

---

[207] Dale, *Christian doctrine*, pp. 165–16, 306–7.

[208] Oriel College, Oxford, Edwin Hatch papers, Orielensia H50, anonymous typescript (unnumbered pages); 'Barrow's sermon on the aversion of the Philosophers in the early centuries to Christianity—not well treated—gave the old solution—pride of human intellect—but suggested interesting thoughts': Bodleian Library, MS Pattison 129/100–101, M. Pattison diary entry for 10 April 1853.

[209] Oriel College, Oxford, Edwin Hatch papers, Orielensia H50: M. Müller to E. Hatch, 5 February 1882 (unnumbered pages).

[210] Oriel College, Oxford, Edwin Hatch papers, Orielensia H50: T.H. Green to E. Hatch, n.d. (unnumbered pages); Hatch, 'Biographical notices', xxxviii–xliii.

Greek metaphysics overspread the faith with contaminating hyphae in his own rehabilitation of the Greek fathers. 'The intuitions of Revelation', Cruttwell argued, 'to be presented to the universal consciousness, must need be recast in the form of thought which nearest approaches universality.'[211] Charles Gore, who had earlier faulted Hatch as a Bampton Lecturer for always remaining 'on the outskirts of Christianity', answered the Hibbert Lectures in his own Bampton series by declaring that 'Christianity became metaphysical simply and only because man is rational.'[212]

The way in which high church replies to an attack on orthodoxy now contained an idealist tincture that would have disturbed Burton or Hussey expressed a wider environment in which religious apologists generally preferred to present the history of early Christian thought as a spiritualizing as opposed to a secularizing force. Charles Bigg remarked in his study of *Neoplatonism* that Hatch and Ritschlian theology entirely missed the extent to which Christian assumptions had overmastered Hellenism in the early church.[213] Edward Caird, for whom that process of conceptual supersession resulted from the internal workings of history itself, regarded the Ritschlian hostility to metaphysics as cutting history off from the possibility of its own rational completion. In a sermon he gave to Balliol undergraduates, Caird argued that there was no '*quod semper, quod ubique, quod ab omnibus*' to which it was possible to point as a mode of settling any debated question, for history was an evolving unity. History was also a divine process, however. While the burden that Athanasius and Augustine had once borne on behalf of others in the struggle for righteousness had now become social and individual, that continuing imperative could not jettison—only sublate—the ethical and philosophical results of those earlier strivings.[214] Caird accordingly expressed his dislike for the view of Ritschl or Harnack 'which takes Christianity as an eternal something which is debased or secularized by being brought into relation with Greek philosophy and Roman organization, and which we have to free from philosophy and politics to get it pure'.[215]

Whether from confidence in orthodoxy's participation in absolute ideas, its attestation to the living power of evangelical faith, or some

---

[211] C.T. Cruttwell, *A literary history of early Christianity, including the fathers and the chief heretical writers of the Ante-Nicene period* (2 vols, London, 1893), i, ix.

[212] Gore, *Incarnation*, pp. 20–1; Gore, *The church and the ministry: a review of the Rev. E. Hatch's Bampton Lectures* (London and Oxford, 1882), pp. 65–6.

[213] Bigg, *Neoplatonism*, pp. [134]–44.

[214] E. Caird, 'The great decision', in his *Miscellaneous pamphlets, lay sermons and addresses, 1866–1907*, ed. C. Tyler (Bristol, 1999), pp. 181–96, here at 186–7.

[215] E. Caird to M. Talbot, 14 January 1906, in Jones and Muirhead, *Edward Caird*, pp. 241–2; cf. Caird, *Evolution of theology*, ii, 359–60.

mediation between the two, those who resisted a secularized vision of human time found it difficult to believe, with Hatch, that the doctrinal history of early Christianity amounted to mere corruption. That reluctance was the product of a wider transformation. The suggestion that orthodoxy represented the dynamic incorporation of revelation into the ideas and experience of the early church was shocking when Newman and Bunsen had thrown down their challenges to the conventional divinity of their day. But by the century's end, liberal and conservative renderings of the idea that historical subjectivity was sacred had become notably widespread and conventional modes of defending doctrine's claims to acceptance. Now that Victorian orthodoxy was less and less enforced by external legal and ecclesiastical constraints, and increasingly by the conscientious self alone, reflection on subjective experience in time made early church history into a crucial locus of religious authority. Medieval Christianity, once widely decried as an aberration from primitive orthodoxy, was to be analogously transformed into its constructive successor phase by the rising power of developmental historicism.

3

Latin Christianity

MEDIEVALISM AND PROGRESS

Whereas previous accounts have generally treated Victorian preoccupation with the medieval period as a broadly constant cultural phenomenon, this chapter focuses on one important way in which conceptions of that past changed markedly over the course of the nineteenth century. This concerned its place as an episode in the history of religion. In the early years of Victoria's reign, interest in the church of the Middle Ages tended to be driven by the imperatives of religious or romantic polemic. Evangelicals, old high churchmen, and Tractarians, writing from positions of hostility, ambivalence, and enthusiasm respectively, invested medieval religion, which often stood as a code for present-day Catholicism, with different kinds of significance in the interests of sectarian self-justification. In a change partly symbolized and partly inaugurated by Henry Hart Milman's 1854–1855 *History of Latin Christianity*, however, the Catholic religious life of the Middle Ages increasingly became important for a different reason. It now appeared to represent a providential stage in the world's progress. As part of a development that Milman encouraged but did not control, a new kind of historical sensibility helped to erode the simplifications both of classical anti-Catholicism and romantic anti-modernism in the second half of the century. The idea that medieval Christendom expressed divine purposes, at work through the religious, racial, and national forms proper to that age, now became a common component of wider Victorian understandings of civilizational advance. Present-day Catholicism, created by history's hammers and anvils, accordingly began to wear a newly constructive aspect; whilst its perceived limitations came to rest on different grounds. The intellectual dynamics and ambiguities of that change are explored in this chapter.

Medieval history and Catholic history permeated one another in Victorian intellectual culture. Histories of the Middle Ages were not solely episodes in the history of historiography, but contributed to wider debates about the place of 'medievalism' in modern society.[1] Reference to medieval history saturated contemporary engagement with aesthetic, constitutional, and socio-economic questions, and idealizations of masculinity and femininity.[2] When Victorians discussed medievalism in a religious context, they were very often arguing over the claims of Catholicism—chiefly in its Roman, but also in its newer, Anglo-Catholic form—to religious obedience, intellectual authority, and cultural power and acceptance. The pre-Reformation past was often made an unnervingly immediate component of Protestant Victorians' present by the extraordinary success of the European Catholic revival, and the encroachments it seemed to be making upon Britain's ecclesiastical settlement and social and political life.[3] Catholic Emancipation in 1829, Pope Pius IX's restoration of the English Roman Catholic hierarchy in the 'Papal Aggression' of 1850–1851, and persistent fears over Irish immigration and foreign Ultramontanism, headily mingled with evangelical sensibilities and suspicions over the ultimate direction of the Oxford Movement to feed deep and periodically explosive anxieties over the nation's Protestant character.

This sentiment was generally articulated in an historical language. The Free Church of Scotland polemicist James Aitken Wylie, writing at the time of the 'Papal Aggression'—when public anti-Catholic agitation reached its feverish height—condemned 'Popery, and its modern Anglican form Puseyism' as 'mediaeval error'.[4] 'Medievalism has long been little more than a synonym for darkness', a reviewer disapprovingly remarked of Pope Leo XIII's commendation of scholastic philosophy in his 1879

---

[1] On scholarly engagement with medieval history in the modern period, see I. Wood, *The modern origins of the early middle ages* (Oxford, 2013).

[2] A. Chandler, *A dream of order: the medieval ideal in nineteenth-century English literature* (London, 1971); R.J. Smith, *The Gothic bequest: medieval institutions in British thought, 1688–1863* (Cambridge, 1987); C. Dellheim, *The face of the past: the preservation of the medieval inheritance in Victorian England* (Cambridge, 1982); J. Mordaunt Crook, *The dilemma of style: architectural ideas from the picturesque to the post-modern* (London, 1987); J.W. Burrow, *A liberal descent*, pp. 97–228; M. Girouard, *The return to Camelot: chivalry and the English gentleman* (New Haven, CT, and London, 1981); A. Dwight Culler, *The Victorian mirror of history* (New Haven, CT, and London, 1985), esp. pp. 152–84; Kirby, *Historians*, pp. [75]–131.

[3] On the nineteenth-century Catholic revival and the vociferous resistance it generated, see for example Clark and Kaiser, *Culture wars*; D. Blackbourn, *Marpingen: apparitions of the Virgin Mary in Bismarckian Germany* (Oxford, 1993); R. Harris, *Lourdes: body and spirit in the secular age* (London, 1999); Wolffe, *Protestant crusade*; S. Gilley, 'The papacy', in Gilley and Stanley, *World Christianities*, pp. 13–29; M.B. Gross, *The war against Catholicism: liberalism and the anti-Catholic imagination in nineteenth-century Germany* (Ann Arbor, MI, 2004); D.G. Paz, *Dickens and Barnaby Rudge: anti-Catholicism and Chartism* (Monmouth, 2006); Paz, *Popular anti-Catholicism*; Bentley, *Ritualism and politics*.

[4] J.A. Wylie, *The papacy: its history, dogmas, genius, and prospects: being the Evangelical Alliance first prize essay on popery* (Edinburgh, 1851), p. 402.

encyclical, *Aeterni Patris*.[5] The notion that Catholicism was 'medieval' joined claims that it was also effeminate, superstitious, and despotic as its British opponents sought to classify it as the inverse of masculine and rational Protestant modernity rooted in respect for the morally responsible individual.[6] The equivalence thus drawn between Catholicism and medievalism drew strength from the fact that, for Catholic sympathizers, the connection involved no reproach. The Catholic convert and leading proponent of the Gothic Revival, Augustus Pugin, wrote in his 1836 architectural study, *Contrasts*, of 'the wonderful superiority' of medieval buildings and the faith they expressed over the aesthetic and spiritual impoverishment of their modern successors.[7]

The fact that scholarly studies of the Middle Ages belonged to a wider intellectual complex which persistently assumed a close association between the Middle Ages and Catholic religion led contemporary critics to understand the reinterpretation of medieval history as a vital reassessment of Catholicism as a whole. The following discussion explores that dynamism, by focusing on the contexts, arguments, and afterlives of Milman's great *History*. Amidst the polarizations of the early Victorian period, evangelical Protestants became increasingly inclined to apply scriptural prophecy to present the medieval church in newly dark colours, whilst high churchmen divided between scholastic self-justification and Puginesque romantic reaction in their own encounter with the subject. For Milman, on the other hand, writing shortly after the fiercest waves of anti-Catholic and Tractarian agitation had broken, medieval religion became, in a radically different sense, 'Latin Christianity'. It was now an autonomous epoch, immediate to God, which for a time encompassed the progressive movement of civilization. That progress did not solely involve the institutional church, but extended to the whole of the political, social, and intellectual life of Western Europe. The history of medieval Europe, on this view, could neither be indiscriminately denounced nor childishly extolled. Instead it had to be accommodated within a newly elevated sense of the religious meaning of history in its progressive entirety. Milman's researches into medieval Christianity followed on from his earlier studies of Judaism and the early church; towards the end of his life, he would become interested in the roles of Savonarola and Erasmus in foreshadowing the Reformation.[8] Just as religious history animated general history,

---

[5] [B. Maitland], 'Thomas Aquinas and the Vatican', *QR*, 152:303 (1881), p. 106.

[6] Wheeler, *The old enemies*, pp. 25–6; on European parallels, see Borutta, *Antikatholizismus*, esp. pp. [267]–389.

[7] Quoted in R. Hill, *God's architect: Pugin and the building of romantic Britain* (London, 2007), pp. 155–6.

[8] H.H. Milman, *Savonarola, Erasmus, and other essays* (London, 1870).

so did the spiritually driven course of civilization give life, and historically recoverable meaning, to the individual religious forms it nurtured.

Milman's *Latin Christianity* possessed rich significance for the subsequent development of British engagement with the Catholic phase of European history. He removed the subject from narrowly confessional frameworks, not by a secular method, but by treating the movement of history itself as the weightiest authority, after scripture, for discerning the purposes of God. Within that scheme, the medieval Catholic ascendancy became the tool by which providence had guided civilization from childhood to manhood, a metaphor he and many other liberal Protestants favoured. Milman won many admirers and several imitators among a liberal Protestant public for the double-edged kind of ecumenism this implied. On the one hand, the dean of St Paul's offered a means by which a Protestant culture could come to terms with Catholicism, and even appreciate its merits, by using a newly impartial form of scholarship to understand why Catholicism had arisen, and what its creative role had been in Protestants' own history. On the other, he had reassuringly shown how the sovereign authority of divinely animated history itself had rendered Catholicism obsolete, and ushered in a Protestant present and future for occidental civilization. Although its approach also attracted significant criticism, the *History of Latin Christianity* thereby contributed to a wider reorientation in which earlier intellectual stances towards medieval religious history evolved in response to the progressive strand of analysis which Milman helped to consolidate. In the late-Victorian decades, anti-Catholicism remained a live force, whilst ecclesiological commitments continued to shape high church medieval scholarship. But the desire to identify progressive continuities between Catholic history and Protestant modernity increasingly spread beyond the liberal Protestant writers who had first drawn attention to them, as the desire to secure a theistic idea of history against secularizing dangers began to overshadow the urgency of Catholic error or modern sinfulness in British imaginations.

REVIVAL AND ROMANISM

Medieval history had become a crucial medium for discussing the rights and wrongs of Catholicism long before the first three volumes of Milman's *Latin Christianity*, breaking through many previously established lines of discussion, reached the booksellers in 1854. In the early decades of the nineteenth century, different species of ancestral British hostility to popery and its misdoings were joined by alarms to the unconverted from post-revolutionary millenarians, together with newer, wistful exaltations of a lost world of medieval religious and social cohesion issuing from the pens of Tractarian social critics. Together these gave medieval history a vivid intensity, and controversial significance, which it had not previously possessed. An undercurrent of dissatisfaction with this growing and rumbustious chorus found expression in the persistence of Enlightenment-era approaches to the history of the Middle Ages, and the appearance of histories of the papacy which professed to spurn controversial intent. But a new and influential mode of answering that discontent was not to appear in English before Milman.

Evangelical historians painted the centuries of popery in dark colours, so as to throw the pure light of the gospel and the invigorating work of the Reformation into sharper relief. At the same time, Christ's promise that 'I am with you alway, even unto the end of the world', obliged them to search for signs of the true church's perseverance even in the times of its greatest tribulation.[9] The question of where the emphasis within that twofold obligation was to be placed provoked a revealing and, to some extent, generationally specific tension within evangelicalism over the status of the medieval church in the first half of the nineteenth century. Joseph Milner's *History of the Church of Christ*—in Julius Hare's words, 'the main, if not the sole, source from which a large portion of our Church derive their notions of ecclesiastical history'—recorded attitudes typical of the earlier phase of revival, even whilst its influence stretched far into the nineteenth century.[10] Milner deplored the creation of an allegedly dictatorial papacy and, above all, the pace at which idolatrous masses and prayers flooded into the medieval church. He endorsed the classically Protestant idea that the Roman system eventually showed itself to be the work of Antichrist, radically separate from real Christianity.

At the same time, Milner's Tory Anglican form of evangelicalism, and the fact that he wrote before the danger of a resurgent papacy began to press itself upon British audiences, encouraged him to find the continuity of evangelical religion which he devoted his *History* to describing within the visible church, as well as beyond it, during the medieval period. Milner accordingly sought to vindicate the 'piety, integrity, and humility' of Pope Gregory the Great from the imprecations that had been cast upon him.[11] Suspicious of contemporary dissenters, Milner showed limited sympathy for sects on the fringes of the church such as the Paulicians, whose scriptural and godly religion showed the continuing operation of divine grace in Asia Minor from the seventh century until the ninth, when they

---

[9] Matthew 28:20.
[10] Quoted in Walsh, 'Joseph Milner's evangelical church history', at p. 174.
[11] Milner, *History of the church of Christ*, ii, 373–4.

rebelled against the established government.[12] Later, the Waldensians had kept the gospel alive in the valleys of Piedmont at a time when there was scarcely 'a visible Church of Christ to be found'; but even then, from the twelfth century to the Reformation, there were 'some "individual souls in Babylon," who loved the Lord,' and whom Milner was gratified to identify.[13] It was in keeping with this emollient attitude that Milner should have ascribed a comparatively late date to the emergence of the papal Antichrist; and he did not make this motif integral to his narrative in the way some did after him.[14] It was only beginning with the eighth-century Pope Gregory II that the scriptural reader, thought Milner, would find 'the MAN OF SIN matured in all his gigantic horrors', a reference to the premillennial rise of an antichristian power prophesied by St Paul.[15]

The advent of an age of revolutions and Catholic revival fed the freshly intense kind of anti-Catholicism which inspired a new generation of evangelical historians writing after 1829. This transition often became bound up with a shift, also rooted in the shocks of the new century, towards historicist premillennialism as the favoured world-historical paradigm of Anglican (though not exclusively Anglican) evangelicals between roughly 1820 and 1860. This involved the decline of an eighteenth-century Protestant expectation that Christ would return at the end of the millennial age of the worldwide spread of the gospel, in favour of a more urgently dramatic—but not necessarily pessimistic—expectation that the millennium would begin with Christ's imminent second coming.[16] The rising apocalypticism took root in a newly historicist culture. Emerging evangelical historians, seeing the history of Europe foretold in the mysterious pages of scriptural prophecy, now keenly stressed the actively Antichristian role of Rome in salvation history.[17]

Milner's approach could now seem to concede too much to Rome's historical pretensions. Robert Benton Seeley, a scion of the evangelical publishing family and father of the more heterodox John Robert Seeley, criticized Milner in his 1845 contribution to *The Christian's Family Library*, a series edited by the premillennialist evangelical Anglican leader,

---

[12] Ibid., ii, 491–9; Walsh, 'Joseph Milner's evangelical church history', pp. 183–4.

[13] Milner, *History of the church of Christ*, iii, 155, 181–206.

[14] J.D. Walsh, 'Joseph Milner's evangelical church history: a biography' (MS, forthcoming), p. 29; I am grateful to John Walsh for permitting me to cite from this unpublished essay.

[15] Milner, *History of the church of Christ*, i, xviii, ii, 445–66.

[16] M. Spence, *Heaven on earth: reimagining time and eternity in nineteenth-century British evangelicalism* (Eugene, OR, 2015); Spence, 'The renewal of time and space: the missing element of discussions about nineteenth-century premillennialism', *Journal of Ecclesiastical History*, 63:1 (2012), pp. 81–101; Bebbington, *Dominance of evangelicalism*, pp. 179–84.

[17] Spence, *Heaven on earth*, p. 49.

Edward Bickersteth. In *The Church of Christ in the Middle Ages*, Seeley argued that Milner had missed the '*total change*' that had swept over the church in the sixth or seventh century. For at that time the 'western Antichrist' had showed her face, and the Book of Revelation became the historian's only correct methodological tool for construing the subsequent history of the western church. Popes and councils thereafter belonged to 'the Apostasy' that grew drunk on the blood of the saints. These witnesses in the wilderness were the Waldenses in the West and the Paulicians in the East, in respect of whom Milner's broadly positive attitude had been tempered by doctrinal and political reservations.[18] The eight hundred years between the rise of the papacy and the Reformation, Seeley believed, had left 'literally *nothing*' of religious worth besides proto-Protestant devotional writings.[19] James Aitken Wylie, a popular Scottish writer and minister who followed the Original Secession Church into union with the Free Church in 1852, won the Evangelical Alliance's competition for a prize essay on 'popery', set in 1850, with a history of the papacy interwoven with allusions to prophecy. Wylie, for whom the papacy was, next to Christianity, 'the great FACT of the modern world' and worse than paganism, likened the papal tiara to the crown of thorns which had mocked Christ, and ended by looking forward to its imminent destruction with a shower of exclamation marks.[20] Milman, whose view of the office of scriptural prophecy could hardly have been more different, would seek to lessen the astringency of such denunciations. He would, however, quietly establish a new kind of division between Protestantism and Catholicism in turn.

Old-fashioned high churchmen were as interested as evangelicals in the rise and progress of popery, but situated it within a very different intellectual framework. They contemplated that history more with indignation than with fear and prophetic foreboding. Where stronger Protestants traced the rise of Antichrist in the history of the Middle Ages, these writers chiefly approached the subject as a way of vindicating Anglican ecclesiology. Robert Hussey organized his series of professorial lectures on *The Rise of the Papal Power* between the fourth century and the fourteenth around an attack on the doctrine of papal supremacy, which was an unacceptable

---

[18] [R.B. Seeley], *The church of Christ in the middle ages: an historical sketch compiled from various authors* (London, 1845), [v]–vii, pp. 186–236; Milner, *History of the church of Christ*, ii, 491–9, iii, 99–155; Walsh, 'Joseph Milner's evangelical church history: a biography' (MS), pp. 34–9.

[19] [Seeley], *Church of Christ*, pp. 471–2; cf. T. Stephen, *The spirit of the Church of Rome, its principles and practices, as exhibited in history* (London, 1840).

[20] Wylie, *Papacy*, pp. [1], 8, 55–6, 548–52; L.A. Ritchie, 'Wylie, James Aitken (1808–1890)', *ODNB*.

'"developement"' upon what the fathers of the first three centuries had authorized.[21] William Palmer of Worcester College, Oxford, who turned away from Tractarianism when its 'restorative' character became unacceptably innovative, wrote an influential *Treatise on the Church* (1838) along comparable lines.[22] He organized his text not as a narrative history, but as a series of controversial theses supported by proof-texts from scripture, patristics, and standard Anglican divinity. Palmer contended for the validity of the Church of England and its sister communions in the British Isles as branches of the Catholic Church. It was therefore necessary for him to disparage Roman innovations, whilst also emphasizing the continuing presence of the Holy Spirit in the institutional church throughout the ages. Palmer deprecated the growth of Roman error, especially the rise of an overweening papacy, but he argued that the doctrine of papal supremacy did not amount to heresy in the formal sense, for it arose from a groundless legend rather than from the obstinate denial of truth.[23] In a way that evangelical writers did not, Palmer stressed that the fact that the Roman church continued to baptise and ordain down to the Reformation, whereupon the Church of England had reasserted its independent apostolicity, marked it out as a true church. He correspondingly greeted Seeley's application of the sure word of prophecy to papal history with scepticism.[24]

Tractarians deepened this technical, ecclesiological approach to medieval history by holding up a romantic picture of the Middle Ages as a lost world of social solidarity and religious piety, to the reproach of their own time. The revival of the monastic principle and national holy days, they often imagined, would counteract the corrupting effects of commercialism, Protestantism, and the subordination of the church to the state.[25] 'The high church party of the twelfth century endeavoured as much as possible to make common cause with the poor and the defenceless', wrote Richard Hurrell Froude, one of Newman's strong-spirited protégés among the Oriel College fellowship, in his study of the twelfth-century archbishop of Canterbury and anti-Erastian martyr, Thomas Becket.[26]

---

[21] R. Hussey, *The rise of the papal power treated in three lectures* (Oxford, 1851), v.

[22] Palmer, *Treatise on the church*, i, 71–101.   [23] Ibid., i, 213–21.

[24] Ibid., ii, [452]–61. Palmer refers to the objections levelled against his treatise in *Essays on the church*, whose author he does not give, but which was certainly R.B. Seeley: ibid., ii, [452] and n.; [R.B. Seeley], *Essays on the church, by a layman*, new edn (London, 1838), pp. 350–6.

[25] S.A. Skinner, *Tractarians and the 'condition of England': the social and political thought of the Oxford Movement* (Oxford, 2004), pp. 203–13.

[26] R.H. Froude, 'History of the contest between Thomas À Becket, Archbishop of Canterbury, and Henry II, King of England', in his *Remains of the late Reverend Richard Hurrell Froude, M.A.*, ed. [J.H. Newman and J. Keble] (4 vols, London, 1838–1839), iv, 31.

Another, ultimately more unsteady Oriel Tractarian, Mark Pattison, dreamt of writing medieval history to the glory of the Catholic Church during his period of close association with Pusey and Newman in the 1830s and early 1840s. He even contributed two *Lives of the English Saints* to Newman's series on the subject.[27] Staying with Newman at Littlemore in 1843, while undertaking part of that research, Pattison noted in his journal the assembled company's dinner-table talk of wonderful monastic abstinences. 'S. Godric stood all night in the river up to his neck—& frozen.'[28] Newman himself, in one of the hagiographies he wrote for the series, nostalgically contemplated 'the whole island once covered with fair monasteries'.[29] Milman and his intellectual sympathizers were to be as distant from this brand of anti-modernism as they were from evangelical anti-Catholicism.

As accounts of medieval religion which took their cue from different kinds of religious conservatism became both louder and more common, signs of dissatisfaction with them also surfaced. The whiggish Henry Hallam's often-reprinted *View of the State of Europe during the Middle Ages*, first published in 1818, kept a late-Enlightenment conception of medieval church history before Victorian audiences, organized around rising papal usurpations of legal powers properly belonging to national churches and the civil government.[30] The advanced theist Francis Newman praised Hallam's work in 1848 as pleasingly out-of-step with the contemporary vogue for medievalism in religion and politics.[31] Nineteenth-century religio-historical polemic had not yet assumed its standard forms at the time Hallam was first writing, and so he did not denounce it. But the atmosphere had changed by the 1850s, at which point a new genre of ecclesiastical-historical writing began to appear. Protestant historians wearied by the new wave of evangelical invective unleashed during the 'Papal Aggression', whilst still resistant or even hostile to the papacy's claims to an historical mandate, began to think it desirable to make and stress a distinction between the unchallengeable authority of historical fact, and the false pretensions of theology to determine historical interpretation. Whilst this manoeuvre marked a significant departure from the modes of approaching papal history

---

[27] Pattison, *Memoirs*, pp. 100–1.

[28] Bodleian Library, MS Pattison 128, M. Pattison diary entry for 10 October 1843, p. 20.

[29] [J.H. Newman], *The Cistercian saints of England: S. Stephen Harding* (London, 1844), p. 2.

[30] H. Hallam, *View of the state of Europe during the middle ages*, 4th edn (3 vols, London, 1826), ii, 198–373. T. Lang, 'Hallam, Henry (1777–1859)', *ODNB*.

[31] [F. Newman], 'Hallam's Supplemental Notes', *PR*, 16 (1848), p. 521. Hallam's *View of the state of Europe* appeared in 14 editions through to 1878.

that had taken shape during the early Victorian period, it did not itself amount to the alternative philosophy of medieval Catholicism which many Victorian readers credited Milman with developing.

Factualist rhetoric, combined nevertheless with a lingering inclination to believe that writing Catholic history required a moral that was primarily anti-papal, were especially visible in two works that took shape in this context. Edward Shepherd, rector of Luddesdown in Kent, began his 1851 *History of the Church of Rome* by stating that he was 'not aware that there is any account of the Church of Rome, framed on the simple and obvious principle of merely collecting and arranging the testimony of History with regard to facts'.[32] Shepherd's history, which focused closely on the individual popes, nevertheless amounted to a Protestant Pyrrhonist reply to Roman Catholic revival. By a close examination of the 'facts' relating to the popes from the first century to the end of the fourth, he concluded that, in truth, very few facts were ascertainable. It followed that the papal claims were unsupportable. 'Truth has recorded nothing of Rome's earlier centuries', thought Shepherd, beyond materials for unflattering conjectures about the pontiffs.[33] Thomas Greenwood, a barrister and reader and fellow in history and polite literature at the University of Durham, offered a comparable interpretative paradigm. In composing his monumental *Cathedra Petri*, published in six volumes between 1856 and 1872, Greenwood sought to take refuge from 'any theological position whatever' by compiling a minute political history of the papacy from its earliest days to the pre-Reformation period.[34] A political rather than a theological focus, which he hoped would guarantee his historical impartiality, still led him to become more strongly convinced than he had been at the outset that the history of the papacy showed civil liberty to be incompatible with religious servitude.[35] Thus, even while Shepherd and Greenwood distanced themselves from revivalist agendas, their starting points still led them to dwell on the ills created by the papacy and the institutionalized clerical caste. An historically, and theologically, influential account of the progressive and constructive relationship between those forces and wider civilization was to come from an historian with a more imaginative and much wider-ranging frame of reference.

---

[32] E.J. Shepherd, *The history of the Church of Rome, to the episcopate of Damasus, A.D. 384* (London, 1851), [iii].

[33] Ibid., pp. 71, 93–4.

[34] T. Greenwood, *Cathedra Petri: a political history of the great Latin patriarchate* (6 vols, London, 1856–1872), i, [iii]–v; E.I. Carlyle, rev. M. Lloyd, 'Greenwood, T. (1790–1871)', *ODNB*.

[35] Greenwood, *Cathedra Petri*, v, [iii]–iv.

MILMAN'S *HISTORY OF LATIN CHRISTIANITY*

Henry Hart Milman's *History of Latin Christianity*, published in two instalments of three volumes between 1854 and 1855, was the last major component of the history of the Judaeo-Christian dispensation since Abraham which he made his life's work. His 1829 *History of the Jews*, with its scandalous description of Abraham as a 'Sheik', was the first extended exhibition of Milman's generational, physical, and intellectual distance from Victorian revivalism.[36] His 1840 *History of Christianity*, a heavily sociopolitical study of the first three Christian centuries, deployed Gibbonian irony to marginalize the importance of dogmatic theology where Stanley had used literary word-painting.[37] Milman never outwardly dissented from orthodox doctrine. But he always treated doctrinalism as though it were no real part of the essence of the Christian religion, and did not join idealist attempts to reinvigorate it. Milman's peculiar combination of moralized, secular-sounding Christianity with ironical detachment from theological enthusiasm showed a level of indebtedness to the eighteenth century that made him unique among Victorian clerical historians. His romantic poetical sensibility, and his early openness to continental scholarship concerning the Bible and ecclesiastical history, nevertheless confirmed his son Arthur's later claim that his father's books exemplified the change which came across 'the proper methods of dealing with religious history' during his lifetime.[38] Nowhere was this truer, nor Milman's influence more widely felt, than in his account of *Latin Christianity*. By placing Catholicism at the centre of a past epoch of the world's growth, on the basis of a theology of history that treated liberal Protestantism as the normative condition of the modern mind, Milman's *magnum opus* won widespread admiration among the mid-Victorian reading public.

Milman's peculiar intellectual disposition, forming something of a bridge between the eighteenth and nineteenth centuries, left him unusually free from the anti-Catholic and anti-papal religious anxieties of the evangelical age. Historical agendas which proceeded from evangelical trembling before the impending Second Advent, or high church searching for legal precedent and Catholic social ideals, simply did not trouble him—though Milman, as will be seen, was to trouble them. He had long left Oxford by the time of the Oxford Movement and the

---

[36] [H.H. Milman], *The history of the Jews* (3 vols, London, 1829), i, 9; cf. S. Goldhill, 'What has Alexandria to do with Jerusalem? Writing the history of the Jews in the nineteenth century', *Historical Journal*, 59:1 (2016), pp. 125–51.

[37] Milman, *History of Christianity*.

[38] Milman, *Milman*, p. 2; Forbes, *Liberal Anglican idea*, p. 2.

common room ascendancy of the alluring personalities through whom it spread. The Catholic revival left him rather amused than alarmed. 'After the drama,' Milman would say dismissively of the transition from Tractarianism to Ritualism, 'the melodrama!'[39] He was also a world away from the Protestant cries of 'no-popery' seldom dormant at that time. Writing to the American historian W. H. Prescott in November 1850, he condemned the 'Papal Aggression' because of the affront it offered to 'the long years during which so many wise and good persons have been endeavouring to allay religious animosities, to soften religious asperities, and to enable us to live, if not in mutual respect, yet without violent collision'.[40] He hoped that his own historical writing would aid in that work of cultural integration, as did a number of historians who followed him.

Over those late-Hanoverian and early-Victorian decades, Milman's literary work and intellectual connections were furnishing him with the ingredients of an eventual assessment of Catholic history that was to take points of departure altogether different from those favoured by religious alarmists. Milman's commitment to the power of poetry to create sympathy between different religious and cultural outlooks has already been noticed, a position with which his work as an historian was in recognizable continuity.[41] His reimagining of biblical prophecy through a poetic medium also paralleled and prefigured his entry into a new field. Milman's critical interest in the Old Testament, bearing its earliest fruit in his *History of the Jews*, here informed his literary activities. In opposition to the evangelical tendency to apply Hebrew prophecy to specific historical events in order to bring the end of days within the scope of measurable anticipation, Milman argued—in an Enlightened and postmillennial idiom—that such premonitions were in fact 'a vast vaticination' of the era of gradually spreading Christian righteousness in which progressive civilization now found itself.[42] The religious poetaster gave colour to the critical stance of the Old Testament scholar. Milman's ode on *The Deluge*, written some time before it was published in 1840, offered a meditation on the account in the Book of Genesis of the destruction of the antediluvian world at the hands of divine vengeance. In the final stanza, the prophetic narrator turns his eyes from a scene of purgative tribulation, to contemplate the renovated earth to which the Son of Man will ultimately return. 'Oh Earth! Shall not thy soften'd face present / A fairer, holier

---

[39] Quoted in [W.E.H. Lecky], 'Dean Milman', *ER*, 191:392 (1900), p. 525.
[40] Milman, *Milman*, pp. 177–8.   [41] See chapter one of this volume at p. 25.
[42] H.H. Milman, *Hebrew prophecy: a sermon preached before the University of Oxford, 26 March, 1865* (Oxford and London, 1865), p. 6; cf. [Milman], *History of the Jews*, i, 278, 297–9.

aspect than the last?', where 'Majestic Order and all-reverenced Law / Rule o'er the nations' and 'social Harmony / Gather mankind in one calm family'. The action closes with the question, 'Shalt thou not find, God's, Love's eternal Son, / Thy kingdom here of truth, of peace, of love, begun?'[43] Thus Milman versified the heavenwards movement of secular time within an expanded notion of sacred history. He would transpose the fundamentals of that narrative structure into his *Latin Christianity*, making it possible for him to construe medieval Christianity not as an abomination, but as an increment of a larger ascent whose consummation was as yet unseen.

Milman's transition from historical poetry to narrative history brought him into contact with a new range of intellectual influences. The reviews and letters he wrote during the 1830s and 1840s show him moving towards a conception of the medieval period's importance that lay not in its apostasy, usurpation or beatific felicity, but in its progressive role in the purposive history of religion and civilization. In common with Gibbon, of whose writings he was unusually fond, Milman was more open than many of his contemporaries to continental intellectual breezes, and turned to face them instead of heading into the storms then besetting his former university. As part of his editorial interest in the *Decline and Fall*, he published an essay on François Guizot's edition of that work in 1834 which identified the liberal scholar and statesman as a fellow-spirit in the necessary work of absorbing Gibbon's accuracy and candour into a genuinely Christian interpretation of European history.[44] Guizot's own extended foray in this direction was his lecture course delivered before the University of Paris in 1828, and published as the *Histoire de la Civilisation en Europe*. Guizot, a Protestant, argued that the Catholic Church had given human experience a depth previously unknown. But its vices, he averred, had been to separate its hierarchy from the people and alternately to support theocracy or empire when, in truth, society could only be truly Christianized when individuals were free from compulsion.[45] This was an approach with which Milman could sympathize. On one occasion

---

[43] Milman, 'The Deluge: an ode', in his *Poetical works*, iii, [339], 346–7; Gen. 6:5–8:19.
[44] [H.H. Milman], 'Guizot's *Edition of Gibbon*', *QR*, 50:100 (1834), p. 292; E. Gibbon, *The life of Edward Gibbon [by himself], with selections from his correspondence*, ed. H.H. Milman (London, 1839); E. Gibbon, *The history of the decline and fall of the Roman Empire*, ed. H.H. Milman (12 vols, London, 1838–1839).
[45] M. Guizot, *Histoire générale de la civilisation en Europe depuis la chute de l'empire romain jusqu'à la révolution française*, 4th edn (Paris, 1840), pp. 163–96; see also his preface to the sixth edition (1855), printed in Guizot, *Histoire de la civilisation en Europe depuis la chute de l'empire romain jusqu'à la révolution française*, 8th edn (Paris, 1866), (xi)–xiv, where he replies to Catholic critics of the lectures.

he asked the writer and sometime Benthamite Sarah Austin, who kept Milman abreast of developments in Parisian intellectual society during her residence there in the 1840s, to give his 'homage' to Guizot.[46]

Together with liberal French assessments of Catholicism that were *laïque* but not *athée*, the Berlin historian Leopold von Ranke's original approach to the history of the post-Reformation papacy was attractive to Milman (as it was to Austin) for its separation of historical explanation from confessional imperatives.[47] Milman never took to the speculative or subjectivist German approaches to religious history, such as those of Schelling or Neander, which became attractive to other early Victorian liberal Protestants. But he was early in introducing Ranke's political and yet providential approach to the *History of the Popes* to a British audience, even if his indifference to philosophical readings of history caused him to glide over the interpretative depths of Ranke's work.[48] Before the appearance of Sarah Austin's translation in 1840, which made the work more accessible to English speakers, Milman wrote two long reviews of Ranke's history of the pontiffs in the sixteenth and seventeenth centuries. They appeared in the *Quarterly Review* in 1836 and 1837.[49] Milman opened his first essay by contrasting the 'dispassionate and philosophical serenity' of 'the German historian' with 'the still-reviving, and, it is almost to be feared, unextinguishable animosity between conflicting religious parties' which marred British writing on the subject.[50] In both essays, Milman voiced his appreciation for how Ranke had made possible an understanding of papal history which both recognized its once-purposive function in taming and organizing the barbarian peoples, and its capacity for spiritual regeneration. 'The Papacy, during the dark ages, notwithstanding its presumptuous and insulting domination over the authority of kings and

---

[46] Milman, *Milman*, p. 159; J. Hamburger, 'Austin (née Taylor), Sarah (1793–1867)', *ODNB*.

[47] On Ranke's curial disrepute, see H. Wolf, D. Burkard and U. Muhlack, *Rankes 'Päpste' auf dem Index: Dogma und Historie im Widerstreit* (Paderborn, 2003).

[48] L. Ranke, *Die römischen Päpste: ihre Kirche und ihr Staat im sechszehnten und siebzehnten Jahrhundert*, 2nd edn (3 vols, 1838–1839): first edition 1834–1836.

[49] [H.H. Milman], 'The popes of the sixteenth and seventeenth centuries', *QR*, 55:110 (1836), pp. [287]–323; [Milman], 'Ranke *on the popes of Rome in the sixteenth and seventeenth centuries*', *QR*, 58:116 (1837), pp. 371–406; L. Ranke, *The ecclesiastical and political history of the popes of Rome during the sixteenth and seventeenth centuries*, trans. S. Austin (3 vols, London, 1840). It was mainly as a result of Milman's articles that Austin decided to translate Ranke's work into English: H.H. Milman, 'Preface to the fourth edition', in L. Ranke, *The popes of Rome: their ecclesiastical and political history during the sixteenth and seventeenth centuries*, trans. S. Austin, 4th edn (3 vols, London, 1866), i, vi.

[50] [Milman], 'The popes of the sixteenth and seventeenth centuries', p. [287].

the rights of nations, was a great instrument in the hand of Divine Providence.'[51]

Milman's view, like Ranke's, represented a considerable affront to the conventional evangelical assumptions of the 1830s. He was also unusual in being able to read Ranke's work in the original language, and he juxtaposed its scholarly standards and historical perspectives to insular and crabbier British writing. But he unselfconsciously omitted those epistemological features of Ranke's account which originated in German philosophical debates, and which were the most foreign to English minds. Where Ranke had refrained from making moral judgements out of his belief in the sovereignty of history, in these essays Milman actively deplored papal baseness where he saw it. Nor did Milman discern, or take an interest in, the dialectical interaction between the real and the ideal in history that was as Fichtean magma to the external surface of Ranke's text.[52] This unspeculative bent was to limit Milman's appeal to more anxious and younger thinkers.

The nature of Milman's interest in Gibbon, Ranke, and French liberal thought makes clear that his developing interest in Catholic history was leading him towards an interpretation of its progressive effects as lying on a concretely sociopolitical rather than a speculative plane, albeit one contained within a theologically rooted historical scheme. This disposition had already been evident in his *History of Christianity*.[53] His receptivity to the critical perspectives of German scholarship, yet his deafness to the hidden or overt faith in *Geist* which animated so much of it, were part of his wider self-distancing from readings of history which proceeded from avowedly philosophical bases. He was disappointed to find that Christoph Friedrich Ammon's *Fortbildung des Christenthums zur Weltreligion* was not an historical account of the past 'change of Christianity into the religion of the world', but that the advanced Lutheran professor had instead offered a prospective, Lessing-like call for the reconciliation of Christianity and reason out of his disenchantment with the Augsburg Confession.[54]

[51] Ibid., p. 292.

[52] P. Bahners, '"A place among the English classics":Ranke's *History of the Popes* and its British readers', in Stuchtey and Wende, *British and German historiography*, pp. [123]–57; On Ranke's early contact with Fichte, see F. Tessitore, 'Rankes "Lutherfragment" und die Idee der Universalgeschichte', in W.J. Mommsen (ed.), *Leopold von Ranke und die moderne Geschichtswissenschaft* (Stuttgart, 1988), pp. 7–36.

[53] Milman, *History of Christianity*, i, v–x.

[54] Milman, *Milman*, p. 153; C.F. v. Ammon, *Die Fortbildung des Christenthums zur Weltreligion in kirchlicher Rücksicht*, 2nd edn (4 vols, Leipzig, 1836–1840); F. Lau, 'Ammon, Christoph Friedrich (1766–1850)', in *Neue Deutsche Biographie*, 1 (1953), p. 253 f.

Milman was more open to sociological approaches to history than he was to such transcendental theorizing. He told Austin of his admiration for the liberal political economist Charles Dunoyer, whose argument that civilization could purify Christianity, as well as Christianity purify civilization, he had deployed against John Henry Newman's *Essay on Development*.[55] As in Macaulay, whom his friend Milman was inclined to present as a religiously as well as a politically sensible figure, traces of Enlightenment conjectural history occasionally surfaced in his writings.[56] Though no apologist for the court of Leo X, the pope who excommunicated Luther, Milman made a slightly *démodé* implicit defence of papal luxury in his 1836 essay on Ranke's *History of the Popes*.[57] The differing economic fortunes of Italy and South America during the period of the Counter-Reformation also prompted a telling observation. In the sixteenth and seventeenth centuries, 'how singular the contrast between the Campagna of Rome and the *haciendas* of Rome's faithful servants in South America!', he exclaimed by way of conclusion to his 1837 essay. 'Here, is Romanism subduing ferocious or indolent savages to the arts and the happiness of civilized life . . . there, close at home, turning a paradise into a desert!—so completely does even the same form of Christianity differ in its effects, according to the circumstances of time and place, and the state of society.'[58] In another instance of the ways in which his scriptural researches fertilized his approach to other periods, Milman was at this point giving expression to a modification of eighteenth-century accommodation theory.[59] The idea that certain forms of religion spontaneously expressed certain stages of society, but grated against others, was to be central to his *Latin Christianity*.

Encouraged by the discovery of the *Philosophumena* and the light it threw on an 'extremely dark' period in Roman affairs, Milman finished writing his *History*, on which he had been working for some years, after his

---

[55] Milman, *Milman*, p. 157; on Milman and Newman, see chapter two of this volume at pp. 72–3. Dunoyer was more anticlerical than Milman himself: C. Dunoyer, *De la liberté du travail ou simple exposé des conditions dans lesquelles les forces humaines s'exercent avec le plus de puissance* (3 vols, Paris, 1845), i, 223–4.

[56] H.H. Milman, *A memoir of Lord Macaulay*, 2nd edn (London, 1862), pp. 14–15.

[57] [Milman], 'The popes of the sixteenth and seventeenth centuries', pp. 298–9.

[58] [Milman], 'Ranke *on the popes*', p.406. Not every liberal Anglican historian was as uniformly hostile to conjectural history as Forbes supposes: *Liberal Anglican idea*, p. 7.

[59] Cf. [Milman], *History of the Jews*, i, 100; Milman, *The History of the Jews: from the earliest period down to modern times*, 3rd edn (3 vols, London, 1863), i, ix–x. On neological accommodation theory and its nineteenth-century supersession, see H.W. Frei, *The eclipse of biblical narrative: a study in eighteenth and nineteenth century hermeneutics* (New Haven, CT, and London, 1974), pp. 60–1, 234–5.

appointment as dean of St Paul's in 1849.[60] The completed text, though indebted at many points to earlier scholarship, offered a boldly original scheme for interpreting the history of medieval Christianity. Its organizing principle was not the delineation of apostasy, impudence, or superstition, but the belief that 'Latin Christianity' had been a purposeful and formative stage in the organic, spiritual development of the world: development in which Milman made religion, after God, the prime mover. Central to Milman's account of Latin Christianity, arising after the religion's Greek and ultimately giving way to its Teutonic form, was the idea that it possessed 'a remarkable historic unity'.[61] Taking root not in luxurious, late-imperial Rome, but in the sun-bleached and stony ground of North Africa, the Latin-speaking church fathers Tertullian, Jerome, and Augustine quintessentially expressed its hard and forceful characteristics.[62] Latin Christianity was despotic, imperious, superstitious, fanatical, practical, and rigid, with none of the subtle intellectualism and soft humanism which Milman supposed to inhere to Greek Christianity and the language which sustained it. The Latin system had limitations which became manifest at a later stage of historical development. But it was, for a time, the indispensable precondition for the conversion and elevation of the western European barbarians, without which the Christian nations and Teutonic Christianity of modern Europe could not have been formed, and by which conventional Christianity was itself purified.[63]

The notion that there was such a thing as 'Latin Christianity' may first have been suggested to Milman by Ranke, who had written of a 'lateinischen Christenheit' common to the medieval 'Germanic' and 'Romanic' peoples, or by Neander, who posited that it was temporarily necessary for Christianity to adopt an 'Old Testament form' comprehensible to 'raw peoples' as yet unable to apprehend the gospel in its purity.[64] Whatever its original provenance, Milman gave the concept a wide content and systematic application which Ranke's political and Neander's theological interests had not ascribed to it. For Milman, Latin Christianity was a cultural whole before it was an institutional hierarchy, accessible through the history of literature, law, art, and religious legend, as well as through political and ecclesiastical history in the narrower senses. In composing his account, Milman weighed the more conventional evidence of chronicles,

---

[60] Milman, *Milman*, p. 223; *HLC*, i, [iii]; on the *Philosophumena*, see chapter two of this volume at p. 76.

[61] *HLC*, i, [iii].   [62] Ibid., i, 29–30, 74, 115.   [63] Ibid., i, [1]–10.

[64] L. Ranke, *Geschichten der romanischen und germanischen Völker von 1494 bis 1535*, vol. 1 (Leipzig and Berlin, 1824), [iii], xviii; Neander, *Allgemeine Geschichte*, iii, 3–4. Although Milman counted both authors among his authorities, he nowhere cited them in this particular: *HLC*, i, iv, vi, 552 n.

law codes, and, where he could readily obtain them, manuscripts, sometimes—as in his treatment of Islam—leaning heavily though never credulously on secondary authorities where scholarly judgements were beyond his linguistic or bibliographical resources.[65] But he extended his range of historical vision to encompass poetry, language, popular ballads, and saints' lives, provocatively taking the latter, with hints of Niebuhr, to be Christianity's 'mythic literature'.[66] Milman's capacious sense of the province of ecclesiastical history, together with his tripartite division of Christian development into Greek, Latin, and Teutonic stages, were predicated on a broad conception of the church that was to prove controversial. 'As an historian I can disenfranchise none who claim, even on the slightest grounds, the privileges and hopes of Christianity.'[67]

In order to present Latin Christianity as a phase of progress, rather than as aberration or decay, Milman's earlier claim that different religious types complemented different social forms now became the more spiritualized and organic idea that history was purposefully growing from childhood to manhood. Whereas the Greek world, and the theology it inspired, were close to expiration in the early Middle Ages, 'Latin Christianity . . . seemed endowed with an inexhaustible principle of expanding life.'[68] Humanity, in this account, had a soul; and its training to maturity demanded the application of successive educational dispensations. 'Human thought is almost compelled to assert, and cannot help asserting, its original free-dom', but discipline and Christian ethics were the necessary preconditions of its productive exercise, and hence of the progress compassed in divine counsels.[69] These starting points guided the ways in which Milman conceptualized the process which lay at the heart of his six volumes: the reception of Christianity by the new, Teutonic peoples who settled amidst the ruins of the Roman Empire, and their growth towards national, intel-lectual, and spiritual maturity through the tutelage of religious Latinity.[70] Under the influence of a hard and inflexible religious system which Milman was given to treating in a personified way, as though it were a kind of schoolmaster, and helped on by the native vigour and independent-mindedness of the Teutonic nations, 'mankind might seem renewing its

---

[65] *HLC*, ii, [4]–33. Milman borrowed several manuscript accounts of papal conclaves from the antiquarian, Thomas Phillipps: Bodleian Library, University of Oxford, Phillipps-Robinson papers, c. 519/246–247: H.H. Milman to [T. Phillipps], 3[?] July 1852.

[66] *HLC*, v, 140–2, vi, 422.   [67] Ibid., i, 9.   [68] Ibid., i, 5.

[69] Ibid., i, 10.

[70] Noticing that the barbarian nations who settled in the western empire had generally converted to Arian Christianity before they accepted its orthodox form at Latin hands, the undogmatic Milman regretted that little could be known of this prehistory on account of 'the total silence of the Catholic historians, who perhaps destroyed, or disdained to preserve the fame of Arian conquests to the common Christianity': ibid., i, 273.

youth' as one leafed through the pages of medieval history.[71] Thus Milman, the erstwhile poet, created a purposeful role for medieval Catholicism within a world-historical drama. Many of his readers welcomed this as an advance on sectarian or impious historiography, even while they disagreed with particular details of Milman's plot. Later accounts of medieval religion which omitted its role in the divine government of the world, such as William Lecky's, were capable of provoking considerable anxiety among those more in sympathy with Milman's analytical approach, and the metaphor of individual growth which symbolized it.

The way in which Milman accounted for the development of the medieval religious system placed him at variance with accounts which attributed it to papal ambition or to the original tendency of the human heart to sin. Ecclesiastical power was more the expression, than the cause, of the specifically Latin form of Christianity, which assimilated to itself the governing assumptions of the Roman polity; the unifying potential of the Latin language; and the affective power of popular superstition. Institutionally, the Latin Church 'was the Roman empire, again extended over Europe' by a universal code and a hierarchy of 'religious praetors or proconsuls', extending from the meanest ranks of society up to a 'spiritual Caesar'; Milman attributed the power vested in the clergy by canon law to the Roman political tradition of arbitrary power.[72] But such a church could not have flourished but for its harmony with a whole society. Jerome's Vulgate Bible, Milman reflected, helped to establish Latin as the language of the church, 'and still tends to maintain the unity with Rome of all nations whose languages have been chiefly formed from the Latin'. In one of his many offences to current Protestant pieties, he called this 'a wonderful work ... even more, perhaps, than the Papal power the foundation of Latin Christianity'.[73] Milman's interest in German scholarship on folklore and pagan belief led him to treat what earlier evangelicals and Enlightenment historians had scorned as superstition in the more imaginatively sympathetic terms of legend and myth.[74] The 'Christian mythology' of the Virgin Mary and the saints, more than 'speculative and dogmatic theology', was for a time the agent of that 'popular, vital, active Christianity' by which religion penetrated to the heart of man and society. This popular belief was neither 'fraud' nor philosophical 'folly', but the parent of art and poetry, and hence of that educative mental quickening eventually given mature expression at the Reformation.[75] The secret to the

---

[71] Ibid., i, 137–8, vi, 400.   [72] Ibid., i, 8, 399–408.   [73] Ibid., i, 70–4.
[74] Milman frequently referred to Jacob Grimm's *Deutsche Mythologie* (Göttingen, 1835): *HLC*, i, 259 n., vi, 408 n.
[75] Ibid., i, 465–76.

growing papal power lay in 'Rome's complete impregnation with the spirit of the age; and this lasted, almost unbroken, till the Reformation'. This was neither 'worldly policy', nor dishonesty, but the unity of the ecclesiastical system with 'the general mind of Christianity'.[76] Milman's account of historical origins controversially posited that there had been a time when Romanism was the sole normative expression of mankind's religious spirit.

Milman constantly stressed the purposive direction of that phase of world history. Pregnant remarks and constructions betrayed his belief, suffusing the text, that historical development was rooted in something beyond human agency alone. The papacy 'must be a counterbalance to barbaric force'; 'Latin Christianity had yet to discharge some part of its mission'.[77] Within this broad scheme, the chief advance made by Latin Christianity on its Greek predecessor lay in its intensely practical character. The Greek Church 'had almost ceased to be aggressive or creative' by the time of the conversion of the empire; unable to win new converts, and promoting a form of monasticism that withdrew energetic citizens from active life, the Greek patriarchs 'sank into administrators of a tolerated religion under Mohammedan dominion' and 'yielded to that worst barbarism—a worn out civilisation'.[78] Nor did Milman sympathize with the eastern predilection for doctrinal theology. 'Early Christianity, it may be observed, cannot be justly estimated from its writers', Milman curtly declared in one of the semi-Gibbonian footnotes he occasionally introduced so as quietly to dismiss the importance of theological controversy.[79]

Milman did not apply this assessment, which had strong notes of Gibbon about it, to western religion, which progressively guided occidental youth while the Christian orient sank into decrepit old age. Western monasticism, Milman wrote with a hint of Enlightenment historical thought, had beneficent unintended consequences. Whereas eastern anchorites self-macerated on the tops of pillars, Benedictines—obliged to employ time not spent in study or worship by useful work—cultivated wildernesses, and extended arts and husbandry to barbarous regions.[80] Though Milman did not set himself above noticing the material side effects of medieval religion, societal moral elevation was more fundamental to his account of the historical role played by external and repressive ecclesiasticism. It had been, Milman believed, the only means by which Christianity could take hold of innumerable individuals since lost to history amidst the barbarous conditions of medieval Europe. The development of ecclesiastical law, which brought every moral and religious act

[76] Ibid., i, 121.   [77] Ibid., i, 430, vi, 332–3.   [78] Ibid., i, 4–5.
[79] Ibid., i, 58 n.   [80] Ibid., i, 409–22.

within its purview under the ultimate sentence of excommunication, was 'a moral and religious discipline'.[81] The controlling impulses of domineering popes—especially Gregory the Great and Hildebrand—won new nations for Christ, stopped the church from becoming a mere feudal patrimony, and checked the buccaneering instincts of medieval monarchs.[82] Milman certainly objected to the ways in which the Latin system, especially as distilled by Augustine, treated the church of God as coterminous with an external, sacerdotal order.[83] He also wrote with Enlightened frankness and sarcasm about the Latin Church's horror of sexuality.[84] But Latin Christianity nevertheless implanted humane feelings previously unknown or else only coldly commanded by mere philosophy; it gave ideas of innate human dignity to a Roman world that had known only despotism; it sacralized the marriage bed.[85] It was the system over which the popes had presided, according to Milman, which had first given western civilization its creative and ethical character.

That development was only made possible, however, by the nature of the ore on which Latin Christianity worked its impress. Milman wrote before it became common to use scientific metaphors to render the significance of the religious past; and the advent of social Darwinism, which made it popular to define Latins and Teutons in pseudo-biological terms, still lay in the future. But he possessed an unsystematic notion that 'race', a word he tended to use only in passing and an idea to which he primarily attached a religious and linguistic meaning, might be shaped by factors arising from a group's common descent.[86] He accordingly presented the latent religious sensibility, and social and political characteristics, of the Teutonic peoples who succeeded Roman hegemony in the West as conditioning the effects of Latin Christianity quite as much as the inherent tendencies of Latin Christianity itself. Latinity, left to its own devices, tended to force and uniformity; it did not itself contain the elements necessary for the ultimate supersession of the papal despotism.[87] In the mob violence which broke out in fourth-century Rome over the succession to Pope Liberius, Milman thought he saw a reanimation of the spirit of ancient Rome, so long crushed under despotism. 'The Roman populace appears quickened by a new principle of freedom', deriving

[81] Ibid., i, 404–8.   [82] Ibid., i, 430–66, iii, 97–109.   [83] Ibid., i, 115–17.
[84] Ibid., i, 117–21.   [85] Ibid., i, 24–5.
[86] The reverse was also true, in that, for Milman, religion and language might efface inherited attributes. He regretted the effective supersession of the Teutonic element in the French nation by the resurgence of the Latin language in the years after Charlemagne: ibid., vi, 519–26, cf. i, 8–9 and n. For an instance of Milman's typically incidental use of the word 'race', see ibid., ii, 312. Cf. Mandler, '"Race" and "nation"'.
[87] *HLC*, i, 159.

from their conversion to Christianity, though it remained as yet a chaotic freedom marked by 'blind partisanship' and 'headstrong and stubborn ferocity'.[88]

The Teutons, in Milman's account, possessed qualities which eventually returned Christianity and Christian liberty to their true natures. The Greeks had been drawn to Christianity by the void in their religion and by the incongruity between their poetic anthropomorphism and 'the progress of [their] discursive reason'; the Romans by their historic uprightness and vigour. But for Christianity to be accommodated to their native dispositions, it had to be ritualized and intellectualized to the detriment of its original simplicity. The Teutons, however, already possessed an illimitable and mysterious sense of deity, which conduced to a subjective and democratic more than an objective and hierarchical form of religion.[89] Their priesthood was not a separate caste, but a judging and disciplining elite: hence the ultimately fateful tendency of Teutonic societies to resist clerical aggrandizement. The Teutons' respect for women prepared them for Christian purity.[90] Milman admitted that it was Teutonic, not Christian, usage which reduced the application of the death penalty in barbarian law codes.[91] Thus the kernels were formed of the northern European nations, in particular England and Germany, which, partly through interaction with papal politics, grew to maturity over the medieval centuries: a process aided by the growth of vernacular languages.[92] The independence, individuality, and self-control of the Teutonic peoples were Christianized by the Latin Church, yet survived to undo papal corruption once that church's allotted time had passed. Milman's incorporation of racial factors into ecclesiastical history was not to pass without critical comment; but it was soon to become conventional, as ideas of what constituted the boundaries of the church, and so of church history, became more blurred at the edges.

Milman's treatment of the Teutons signalled that the ground of his complaint against the survival of Latin Christianity into the nineteenth century was not that it was evil, but that it no longer synchronized with the higher authority of teleological historical development, the providential ends of which Milman felt able to discern. Milman was given to emphasizing the supposedly anachronistic qualities of medieval reform movements and intellectual innovations in explaining their failures, whilst

---

[88] Ibid., i, 67.   [89] Ibid., vi, 629–32.

[90] Ibid., i, 255–90.   [91] Ibid., i, 395.

[92] Ibid., iv, 246–7, v, *passim*, vi, 391–3. Milman cited L. Ranke, *History of the Reformation in Germany*, trans. S. Austin, 2nd edn (3 vols, London, 1845–1847), on Germany's growing independence at the time of the conciliar movement: *HLC*, vi, 551 and n.

weaving intimations of future developments into his account of them. The official iconoclasm sponsored by eighth-century Byzantine emperors, imposed by rulers instead of rising up from the people, failed, in his view, because there was as yet no intense inner spiritual life which could support religion in the absence of images. 'It was a premature Rationalism, enforced upon an unreasoning age.'[93] At a slightly later period, Milman alternated between scorning scholasticism, in an Enlightenment register, as pyramidal in its uselessness, and giving voice to a newer fashion for seeing it as the premature, half-formed expression of the western mind's yearning for freedom from external authority.[94] The text's ambivalence on this point can be understood as the result of a natively sceptical, sometimes Lockean Milman coming into intellectual contact with nineteenth-century histories of scholastic philosophy which, under the influence of German Idealism and the eclectic philosophy of Victor Cousin, sought to disinter a subject which the Enlightenment had buried alive.[95]

If proto-Protestantism had been out of step with the world's movement before the Reformation, an event anticipated in the growing restlessness of vernacular poetry, Catholicism had ceased to fulfil a progressive function after it.[96] Latin Christianity, Milman conceded, 'may point to still surviving Foundations for the good—the temporal, the intellectual good—of mankind; her Hospitals and her Brotherhoods, her Universities and her schools, her Churches and her Missions'.[97] But the purposive movement of the modern period towards individuality and subjectivism rendered it obsolete, just as western medievalism had previously displaced the eastern Christianity that lingered on, uncreatively, in Russia, the Levant, and the farther East. Latin Christianity, in the form of modern papalism, was today more of a danger to religion than its support, Milman argued. 'A religion of outward form' could today only appeal to 'more religious minds' unable or unwilling to think, and to women; but to seek to impose

---

[93] Ibid., ii, 146–7.   [94] Ibid., iii, 346–77, vi, 449.

[95] For example: H. Ritter, *Geschichte der christlichen Philosophie* (8 vols, Hamburg, 1841–1853), i, 5–52, iii, 119–27; Milman quoted Ritter's remark at ibid., iii, 37 that 'the philosophy of the middle ages was not of the times when the German element ruled; it was of primarily Latin nature': *HLC*, vi, 436 n.; B. Hauréau, *De la philosophie scolastique* (2 vols, Paris, 1850), i, [1]–6, ii, 497–525. Milman cited Hauréau to illustrate his observation that while the scholastic philosophers had not solved any of the great problems of human existence, neither had they shown them to be insoluble: 'Il est donc bien difficile aux philosophes d'avouer que la philosophie consiste plutôt à reconnaître la limite naturelle de l'intelligence humaine qu'à faire de puérils efforts pour reculer cette limite. – Haureau [*sic*], ii. p. 45, quoting Locke, whose whole, wise, wise, but strangely misrepresented work is a comment on that great axiom.' *HLC*, vi, 452 n. On Cousin's significance in the history of intellectual history, see D.R. Kelley, *The descent of ideas: the history of intellectual history* (Aldershot, 2002), pp. 9–29.

[96] *HLC*, v, 142.   [97] Ibid., vi, 383.

it on the generality of mankind would only drive them away from Christianity.[98] Though Milman hesitated to foretell the future of Christianity, he believed its ideal future development lay in Teutonic, Protestant Christianity and the supposed compatibility of its subjective, internal character with the advance of knowledge and society. 'I have no more faith in the mathematical millennium of M. Comte (at all events we have centuries enough to wait for it) than in the religious millennium of some Judaising Christians', Milman claimed.[99] But the self-guided and intelligent nature of Teutonic Christianity would, he ended by hoping, lead Christianity to approximate more and more to 'the absolute and perfect faith of Christ'; to 'discover and establish the sublime unison of religion and reason'; to 'assert its own full freedom, know the bounds of that freedom, respect the freedom of others'. His closing sentence caught the prophetic aspirations of the religious poet: 'Christianity may yet have to exercise a far wider, even if more silent and untraceable influence, through its primary, all-penetrating, all-pervading principles, on the civilisation of mankind.'[100] This reading of the present-day relationship between Protestantism and Catholicism was to become a hallmark of religiously liberal thought in the following years.

By the wide and original argumentation of his six volumes, Milman lessened the attraction of many of the earlier vantage points from which historians had perceived Catholicism. Though the *History of Latin Christianity* could not have taken the form it did without Milman's familiarity with French and German scholarship, in Britain it marked a new phase of debate. Milman by no means swept aside those accounts of Catholic history that were conditioned by Protestant evangelicalism and high church Anglicanism. But he provocatively synthesized many of those intellectual developments which tended to separate the discussion of religious medievalism from the immediate requirements of Biblicist and confessional polemic. Latin Christianity was now presented as a phase of political, social, cultural, and above all religious history, of which popes and councils were more the expressions than the controllers. Created by history, it was by history that it now stood condemned; Milman's eirenicism was always double-edged. His intellectual manoeuvre was itself underpinned by a theology of history which lay not far beneath the surface of his text. His conception of ecclesiastical history sacralised the socio-political changes wrought by language, race, and the free individual. The historical progress discernible by the historian was equivalent to the action of God within mankind. The rights and wrongs of Catholicism, in this

[98] Ibid., vi, 628–9.   [99] Ibid., vi, 627–8.   [100] Ibid., vi, 633–4.

scheme, became a much less significant question than that of the place of Catholicism in the divinely guided movement of history, in relation to which Catholics, Protestants, and unbelievers alike ought properly to estimate themselves. The changed understanding of the relationship between revelation, man, and time upon which Milman's historical philosophy relied was to spread widely in the succeeding decades; and it animated much of the controversy which the *History* generated on its first appearance.

MILMAN'S READERS

Milman's work was generally regarded as answering the reproach that England had produced no ecclesiastical history worth reading since Gibbon. After his final three volumes appeared in 1855, Macaulay wrote to tell him that it was his best work, destined for 'a high and permanent place in literature'.[101] Stanley publicly hailed the *History* as 'what may fairly be called the most important work on ecclesiastical history that the English language has produced'.[102] James Anthony Froude, in a letter to Milman, went still further: 'what can I say, except that you have written the finest historical work in the English language?'[103] After his retirement, Lord John Russell expressed his gratification that such a performance should have come from one whom he had nominated to the deanery of St Paul's.[104] In the country at large, congregations presented copies of Milman's work to favoured ministers.[105] Not all readers were so complimentary. But they generally agreed that Milman's history offered, for better or worse, no conventional account of its subject. Whether a Protestant historian of Catholicism was under an obligation to see himself as an anti-Catholic paladin remained a contentious point. Milman's text achieved such resonance, however, partly because it struck at a newer issue, which was coming to seem more fundamental than sectarian division. Milman's characteristic positions—liberal Protestant impartiality, topical and religious breadth, a certain doctrinal indifference—added fuel

[101] T.B. Macaulay to H.H. Milman, 29 December 1855, in T.B. Macaulay, *The letters of Thomas Babington Macaulay*, ed. T. Pinney (6 vols, Cambridge, 1974–1981), v, 484.

[102] [A.P. Stanley], 'Latin Christianity', *QR*, 95:189 (1854), p. 38.

[103] Quoted in Milman, *Milman*, pp. 224–5.

[104] J. Russell, *Essays on the rise and progress of the Christian religion from the reign of Tiberius to the end of the Council of Trent* (London, 1873), xi.

[105] [Anon.], 'Handsome presentation to a clergyman', *Sheffield and Rotherham Independent*, 2 January 1862, p. 3; [Anon.], 'Longborough', *Jackson's Oxford Journal*, 2 March 1867, p. 7.

to a growing contemporary debate about how the history of religion should be read, and how the relationship between religion and historical progress should be conceptualized. Arthur Milman, at the beginning of the twentieth century, would complain that some of the criticisms aimed at his father's great work had depended on 'some confusion between the respective provinces of the theologian and of the historian'.[106] Milman had himself richly interwoven those provinces in his own writing, in ways that invited subtly differing shades of appreciation and repudiation from contemporary reviewers and subsequent historians.

Although it was to become a commonplace later in the century, Milman's effort to establish the notion that Christianity could be divided up into 'Greek', 'Latin', and 'Teutonic' historical forms—each the holistic religious expression of a particular historical context, and none representing wilful apostasy from a shared religion—still appeared new and even subversive in the 1850s. Roman Catholic critics, and some conservative Protestants, resisted Milman's assessment of 'Latin Christianity', out of reluctance to accept the relativizing or conciliatory implications of positing that no one form of Christianity was necessarily true for all time. Charles William Russell, professor of ecclesiastical history at St Patrick's College, Maynooth, and president of the college from 1857, treated Milman's idea of 'Latin Christianity' as a polemical attack on the antiquity of the papal claims.[107] In one of his two rather straitjacketed lunges at Milman in the *Dublin Review*, Russell even called him 'Dr Milner' in a revealing slip of the pen.[108] From the opposite end of the ecclesiastical spectrum, a staunchly Protestant writer in the *Dublin University Magazine* thought that he saw something dangerous in Milman's confusing attempt to render the history of 'Latin Christianity' as something other than the history of an iniquitous papacy. 'We cannot but think Mr. Milman's language unguarded; and that there is an implied approval of the Papacy in this mode of viewing the history of Christianity.'[109]

A wide range of readers were receptive to Milman's historical scheme on its own terms, however. They welcomed Milman's argument that Latin Christianity had been an engine of European historical progress, and lauded its potential both to separate historical explanation from Protestant polemic, and to soften anti-Catholic sentiment. The *Morning Chronicle* spoke for many when it regretted England's long indifference to the

---

[106] Milman, *Milman*, p. 227.
[107] [C.W. Russell], 'Milman's History of Latin Christianity', *DR*, 37:74 (1854), pp. 404–49; A. Macaulay, 'Russell, Charles William (1812–1880)', *ODNB*.
[108] [C.W. Russell], 'Milman's Latin Christianity', *DR*, 40:80 (1856), p. 292.
[109] [Anon.], 'Milman's Latin Christianity', *DUM*, 44:262 (1854), p. 498.

history of the pre-Reformation church. Hallam, Guizot and now supremely Milman had rightly 'familiarised the minds of all educated Protestants with a truer estimate of the high genius and eminent goodness displayed in the prominent representatives of Latin Christianity, and have implanted a keen sense of gratitude to a Church which was at one period the great instrument in making modern society free, honourable, and courteous'.[110] The progressively inclined *Fraser's Magazine* greeted Milman's work as the latest and most comprehensive English contribution to 'historical *narrative*' in ecclesiastical history, as opposed to the scattered 'treatises, disputations, attacks, replies, rejoinders' which had traditionally dominated the field at home.[111] Addressing himself to a more confessionally Protestant audience, an anonymous writer in the *Journal of Sacred Literature* welcomed Milman's *History* as the best antidote to that fashionable millenarianism which falsely supposed that some 'master spirit... in the fourth and fifth centuries threw its prophetic glance upon the future, and then laid out a plan of aggrandizement which after-ages were to work out and complete'.[112] The breadth of Milman's conception of what an historian of Christianity could take his subject to encompass was itself a rebuke to bigotry, he continued.[113] These views were compatible with the reviewer's conservative evangelicalism. He took comfort from the hope that the Roman Catholic Church might change in the future, just as Milman had shown that it had changed in the past, as Bible societies spread the Word of God on the Continent. Being in accordance with the development of modern societies, it was scriptural evangelism, not apocalyptic denunciation, which appeared to be the best way to save Roman Catholic souls.[114] Milman's *Latin Christianity* was widely read as an eirenical text, which yet did not necessarily abnegate distinctively Protestant intellectual commitment.

Milman's belief that religion was an essential determinant of historical change was widely shared. The way in which he applied this idea, by treating the historical significance of religious change as coterminous with its racial, social, and political causes and effects, was more contentious, but it also found numerous supporters. The moderately conservative *Saturday Review*, whose editor John Douglas Cook tried to keep the journal out of theological controversy, carried reviews which looked favourably on Milman's sociopolitical understanding of the beneficial effects of

---

[110] [Anon.], 'History of Latin Christianity', *Morning Chronicle*, 19 April 1854, p. 7.
[111] [Anon.], 'Milman's Latin Christianity', *FM*, 50:298 (1854), p. 430.
[112] [Anon.], 'Milman's History of Latin Christianity', *JSL*, 7:13 (1854), pp. 3, 21.
[113] Ibid., p. 14.   [114] Ibid., pp. 22–4.

Latin Christianity on European development.[115] Stanley, writing in the thoughtfully conservative *Quarterly Review*, presented a comparable and more religiously pointed analysis. He began his essay with a characteristically picturesque invocation of those worthies who had, in the past, flourished in the environs of St Paul's: Colet and Donne, Wren and Butler. How congruous it was, he thought, that Milman, who combined 'poetic temperament' with 'industry and experience', should now have made such a contribution to the intellectual life of the nation.[116]

The rendition of Milman's *History* which followed exhibited Stanley's classically broad church desire to lessen religious divisions by setting them in historical perspective, whilst also insisting that a clear division existed between progressive and regressive modern-day religious types. Stanley connected Milman's enterprise to Neander's, for Milman had shown, like Neander, how much common Christianity thrived across each of the religion's several forms. Stanley considered that it was 'useful to trace how large a share in our ecclesiastical diversities is to be ascribed not to theological or religious causes, but to the more innocent, and in one sense, more inevitable influences of nation, of climate, of race, of the general stream of human history'.[117] Endorsing Milman's division of that stream into three cataracts, he argued that although the Latin Church was superstitious and fanatical in comparison with reformed denominations, 'in comparison of the Greek Church it is enlightened, progressive, in one word, Protestant'.[118] It was valuable for present-day Protestants to reflect on how, in the centuries of barbarism, Latin Christianity 'stood in the vanguard of civilization, whilst it represented the unborn Protestantism of Europe', as the Eastern Church—symbolically administering first communion to uncomprehending infants rather than to reasonable youths, and fostering eremitic rather than practical monasticism—slid into oriental immobility. It fell to modern, Teutonic Protestantism to absorb its parent and grandparent communions into some higher unity.[119] Stanley, sharing the ambiguities of Milman's kind of religious inclusivism, would further develop these themes in his own professorial lectures at Oxford.

Milman's *History* evidently encouraged mid-Victorian Protestants to think that Latin Christianity was not straightforwardly an anti-type of themselves, but had in fact formed a constructive part of their own history. Its present-day manifestations might be outdated; but they stemmed from

---

[115] [Anon.], 'Milman's Latin Christianity', *SR*, 1:15 (9 February, 1856), pp. 277–8; [Anon.], 'Milman's Latin Christianity', *SR*, 1:17 (23 February, 1856), pp. 324–5; B.Q. Schmidt, 'Cook, John Douglas (1808?–1868)', *ODNB*.
[116] [Stanley], 'Latin Christianity', p. 38.   [117] Ibid., pp. 40–1.
[118] Ibid., p. 56–7.   [119] Ibid., pp. 69–70.

a common root, towards which Protestant historians could safely become more curious, and even indulgent, than they had once been. The reflection on Catholicism which Milman's text invited proved to be inseparable from a further question. This was the issue of whether, and in what ways, an historian of religion ought properly to be a religious interpreter. Milman's readers, of whatever denomination, generally agreed that history should be more than a field for partisan or scholastic polemic. They found the suggestion that the historian should seek to trace continuous historical progress, over a broad narrative sweep, much more congenial. The question of the stance from which he should reconstruct and evaluate that progress was a more contentious one, to which no universally compelling answer was returned. Beneath the ascription of a historically creative role to Catholicism commonly lay an affirmation, which could not have been present in the same way twenty or thirty years earlier, of the importance of historical interpretation as a form of religious apologetic. Milman and his readers belonged to a shared intellectual space in this respect. But what it was that gave history its ultimate significance was a more divisive subject. The strongest admirers of the *History of Latin Christianity*, such as Stanley, thought that the sheer fact of the congregational, social, and political life which Christianity had underpinned down the centuries constituted intrinsically strong evidence of the truth of the religion. Others, though open to developmental views of history, criticized Milman for neglecting the inward spiritual and intellectual sides of religious growth: which was to say, the religious dimension of religion. The debate which opened up in the periodical press on this question of the religious implications of historical interpretation was to rumble on until the turn of the century.

Milman's conservative Protestant critics did not doubt that historical interpretation should serve a religiously didactic purpose, but they were hotly suspicious of any suggestion that the religious outgrowths of human historical experience could rightly clarify, or temporarily modify, the clear truths of the Bible. The Methodist *London Quarterly Review* blackened Milman, and his developmental theorizing, by associating him with Bunsen and Newman. 'There is an awkwardness in even seeming to supplement that which is divine, by human additions'. Myth, the essayist argued, was no 'amusement' but instead dangerous fiction and dishonesty.[120] W. E. Rawstorne, writing in the Free Church-aligned *North British Review*, suggested that Milman had not taken the bearing of ecclesiastical history 'on our own trial with respect to truth' sufficiently seriously. Newman's *Essay* had thrown down a challenge to Protestant historians to come to a right

---

[120] [Anon.], 'Latin Christianity', *LQR*, 4:7 (1855), pp. 146–9.

understanding of Christian history, to which Milman—though undoubtedly
a scholar of the first rank—had responded only defectively.[121] For Milman
seemed to judge history from a position curiously detached from positive
doctrinal commitment. He appeared indifferent to theology, and hence
inclined to avoid questions of what was right and true, seeming 'too apt to
judge both with reference rather to the effect that they have produced on the
world, than to the relation which they bear to abstract truth and right'.
Milman was too ready to let history, populated after all by the children of
wrath, stand as its own justification.[122]

A number of Milman's readers were closer to his own view that it was not
impious to treat history itself as a kind of supplement to Holy Scripture.
Milman's *History*, it could appear, vindicated the benignly providential
character of what had once seemed the most benighted of historical eras.
'The course of the Christian religion, in spite of all the impediments it has
encountered', ran the final moral of Stanley's essay, 'has always moved
onwards, and from that onward movement derived its main strength.'[123]
'Amidst the turmoil of human passions, the acrimony of contending sects,
their sanguinary strifes and mutual cruelties, the interminable discords
within, and the deadly assaults from without, under which any merely
human institution must have perished utterly, Christianity itself has ever
stood forth in unsullied purity and dignity, laying its foundations yet deeper
and deeper', another reviewer reflected.[124] Milman made tangible the
activity of the divine in human time.

Whilst liberal Protestant commentators typically agreed that Milman's
subject had the potential to add another buttress to the edifice of Christian
credibility, greater doubt existed as to whether he had gone about this
work in the right way. Without maintaining that religious history should
be structurally determined by dogmatic prepossessions, some came close
to the opinion once voiced by John Henry Newman that Milman looked
on religious experience in a manner akin to how an external observer
would view some natural fact.[125] To these writers, religious history was in
truth the reverse of inanimate. Being a moral and at least in part a
transcendental phenomenon, that history could not be written without
moral and transcendental commitment. Christianity involved, after all,
belief in the reality of a spiritual world. But Milman had persistently
baulked, or else smiled with Gibbon, at the history of the intellectual and

---

[121] [W.E. Rawstorne], 'Milman's *History of Latin Christianity*', *NBR*, 22:43 (1854),
p. 86 and n.
[122] Ibid., pp. 111–12.   [123] [Stanley], 'Latin Christianity', p. 70.
[124] [Anon.], 'History of Latin Christianity', *NQR*, 3:11 (1854), p. 315.
[125] [J.H. Newman], 'Milman's *History of Christianity*', *BC*, 29 (1841), pp. 71–114; for
attribution, see Newman, *Letters and diaries*, viii, 7 n. 2.

doctrinal formulations by which past minds had sought to articulate the implications of that conviction. Race, law, language, and nation, though historically important, might seem religiously epiphenomenal. John Tulloch, who developed a high view of the importance of the history of thought in his own struggles against materialism, criticized Milman for his lack of attention to the history of doctrines.[126] In a comparable vein, the *Westminster Review* thought Milman had offered a history of the church rather than a history of Christianity; and the 'progressive revelation of the Central Mind of the universe' spoke more through the latter than the former.[127] John James Tayler, a Unitarian minister and historian, disapprovingly placed Milman in the 'philosophic' tradition of Hume and Hallam rather than alongside the more religiously 'poetic' Carlyle in an essay for his denomination's *Prospective Review*.[128] 'He has so closely bound up the history of Christianity with that of civilisation, that we are often at a loss to know what is due to each'.[129] The essence of Christianity, the wellspring of its heroism and self-sacrifice, was indeed to be found in history, and not in Strauss; it would be part of the religious philosophy of the future. But Milman's critical eye was of little use to Tayler in discerning what this was.[130] Viewed in this light, Milman's Enlightened self-distancing from directly theological or philosophical discussion, in some ways redolent of an eighteenth-century world, may have betrayed a degree of assumed confidence in the basic premises and historical foundations of Christianity increasingly unusual among its liberal and even conservative apologists.

There was a sense in which Milman was the last of a line. In an obituary published after his death in September 1868, the *Pall Mall Gazette* lamented that he 'was, we fear, almost the last member of one of the most useful and characteristic classes of English society'. The church no longer produced men who combined 'learning, genius, and piety' in the same degree, as they had so often done in the eighteenth century.[131] In another respect, however, Milman's *History of Latin Christianity* marked the beginning of a new phase. The public responses to Milman's work, which reflected the complex and intersecting layers of his argument, pointed to a changing intellectual climate. Milman's text generated such controversy in no small measure because it assembled in a symmetrical and compelling form ideas and arguments which were already playing on

---

[126] [J. Tulloch], 'Stanley's *Eastern Church*', *NBR*, 35:69 (1861), p. 85.
[127] [Anon.], 'The fact and principle of Christianity', *WR*, 62:121 (1854), pp. 202, 218.
[128] [J.J. Tayler], 'History of Latin Christianity', *PR*, 39 (1854), p. 314.
[129] Ibid., pp. 319–20.   [130] Ibid., pp. 319–25.
[131] [Anon.], 'The late Dean Milman', *Pall Mall Gazette*, 25 September 1868, p. 10.

mid-Victorian minds. Revivalist writers, often suspicious of the worldly
and doctrinally insouciant progressivism they seemed to see in Milman,
remained prominent in the succeeding years. But the belief that the
Catholic centuries of religious history had not been squandered would
more and more spread beyond the liberal circles which had first promoted
it, as the notion that history was central to religious apologetic won wider
acceptance.

PROGRESS AND ITS LIMITS
IN MEDIEVAL RELIGION

The *History of Latin Christianity* helped to stimulate a wider reconfigur-
ation of Protestant responses to Catholicism. Milman's work continued to
inform that reorientation until late in the century; but it soon ran beyond
the parameters he had laid down for it.[132] The idea that Catholic belief
and practice were the products neither of pristine fidelity, nor papal
design, but of the historical process they in turn helped to mould, came
to undergird much British writing on the Middle Ages. Whether the
period of Europe's incubation yielded a rich harvest of wheat to posterity,
or a crop of tares which the Reformation had been right to uproot, was a
question that nevertheless continued to issue in a range of replies, from a
spectrum of starting points. Liberal Protestant clerical historians typically
followed Milman in identifying Latin Christianity as a providentially
ordained training ground for a freer, Teutonic religion. They often drew
on his favoured metaphor of a movement from childhood to manhood to
capture the spiritually purposeful character of that transition. For the
rationalistically Protestant William Lecky, however, the late dean's prising
of medieval history from confessional grooves informed his own more
secular and sociological conception of the subject. Yet this remained an
unusual, and unsettling, interpretative mode. High Anglicans' continuing
idealisation of medieval religious and social practice was now joined,
among a new generation, by a humanizing progressivism that broke
from the stern ecclesiasticism of their forebears. Evangelical writers held
their strident opposition to the religiously baneful aspects of medievalism
together with a newer recognition that medieval religion had, at least
in some respects, nurtured piety and civilization. To a certain extent,
anti-Catholicism remained vital. G. G. Coulton represented a new

---

[132] The final nineteenth-century British impression was published in 1883:
H.H. Milman, *History of Latin Christianity: including that of the Popes to the pontificate of
Nicolas V*, 4th edn (9 vols, London, 1883).

permutation of that tradition as he cut his authorial teeth at the beginning of the twentieth century, with denunciations of medieval religion that gave voice less to classical Biblicism than to a secularized and scientifically inflected kind of cultural Protestantism. Yet appreciation of the theological and intellectual depths of medieval religion—going beyond Milman— became more general as the attractions of finding spiritual continuities between the medieval past and the progressive present began to spread across denominations and church parties.

William Lecky, a friend of Milman's who developed his historical promise in a sociological rather than a providential direction, appeared to make the dangers of not pursuing the latter course disturbingly visible in his *History of European Morals*. The work resulted from a complex history. Having declined to pursue holy orders in his ancestral Church of Ireland after leaving Trinity College, Dublin, Lecky settled in London in 1866 to pursue a life as a man of letters. There he was elected to the Athenaeum in 1867, and became acquainted with the lights of London literary and political society, including Milman and Russell.[133] Milman's, especially, was to be a guiding hand. In an early essay on 'formative influences', Lecky remarked on how 'the great predicted apostasy, the mystery of iniquity' he had been taught about in his youth, by which he meant the Catholic Church, became much less of a mystery under the later 'influence of the historic method'.[134] Integral to that process of demystification had been his contact with Milman's *Latin Christianity*. In an affectionate essay prompted by the 1900 publication of Arthur Milman's memoir of his father, Lecky hailed the volumes as still the finest ecclesiastical history in English. They were, he wrote, representative of that 'broad stream of English thought' during the nineteenth century which had also gathered Macaulay, Mill, Buckle, and Eliot into its rejuvenating flow, and in relation to which Newman and the Oxford Movement were merely passing disturbances.[135]

Milman's unpartisan historical candour and breadth of research resonated more strongly with Lecky, however, than did his providential conception of medieval religion.[136] Lecky's keen sense of the constraints which Catholicism had imposed on the social and political development of his home country, accentuating his natively anti-dogmatic and unpriestly

---

[133] E. Lecky, *A memoir of the Right Hon. William Edward Hartpole Lecky* (London, 1909), p. [50].
[134] W.E.H. Lecky, 'Formative influences', in his *Historical and political essays*, ed. E. Lecky (London, 1908), p. 98.
[135] [Lecky], 'Dean Milman', pp. 510–12.   [136] *HEM*, i, ix–x.

disposition, coloured his wider approach to ecclesiastical history.[137] His first book, his 1861 *Leaders of Public Opinion in Ireland*, sought to encourage the growth of secular Irish national feeling which would, he hoped, check clerical power and encourage Ireland's mental coalescence with England.[138] The rise of agrarian agitation and popular Ultramontanism sapped this early confidence and, whilst he supported Irish disestablishment in 1869, fostered the growing hostility to nationalism, and doughty support for landlord privilege, which he showed as a Liberal Unionist Member of Parliament for Dublin University after 1895.[139] Though determined to follow Milman in freeing Catholic history from confessional bonds, a resolution in which he was aided by Comte and Buckle, stronger barriers remained in Lecky's mind than in those of many of his English and Scottish contemporaries to regarding Catholicism as a progressive historical force.[140]

This combination of liberal Anglican historiography, early sociology, and an anti-clerical bent pricked and bitten by Irish affairs shaped Lecky's 1869 *History of European Morals*, a study of the causes and results of the transition from Roman to medieval ethics. Lecky began the work with an encomium to the recently deceased dean of St Paul's, and an insistence, reminiscent of Milman, that historical impartiality necessitated the laying aside of 'all considerations of a purely theological or controversial character'. But whereas Milman had found his alternative to theological controversy in a personified and sacralized conception of historical development itself, Lecky posited a more detached relationship between the historian and his subject matter. He would, he pledged, assess the role of the church in Christian Europe as 'a moral agent', in exactly the same way as he would treat the moral influence of the Stoic or Epicurean philosophies on pre-Christian societies.[141] Lecky combined this dispassionate conception of the scholarly office with a theory of intuitive morals, which argued that mankind's innate ability to distinguish between humanity and cruelty was given definite form and content by the often ambivalent influences operative at different stages of society.[142]

The result was that Lecky's *History* treated the Middle Ages less as a scene of divine education than as a kind of laboratory, in which

[137] D. McCartney, *W. E. H. Lecky: historian and politician 1838–1903* (Dublin, 1994), pp. 4–18; J. Spence, 'Lecky, (William) Edward Hartpole (1838–1903)', *ODNB*.
[138] W.E.H. Lecky, *The leaders of public opinion in Ireland* (London, 1861).
[139] Arx, *Progress*, pp. 64–101; McCartney, *Lecky*, pp. 21–2, [85]–113, [162]–185.
[140] On Lecky's engagement with Comte and Buckle, see chapter five of this volume.
[141] *HEM*, i, vii–x.
[142] Ibid., i, [1]–158; on Lecky's conception of intuitive ethics, see chapter five of this volume.

Christianity became one force among many in shaping social morals, and a force that was spread more by external and secondary causes than by its inward and primary powers. Lecky explained the rise of Christianity, not from its innate validity, but by its relation to 'the general tendencies of the age'.[143] Christianity converted the Roman Empire where Judaism, Mithraism, or the Egyptian deities did not, Lecky argued, because it was favoured by a powerful structure, its freedom from local ties, its noble code of ethics, and the great credulity of the age towards signs and wonders.[144] When it came to the benefits of Christianity for medieval society, Lecky did not write of a slow training or a moral transformation, but instead neutrally assembled the advantages alongside the disadvantages of conversion for social and sexual mores and, notably, the position of women. Christian compassion softened, even feminized ethical habits; but the classical political economy which Lecky endorsed, and which many contemporary Irish critics were turning against, showed how the praise of mendicancy and institutional support for idleness were socially counter-productive.[145] The new religion cultivated purity; but its medieval ascetic form caused undue revulsion from sensuality.[146] Christianity exalted the feminine virtues of gentleness and humility, and the Catholic reverence for the Virgin improved the ideal of womanhood; but asceticism degraded women by blaming them for all ills, and by insisting on mystical lifelong matrimony, Christianity obscured the advantages of other forms of union.[147] Although Lecky allowed that there were exceptions to Catholicism's deadening historical effects, he never tried to invest them with divine qualities.

Lecky, the patriotic but pessimistic Anglo-Irishman, thus explained how the age of Catholic theology, still continuing in some parts of the world, had repressed society as much as it had advanced it.[148] He was no polemical secularist, however. Lecky identified with the Christian rationalism of Joseph Butler and Richard Whately.[149] He did not argue that early medieval Europe represented a degeneration from heathenism, but emphasized that Christianity had sacralized human life and brotherhood.[150] If this did not prevent inquisitorial killings or abolish slavery, it

---

[143] *HEM*, i, 410. [144] Ibid., i, 357–498.

[145] Ibid., ii, 96–106; T.A. Boylan and T.P. Foley, *Political economy and colonial Ireland: the propagation and ideological function of economic discourse in the nineteenth century* (London and New York, 1992), esp. pp. [113]–156; C. Boylan, 'Ireland, religion and reform: Archbishop Richard Whately, 1831–63', (Oxford Univ. Dphil thesis, 2008).

[146] *HEM*, ii, 107–48. [147] Ibid., ii, 292–392. [148] Ibid., ii, 16, 219–20.

[149] Lecky, 'Formative influences', pp. [90]–103.

[150] Jeffrey Paul von Arx, seemingly conflating Lecky's dim view of theology with his estimation of Christianity, characterises the *HEM* as 'about historical retrogression': *Progress*, pp. 93–101.

at least established a new ideal, and dignity for the servile classes.[151] Even if
Christianity had spread by natural influences, therefore, these had ultimately served moral ends; and he later expressed satisfaction when he
learned that a speaker had used his *History* to rout an atheist lecturer at
a public debate in London.[152] But he maintained that Christianity could
not realise its inherent potential to regenerate the world until the sixteenth
century, when theologians' rule over the human mind came to an end.[153]
This was a theme which Lecky had explored in his earlier *History of
Rationalism*, a recognizably liberal Protestant companion volume to his
European Morals, examining European intellectual progress since the
Reformation and which, it appears, had first brought Lecky to Milman's
approving attention.[154]

Although Lecky's historical sympathies ultimately lay with the simple
gospel, and not unbelief, a number of reviewers faulted him for treating
the Christianisation of Europe as the product of chance, ultimately
dependent upon the vagaries of social circumstance rather than the
internal powers of the faith. Charles Merivale, whom Gladstone nominated to the deanery of Ely in 1869 after he declined the Regius Professorship of Modern History at Cambridge, was one such critic.[155] Though
disinclined to identify with any church party, Merivale had been among
the mourners behind the coffin at Milman's funeral in St Paul's whilst he
was serving as chaplain to the House of Commons, and he shared more of
his friend's historical sensibility than Lecky did.[156] Writing in the *North
British Review* for 1869, by which time the journal had shed its earlier Free
Church leanings in favour of a religiously broader outlook, Merivale
connected Lecky's *History of European Morals* to his earlier attempt in
the *History of Rationalism* 'to trace our modern discoveries in moral truth
to the defeat and discomfiture of all ideas founded upon the belief in the
supernatural'.[157] Lecky's book conjured eighteenth-century spectres. He
was a 'philosophical' historian, at pains to show 'the sufficiency of strictly
natural causes' for Christianity's success. Merivale nevertheless distanced
himself from older ecclesiastical writers who attributed the conversion of
the world 'to a continuous miracle'. The divine counsels lay in 'the
preparation of the world for Christianity', rather than in interventions in

[151] *HEM*, ii, 19–91.   [152] Lecky, *Memoir*, p. 79.   [153] *HEM*, ii, 18–19.
[154] Bodleian Library, Oxford, Milman letters, MS Eng. lett. d. 166/42–43: W.E.H. Lecky
to H.H. Milman, 4 March 1865.
[155] J.M. Rigg, rev. J.D. Pickles, 'Merivale, Charles (1808–1893)', *ODNB*.
[156] [Anon.], 'Funeral of the Dean of St Paul's', *Standard*, 2 October 1868, p. 6. The
correspondent gave his name as 'the Rev. Herman Merivale, chaplain of the House of
Commons'; apparently confusing Charles with his brother, the economist.
[157] [C. Merivale], 'History of European Morals', *NBR*, 50:100 (1869), p. 383.

the actual course of its conquests. Yet Christianity was not merely continuous with the paganism of the ancient world. 'We must insist strongly on the scandal of the Cross of Christ', so unlike anything in the heathenism it ultimately overcame.[158] There were failures in the working out of Christian ethics, in the past as in the present, but the gospel did not undertake to make the world righteous: it was given primarily to reconcile God to man.[159]

Merivale's own interpretation of the period covered by Lecky, expounded in his 1864 and 1865 Boyle Lectures given in the Chapel Royal in Whitehall, ran in a very different direction to that which the latter had adopted. These addresses, examining the conversions of the Roman Empire and of 'the northern nations', were sermons as much as they were historical lectures. Merivale described his audience as his 'congregation', and used a scriptural passage for the heading of each address.[160] The primary aim of both series, he explained, was 'to impress upon the hearer or reader the conviction' that there had always been a 'gradual and constant preparation of mankind' under providence 'for the full development of religious life under the revelation of Jesus Christ'.[161] Merivale treated the religion's development over time, and its slow permeation of European societies, in the personalized, soulful terms of the ages of man which Milman had used, but which Lecky had left to one side. Thus he took as his theme for his lecture on the 'expansion of Heathen belief by the ideas of Roman jurisprudence' the Arnoldian moral of Galatians 3:24: 'the law was our schoolmaster to bring us unto Christ.'[162] Conversion to Catholicism laid the foundations of Protestant moral responsibility amongst the Teutonic races. With more of the religious liberalism of Frederick Temple than that of Matthew Arnold, Merivale challenged modern philosophers, with their 'natural filiation from the sceptics of Greece and Rome', to give a biological account of the spiritual movements of history.[163]

Merivale was thus led to his rebuttal of Lecky by his conviction that the history of religion answered materialist interpretations of human experience. The idea that medieval Christendom should not be attacked, but instead reinterpreted as an educative phase of human progress that

---

[158] Ibid., p. 390.   [159] Ibid., pp. 404–5.

[160] C. Merivale, *The conversion of the Roman Empire: the Boyle Lectures for the year 1864 delivered at the Chapel Royal, Whitehall* (London, 1864), [vii]–viii.

[161] Merivale, *The conversion of the northern nations: the Boyle Lectures for the year 1865 delivered at the Chapel Royal, Whitehall* (London, 1866), x.

[162] Merivale, *Roman Empire*, viii–xv, p. 64.

[163] Merivale, *Northern nations*, pp. 56–96, 118–58, here at 86–7; Temple, 'The education of the world'.

vindicated the reality of providence, became a widespread motif in the late-Victorian public sphere. The Society for Promoting Christian Knowledge published a popular rendition of the dean of Ely's account of the Christianisation of the Teutons, notably informed by Milman, in its new series on the *Conversion of the West* launched in 1878.[164] Latin Christianity, wrote Milman's broad church admirer, George Cox, prepared the Teuton for that 'spontaneous obedience to law' and 'versatile freedom' in favour of which he revolted at the Reformation. It was these qualities, Cox believed, that lay at the basis of constitutional government and tolerant, inquiring religion.[165] The Idealist Church of Scotland historian, George Matheson, comparably treated medieval religion, and especially scholastic philosophy, as representing Christianity's school life in his 1877 *Growth of the Spirit of Christianity*, a two-volume speculative history published by T. & T. Clark. The movement of progress in the Middle Ages, observed the sometime Glasgow pupil of John Caird's, was towards 'mind over matter', 'intellect over force', 'human liberty over the chains of slavery'.[166] By 'the dawn of the Lutheran era', these forces were ready to claim their religious rights.

The liberal Protestant idea that the medieval dispensation, though valuable in its time, had passed into obsolescence with the coming of Teutonic maturity was not one that a vigorous high church scholarly tradition could readily endorse. For these writers, the Middle Ages remained a source of authoritative precedents. With time, however, the period could also become in their eyes a kind of kindling-fire of modern Europe, albeit one whose rightful energy was not, as more liberal minds supposed, extinguished at the Reformation. Old high church historians writing in the second half of the century, though showing a new attentiveness to the social and cultural breadth of church history, continued to treat the period as a normative resource for delimiting the proper province of ecclesiastical institutions, and for vindicating the anti-papal rights of national churches.[167] In a more Tractarian register, William Stubbs, sometime disciple of Pusey and Oxford's Regius Professor of Modern History from 1866 until his elevation to the see of Chester in 1884,

---

[164] C. Merivale, *Conversion of the West: thecontinental Teutons* (London, 1878), pp. 154–5, 163–4.

[165] G.W. Cox, *Latin and Teutonic Christendom: an historical sketch* (London, 1870), vi–vii, pp. 13–14, 216–18.

[166] G. Matheson, *Growth of the spirit of Christianity to the dawn of the Lutheran era* (2 vols, London, 1877), ii, 394; D. Macmillan, *The life of George Matheson D.D., LL.D., F.R.S.E.* (London, 1907), pp. 24–46, 87–129.

[167] J.C. Robertson, *History of the Christian church* (4 vols, London, 1854–1873); C. Hardwick, *A history of the Christian church: Middle Age* (Cambridge, 1853). The latter reached a third edition, under Stubbs's editorship, in 1872.

ululated over the dissolution of ecclesiastical charitable endowments at the Reformation in his *Constitutional History of England*.[168]

For other members of the Oxford Movement's second generation of adherents, however, abiding commitment to the authoritative character of the Middle Ages could pass into a newer and significantly different interest in the progressive connections subsisting between medieval Christianity and modern civilization. The writings of Richard William Church gave voice to that tonal modification. Church had been an undergraduate at Oriel College, Oxford, in the 1830s, where in common with his approximate contemporary Mark Pattison he fell under Newman's spell. Unlike Pattison's, however, Church's high church allegiance was to be lifelong, though it was rendered less mortifying and more cosmopolitan than that of the Oxford fathers by his upbringing in Florence as the son of a wine merchant. Having co-founded the *Guardian* newspaper in 1846, he devoted his years after vacating his Oriel fellowship in 1852 to religious journalism, parish ministry, and historical scholarship. He became dean of St Paul's in 1871, after the death of H. L. Mansel, Milman's successor in that preferment.[169]

Running through Church's historical writings was his belief, one emphatically not shared by his Tractarian forebears, that the historian of Christianity should join together the relative claims of divinely authored secular civilization and absolute religion in an imaginative unity.[170] Reviewing Lecky's *European Morals* for the leading literary review, *Macmillan's Magazine*, in 1869, Church argued that its author's deliberate separation of positive religious profession from historical analysis led him to miss the leading truth about medieval Europe: that it was a self-reforming, self-renovating period of law that necessarily preceded the growth of freedom.[171] Church thus reiterated, in an important respect, the characteristic theme of liberal Anglican writers. But Newman's admirer made it clear in his essays and occasional pieces that he believed Stanley and Milman to suffer from something of the same externality—that cool

---

[168] W. Stubbs, *The constitutional history of England in its origin and development*, library edn (3 vols, Oxford, 1880), iii, 647–8 (first edition 1873–1878); J. Kirby, 'An ecclesiastical descent: religion and history in the work of William Stubbs', *Journal of Ecclesiastical History*, 65:1 (2014), pp. 84–110; J. Campbell, 'Stubbs, William (1825–1901)', *ODNB*.

[169] G. Martin Murphy, 'Church, Richard William (1815–1890)', *ODNB*.

[170] R.W. Church, 'Carlyle's Cromwell', in his *Occasional papers selected from the Guardian, the Times, and the Saturday Review 1846–1890*, ed. M.C. Church (London, 1897), pp. [1]–3; R.W. Church, *Civilization and religion: a sermon preached before the University of Oxford, at St. Mary's Church, on the fifth Sunday in Lent, March 29, 1868* (Oxford and London, 1868).

[171] [R.W. Church], 'Lecky's 'History of European Morals'', *MM*, 20:115 (1869), pp. 76–88.

indifference to the inward and intellectual power of historic Christianity—which desiccated Lecky's writing.[172]

Church therefore applied himself to developing a more spiritualized interpretation of the theological and worldly forces which had first entwined civilization and Christianity together during the conversion of Europe. Milman's institution of evening services at St Paul's, under pressure from Bishop Tait of London, afforded Church an opportunity to deliver occasional lectures to his congregation, in one of which he mused that the decay of Rome's admirable political and ethical traditions into sceptical and oriental habits arose from its lack of an eternal spring of spiritual renewal.[173] The coming of Christianity, separating the ancient from the modern world, provided the source of moral seriousness and commitment to human dignity that Rome lacked. Church's 1877 study, *The Beginning of the Middle Ages*, explored how these attributes of the new religion had shaped secular phenomena into earthly footstools of the heavenly kingdom. Playing down the deterministic importance some ascribed to race, Church thought of the Latins and Teutons not so much as active powers as soils to which religion gave form. To the warlike Teutons, the church taught the value of persuasion and hope in place of the brute force to which they were accustomed.[174] The conversion of the Latins to the religion of the Beatitudes, he told a lecture audience in St Paul's, softened their old hardness, explaining why Italy later became the spring of art and poetry. The transition, as Church made use of Matthew Arnold to explain, was symbolized by the difference between the repressed religious emotion of Marcus Aurelius' *Meditations* and Augustine's *Confessions*, where feelings for the divine had learned to pour out their fullness.[175] Latin Christianity was no less a purposeful and educative force in Church's account than in Milman's. But for the urbane Tractarian, its relevance to modern individuality had not yet receded into the past. Similar arguments began to filter into more popular attempts at high church edification. 'You have all heard of the crusades...?', the author of a moderately Anglo-Catholic Sunday school primer of 1902,

---

[172] R.W. Church, 'Stanley on the study of ecclesiastical history', and 'Dean Milman's essays', in his *Occasional papers*, pp. [66]–73, [155]–65.

[173] Church, 'Civilisation before and after Christianity: two lectures delivered in St. Paul's Cathedral, at the Tuesday evening services, January 23rd & 30th, 1872', in his *The gifts of civilisation and other sermons and lectures delivered at Oxford and at St Paul's*, new edn (London, 1880), pp. [147]–76; Church, *Dean Church*, p. 209.

[174] R.W. Church, *The beginning of the middle ages* (London, 1895), pp. 56–63. (First edition 1877.)

[175] Church, 'Christianity and the Latin races', in his *Gifts of civilisation*, pp. [254]–99.

Georgiana Forde, asked her pupils. 'The crusades helped to waken people up and enlarge their ideas', she continued.[176]

The coexistence of progressive and pluralistic perspectives with older typologies was also evident, in a different way, amongst the self-consciously Protestant writers who rose to prominence after 1850. These authors did not shed their historic antipathy to the ecclesiastical tradition which high churchmen, in changing senses, continued to venerate. But that hostility came to be joined, and sometimes weakened, by their growing awareness of the medieval church's services to society, and even to religious edification. Evangelicals continued vigorously to expose what they took to be the religious weaknesses of the medieval church, now seeing the need to rebut newer ideas of history which presented these as unimportant or temporarily beneficial. John Stoughton's 1855 Congregational Lectures on the *Ages of Christendom* dissented from the newly fashionable opinion that medieval Catholicism's obscuration of timeless Christian verities could be ignored or excused on the grounds that it had contributed to the advance of civilization. Stoughton interpreted the progressive degeneration of the institutional church from apostolic purity, via patristic innovation, to medieval traditionalism as a cycle of corruption latterly repeated in the course of the Oxford Movement. Probably alluding to that facet of Milman's argument which had also irked his more hardline reviewers, Stoughton rejected the idea that medievalism amounted to 'a kind of intermediate dispensation' akin to Judaism, for this was to imply that 'the system had a sort of Divine sanction'.[177] Amongst evangelical Anglicans, the anti-ritualist Henry Wace continued keenly to feel medieval religion's failings. The historical component of his *Foundations of Faith* leapt straight from 'the faith of the early church' to 'the faith of the Reformation', bypassing the intervening centuries.[178] In his Warburton Lectures for 1894 to 1898, Wace reiterated a prophetic interpretation of papal history of the kind that also persisted amongst conservative Presbyterian historians in Scotland and Ulster. 'Now little as we may be disposed to denounce another communion, we cannot, as Protestant churchmen, disguise our belief that a great apostasy, and an apostasy bearing a great resemblance to some of the marks indicated by St Paul, has arisen in the Christian Church.'[179]

---

[176] G.M. Forde, *A goodly heritage: a simple church history* (London, 1902), pp. 124–5. On Sunday school culture in the period, see S.J.D. Green, *Religion in the age of decline: organization and experience in industrial Yorkshire, 1870–1920* (Cambridge, 1996).

[177] Stoughton, *Ages of Christendom*, pp. 327–8, 453.

[178] Wace, *Foundations of Faith*, pp. [138]–88.

[179] H. Wace, *Prophecy Jewish and Christian considered in a series of Warburton lectures at Lincoln's Inn* (London, 1911), pp. 189–90; cf. J.A. Wylie, *The history of Protestantism*

Wace's semi-embarrassed reference to the importance of ecumenical sentiment was nevertheless significant. For even evangelicals who continued sharply to protest against the evils of the medieval clerical caste and its modern successors, made more of a distinction than their forebears had done between the falsity of an ecclesiastical system and the ways in which other aspects of medieval Christianity had guided civilization, or nurtured healthful forms of thought and piety. Even though 'a terrible temptation was placed in the hands of a hierarchy' in the medieval era, Wace explained in his introduction to a collection of Luther's works, 'these ages had been a stern school of moral and religious discipline', entrusted with 'the special mission . . . to tame the fierce energies of the new barbarian world'.[180]

Stoughton's earlier suspicion of the relativizing implications of the argument Wace here countenanced underwent significant modification over time. It had always coexisted with a desire to expand his readers' ideas of the operation of the Holy Spirit during a period of darkness. His *Ages of Christendom*, though it warned against the dangers of medievalism, quarried Neander for worthy instances of medieval piety.[181] Stoughton developed this theme more distinctly in his later *Introduction to Historical Theology*, published as a students' handbook in 1880 by the Religious Tract Society. Medieval hymnody, which the archbishop of Dublin R. C. Trench's *Sacred Latin Poetry* helped him to appreciate, and the underestimated sermons of those days, led Stoughton to argue that the medieval church shared more extensively than was sometimes acknowledged in that stream of evangelical experience which ran from the primitive era down to the present day.[182] Medieval art, he wrote, composed 'sermons . . . in stone'.[183] Mystical and scholastic writings showed that 'the theoretical divinity of Christendom' was far higher than its 'actual life', and so contained 'hope for the future'.[184] It was perhaps not so great a leap to move from this outlook, to an implicit acceptance in his old age of the educative view of medieval religion which he had once dismissed. His

---

(3 vols, London, Paris, and New York, 1874-1877), i, 22–3; W.D. Killen, *The Old Catholic Church: or the history, doctrine, worship, and polity of the Christians traced from the apostolic age to the establishment of the Pope as temporal sovereign, A.D. 755* (Edinburgh, 1871), p. 394 and n.

[180] H. Wace, 'On the primary principles of Luther's life and teaching', in Wace and C.A. Buchheim (eds), *First principles of the Reformation or the Ninety-Five Theses and the three primary works of Martin Luther* (London, 1883), xi–xiii.

[181] Stoughton, *Ages of Christendom*, pp. 311–12 and n.

[182] Stoughton, *Historical theology*, pp. 287–306; R.C. Trench, *Sacred Latin poetry, chiefly lyrical, selected and arranged for use; with notes and introduction* (London, 1849).

[183] Stoughton, *Historical theology*, pp. 299–300.   [184] Ibid., pp. 361–2.

later writings showed notable respect for Milman and Merivale.[185] In the preface to his *Golden Legends of the Olden Time*, a work consisting mainly of stories about medieval saints, Stoughton accepted that legends derived from 'the childish ages of Christendom'. It was true, nevertheless, that grown men and women 'can find even in childish things profit as well as pleasure' once they had followed the Pauline injunction to put them away.[186] Spiritual manhood's overmastering of religious childhood, which Temple and other liberal Protestants were inclined to celebrate, was something that Stoughton's growing sense of gratitude to the medieval church led him to temper. His subsequent autobiographical acknowledgement that the Protestant reaction to 'Papal Aggression', against which he had himself once petitioned the Queen, had been, in retrospect, 'unreasonable', was of a piece with the ameliorative character of his later works.[187]

There were evangelical critics for whom the two-mindedness shown towards medieval religion by Stoughton or Wace passed into a more insistently affirmative desire to incorporate it into a providential conception of the world's growth as a whole. Some explicitly related the point to the challenge of unbelief. Thomas Martin Lindsay, lecturing to his students at the Free Church's Glasgow theological college in 1875, intoned that what the Enlightenment had miscalled 'the Dark Ages' were in fact 'instinct with the beginnings of that life' whose manhood Europe was now experiencing. 'For a century to come I venture to say that part of the battle between Christianity and the unchristian spirit will be fought out on the field of mediaeval history.'[188] Principal Cairns comparably used the period, replete with national conversions and orthodox religious philosophy, to demonstrate how Christianity had a unique capacity to '"renew its youth"'—paraphrasing Milman—in a popular pamphlet on Christian evidences which he wrote for the Religious Tract Society.[189] The Methodist historian, Herbert Brook Workman, placed the idea that the child had first to learn obedience, before the youth could start to learn the higher truths of the soul, at the heart of his more scholarly 1898

---

[185] Stoughton, *Primitive Christendom*, pp. 206–7 and n. 1; Stoughton, *Church life*, pp. 290 and n. 1, 342–3 and n. 1.

[186] J. Stoughton, *Golden legends of the olden time* (London, 1885), xii; cf. 1 Cor. 13:11. On the rehabilitation of saints in the period, see G. Atkins (ed.), *Making and remaking saints in nineteenth-century Britain* (Manchester, 2016).

[187] Stoughton, *Recollections*, pp. [101]–03.

[188] Lindsay, 'The study of church history', p. 97.

[189] [J.] Cairns, *Christ the central evidence of Christianity and other present-day tracts* (London, 1893), pp. 16–17.

Church of the West in the Middle Ages.[190] He listed Milman, Neander, Thomas Carlyle, and R. W. Church among his favoured authorities.[191] Slightly later, Workman came to advocate a vision of spiritual history in which Catholicism here, Methodism there, became but transient phases of faith in the steady movement of the world towards some unseen goal.[192] Anti-Catholicism, in Workman as in many others, faded away as a distinctive intellectual position as Catholicism, as well as their own churches, came to seem as moments in the progressively unfolding mind of God.

As evangelical hostility to medieval religion lost something of its older systematism, and sometimes all but dissolved, the inscrutably agnostic G. G. Coulton's early writings articulated a newer, semi-secularized variety of anti-Catholicism at the turn of the twentieth century. Coulton had drifted away from Christian belief since his ordination to the diaconate in 1883. But the autobiography he wrote towards the end of his life, which spoke of the churches' services to civilization and his anxiety over what would become of the social benefits of the Anglican parish system in 'an unclerical age', recorded the culturally Protestant commitments that had powerfully informed the medieval researches which first made his name.[193] His preface to his 1906 edition of the fourteenth-century English poem *Pearl*, in which a deceased daughter returned to extend heavenly consolations to her grieving father in a dream, expressed satisfaction at the text's display of the '"evangelical rather than ecclesiastical"' attitude of 'the Englishman' of those days.[194]

The counterpart to Coulton's interest in Protestant origins was the highly negative estimation of medieval religion that informed his edition of the chronicle of the thirteenth-century Italian Franciscan, Salimbene, which appeared in the same year. 'Medieval history', he complained, 'has been too exclusively given over the poet, the romancer, and the ecclesiastic'; Coulton's aversion to what he regarded as Catholic historical dishonesty registered his consciously modernizing commitment to 'the scientific spirit'.[195] Although Coulton understood that spirit to require

---

[190] H.B. Workman, *The church of the west in the middle ages* (2 vols, London, 1898).

[191] Ibid., i, 91–4, 246, ii, ix.

[192] H.B. Workman, *The place of Methodism in the catholic church*, new edn (London, 1921); the piece had first appeared in 1909 as the introduction to W.B. Townsend, G. Eayrs and H.B. Workman (eds), *A new history of Methodism* (2 vols, London, 1909), i, 3–73.

[193] Coulton, *Fourscore years*, pp. 299, 350.

[194] Coulton, *Pearl: a fourteenth-century poem* (London, 1906), vi-vii.

[195] Coulton, *From Francis to Dante: a translation of all that is of primary interest in the chronicle of the Franciscan Salimbene; (1221–1288) together with notes and illustrations from other medieval sources* (London, 1906), [v], pp. 8–9.

the integration of church history with social history, Salimbene's testimony disclosed that there had been no 'harmonious growth of one great body through the Middle Ages' such as romantic reactionaries and liberal historians had, in their different ways, imagined.[196] Rather, Salimbene showed that medieval history was really 'a history of many divergent opinions violently strangled at birth'. In the Italy of his day, proto-puritan monasticism, scandalous corruptions, unhygienic friars, worldly prelates, unscrupulous factions, murderous inquisitors, persecuted heretics, and worthily indignant commentators such as Dante and Salimbene himself clashed and struggled for air, before the Reformation pointed the way to the liberation and consecration of civilized life.[197] Coulton's unsentimentally Darwinian metaphor expressed his own sense of moral distance from Catholic history. It also conveyed his post-theological conception of history as a whole. Where believing historians had become widely inclined to deploy personal and soulful images to understand medieval history, and historians of early orthodoxy had sometimes invoked more spiritual images of biological evolution to depict doctrinal history, Coulton's understanding of historical movement quietly removed providence from human time.[198]

Coulton's uncompromising hostility to Catholicism was, by the time he was writing, notably unusual. With a certain irony, it reflected his secular-minded distance from the theological kinds of historicism that increasingly enabled orthodox Protestants to incorporate its history within a spiritualized narrative structure. The lingering Enlightenment criticism and the heightened evangelical and high church agitation of the early Victorian years variously impugned and extolled medieval religion, treating it as a proxy for present-day Catholicism and the intellectual and societal attitudes it supposedly represented. But amongst liberal Protestants of Milman's type, and, less uniformly, high churchmen and evangelicals too, the belief that the period represented a phase in the education of the world exercised a growing appeal. It was an idea that helped early-Victorian ecclesiastical contentions to continue to recede, and creeping, secular understandings of the medieval church to be contained. The growing apologetic importance of the belief that no formative historical period had been a mistake, and the assumption that a progressive society could not safely cast aside its religious inheritances, were also to shape how Victorian moralists understood their Protestant ancestry.

---

[196] Ibid., pp. 34–5.   [197] Ibid., p. 68.
[198] See chapter two of this volume at pp. 86–90.

4

Reformation Protestantism

HISTORIC PROTESTANTISM AND MODERN CULTURE

> All which Protestantism was to itself clearly conscious of, all which it succeeded in clearly setting forth in words, had the characters of Hebraism rather than of Hellenism.[1]

Matthew Arnold's limpid deconstructions of his countrymen's supposedly Philistine narrowness in his 1869 *Culture and Anarchy* relied on the assumption that the historical forces of the Reformation era remained active agents in a fragmented present. The oppositions he established between active, Biblicist 'Hebraism' and reflective, humane 'Hellenism' would, he hoped, encourage his contemporaries to sweeten and lighten the overbearing puritanism he thought to be stifling culture, which was properly the study of perfection, by rediscovering the principles prized by Greece and the Renaissance. Arnold, son of the broad church patriarch Thomas Arnold and a votary of the *Bildungsstaat*, emphasized the civilizing influence of the national church and national education in making 'reason and the will of God prevail'.[2] In *Culture and Anarchy*'s less-remembered successor-volume of 1870, *St Paul and Protestantism*, Arnold applied a particular idea of the history of Protestant doctrine to the same end. Contemporary philistine 'Hebraisers', he wrote, depended on Luther's and Calvin's cramped understanding of the Pauline epistles, which construed religion as a mechanism for instantaneous salvation through acceptance of the doctrines of predestination and justification by faith alone. The revival of 'philosophy and criticism' since 'the Renascence', however, ensured that what Goethe had called the '*Zeit-Geist*' was slowly leading critical opinion to recognize Paul's original master-idea of religion, which expressed Hebraism's true rather than its distorted self.[3]

---

[1] Arnold, *Culture and anarchy*, p. 103.   [2] Ibid., p. 34.
[3] M. Arnold, *St. Paul and Protestantism; with an introduction on puritanism and the Church of England* (London, 1870), xi, pp. 3, 34–6, 104.

This was *'the desire for righteousness'*.[4] To Arnold, it was the national church's special obligation here to manifest 'the principle of development' in doctrine which Newman had been right to defend, albeit in too narrowly ecclesiastical terms.[5] An historic church that overcame the errors of historic Protestantism, Arnold assumed, would thus lead latter-day Puritans towards the ethical idea of religion which culture had attained.[6]

Arnold's essayistic swipes at his contemporaries marked him out as a decidedly advanced critic. He was far more equivocal than many of his contemporaries had been in welcoming the supersession of Christianity's Latin by its Teutonic form. Committed to the study of medieval Celtic literature as a means of infusing Anglo-Saxon sturdiness with sentiment and gaiety, and vocally sympathetic to the imaginative 'poetry' of Catholicism, he hoped to improve the English and British national types by bringing native puritanism into contact with these more cosmopolitan influences.[7] But in his assumption that post-Reformation Protestantism remained a pervasive and sometimes problematic influence in British culture, and by bringing it into evaluative relationship with European and universal frameworks, Arnold was joined by many who approved of the Reformation's original achievement, as well as those who disparaged it. This chapter reconstructs the texture of that longer-running argument. More so than when Victorian critics thought about the early church or medieval religion, Protestantism was immediately their own. Evangelicals, anti-Protestant Tractarians, liberal Protestants, and secularizing thinkers all found themselves drawn towards the age during which Protestantism had held supreme social and intellectual sway in Britain and much of Europe, a period generally taken by Victorians to encompass a 'long Reformation' running from the sixteenth to the later seventeenth centuries.[8] The era provided them with a vocabulary for debating two central and interrelated questions. These centred on whether Protestant doctrine was true or not, and whether the culture that had grown out of that teaching had benefited European civilization, or else discoloured it.

As Protestantism came to be regarded as the product of historical development, and a factor in historical progress, conventional understandings

---

[4] Ibid., p. 97.   [5] Ibid., p. 24–30.   [6] Ibid., pp. 70–1.

[7] M. Arnold, *On the study of Celtic literature* (London, 1867); Arnold, 'Irish Catholicism and British Liberalism', in his *Essays religious and mixed*, ed. R.H. Super (Ann Arbor, MI, 1972), pp. 321–47 (repr. from the *FR* for 1878). Arnold wrote of Philistinism as a British, and not solely as an English phenomenon: 'the body of British Protestant dissenters' amounted, in his view, to 'the Church of the Philistines': *Paul and Protestantism*, xxvii.

[8] J. Morris, 'Afterword', in P. Nockles and V. Westbrook (eds), *Reinventing the Reformation in the nineteenth century: a cultural history*, *Bulletin of the John Rylands Library*, 90:1 (2014), p. 379.

of its meaning and value changed substantially. It became clear that classical Protestant orthodoxy did not reprise unmediated the tenets of scripture, but possessed a history of its own. The Reformation, it became more and more plausible to argue, did not descend to earth by a sudden outpouring of divine grace, but grew from the soils of later medieval Europe. Critics of Protestantism, seeing in it the lingering scholasticism of the Middle Ages, enthusiastic novelty, or a tumorous extrusion from secular history, turned these historicist perceptions against it. It was more common, however, for historical study to forge Protestant commitment anew. Liberal and, increasingly, conservative Protestant historians and theologians became inclined to melt Reformation religion from the dogmatic moulds into which it had been hastily poured and imperfectly set, so that the hot metal might be refashioned for a new age. The idea that Protestantism grew out of, or disciplined, antecedent currents of religious and aesthetic reform reinforced the newly contentious case that the Reformation constituted the foundation stone of modern culture.

These apologetic shifts tell against Peter Nockles' recent suggestion that the significant transformation in Victorian conceptions of the Reformation lay in a movement from the sectarian and evangelical assumptions predominant at the beginning of the period, to the ascendancy of secular and liberal nationalist ones at its end.[9] There were certainly historians who sought thoroughly to secularize the Reformation's historical significance, or to apply Reformation history to secularist ends. But even around 1900, these positions remained knowingly counter-cultural points on a spectrum of responses. They should be distinguished from attempts by Victorian prophets to shake their contemporaries out of what they took to be complacent forms of identification with the Reformation and the values it expressed. James Anthony Froude's crisis-stricken belief that the historical conditions which had given power and intellectual authority to Protestant theology had passed away gave a melancholy tincture to his efforts to reinvigorate Protestantism as a cultural principle.[10] Froude's mentor, the convulsively heterodox Thomas Carlyle, reproached his countrymen by leading the mid-Victorian rehabilitation of puritanism and the erstwhile tyrant, Oliver Cromwell.[11] But their pessimism over

[9] P. Nockles, 'The Reformation revised? The contested reception of the English Reformation in nineteenth-century Protestantism', in Nockles and Westbrook, *Reinventing the Reformation*, pp. [231]–56.

[10] On Froude, see C. Brady, *James Anthony Froude: an intellectual biography of a Victorian prophet* (Oxford, 2013), pp. 247–9; Garnett, 'Protestant histories'.

[11] R. Samuel, 'The discovery of Puritanism, 1820–1914: a preliminary sketch', in Garnett and Matthew, *Revival and religion*, pp. 201–47; on the afterlife of Victorian-era puritanism in the next century, see M. Grimley, 'The religion of Englishness: Puritanism,

the outlook for conventional Protestantism was the counterpart of a more constructive wish fundamentally to overhaul national religion, in ways that drew upon Protestant tradition. Whether in the relatively moderate forms sought by authors and preachers at the conventional centre of Victorian Protestantism, or the radical ones promoted by the iconoclasts who addressed themselves to that centre, nineteenth-century critics generally hoped for the reconstruction rather than the supersession of Protestantism. They pursued it through newly progressive readings of Protestant history.

The following discussion develops this observation by considering several interrelated trajectories in the nineteenth-century reimagining of the Reformation. Beginning especially in the 1830s, and rumbling on thereafter, polemical exaltation of the religious history of the sixteenth and seventeenth centuries became integral to English and Scottish evangelicals' respective criticisms of Tractarian repudiation and Erastian betrayal of the Reformation inheritance. Reformation history, witnessing to the redemption of fallen humanity by the intervention of divine grace, became a macrocosmic projection of the individual Christian life and the dualistic, atonement-centred theology in terms of which evangelicals across denominations understood it. Reformation era doctrinal standards—the 1571 Thirty-Nine Articles in the Church of England, and the 1646 Westminster Confession to which Scottish Presbyterians subscribed—attracted renewed professions of fidelity in this environment. As theologians became more acquainted with and reliant upon the Articles and the Confession, however, the creeds' ambiguities and historical limitations became more obvious. From around the mid-century, liberal Protestants began to treat these symbols as the product of historical development. They appealed to the underlying principles of the Reformation so as to justify reverent departures from its formal theology. A number of evangelical writers, hoping to reinvigorate a more maximalist view of Reformation fundamentals than liberal Protestants defended, made a similar case. Where developmental historicism had often reinvigorated primitive orthodoxy, it tended to lessen the authority of Reformation-era formularies and systematic theology. The theologians who employed such historicism,

providentialism and "national character," 1918–1945', *Journal of British Studies*, 46:4 (2007), pp. 884–906; cf. Green, *Passing of Protestant England*, pp. 135–79. B. Worden, 'The Victorians and Oliver Cromwell', in Collini, Whatmore, and Young, *History, religion, and culture*, pp. 112–35. On Carlyle and Cromwell, see T. Carlyle, *Oliver Cromwell's letters and speeches, with elucidations*, 2nd edn (3 vols, London, 1846), first edition 1845; B. Worden, 'Thomas Carlyle and Oliver Cromwell', *Proceedings of the British Academy*, 105 (2000), pp. 131–70. On Victorian historians and the wider sociopolitical legacies of the seventeenth century, see Lang, *Victorians and the Stuart heritage*; Bennett, *Victorian high church*.

however, generally did so in order to commend the perennial power of Reformation religion to a generation doubtful of the doctrines of biblical inerrancy or divine vengefulness with which it had popularly and errone-ously been connected. A new fashion redoubled the urgency of that pro-cedure. After 1870, especially, the Reformation's claim to have given birth to the modern spirit came under pressure from secular-minded critics' growing interest in the Renaissance as an alternative locus for that achieve-ment. Liberal and evangelical Protestants, together with Froude, accord-ingly became embroiled in another sphere of debate, which compelled them to re-examine and vindicate the Reformation's role as a progressive moment in world history, rather than simply to assume it.

THE REFORMATION REVIVED

In their struggle against the pretended authority of false religious tradi-tions, nineteenth-century British evangelicals were aided by a distinct sense of tradition of their own. As the passing of the years encouraged Protestant stalwarts to begin to set the evangelical revival they continued to champion in critical retrospect, the Reformation burned brightly as a lodestar of comparison. 'The *theology* of the Evangelical Revival, both in its affirmations and denials, was substantially the theology of the Reforma-tion', R. W. Dale explained to his Carr's Lane congregation in a sermon of 1879.[12] 'This Evangelical Movement links us with the teachers, the heroes, the martyrs of the Reformation in our own country as well as in other countries', wrote one Anglican layman in a later, anti-ritualist volume.[13]

This sense of historical indebtedness had not been absent from the hotter gospellers of earlier times. But it had first arisen in its acute form amidst the historicist impulses and religious fractures of the earlier nine-teenth century. The evangelical answer to Tractarian 'patrolaters' and 'romish' enthusiasts for the Middle Ages was to rediscover and restore the Reformation in its doctrinal purity. Where, exactly, the emphasis was to be placed in Reformation doctrine—justification by faith, scriptural supremacy, the divine decrees, the priesthood of all believers—varied from denomination to denomination, and very often within them. But Prot-estants across Britain who held to a high view of Christ's atonement, felt their reliance upon sovereign grace, and feared the encroachments of

---

[12] R.W. Dale, 'The evangelical revival', in his *Evangelical revival*, p. 18.
[13] R. Temple, 'The evangelical movement in the Church of England', in H. Wace et al., *Church and faith: being essays on the teaching of the Church of England* (Edinburgh and London, 1909), p. 398.

'popery' at home and abroad, all became increasingly inclined to define themselves as the heirs of the Reformers, Puritans, and Covenanters of former days. The fundamental doctrines evangelicals shared with one another also shaped a common view of how history moved. The Reformation, irrupting into the medieval darkness of which it was the luminous anti-type, was to them not the result of worldly development, but of the divine grace that led its champions to restore scriptural truth. Its history was to be approached as a means of exhibiting and promoting that truth, which was often taken to be pristinely distilled in Reformation era creeds. Writers who wished to challenge evangelicalism's understanding of Protestantism, necessarily also had to confront its account of Protestant origins, and of the Reformation's doctrinal results.

Evangelicals in England and Scotland were first led to reassert the Reformation's foundational importance by rising threats to its achievement. Although this affirmation was founded upon a pan-evangelical sense of the Reformation's universal truth, the differences between the two countries' ecclesiastical polities had their effect. In England, the Oxford Movement was amongst the strongest of the negative factors that pushed evangelicals towards a more concretely historical articulation of Protestant traditionalism. The Tractarians shattered the brittle Anglican consensus on the English and European Reformations, and the religious principles to be extracted from them, by adopting a more hostile attitude towards Protestantism than that generally assumed by old high churchmen.[14] The latter, less radical divines valued the English Reformers and doughtily defended the Church of England's right to its rubrics and Articles, as warranted by scripture understood in the light of antiquity.[15] They also accepted that the continental non-episcopal churches were true churches, for they had not found it possible to maintain purity of doctrine alongside the episcopal system during the turbulence of the sixteenth century.[16]

The Tractarians, however, condemned the continental Reformation, and at least the political dimension of the English Reformation, in terms of quasi-Augustinian moral analysis. The sixteenth century seemed to them a period when impetuous spirits, spurred on by political self-interest and overreacting to ecclesiastical abuses, had divided the Catholic Church—or in England's case, either gave or came perilously close to giving the appearance of having dividing it. These theological mistakes had ushered in the modern world, but in no positive sense. James Bowling Mozley and Walter Farquhar Hook blamed what they represented as

[14] Nockles, 'The Reformation revised?'; Nockles, *Oxford Movement*, pp. 20–1.
[15] Ibid., pp. 112–42.   [16] Ibid., pp. 156–7.

Luther's subjective principle of private judgement for planting the seeds of that religious rationalism which had subverted the gospel and destabilized political order in modern times.[17] Like-minded authors lamented the theological and societal implications of the English Reformation in comparable, if significantly qualified ways. In an early example of how critiques of Protestantism often also became criticism of Victorian society, Tractarian and Tractarian-inspired novelists and historians—echoing from a different ideological standpoint the arguments of Thomas Carlyle's contemporaneous *Past and Present*—traced the disintegrative rise of commercialism to the dissolution of the monasteries.[18] Keble's and Newman's posthumous edition of Hurrell Froude's *Remains* scandalized conventional readers by publicizing their subject's belligerent descriptions of the 'shocking' English Reformation as 'a limb badly set'.[19] Unlike continental Protestant churches, however, the post-Reformation Church of England had preserved apostolic succession through its episcopate, and the rule of antiquity. It accordingly possessed the means by which to break the limb in order to right it.

The danger of what was perceived as Oxford's rising popery, which proved difficult to separate from a more general Catholic revival at home and abroad, drove English evangelicals to anchor themselves more definitely in Protestant history. This new interest manifested itself in several ways. English evangelicals' invocations of the Reformation in public controversy, noticeable from the 1820s, became at once more systematically combative and historically particular as pessimism over the prospects of Irish conversion, and alarm at the Oxford Movement, intensified during the 1830s. The first of many commemorations of Protestant events and heroes in nineteenth-century England, the tercentenary of the publication of Miles Coverdale's English Bible, took place in 1835. In a pattern that was to become common, replicated for instance in the commemorations marking Martin Luther's four-hundredth birthday in 1883, the event temporarily drew Anglican and nonconformist evangelicals together.[20] The

---

[17] W.F. Hook, *The three Reformations: Lutheran-Roman-Anglican* (London, 1847), p. 33; J.B. Mozley, 'Luther', reprinted in his *Essays historical and theological* (2 vols, London, 1878), i, 348–54, 425–33.

[18] S.A. Skinner, '"A triumph of the rich": Tractarians and the Reformation', in Nockles and Westbrook, *Reinventing the Reformation*, pp. [69]–91; cf. T. Carlyle, *Past and Present* (London, 1893), pp. [58]–59 (first edition 1843).

[19] Froude, *Remains*, i, 325, 433.

[20] J. Wolffe, 'The commemoration of the Reformation and mid-nineteenth-century evangelical identity', in Nockles and Westbrook, *Reinventing the Reformation*, pp. [49]–68; cf. J. Bennett, 'The British Luther commemoration of 1883–1884 in European context', *Historical Journal* 58:2 (2015), pp. 543–64. Wolffe notes that the Coverdale tercentenary took place shortly before evangelical concerns about Tractarianism became acute.

fragile hope that orthodox Protestant denominations might be drawn to unite on a shared basis in 'Reformation' principles surfaced and resurfaced in the historical imagination of nineteenth-century evangelicalism.

The commemorative and historicist impulses now animating conservative Protestantism informed edificatory publishing initiatives. New editions of dormant Reformation era texts began to circulate, furnishing disputants with intellectual archaeologies for their favoured doctrinal systems. Anglican debates proved especially fruitful in this respect. The evangelical publishers, Seeley and Burnside, announced a new edition of John Foxe's *Acts and Monuments*—the classic text of Protestant martyrology—in the late 1830s, at the height of Tractarian advance.[21] Anti-Tractarian Anglicans, newly aware of the need to assert the Protestant origins of the Church of England, formed the Parker Society in 1840; the evangelical campaigner Anthony Ashley-Cooper, seventh earl of Shaftesbury, served as its president. The Society aimed to republish, in affordable editions, the reformed divinity of the early fathers of the Church of England, including the works of Nicholas Ridley, Edmund Grindal, and John Jewel.[22] The thirteenth and final report of the Council of the Society, issued in December 1855, declared at the completion of the series that these works had been issued because 'they contain proved weapons for the whole encounter with popery, and maintain the doctrine and order of the Church of England against those who afterwards rose up from her own bosom to assault her.'[23] Higher church editors replied to the Parker Society's promotion of Tudor divinity by launching the *Library of Anglo-Catholic Theology*, giving prominence to the more amenable Caroline theology of the next century.[24]

Scottish evangelicals were comparably drawn to celebrate the heroes of their own Reformation, and to reaffirm the historic divinity the latter had composed, by a different kind of challenge. No powerful Scottish party attempted to disavow the Reformation. For a growing number of ministers within the Church of Scotland, however, the establishment had become too forgetful of the spiritual freedoms and responsibilities which

[21] S.R. Cattley and G. Townsend (eds), *The acts and monuments of John Foxe* (8 vols, London, 1837–1841). On this project, see D. Andrew Penny, 'John Foxe's Victorian reception', *Historical Journal*, 40:1 (1997), pp. 111–42.

[22] N. Ridley, *The works of Nicholas Ridley, D.D. sometime lord bishop of London, martyr, 1555*, ed. H. Christmas (Cambridge, 1841); E. Grindal, *The remains of Edmund Grindal, D.D. successively bishop of London, and archbishop of York and Canterbury*, ed. W. Nicholson (Cambridge, 1843); J. Jewel, *The works of John Jewel, Bishop of Salisbury*, ed. J. Ayre (4 vols, Cambridge, 1845–1850).

[23] Prefixed to H. Gough, *A general index to the publications of the Parker Society* (Cambridge, 1855), [iii–iv].

[24] Nockles, *Oxford Movement*, pp. 127–8.

the break with Rome had won for it. The Disruption of 1843, immediately occasioned by a dispute over lay patronage, expressed long-simmering anxieties over state intrusion on the spiritual authority that rightly belonged to presbyteries, and the vitality of the classically Reformed theology embodied in the Calvinist Westminster Confession. The decision of one third of the Church of Scotland's ministers to exit the General Assembly occurred amidst, and further stimulated, the rediscovery and exaltation of Reformation religion by Scotland's conservative Presbyterians. Whilst, from London, Carlyle's praise of John Knox's heroism made no attempt to rescue Calvinist theology, a larger number of contemporary Scots found history to be a means of revivifying their historic divinity.²⁵ Where England's anti-Erastian insurgents turned the mandate of history against the Reformation, Scotland's invoked a defiantly Reformed theological heritage, which they shared with Irish and continental churches.²⁶ The rehabilitation of that inheritance had been underway for some years. Thomas McCrie, an Original Secession minister and author of a much-reprinted 1811 *Life of John Knox*, and James Seaton Reid, an Ulster Presbyterian who served as professor of ecclesiastical and civil history at Glasgow from 1841 to 1851, were early and influential challengers of David Hume's and William Robertson's Enlightened disparagement of the Scottish Reformation.²⁷ 'How criminal must those be', apostrophized McCrie, 'who sitting at ease under the vines and fig-trees...watered by the blood of these patriots...misrepresent their actions, calumniate their motives, and cruelly lacerate their memories!'²⁸ Scotland's experience of the destabilization of its post-Reformation settlement, in common with England's, made it necessary to control the meaning of sixteenth- and seventeenth-century history.

Disruption era Free Churchmen, more than Establishment ministers, idealized Scotland's Reformers, and the Covenanters who had defended their teaching against a Romanizing prelacy backed by the Stuart monarchs. John Tulloch expressed and exemplified the temperamental difference when he wrote in the *Contemporary Review* that Free Churchmen played 'the part of defenders of the pure confessional faith of Scotland, for which

---

²⁵ T. Carlyle, *On heroes, hero-worship and the heroic in history* (London, 1893), pp. 133–41; first edition 1841.

²⁶ A.R. Holmes, 'The Scottish reformations and the origin of religious and civil liberty in Britain and Ireland: Presbyterian interpretations, c. 1800-60', in Nockles and Westbrook, *Reinventing the Reformation*, pp. [135]–53.

²⁷ Ibid.; J. Kirk, 'McCrie, Thomas (1772–1835)', *ODNB*.

²⁸ T. McCrie, *The life of John Knox with biographical notices of the principal Reformers, and sketches of the progress of literature in Scotland, during a great part of the 16th century* (London, Edinburgh, and New York, 1889), p. 15.

the martyrs of the seventeenth century had perished, and the Church had witnessed in its purest days'.[29] Free Church emotions particularly centred on the spiritual independence of presbyteries, God's sovereignty in grace over fallen man, and the supreme authority of the Bible. What, exactly, was involved in the latter two positions, especially, became an increasingly fraught issue as the century wore on; but that saints and martyrs had fought and died for them all was an awful fact. Free Churchmen did not disclaim the names of John Calvin or Calvinism. These terms were etched into their hearts rather less deeply, however, than the memory of Scotland's own Reformers and the persecuted adherents of the Solemn League and Covenant.[30] A set of *Communications on the Principles of the Free Church of Scotland*, representative of this frame of mind, was issued in 1855 by a committee appointed by its General Assembly to defend the position of the church and to vindicate its dramatic separation over ten years earlier. It was replete with allusions to 'the characteristic contendings of our ancestors in the same great cause of Christ's Crown and Covenant' during the anti-popish and anti-Pelagian Scottish Reformation.[31]

Such attitudes died hard. The unbending James Aitken Wylie edited a lavish hagiographical memorial to the *Disruption Worthies*, first published in 1876, intended to instruct a younger generation, with no personal experience of 1843, of the momentous issues on which the Disruption turned. The collection situated Alexander Keith, William Hetherington, and other early Free Church patriarchs on a shared religious plane uniting the Old Testament, the Reformation, the 'killing time', and the nineteenth-century revival. They belonged to 'a party whose theology was in accordance with the standards of the first and second Reformation, and whose principles were those of the Puritans and the Covenanters, and whose preaching, faithful and fervent, had the scarlet thread through it, and the blood-bought salvation in its freeness and fullness, as its constant and urgent theme'.[32] Those who wished to modernize Protestantism, whom early Free Churchmen often castigated as loyal to that impudently secular 'Moderatism' which had withered the eighteenth-century Establishment, would have to

---

[29] J. Tulloch, 'Progress of religious thought in Scotland', *CR*, 29 (1877), p. 538.

[30] British evangelicals generally preferred to stress the moral and voluntary rather than the natural and necessary inability of the sinner, and accordingly often found it difficult to relate to Calvin: D.W. Bebbington, 'Calvin and British evangelicalism in the nineteenth and twentieth centuries', in I. Backus and P. Benedict (eds), *Calvin and his influence, 1509–2009* (Oxford, 2011), pp. 282–305.

[31] 'Preliminary statement', T. McCrie et al., *Communications on the principles of the Free Church of Scotland: issued by the Committee of the General Assembly* (Edinburgh, 1855), p. 2.

[32] [J. Craufurd], The Hon. Lord Ardmillan, 'Introduction', to J.A. Wylie (ed.), *Disruption worthies: a memorial of 1843* (Edinburgh, 1881), xiv–xv.

confront the thought-worlds which their opponents had sought to reanimate.

Important though localized anxieties over Romanism or Erastianism were in fostering the excavation and popularization of Reformation history, the grateful tones in which English and Scottish evangelicals prosecuted these labours also expressed more positive convictions. Evangelicals' determination to overcome anti-Protestant dangers drew energy from the belief that the Reformation represented a universal and ineradicable historical achievement. The spread of popular histories of the Reformation, stressing its benefits for Protestants of all nations, made this awareness newly vivid, and inspired new kinds of Protestant solidarity. Jean Henri Merle d'Aubigné's 1835–1853 *Histoire de la Réformation du Seizième Siècle* gave a particular impetus to the Protestant historical imagination across the English-speaking world, where it was far more widely read in translation than its French text had been in Europe. Merle d'Aubigné expressed an enthusiasm for the Reformation's recovery of the spiritual equality of all believers, and its alignment of social life with godly principles, that ran deeper than the author's declared anti-papal sentiments.[33] Whereas high church Anglicans, especially Tractarians, drew an essential distinction between the episcopal Reformation in England and its schismatic continental varieties, Merle d'Aubigné powerfully answered British evangelicals' wish to hear of the Reformation's universal restoration of the truths of *sola scriptura* and justification by faith alone. His romanticized Calvinist allegiances, tinctured with a modishly pietistic sensibility indebted to August Neander, told in his reverence for the sovereignty of God over history. But his pan-European narrative focus, incorporating the German, English, and Swiss Reformations into the history of a common achievement, reflected his belief that the Reformation should engage the imaginations of all mankind.[34] The popularity of the itinerant Genevan pastor and luminary of the international and cross-denominational Evangelical Alliance, formed in 1846, soon rivalled that of the Milners in evangelical circles.[35]

[33] J.H. Merle d'Aubigné, *Histoire de la Réformation du seizième siècle* (5 vols, Paris and Geneva, 1835–1853). Partly in order to establish a standard English text to replace an array of unauthorized and, to his mind, inadequate renderings, Merle cooperated with one translation project in particular: Merle d'Aubigné, *History of the Reformation of the sixteenth century*, trans. H. White (5 vols, Edinburgh, 1846–1853), i, [3]–7, iv, [iii].

[34] Merle d'Aubigné, *Histoire*, i, [i].

[35] J.B. Roney, *The inside of history: Jean Henri Merle d'Aubigné and romantic historiography* (Westport, CT, and London, 1996), esp. pp. [109]–130, [157]–181; N.M. Railton, *No North Sea: the Anglo-German evangelical network in the middle of the nineteenth century* (Leiden, 2000), pp. 32–3.

This pan-evangelical enthusiasm for the Reformation and its legacies rested on a deeper consensus as to what drove history. That underlying agreement itself pointed to a certain doctrine of man, and his relation to divinity, which the Reformation had restored and secured. Evangelical historians deliberately reversed Enlightenment era accounts of the Reformation's causes. These were now seen to lie in God's plan and the activity of the Holy Spirit; and not in the self-willed movements of earth's proud empires. Eager to rescue church history from eighteenth-century historians' idolatry of secondary causes, Joseph Milner and his continuator, his brother Isaac, placed the Lutheran Reformation at the apogee of their *Church History*. They depicted it as flowing from immediate effusions of the Holy Spirit, significant for its definitive recovery of justification by faith and the open Bible: an evaluation with which they rebuked those who thought of the Reformation primarily in terms of its secular contexts and results.[36] The Milners 'saw the FINGER OF GOD in every step of the Reformation'.[37] On the classically evangelical reading, the Reformation was second only to the foundation of Christianity as an event in salvation-history. The implication was that similar forces were at work in both. The early Free Church leader, William Cunningham, opened an essay on the subject by claiming that 'the Reformation from Popery in the sixteenth century was the greatest event, or series of events, that has occurred since the close of the Canon of Scripture.'[38] 'The heavenly forces which had slumbered in humanity since the first ages of Christianity', wrote Merle d'Aubigné, 'awoke during the sixteenth century, and with them awoke modern times.'[39] God's interventions, through the spirit, gave to history whatever glory it possessed.

This high view of providential action encouraged, indeed required, evangelical historians to isolate the transcendent motor of the Reformation from profaner contexts. It was not so much a lack of specialized monographs that made the Reformation appear to them to be a dramatic rupture, as an Augustinian vision of human experience, emphasizing the sovereignty of grace and Manichaean separation between the cities of God and man, which historical as well as individual life confirmed. Especially for those earlier evangelicals to whom the medieval church was a kingdom of darkness, the Reformation represented a shaft of light originating

[36] Walsh, 'Joseph Milner's evangelical church history: a biography' (MS), pp. 39–47.

[37] I. Milner, 'Preface to the fourth volume', in Milner, *History of the church of Christ*, i, xxv.

[38] W. Cunningham, 'Leaders of the Reformation', repr. in his *The Reformers and theology of the Reformation* (Edinburgh, 1862), p. 1.

[39] Merle d'Aubigné, *Histoire*, v, [1]. With Neander, Merle also regarded the role of Christianity in history as a slowly-working leaven, however: J. Winkler, *Der Kirchenhistoriker Jean Henri Merle d'Aubigné* (Zurich, 1968), pp. 90–1.

beyond and triumphantly dispersing what had preceded it. 'Of the doctrine of Christianity, scarce anything remained but the name', wrote Thomas McCrie of the pre-Reformation church in Scotland.[40] Such writers were likewise disinclined to connect the Reformation with the preceding recovery of Greek and Latin literature, and the expansion of artistic sensibility. Evangelicals wrote of the 'revival of letters' as part of God's preparation for the Reformation, to which it was firmly subordinate. But they took the significance of this revival to lie in its making available scriptural exegesis to the faithful once again, rather than in any general renewal of the human spirit.[41] Partly this was because 'the Renaissance', as shorthand for an autonomous, extensive event in cultural history, did not come into being before the mid-century. But it also witnessed to the cultural power of that view of mankind's estate that was predicated upon humans' total depravity. Later Victorian Protestants' re-examination of the relationship between the Reformation and the Renaissance in the light of the latter's newly apprehensible content and secularizing potential, simultaneously involved the reconsideration, and often the elevation, of the moral status of humanity's natural reason and fleshly wants.

The filtration of Reformation history beyond learned treatises, to become integral to religious argument in a wider and often urgently practical sense, was apparent in the movement of Reformation era creeds to the centre of ecclesiastical contention. Contemporary anxieties over biblical and church authority, human freedom, and the capacity of the human mind to know God's purposes thereby acquired an historical form, and the creeds became a flashpoint for different understandings of history. Staunch Protestants advanced the most uncomplicated defences of these texts. In Scotland, Presbyterian revivalists paraded their allegiance to the Westminster Confession. Among other doctrines that were to cause difficulties to liberal theologians, this symbol proclaimed the infallibility and all-sufficiency of scripture; the predestination of some to eternal life and the foreordination of others to death; and the penal theory of the atonement whereby Christ voluntarily accepted death to satisfy the demands of divine justice and extend salvation to the elect. Free Churchmen pointedly celebrated the 1843 bicentenary of the Westminster Assembly of Divines, which had drawn up the Confession, shortly after their exodus from the Church of Scotland General Assembly.[42]

---

[40] McCrie, *life of John Knox*, p. 11.   [41] Merle d'Aubigné, *Histoire*, i, 112–13.
[42] T. Chalmers, *Christian union: address of the Rev. Dr Chalmers at the bicentenary commemoration of the Westminster Assembly, July 13, 1843* (London, 1843); W.M. Hetherington, *History of the Westminster Assembly of divines* (Edinburgh, 1843), [iii], pp. 306–7.

William Hetherington hailed the text as 'almost perfect', its 'syllogistic form' witnessing to an 'astonishing precision of thought and language'.[43]

The Thirty-Nine Articles, partly on account of their inescapable capaciousness, never quite served as the emotional emblem of reformed religion in the Church of England in the way that the Westminster Confession became further north. But their affirmation of the salvific sufficiency of scripture and justification by faith alone, and their repudiation of Purgatory and church infallibility, made them less problematic for evangelical and Protestant high church than for Catholicizing Anglicans. They might be seen to immortalize a Protestant achievement.[44] John Charles Ryle, a moderate Calvinist, future bishop of Liverpool, and popular author, sounded 'the trumpet of ecclesiastical history' in their defence before the Derby Church Association meeting in 1878.[45] The old orthodox canon of Westminster and future bishop of Lincoln, Christopher Wordsworth, esteemed the Articles as the fruit of the Holy Spirit and purified by 'the fires of martyrdom'; their fundamental principle, he thought, was the supremacy of scripture as the rule of faith.[46]

Although a number of theologians down the century continued to regard sixteenth- and seventeenth-century formularies as timeless sources of religious authority, the potential difficulties of so doing became evident at an early point. Within the Church of England, strains appeared over the status and meaning of the Articles as soon as the Oxford Movement began to disturb Anglicanism's delicate ecclesiological consensus. Whereas Protestant churchmen of both evangelical and high church dispositions understood the Articles to safeguard the rule of scripture, the defenders of 'church principles' started to give them a distinct and potentially subversive signification as the expression of church authority, and the guarantor of Oxford University's ecclesiastical character. Oxford's Bampton Lecturer for 1832, Renn Dickson Hampden, played an important role in precipitating this change of tone. In a series published as *The Scholastic Philosophy*, Hampden argued that 'church-creeds and Articles' were 'records of Opinions' and hence not immutable, though he was careful to insist that he did not believe that any modification of them was in fact required.[47] He soon

---

[43] W.M. Hetherington, 'Introductory essay', to R. Shaw, *An exposition of the Confession of Faith of the Westminster Assembly of Divines* (Edinburgh, 1845), xvi–xviii.

[44] [Anon.], *Pamphlets in defence of the Oxford usage of subscription to the XXXIX Articles at matriculation* (Oxford, 1835), p. 8.

[45] J.C. Ryle, *Church principles and church comprehensiveness* (London, 1879), pp. 13–14.

[46] C. Wordsworth, *The two tercentenaries: the Thirty-Nine Articles and the Council of Trent: a sermon, preached in Westminister Abbey, on Sunday, December 13, 1863* (London, 1863), pp. 5–6.

[47] R.D. Hampden, *The scholastic philosophy considered in its relation to Christian theology* (Oxford, 1833), p. 381.

applied his alarming stance in support of the separately offensive rising clamour to admit nonconformists to academic degrees, thus completing the preconditions for the vociferous high church opposition to Melbourne's whiggishly anticlerical decision to appoint him as Regius Professor of Divinity in 1836.[48]

In this disturbing climate, old orthodox divines or those caught in the whirlpool of Tractarianism began to argue that with the Articles stood or fell every principle of dogmatic authority. Suddenly assailed on what seemed to be every side, they were disinclined to press historically minded distinctions between the claims of the Articles to whole-hearted obedience, and those of the Nicene or Athanasian creeds.[49] The Catholicizing direction of the Oxford Movement, however, soon grated against such a high view of the Articles. John Henry Newman, whose overpowering conscience had temporarily subordinated his private dislike for the formulary's flirtation with 'vile Protestantism' to the larger principle that religion should 'be approached with a submission of the understanding', made that tension acute when he argued in his 1841 *Tract 90* that the Articles' opposition to 'Romish' error did not exclude their compatibility with Tridentine teaching.[50] The storm generated by Newman's inflammatory treatise helped to push the first phase of the Movement on to its 1845 denouement. For the successors to those Tractarians who remained within the Church of England, the preferred mode of dispelling the Articles' constraints would not be Newman's logical ingenuity. Rather, it would be a pious form of historical relativism. A comparable procedure commended itself to a wider spectrum of more Protestant theologians in England and Scotland, as they looked for ways of detaching Protestantism's lasting relevance from the restrictive dogmatic forms history had led it to assume.

---

[48] See chapter two of this volume at p. 71. H.C.G. Matthew, 'Noetics, Tractarians, and the reform of the University of Oxford in the nineteenth century', in *History of Universities*, 9 (1990), pp. [195]–225; R. Brent, 'Hampden, Renn Dickson (1793–1868)', *ODNB*. Hampden largely withdrew from public controversy thereafter, and accepted Russell's offer of the diocese of Hereford in 1847. At one of his most Gibbonian moments, Milman regretted that Hampden, rather than fulfil his promise to be 'the English historian of this remarkable chapter in the history of the human mind', had 'sunk into a quiet bishop': *HLC*, vi, 435 n.–436 n.

[49] W. Palmer [of Magdalen College, Oxford], *A letter to the Rev. Dr Hampden, Regius Professor of Divinity in the University of Oxford* (Oxford, 1842), pp. 18–19; R. Parkinson, *The moderation of the Church of England, a sermon, preached in the Collegiate Church of Christ, in Manchester, on Sunday the 27th of April, 1834* (London, 1834), pp. 6–7.

[50] J.H. Newman to R.F. Wilson, 13 May 1835, in Newman, *Letters and diaries*, v, 70; J.H. Newman to A.P. Perceval, 11 January 1836, in Newman, *Letters and diaries*, v, 196; [Newman], 'Remarks on certain passages'; Nockles, *Oxford Movement*, pp. 136–42.

Early-Victorian evangelicals were disappointed in their hopes of recalling contemporaries to the standards set by the sixteenth-century religious revolution, as were their Tractarian opponents in wishing to reverse it. They were not, however, without success in their more restrained desire to encourage greater familiarity with the principles and personalities of the sixteenth and seventeenth centuries. By 1845, the Reformation and its defenders conventionally featured in the rhetoric of Victorian religious argument. Luther and Calvin, Tyndale and Knox, were living and familiar personalities once more. Evangelical theology and Biblicist conviction now seemed rooted in concrete historical conflicts and triumphs. This reaffirmation of tradition offered a stable resting point to a considerable number of writers. Self-conscious traditionalists, however, did not monopolize the meaning of Protestant tradition. Those who wished either to liberalize Protestant self-understanding, or to free evangelical religion from the intellectually problematic encumbrances it had acquired after its release from Babylonian captivity at the Reformation, felt the weight of Protestant history in a different way.

HISTORY, DOGMA, AND PROTESTANT LIBERTY

The religious history of the sixteenth and seventeenth centuries acquired new kinds of significance as the classical Protestantism celebrated by early revivalists came under increasing strain in the years after 1850. That restlessness was experienced at several levels. The spread of biblical criticism made belief in the verbal inerrancy of scripture more difficult to sustain. A wider change of sensibility, elevating human moral subjectivity as the expression of the divine image, eroded the popularity of the traditional tenets of Reformed theology such as the Westminster Confession had quintessentially expounded.[51] Difficulties with Reformation era theology inevitably gave rise to unease with the doctrinal standards into which it had been cast. One reaction to such unsettlement was defensiveness, manifested in periodic ecclesiastical prosecutions of clerics for having breached the limits these symbols laid down. Another, ultimately more enduring response was to make room for greater critical freedom and latitude of belief in inessentials, however defined. Along these lines, British churches controversially started to modify the terms of subscription to their historic formularies. The Clerical Subscription Act of 1865 replaced the complex and narrow earlier formula of Anglican clerical subscription to

---

[51] For a general survey, see B.M.G. Reardon, *Religious thought in the Victorian age: a survey from Coleridge to Gore*, 2nd edn (London, 1995), pp. 293–317, 237–65.

the Thirty-Nine Articles with a more general, and ambiguous, declaration of endorsement.[52] Church of Scotland divines became more articulate in distancing themselves from the Westminster Confession to which they were legally bound. Among the Scottish free churches, the United Presbyterians, guided by John Cairns, modified their subscription to the Confession in 1879, by declaring that it did not exclude uplifting beliefs such as the free offer of salvation to all and the operation of the Holy Spirit in fallen man. The General Assembly of the Free Church approved a similar measure thirteen years later.[53]

Although the spread of a more critical approach to Protestant theology is a familiar feature of nineteenth-century religious history, less so is the centrality which Reformation and post-Reformation history acquired for criticism's proponents. Early revivalists had sought to invest Reformation religion, as the rediscovery of biblical truth, with an absolute authority over the present. Liberal Protestants in England and Scotland were no less invested in Protestant history. But they interpreted it in a more differentiated way, as the result of historical development. By separating the principles of the Reformation from their subsequent stereotyping in scholastic forms, a hardening explicable by a context in which medievalism was as yet incompletely dispersed, they hoped, on the one hand, to lessen the authority of problematic Reformation era doctrinal standards. In another, more positive sense, they aimed to show that an ethicized Protestantism, cleared of its abnormal accretions, remained foundational to progressive intellectual culture, and that Reformation precedent legitimized the kind of reverential biblical criticism which, they feared, too rigid an interpretation of post-Reformation creeds would stymie. John Tulloch in Scotland, and Arthur Penrhyn Stanley in England, deployed Reformation history along these liberal Protestant lines. The application of developmental historicism to Protestant history was not solely a liberal preserve, however. High churchmen, once the Thirty-Nine Articles' strongest defenders, became increasingly inclined to treat them as a localized, historically specific expression of a phase of religious thought. Evangelical writers such as Henry Wace and R. W. Dale, though by no means hostile to systematic theology, began to rearticulate reformed theology by stressing that the circumstances of its first growth reinforced its permanent merit more than its later formulistic statements were able to convey. Across the Victorian spectrum, the doctrinal definitions of the Reformation era began to wear an historically relative aspect, as the

---

[52] O. Chadwick, *The Victorian Church* (2 vols, London, 1966–1970), ii, 132–3.
[53] Drummond and Bulloch, *Late Victorian Scotland*, pp. 29–38, 267–72; Macewen, *John Cairns*, pp. 662–770.

vindication of their underlying principles, scriptural witness, and the ancient creeds came to acquire a more fundamental importance.

John Tulloch conceived of the enlightenment of his fellow Presbyterians, and Protestants elsewhere in Britain, through historical reassessment as an essential part of his public duties after his appointment as principal and primarius professor of theology at St Mary's College, St Andrews, in 1854. As will be seen, in later life Tulloch's primary argumentative target shifted from evangelical traditionalism to rising secularism; but he continued quintessentially to express that strand of high-Victorian criticism which made a progressive understanding of Protestant tradition integral to the liberalization of Protestantism in a wider sense.[54] His inaugural lecture on 'theological tendencies of the age', delivered in November 1854, set out the main lines of the argumentative aims which his subsequent historical writings faithfully developed. The address offered a taxonomy of contemporary wrong-turnings in religious thought, and the broad outline of Tulloch's own answer to them. The traditionalist tendency, evident in anti-Catholic Protestants as much as in Anglo-Catholics, maintained that truth was to be referred to 'some outward authoritative expression... *in reference to which the right of private judgment is not to be exercised.*' Although it was important to respect the past, Tulloch continued, to attempt to bar the reason from criticizing its theological productions rendered religion helpless in the face of 'the seductions of Popery and the assaults of Infidelity'.[55] 'Rationalism' was equally dangerous. In the more recent, *'intuitional'* form of rationalism, which Tulloch especially associated with Schleiermacher, the present Christian consciousness was made the supreme test of religious truth.[56] Religious opinion, Tulloch concluded, properly emerged from the application of the variable, subjective element in criticism, in the recognition that it should always be subordinate to the objective authority of scripture.[57] Tulloch counted it the great failure of traditional Protestantism, represented locally by the early Free Church, that it failed to recognize the subjectively opinionative nature of the sense in which it construed the objective fact.[58]

For Tulloch, the key to true criticism lay in a complex historical method in which the interactions between religious thought, character, and spiritual progress in the past yielded standards by which to guide theology in the present. He did not chiefly apply this approach to the Bible, but instead

---

[54] See chapter five of this volume.
[55] J. Tulloch, *Theological tendencies of the age: an inaugural lecture, delivered at the opening of St. Mary's College on Tuesday, the 28th November 1854* (Edinburgh, 1855), pp. 5–12.
[56] Ibid., pp. 16–17, 20–7.   [57] Ibid., pp. 28–31.
[58] J. Tulloch, 'Dean Stanley and the Scotch "Moderates"', *CR*, 20 (1872), p. 717.

to the fructifications of religious thought which lay between the apostolic period and the nineteenth century, and especially to the history of Protestantism.[59] Tulloch held that history, thus understood, both witnessed to the intrinsic truth of the Christian religion, and furnished a critical principle by which the essence of Protestantism might be freed from the outdated accretions that had hardened around it. To historicize the subjective response of the believing mind to revelation, was therefore to offer a kind of objective guiding authority in future development. Two sources appear to have been formative in leading Tulloch towards this outlook. He praised August Neander for his power of exhibiting the universal, leavening power of Christianity in successive, even opposing individual forms of intellectual culture, whilst avoiding Schleiermacher's excessive psychological subjectivism by cleaving to the objective, redemptive efficacy of revelation.[60] Tulloch's preference for regarding ecclesiastical doctrines as a living stream of spiritual life running down the ages also owed something to Coleridge, who had unlocked 'the transcendental element in all Christian dogma'.[61] These influences combined to make the history of religious movements significant to Tulloch insofar as their peculiar theologies and personalities vivified fundamental principles, which were then taken up and further purified in later stages of growth. 'Deeper intelligence', Tulloch wrote in an 1877 essay in the *Contemporary Review* on the progress of Scottish theology, 'sees through the decay of systems the onward working of principles destined to better and more comprehensive constructions in the future.'[62] As he was to affirm in a series of lectures on nineteenth-century intellectual history which he delivered at St Giles' church in Edinburgh, and published as *Movements of Religious Thought* in 1885, 'I believe in the continuous movement of the Divine Spirit enlarging, correcting, and modifying human opinion.'[63]

Tulloch brought these perspectives to bear on Reformation history in his 1859 study of the *Leaders of the Reformation*, based on lectures he had delivered at the Edinburgh Philosophical Institution in the same year. In this text, Tulloch drew out the right relationship between past and present Protentantism by threading progressive lines of spiritual development

---

[59] Tulloch popularized the results of biblical criticism in order to vindicate the historicity of the New Testament narratives, but he was not himself an original exegete: Tulloch, *The Christ of the gospels and the Christ of modern criticism: lectures on M. Renan's 'Vie de Jésus'* (London, 1864); Tulloch, *Beginning life: a book for young men*, rev. edn (London, 1882), pp. 46–123.

[60] [Tulloch], 'Augustus Neander', *BQR*, 24 (1850), pp. [297]–337. On Neander, see chapter one of this volume at pp. 28–9.

[61] J. Tulloch, 'On dogma and dogmatic Christianity', *CR*, 23 (1873), p. 924.

[62] Tulloch, 'Progress of religious thought', p. 536.

[63] Tulloch, *Movements of religious thought*, p. 4.

through a succession of Protestant actors. He lifted out and universalized what he regarded as their praiseworthy ideas. The counterpart of this procedure was his localization and dismissal of their overly dogmatic or scholastic stances, as the products of lingering medievalism or personal crotchetiness. In keeping with his dislike of scholastic formalism, Tulloch redefined Martin Luther's principle of justification by faith alone in a 'more general and ethical form of expression' as 'the principle of *moral individualism*'.[64] This was the ground spring of Protestantism, in the past as in the present. Tulloch thought it unavoidable, and correct, that in the course of time this principle should have come to encompass the individual's right privately to judge and interpret the Bible: a right that hardline revivalists were careful to construe as the right of responsible individuals to refer everything to God's word.[65] But Luther's belief in a personal devil was 'medieval', and his reaction against the Catholic religion of works led him unduly to deprecate the importance of moral conduct.[66] Calvin had built on Luther's insights to develop a system of ecclesiastical polity capable of withstanding the Jesuitical Counter-Reformation. Tulloch sounded a Coleridgean note, however, when he insisted that the Christian idea now had to work itself free from the Judaistic or medieval externalism which coloured Calvin's disciplinary and dogmatic systems.[67] By reconceptualizing Protestant history, Tulloch both offered a progressive justification for loyal departures from Reformation religion, as well as—he hoped—a means of harmonizing such freedom with biblical authority and the divine rules unveiled by conscience.

Tulloch made the practical implications of his historical perspective explicit in his interventions over the increasingly contentious status of the Westminster Confession in Scottish intellectual and religious life. In an 1865 address to Edinburgh University students on the ends of theological debate, Tulloch argued that the church ought to make room for differences of opinion as 'the growth of a more complex, philosophical, and historical culture' exposed the limitations of 'the logical nomenclature of the sixteenth and seventeenth centuries'.[68] This was the necessary

---

[64] Tulloch, *Luther and other leaders of the Reformation*, 3rd edn (Edinburgh and London, 1883), p. 163; first edition 1859.

[65] Ibid., pp. 170–1; cf. William Cunningham's review of the work: 'Leaders of the reformation', p. 4.

[66] Tulloch, *Leaders of the Reformation*, p. 144.

[67] Ibid., pp. 255–71; cf. Tulloch's Coleridge-inflected defence of Establishment: J. Tulloch, 'The ideal of the church', reprinted in his *Sundays at Balmoral: sermons preached before her majesty the Queen in Scotland*, ed. W.W. Tulloch (London, 1887), pp. 198–223.

[68] J. Tulloch, *Theological controversy; or, the function of debate in theology: an address delivered to the members of the Theological Society of the University of Edinburgh*, 4th edn (Edinburgh and London, 1866), p. 9.

precondition, in his view, for the emergence of definite statements of Christian doctrine which the intelligence of the century could accept. He added an appendix on the Westminster Confession to the published version of his lecture, sufficiently inflammatory to spark numerous aggrieved replies, which contended that the text should not be studied as a set of propositions to be memorized, but as documenting a particular phase of religious thought. 'Genevan and Dutch theologies', he argued, caused the Confession to state 'such ideas, for example, as *law* and *covenant*—as *forensic justice* and *administrative order* . . . with a confidence hitherto unexampled'.[69]

Although Tulloch accordingly favoured the lessening of the Confession's sway over modern thought, by for example opening up divinity chairs in Scottish universities to those who dissented from it, he was careful to counterbalance his stress on its historical relativity with the insistence that, when properly interpreted, it in fact allowed considerable scope for free theological inquiry.[70] Addressing the General Assembly of the Church of Scotland in 1878, Tulloch claimed that the Confession approved by the Westminster Assembly substantially represented the 'large and liberal' confession of John Knox, and so by extension the common doctrine of all reformed churches. 'It was in this large historical spirit, and not in any rigorous and mere rigid temper, that our national Presbyterianism adopted the Westminster Confession.' The way to resolve the problems it posed for churchmen in the present was therefore to accept it in an historical spirit—which was indistinguishable for Tulloch from a progressive Christian spirit—and make official declarations to this effect, rather than to reject it or to rewrite its defective or excessive parts 'according to modern fashion'.[71]

Tulloch's biographer, the novelist Margaret Oliphant, suggested that his 1865 intervention over the status of the Westminster Confession had given an intellectually systematic legitimation to wider departures from the Church of Scotland's traditionally puritanical religious life. She instanced Robert Lee's promotion of a more liturgical mode of worship, and Norman Macleod's criticisms of his country's unrelenting sabbatarianism, as having helped to initiate this trend.[72] The spread beyond the

[69] Tulloch, *Theological controversy*, p. 29.

[70] J. Tulloch, *The theological faculties of the Scottish universities in connection with university reform* (Edinburgh and London, 1883), p. 3.

[71] J. Tulloch, *Position and prospects of the Church of Scotland: address delivered at the close of the General Assembly of the Church of Scotland: June 3, 1878* (Edinburgh and London, 1878), pp. 30–4.

[72] Oliphant, *Memoir*, pp. 223–9; T. Hamilton, rev. H.C.G. Matthew, 'Macleod, Norman (1812–1872)', *ODNB*; R. Mitchell, 'Lee, Robert (1804–1868)', *ODNB*.

Church of Scotland of approaches to the Confession similar to Tulloch's certainly indicated that his own criticisms of the standard belonged to a wider movement. Robert Mackintosh, a Free Church minister who was to become a reconstructively evangelical Congregationalist in 1890 out of opposition to the Calvinism of his parent communion, published a paper on the *Obsoleteness of the Westminster Confession of Faith* in 1888.[73] There he accused the Westminster divines of having inherited a medieval presumption in favour of logical syllogism as a theological approach. The elaborate mechanism they drew up for the forensic operation of grace, he argued, followed from their medieval doctrine of God as the operator of a legal system.[74] The creed was therefore 'a broken light'— the allusion was to Tennyson—whose theology had to be corrected by a more historical understanding of the Bible than that implied by the Westminster theologians' treatment of the Old and New Testaments as 'not manifold, but one'.[75] The emergence of a new theology from the old foundations, Mackintosh argued, would recognize the complexity of the biblical history, and the hazardousness of making those parts of the Bible which spoke of election logically overrule those which involved probation and moral freedom. He concluded that such a process could be stimulated by the substitution of a general for a precise declaration of adherence to the Confession on the part of church teachers.[76]

The authority of the Church of England's Thirty-Nine Articles came under comparable pressure. Whereas the Westminster Confession's sceptics included liberal and a growing number of evangelical Protestants, English discontent with the Articles originated in an overlapping liberal movement, as well as in autochthonous and continuing high church difficulties in reconciling the formulary to Catholic theology. But the increasingly historicist terms which liberal Anglicans deployed to critique the Articles, and which their once-stalwart supporters now used to distance themselves from their phraseology, gave English and Scottish debates a mutual resemblance. Two years before Tulloch issued his first pronouncement on the status of the Westminster Confession, his friend and intellectual counterpart in the Church of England, Arthur Penrhyn Stanley, had published *A Letter to the Lord Bishop of London* on the Articles while he was Regius Professor of Ecclesiastical History at Oxford. It was to play a significant role in sparking the momentum that led to the Clerical

---

[73] A.P.F. Sell, 'Mackintosh, Robert (1858–1933)', *ODNB*; cf. R. Mackintosh, *Essays towards a new theology* (Glasgow, 1889).

[74] Mackintosh, *The obsoleteness of the Westminster Confession of Faith* (Glasgow, 1888), pp. 11–14.

[75] Ibid., pp. 29, 46–54.   [76] Ibid., pp. 59–63.

Subscription Act.[77] Stanley argued that the requirement that Anglican ordinands subscribe to the symbol, and so commit themselves to abrasive stances concerning original sin and the Catholic Mass, was alienating intelligent young men from the ministry in a way it had not done twenty or thirty years previously. The practice should therefore be ended. Rather as Tulloch had proceeded in relation to the Confession, the future dean of Westminster drew attention to the Articles' origin in 'the heat of vehement struggles which have long since passed away'. At the same time, he loyally ascribed to them an originally broad character, which later subscription requirements, arising from the needs of anti-Puritan and anti-Catholic activism, had unhappily suppressed.[78]

A wider spectrum of liberal Anglican critics echoed Stanley's attempt to lessen the Articles' authority by drawing attention to their historical limitations. The similarly unspeculative Milman agreed with him that clerical subscription was no longer tenable.[79] Benjamin Jowett wrote privately of the impossibility of enforcing agreement on points upon which none could really agree, and the absurdity of supposing English belief to have been definitively settled by the 'compromises and accidents' of the sixteenth century.[80] Lord John Russell's retirement *Essays on the Rise and Progress of the Christian Religion* held that the Judicial Committee of the Privy Council's power of interpreting the Articles afforded the only security that 'the spirit of Laud or the spirit of John Knox shall not indulge itself in prohibitions and exclusions, banishing from the Church such men as Clarke, Middleton, and Hampden.'[81] The Privy Council had not quite lived up to Russell's idea of it in 1871, when it deprived the controversial preacher Charles Voysey of his Anglican living on the grounds that the views he expressed in his best-selling sermons, including the denial of Christ's divinity and saving atonement, were contrary to the Articles. Voysey, who conducted his own defence, alluded to the closing words of Milman's *History of Latin Christianity* in justifying his own rejection of the authority of formulae: 'the words of Christ, and His words alone (the primal indefeasible truths of Christianity), shall not pass away.'[82]

[77] Prothero and Bradley, *Arthur Penrhyn Stanley*, ii, 119–20.

[78] A.P. Stanley, *A letter to the Lord Bishop of London on the state of subscription in the Church of England and in the University of Oxford* (Oxford and London, 1863), pp. [3]–13, 39.

[79] Milman, *Milman*, pp. 244–7.

[80] P. Hinchliff, *Benjamin Jowett and the Christian religion* (Oxford, 1987), pp. 63–4; B. Jowett to [anon.], 6 July 1851, and private paper [1874], in his *Letters of Benjamin Jowett, M.A.:Master of Balliol College, Oxford*, ed. E. Abbott and L. Campbell (London, 1899), pp. 4–6, 41–2.

[81] Russell, *Essays*, pp. 278–9.

[82] Quoted in [anon.], 'The charge of heresy against a clergyman', *Reynolds's Newspaper*, 20 November 1870, p. 6; cf. *HLC*, vi, 633–4.

The rhetorical localization of the Articles in a bygone age was not an argument monopolized by those who desired to make the Church of England doctrinally comprehensive. The more doctrinally conservative challenge to the Articles' authority came not, as in the case of the Westminster Confession, from an evangelical Protestant direction, but from a Catholicizing tendency. As the early Victorian crises passed away and as the revival of Catholic theology and ritual in the Church of England continued, high churchmen found themselves at once less urgently committed to the Articles and more discontented with them. Historicism of the kind which Hampden had once been hounded for promoting thus crept into high church treatments of the Articles in the later part of the century. The high church historian and vicar of Kennington in Oxfordshire, John Henry Blunt, praised the Ten Articles of the orthodox, Henrician Reformers in his often-reprinted history of the English Reformation. By lamentable contrast, he continued, the framers of later versions, ending with the Thirty-Nine Articles, had pared them down with 'Continental Protestantism' and the desire to 'conciliate dissenters'.[83] Richard William Church, reflecting on the controversy over *Tract 90* fifty years afterwards, commented that the Articles did not pose a problem if read as a broad and loosely worded condemnation of an antagonistic, Roman system. 'But take them as scientific and accurate and precise enunciations of a systematic theology, and difficulties begin at once, with every one who does not hold the special and well-marked doctrines of the age when the German and Swiss authorities ruled supreme.'[84] Dynamically conservative, as well as liberalizing imperatives thus combined to reduce the hold of the Reformation theological settlement in Anglican circles.

As the hold of Reformation-era creeds in both England and Scotland waned, it became necessary to find sources of authority elsewhere in history. The relative marginalization of Reformation era standards functioned as a counterpoint to the reinvigoration of the early creeds.[85] Beresford James Kidd, in his high church 1899 exposition of the Articles for the *Oxford Church Text Books* series, argued that they were susceptible of Catholic senses, but stressed the distinction between the Articles and the earlier formularies. The creeds were spontaneous and anonymous growths; the Articles were made. The creeds were 'theological' and

---

[83] J.H. Blunt, *The Reformation of the Church of England: its history, principles and results [A.D. 1514–1547]*, 2nd edn (London, Oxford, and Cambridge, 1869), pp. 444–7; T.F. Tout, rev. H.C.G. Matthew, 'Blunt, John Henry (1823–1884)', *ODNB*.

[84] R.W. Church, *The Oxford Movement: twelve years 1833–1845* (London, 1891), pp. 250–1.

[85] See chapter two of this volume.

'historical', preserving doctrines only as far as they were bound up with the acts and nature of Christ; the Articles, however, were 'anthropological' and 'controversial'.[86] Robert Rainy had made a comparable distinction between the early creeds and the Westminster Confession in the Cunningham Lectures which he delivered to the Edinburgh New College in 1873, the year before he became the institution's principal. He concluded his series by suggesting that the Confession, for historical reasons, involved its adherents in positions to which the universal church was not committed; and that Free Churchmen would eventually have to confront this fact.[87] Rainy was later to be instrumental in securing the modification of the Free Church's adherence to the Westminster standards.[88] Even Milman had favoured continuing subscription to the Book of Common Prayer, on the grounds that this also involved subscription to the catholic creeds.[89] Tulloch, for his part, was led through the contests with anti-theological thinkers of his later life to locate the essence of religion not in any historically fluctuating formula, but in the spiritual consciousness universal to human historical experience.[90]

The increasing inclination to view Reformation era formularies as historically imperfect developments, however, often involved the celebration of the foundational assumptions of the Reformation itself as the perennial wellspring of new life. Liberal and evangelical Protestant critics who sought to reconcile their hearers to biblical criticism, often did so by insisting that it could be a means of reobtaining the Reformation's original liberation of scriptural authority from traditionalist accretions. The imbrication of the Westminster Confession's Calvinism, or at least hardline interpretations of it, with ahistorical approaches to the Bible gave this argument particular charge in Scotland. The young Thomas Martin Lindsay, before he became well-known as a Reformation historian, advanced such an argument in the *Contemporary Review* for 1878 in support of his fellow Free Church professor, William Robertson Smith. Smith, a professor of Hebrew at the Aberdeen Free Church College, was facing prosecution in the church's Glasgow Assembly for allegedly subverting the Westminster Confession by denying the Mosaic authorship of the Pentateuch and the historicity of Deuteronomy, positions which reflected Smith's understanding of the Old Testament as the history of

---

[86] B.J. Kidd, *The Thirty-nine Articles: their history and explanation* (2 vols, London, 1899), i, 1–7.

[87] R. Rainy, *Delivery and development of Christian doctrine* (Edinburgh, 1874), pp. 235–86.

[88] H.C.G. Matthew, 'Rainy, Robert (1826–1906)', *ODNB*.

[89] Milman, *Milman*, pp. 244–7.   [90] See chapter five of this volume.

Israel's growth in faith.[91] Lindsay answered the prosecution by arguing that modern biblical scholars were obliged to challenge both Arnoldian paganism and Manningite dogmatism by resolving 'the Bible into scene after scene of fellowship and communion with God'.[92] The sixteenth-century reformers, he noted pointedly, had accomplished the same for their own age.

Tulloch, one of Smith's more liberal supporters at the time of his prosecution, made a similar case in an essay on Martin Luther published to coincide with the 1883 commemoration of the great Reformer. Luther's contest with Roman apologists, he contended, had led him to recognize, albeit imperfectly, 'the diversity of the Scriptures in meaning and authority'. It was 'an advance which, unhappily, Protestantism did not maintain, and which the Churches are only now beginning to realize as a condition of intelligent Biblical interpretation.'[93] Frederic William Farrar, a provocatively outspoken critic of the doctrine of eternal punishment and canon of Westminster Abbey during Stanley's tenure as dean, argued along the same lines in his 1885 Oxford Bampton Lectures on the *History of Interpretation* of the Bible, which he dedicated to Jowett.[94] The historical criticism of scripture, he contended, was a freedom won, and a duty imposed, by the Reformation. Although Luther and Calvin were imperfect exegetes, especially on account of their inability to distinguish between the weighting properly assignable to different phases of biblical development, Farrar regarded them, in an explicitly Fichtean sense, as gifted men and mediators of the divine spirit. So too were their nineteenth-century successors.[95]

Whereas liberal and late-century evangelical Protestants could agree that the Reformation legitimized reverent inquiry into the history of the biblical text, evangelicals added to this a more definite commitment to

---

[91] Drummond and Bulloch, *Late Victorian Scotland*, pp. [40]–78. Robertson Smith was deposed from his chair in 1881.

[92] T.M. Lindsay, 'The critical movement in the Free Church of Scotland', *CR*, 33 (1878), pp. [22]–5.

[93] J. Tulloch, 'Luther and recent criticism', *NC*, 15:86 (1884), p. 668; cf. Tulloch, 'Progress of religious thought', pp. 544–5.

[94] F.W. Farrar, *History of Interpretation: eight lectures preached before the University of Oxford in the year MDCCCLXXXV* (Oxford, 1886); G. Rowell, *Hell and the Victorians: a study of the nineteenth-century controversies concerning eternal punishment and the future life* (Oxford, 1974), pp. [139]–52; N. Vance, 'Farrar, Frederic William (1831–1903)', *ODNB*. Farrar may have owed the idea for his Bampton Lectures to Jowett's contribution to *Essays and Reviews*: B. Jowett, 'On the interpretation of scripture', in Shea and Whitla, *Essays and Reviews*, p. 482.

[95] Farrar, *History of Interpretation*, pp. 307–54 and esp. 329–30, 353–4 and 353 n.; cf. Farrar, 'The reformers as expositors. II. Luther', and 'Calvin as an expositor', *The Expositor*, 7 (1884), pp. 214–29, 426–44.

rearticulating the formal theology of the Reformation—as they also restated the theology of the early church—in newly experimental terms. They now explained why the doctrines of justification by faith alone or divine election had come to be rediscovered at the period of the Reformation, by relating them to the abiding facets of human moral experience that underlay the contextually particular ways in which the reformers had expressed them. It thereby became possible to free these doctrines from the scholastic forms into which they had once been thrown, or even to invest those definitions with new meaning. In the 1879 sermon in which he discussed the relationship between the evangelical revival and the Reformation, R. W. Dale proclaimed that 'the movement of theological speculation' which began in the sixteenth century and 'assumed a permanent form in the confessions and creeds of the great Protestant Churches' was now coming to an end, and must be reinvigorated for new conditions.[96] The consequences of not doing so, he believed, would be the enervation of the faith those confessions outwardly summarized. 'It was not in the earlier days of Protestantism', Dale mused regretfully in an 1874 address at a London evangelical auditorium, Exeter Hall, 'that Protestant theologians wrote treatises on the external evidences of Christianity and on the historical proofs of the certainty of the Christian revelation.' In those times justification by faith had been a 'fountain of light', rather than the 'mathematical formula' it became in seventeenth-century disquisitions.[97]

Dale sought to make such doctrines live again by examining how the outworn forms of Protestant scholasticism represented attempts to distil the timeless verities which the Reformation had recovered. In an 1867 essay for the *British Quarterly Review*, Dale attempted to rescue the scriptural truth of Christ's atonement for sin from what he took to be the seventeenth-century misunderstanding that God had punished his innocent Son in order to satisfy the requirements of divine justice. It were more scriptural, and more moral, to posit that God had surrendered his Son so that he might voluntarily suffer to meet the 'ill-desert' of sin, and sanctify the race.[98] 'Calvinism is dead', he announced to the congregation of Bradford's Great Horton Lane Chapel thirteen years later, in reference to the Calvinist doctrine of divine election, 'and dead things soon become unlovely, hideous, and disgusting'. Calvinism's imputation of Adam's guilt to his double-predestined descendants had now acquired

---

[96] Dale, 'The evangelical revival', pp. 18–19.

[97] Dale, *Protestantism: its ultimate principle* (London, 1928), pp. 40, 49–50; first edition 1874.

[98] Dale, 'The expiatory theory of the atonement', *BQR*, 92 (1867), pp. 463–504.

those characteristics. But the tradition's founding idea that 'God does not love all men alike'—the reverse of 'the modern gospel'—reflected the scriptural truth that God loved those who followed his commandments more than grievous sinners.[99] Dale, who elsewhere warned intending preachers off reliance on Stanley's geographically descriptive biblical primers as books without salt, thus sought to refresh evangelicalism through historical argument, without permitting evangelicalism to be absorbed into what he castigated as 'modern liberal Christianity'.[100]

Among Anglican evangelicals, Henry Wace turned Reformation history to similar ends. His 1874–1875 Boyle Lectures on *Christianity and Morality*, which sought to demonstrate the correspondence of revelation to man's moral constitution, attempted to vindicate orthodox Protestantism from the strictures placed upon it by Matthew Arnold, among others. The conversion of the doctrine of justification by faith into 'a rigid statement of impersonal transactions' in the post-Reformation period deserved much of the censure heaped upon it in Arnold's *Paul and Protestantism*, Wace conceded. But in truth the doctrine had to be understood not as the theoretical form in which it was stated, but as the fact of experience it denoted, which was to say 'the establishment of confidence and fellowship between the soul and a God of all righteousness'. 'This is the Protestantism which, in the mouth of Luther, gave a new life to the world.'[101] That experience, he further explained in his Bampton Lectures, reprising many of the themes of his *Christianity and Morality*, was not a matter of mere feeling, but the sinner's realization that he must rely on God's word for deliverance.[102] In a later essay, Wace invoked Coleridge's *Aids to Reflection* to argue that sixteenth-century theologians' grappling with the great problems of human existence, including their recovery of man's dependence on God through the doctrine of predestination, recognizably belonged to the century of Shakespeare. This had been 'a century in which human nature, too long confined in the swathing-bands of medieval discipline and philosophy, cast them aside' and 'burst into the realities of the great world of man and nature'.[103] In this latter observation, Wace gave voice to a sentiment which liberal Protestants also shared. The Reformation, by restoring biblical faith

---

[99] Dale, 'The gospel for the church', in his *Evangelical revival*, pp. 194–200.
[100] Dale, 'The forgiveness of sins', in his *Evangelical revival*, pp. 166–7; Dale, 'The intellect in relation to preaching', in his *Nine lectures*, p. 29.
[101] Wace, *Christianity and morality*, pp. 136–8 and n.
[102] Wace, *Foundations*, pp. 176–8.
[103] H. Wace, 'The course of Protestant theology in the sixteenth century', in his *Principles of the Reformation practical and historical* (London, 1910), pp. 140–53 (repr. from *CM* for 1902).

and personal responsibility to a creator, had in crucial respects created modern individuality. The exploration and proclamation of its history became a means of holding intellectual freedom within a framework of religious authority. Meanwhile, a newer fashion for extolling the Renaissance, often seen as an historically articulated code for expressing a broader complex of irreligious ideas, posed a serious challenge to this understanding of the foundations and ultimate direction of modern culture.

RENAISSANCE, REFORMATION
AND PROTESTANT ORIGINS

While British Protestants were hesitantly and controversially developing bolder notions of the liberty won for them by the Reformation, an alternative and potentially secularized understanding of the origins of modern freedom and progressive culture was taking shape. For those deeply discontented with the power of evangelical religion, and the legacies of puritanism in British life, the Renaissance as both an historic event and a present ideal was assuming an attractive form. British writers first began to treat the Renaissance as an integrated, epoch-making historical movement in the 1860s and 1870s. The term 'Renaissance' had been used earlier, to describe a classicizing style of art, architecture, and design. But the sexually and religiously heterodox Oxford aesthete Walter Pater was conscious of imparting something new when he wrote in his 1873 *Studies in the History of the Renaissance* that the word 'is now generally used to denote ... a whole complex movement, of which that revival of classical antiquity was but one element or symptom'.[104] Enthusiasts for the Renaissance began to write of it as the cradle of the supposedly 'modern' spirit of humanity, creativity and fleshly release, with roots stretching back to the fifteenth and fourteenth centuries. The histories of the Renaissance and the Reformation began to intersect, as critics sought to understand the significance of both movements for the past and future of civilization.

This relationship became crucial to a late-century complex of argument, in which Matthew Arnold was a vocal but not a dominant interlocutor, over the relative cultural authority of Hellenism, of which the Renaissance was often taken to be a rediscovery, and Hebraism. The Renaissance's Victorian celebrants generally identified that movement, and themselves, with a reanimation of the Greek ideal of the harmoniously balanced and

---

[104] W.H. Pater, *Studies in the history of the Renaissance* (London, 1873), p. 2.

pleasingly embodied human life, and so with a rather different species of classicism from the chaste Platonism often excogitated by contemporary divines. The Reformation could, by comparison, become a backwards-looking obstacle to progress. In its bolder form, however, this argument was a notably counter-cultural one. It was much more common to look for ways of bringing the two moments into constructive historical relationship. John Addington Symonds, one of the foremost popularizers of the Renaissance as a period and an idea, showed an ambivalence on the question of its historical self-sufficiency which registered wider anxieties over the erosion of Protestantism as a source of value. Liberal Protestant critics, more fulsomely, interpreted both epochs as two branches of a shared spiritual liberation. Late-century evangelicals here detected secularizing dangers. They instead took the rising fashion for the Renaissance as a cue to reaffirm the distinctiveness of the Reformation's contribution, not only to religion, but also to civilization, in a way that complemented their new interest in doctrinal history as a means of humanizing Protestantism. The percolation of secular conceptions of the progress inaugurated by the Renaissance prompted religious critics to re-examine their own assumptions concerning the meaning of history, without displacing theology from the centre of wider British understandings of the origins of modernity (and in many cases reinforcing it).

The British discovery of the Renaissance, in common with so many other fields of intellectual innovation, owed much to Germanophone culture even as it developed along distinctive lines. Writing to a friend on the subject of the Renaissance in 1885, Symonds declared that this 'period of history has only been defined during the last twenty-five years, and its importance recognized'.[105] He was almost certainly alluding to the publication of Jacob Burckhardt's *Die Kultur der Renaissance in Italien*.[106] It was this work, more than any other, which first brought international recognition to the Basel professor and pioneering cultural historian.[107] The Renaissance, in Burckhardt's account, was that period of Italian history, running from the end of the thirteenth to the early sixteenth century, during which the veil of medieval faith was lifted from human

[105] J.A. Symonds to H.F. Brown, 26 June 1885, in J.A. Symonds, *The letters of John Addington Symonds*, ed. H.M. Schueller and R.L Peters (3 vols, Detroit, MI, 1967–1969), iii, 60.
[106] J. Burckhardt, *Die Kultur der Renaissance in Italien: ein Versuch* (Basel, 1860).
[107] L. Gossman, *Basel in the age of Burckhardt: a study in unseasonable ideas* (Chicago, IL, 2000), pp. 239–40. The first English translation was published in 1878: J. Burckhardt, *The civilisation of the period of the Renaissance in Italy*, trans. S.G.C. Middlemore (2 vols, London, 1878).

eyes and the dreams which had bound mankind into a corporate life of guild and church dispelled.

> It was first in Italy that this veil was blown away into the air; there awoke *objective* observation and treatment of the state and all the things of this world in general; but besides that, the *subjective* arose in all its power; man became a spiritual *individual* and recognized himself as such.[108]

A Basel patriot and sometime pupil of Ranke who grew disillusioned with the hieratical Berlin professor, Burckhardt, unlike its British students, did not idolize the Renaissance. His analysis of the naked power politics of the Italian principalities, removed from all traditional restraints, and of the uninhibited egotism which underlay so many undeniable architectural and artistic masterpieces, told of his civilized distaste for the Prussian military state and democratizing, commercialist liberalism.[109] It also recorded the maturation of a changed historical sensibility, or *Sinn*, which was of great significance for the longer-term development of *Historismus*. Burckhardt's 1839 transition from the study of theology in his native Basel, to that of history at Berlin, expressed not simply a change of specialization, but his stoical, unsensational withdrawal from the orthodox Protestant world view of his childhood.[110] For Burckhardt, there was no transcendent spirit or world plan which spoke through distinctive historical epochs, as there was for Ranke and his acolytes. So far as the historian was concerned, there were only concrete historical totalities, or cultures. Burckhardt's own route to rejecting metaphysical readings of history in favour of *Kulturgeschichte* was a peculiarly Germanic one. But it was to find analogies in British debates over how to interpret the moment at which, it appeared to more and more critics, the modern spirit had been born.

For one of the early British students of *Kulturgeschichte*, Karl Pearson, the answer to this problem was relatively uncomplicated. Pearson was to become famous in later life for his statistical work and eugenicist scientism. But led on by his early rejection of conventional religion, and growing socialist sympathies which made him regret the passing of medieval Catholic social solidarity, he devoted much time to ecclesiastical history in the 1880s. His interests focused particularly on the fifteenth and sixteenth centuries as constituting the pivot of European history. Dogmatic Protestantism, in Pearson's hands, became a comprehensively

---

[108] Burckhardt, *Kultur der Renaissance*, p. [131] (Burckhardt's emphasis).
[109] H.R. Trevor-Roper, 'Jacob Burckhardt', in his *History and the enlightenment*, pp. [246]–265; Gossman, *Basel in the age of Burckhardt*, pp. 259–90.
[110] T.A. Howard, *Religion and the rise of historicism: W.M.L. de Wette, Jacob Burckhardt, and the theological origins of nineteenth-century historical consciousness* (Cambridge, 2000), pp. 110–36; Gossman, *Basel in the age of Burckhardt*, pp. 210–13.

destructive aberration from the Renaissance. Whilst his disparagement of individualistic Protestantism drew heavily on German depictions of medieval Catholicism as a flourishing social whole, the second part of his argument—that Protestantism had inhibited enlightened humanism from running its course—reflected more his own, highly public rejection of orthodox religion. During his undergraduate years at King's College, Cambridge from 1875 to 1879, Pearson had rebelled against compulsory attendance at chapel and divinity lectures: a protest that precipitated the abolition of the system in 1878.[111] His motivation lay more in his objections to religious hypocrisy than his commitment to science, which then lay in the future. His formulated alternative to Christianity, akin to Mark Pattison's and Matthew Arnold's, was a personal religion of the intellect formed from reading Spinoza and German philosophy, an attitude which acquired fuller theoretical shape in the time he spent studying at Berlin and Heidelberg after leaving Cambridge.[112]

Pearson's experience of religious disenchantment, and his reading of German cultural historians—especially the Catholic Johannes Janssen—informed two subversive essays on the Renaissance and Reformation in Germany.[113] Published in the radical *Westminster Review* in 1883 and 1884, thus timed so as to puncture the celebrations of Martin Luther then reverberating across the Protestant world, Pearson's essays argued that the birth of the modern spirit preceded Luther, and had only been stymied by him. His first essay explored the promise of the Renaissance. The rediscovery of Greek learning by 'the so-called *Humanists*'—a construction recording the deliberately innovative character of ideas that have since come to seem conventional—enabled philosophy to work itself free from service to ecclesiastical dogma. This process was significant not for having cleared a path to Protestantism, but for having made possible wholly secular sources of value. 'For the first time in the history of culture, Hebraism and Hellenism will step out as conflicting truths', Pearson wrote, alluding to Arnold.[114] The foundation and reform of universities in Germany in the century preceding the Reformation, by encouraging Greek and historical learning, spread a culture that 'must ultimately oppose a theology which had ceased to keep pace with the progress of thought'.[115] The unconventional lives of the German humanists, roving

---

[111] J. Woiak, 'Pearson, Karl [*formerly* Carl] (1857–1936)', *ODNB*.

[112] On Pearson's early life, see T.M. Porter, *Karl Pearson: the scientific life in a statistical age* (Princeton, NJ, and Oxford, 2004), pp. 1–66.

[113] Ibid., pp. 96–105; University College London, Karl Pearson papers, Pearson 3/1 /1/6; ibid., Pearson 3/1/3/17, 1–5.

[114] [K. Pearson], 'Humanism in Germany', *WR*, 119:236 (1883), pp. 315–18.

[115] Ibid., p. 326.

from university to university between drinking bouts and military service, expressed a temperamental gaiety altogether at variance with medieval asceticism.[116]

This revival of humanity, Pearson continued in his 1884 second instalment, was crushed by the Lutheran Reformation. He complained, with hints of speculative anthropology, that Luther's admirers invested the founder of their 'phase of religion' with 'legendary perfection'.[117] Disclaiming redundant 'theological discussion', he challenged those who insisted that modern freedom began at the Reformation by examining its effects on the intellectual and material welfare of Germany.[118] Pearson imagined that, had the humanists Reuchlin and Erasmus been allowed to reform the Catholic Church slowly from within, it might by the nineteenth century have become 'the universal instrument of moral progress and mental culture', counting Huxley and Arnold among its members.[119] But it was not to be. Whereas humanists had placed their faith in the gradual education of the universal church by reason, Luther regarded reason as the arch-enemy of faith; Pearson was especially caustic about his belief in the personal activity of the devil.[120] Not only was Luther uncultivated, but also demonstrably immoral: his invectives against the Jews animated modern German anti-Semitism.[121] Citing the Catholic priest and historian, Ignaz von Döllinger, Pearson maintained that the religious conflict Luther unleashed caused schools and universities, invigorated by the humanists, to fall into decay.[122] Pearson also claimed, agreeing with the tropes of German Catholic anti-Lutheran polemicists, that the Reformation enriched the German princes at the expense of the people; and despite his professed aversion to theological skirmishing, he insisted that the doctrine of justification by faith alone sanctified moral selfishness.[123] It followed from the historical destructiveness of Protestantism that no future progress would come from it. The future lay with Erasmian 'rational reform' and 'the gradual influence of education'.[124]

Pearson's essay on Luther more than once invoked the authority of Mark Pattison, who often framed his commitment to university reform and the life of scholarship—which Pattison liked to experience vicariously—in historical terms diametrically opposed to the claims of

---

[116] Ibid., pp. 331–2.
[117] [K. Pearson], 'Martin Luther: his influence on the material and intellectual welfare of Germany', *WR*, 121:241 (1884), p. [1].
[118] Ibid., p. 3.   [119] Ibid., p. 6.   [120] Ibid., p. 16.   [121] Ibid., p. 19.
[122] Ibid., pp. 24–5.
[123] Ibid., pp. 31–3; cf. J. Janssen, *Geschichte des deutschen Volkes seit dem Ausgang des Mittelalters* (8 vols, Freiburg im Breisgau, 1876–1894).
[124] [Pearson], 'Martin Luther', p. 41.

dogmatic religion on the attention of modern civilization.[125] 'Reformed Europe', Pattison intoned in one of his rare later sermons before Oxford University, possessed an ideal of intellectual culture which it had 'inherited from Greek civilisation'.[126] By the time he ascended the pulpit, in 1865, he had come to rue his youthful forays into religious polemic and ecclesiastical history. Dogmatic Protestantism now became a recurrent target in his writings on the history of literature and scholarship.[127] Pattison's semi-autobiographical biography of *Isaac Casaubon* regretted how the untiring Huguenot classical scholar and philologist had periodically squandered his gifts on patristics, which he approached as a matter of consecrated precedent instead of historical analysis. At the conclusion of the work Pattison quoted a telling remark from the work of Eduard Zeller, one of the German scholars he came to idealize as his departure from Christianity solidified. An adherent of the Tübingen School during the *Vormärz*, Zeller's early interests in radical theology slowly receded as he came to focus on the history of Greek philosophy, though he never completely jettisoned Hegelianism.[128] In a passage that offered a pointed comment on why Pattison had left theology behind, he translated one of Zeller's aphoristic sentences: 'when, in the very conception of the problem, the intellectual activity is engaged in the service of a religious interest, a scientific solution cannot be looked for.'[129] Pattison's study of *Milton* was coloured by the same duality. First published in John Morley's *English Men of Letters* series in 1879, Pattison presented the poet and political theorist as still more torn between two selves than Casaubon had been. 'The Puritan self', on Pattison's reading, constantly wrestled with 'the poet's self', the lover of 'culture and the humanities'.[130] Pattison's inclination to construe the critical and religious currents at work during the sixteenth and seventeenth centuries as radically severed from one another mirrored his secularized vision of the ends of true scholarship in nineteenth-century conditions.

The new vogue for the Renaissance powerfully informed secular interpretations of the roots and ends of modern progress. But a number of advanced thinkers doubted the adequacy of self-development for serving as the basis of social order. The wateriness of Renaissance values as a foundation for ethical commitment, as opposed to the more constructive

[125] Ibid., pp. 5, 22 and n.; Jones, *Intellect and character.*
[126] M. Pattison, *Sermons* (London, 1885), p. 125.   [127] Pattison, *Memoirs*, p. 159.
[128] On Zeller, see chapter two of this volume at p. 85.
[129] M. Pattison, *Isaac Casaubon 1559–1614* (London, 1875), pp. 374–8, 524–5 and 524 n.
[130] Pattison, *Milton* (London, 1913), pp. 67–8.

agency of altruism, ran through George Eliot's *Romola*, set in the superficial and lying world of 1490s Florence, and speaking to contemporary Britain.[131] Even among some of its strongest exponents, the appeal of the Renaissance as a source of value could be qualified by its lack of what the Cambridge moral philosopher Henry Sidgwick, in his criticisms of Arnold's doctrine of culture, called 'fire and strength': the inspiration religion gave to heroism, duty, and triumph over circumstance.[132] John Addington Symonds, one of the most influential figures in impressing the Renaissance into the British cultural lexicon, was drawn to the subject out of his love of Italy and belief in sexual freedom. But his enthusiasm for the 'natural' was always tempered by his residual gratitude, greater than Arnold's, for the historic benefits of Protestant vigour.

Born into a family of Shropshire nonconformists, Symonds spurned a legal career after leaving Balliol College, Oxford, in favour of a life as a man of letters. Though his marriage was affectionate and produced children, Symonds was preoccupied by his homosexuality, and spent much time in Italy from his first visit in 1861 until his death in Rome in 1893 in order to escape from repressive English domesticity. Symonds' *Renaissance in Italy*, his seven-volume, literarily ornate *magnum opus* published between 1875 and 1886, grew out of these experiences. It was while he was completing the first volume, he claimed, that he first encountered and was deeply struck by Burckhardt.[133] Although Symonds' idea of the Renaissance was not demonstrably taken from Burckhardt, his description of it as 'the whole transition from the Middle Ages to the Modern World' indicates why he could appreciate him. The period was, thought Symonds, 'the history of the attainment of self-conscious freedom by the human spirit manifested in the European races', which inspired new achievements in the art, science, literature, and invention. This was not solely an event in the past: 'the truth is that in many senses we are still in mid-Renaissance.'[134] Many of Symonds' descents from the general to the particular amounted to sometimes hidden, sometimes overt defences of the naturalness of same-sex attraction. 'When Luca Signorelli drew naked young men ... he created for the student a symbol

[131] G. Eliot, *Romola*, ed. D. Barrett (London, 1996); first published 1862–3.

[132] Garnett, 'Introduction', to Arnold, *Culture and Anarchy*, xviii–xix; [H. Sidgwick], 'The prophet of culture', *MM*, 16:94 (1867), pp. 271–80.

[133] J.A. Symonds, *Renaissance in Italy* (7 vols, London, 1875–1886); P. Grosskurth, *John Addington Symonds: a biography* (London and Southampton, 1964), pp. 251–2. Grosskurth speculates that Symonds expanded his work to such length in order to avoid comparison with the Swiss historian.

[134] J.A. Symonds, *Renaissance in Italy: the age of the despots*, 2nd edn (London, 1880) [volume 1], pp. 1–4.

of the attitude assumed by fine art in its liberty of outlook over the whole range of human interests.'[135]

Italian painters and sculptors enabled Symonds to idealize and ennoble voluptuous earthly passion, in ways that separated him from the stern puritanism of his forebears. Writing to Henry Sidgwick in July 1880, after destroying a number of his papers, Symonds reported the psychological interest he felt in his own and his ancestors' correspondence before committing it to the flames. 'The ardent faith of the Puritan impulse' evident in his seventeenth-century Independent forebears, after passing through 'formalized Methodism' and 'strict Puritan orthodoxy' in the eighteenth century, faded into the 'robust theistic complexion' of his father's letters. It expanded 'finally into a free and gaseous atmosphere' in Symonds' own aesthetically preoccupied missives. 'The spiritual problem was the main matter of all these letters', he wrote.[136]

The wistfulness with which Symonds related the transmutations of his ancestral beliefs furnishes a presumption against the simplistic claim that Symonds 'celebrated paganism over Christian superstition' in his Renaissance studies.[137] Symonds certainly understood the Renaissance, further developing the ideals of classical Greece, to have released European civilization from the self-denying, ascetic culture of medieval religion. He thought of the growth of religious art as having incubated the worship of the human body for its own sake, thereby undermining the premises of earlier ecclesiasticism.[138] He closed his volumes by relating how the Catholic hierarchy, realizing the danger, set about extinguishing the intellectual and artistic freedoms cultivated during the Renaissance. 'Over the Dead Sea of social putrefaction floated the sickening oil of Jesuitical hypocrisy.'[139] It was not only Catholicism for which the ancestrally dissenting Symonds had harsh words. 'The counter-movement of the modern spirit' crystallized not solely in papal countermeasures, but in 'Protestant establishments'.[140] He even insisted that the medieval asceticism against which he revolted was soundly rooted in Christ's own severity towards fleshliness and earthly ties.[141]

---

[135] Symonds, *Renaissance in Italy: the fine arts* (London, 1877) [volume 3], pp. 23–4.

[136] J.A. Symonds to H. Sidgwick, 8 July 1880, in J.A. Symonds, *Letters and papers of John Addington Symonds*, ed. H.F. Brown (London, 1923), p. 105.

[137] R. Norton, 'Symonds, John Addington (1840–1893)', *ODNB*.

[138] Symonds, *Age of the despots*, pp. 17–18; Symonds, *The fine arts*, pp. 7–8.

[139] Symonds, *Renaissance in Italy: the Catholic reaction: 2 parts: part 1* (London, 1886) [volume 6], p. 67.

[140] Symonds, *Renaissance in Italy: Italian literature: in two parts: part II* (London, 1881) [volume 5], p. 490.

[141] Symonds, *The fine arts*, pp. 24–5 and 24 n.

Symonds nevertheless repeatedly returned to the idea that the Reformation and the Renaissance were two parts of the same movement, still active in the present, which imparted 'recovered energy' and 'freedom of the reason' to religious thought and national politics just as much as to culture, art, and science.[142] These were not points on which Symonds was wholly consistent. Sometimes he wrote of intolerant, post-Reformation Protestantism as though it were a continuation of clericalist bigotry, its progressive significance lying purely in the impetus it gave to scepticism.[143] Elsewhere he thought of the Renaissance and the Reformation as a 'twofold Liberalism', which he hoped would ultimately result in the harmonization of 'the classical ideal of a temperate and joyous natural life' with 'the conscience educated by the Gospel'.[144] Italian thinkers who sought to philosophize Christianity by expressing it in terms of heathen speculation left him cold: 'they lack the vigorous simplicity that gave its force to Luther's intuition.'[145] Symonds' unwillingness altogether to jettison an ethical form of Protestantism as an inspiration for action mirrored his criticisms, expressed in his correspondence, of Matthew Arnold's one-sidedness. Writing to Arthur Galton, a former Catholic priest who had become an Anglican vicar, Symonds complained of the Arnoldian 'Gospel' of culture of which Galton was an apostle. He judged that it 'leaves out a whole & very vital element of human life; the ignoring of which makes his Gospel jejune for disciples, though it has been aptly uttered by himself'.[146] Symonds even called him 'the egotistical Mat'.[147]

The intellectual atmosphere of Symonds' undergraduate college provides some illumination as to what may have lain behind this two-mindedness, not to say confusion, concerning the relationship between the Renaissance and religious commitment. After arriving at Balliol in 1858, Symonds was taught by the newly elected fellow and future Idealist worthy Thomas Hill Green, who later married his sister, Charlotte.[148]

---

[142] Symonds, *Age of the despots*, p. 24.

[143] Symonds, *Renaissance in Italy: the Catholic reaction: in 2 parts: part II* (London, 1886) [volume 7], pp. 422–9; Symonds, *Italian literature: in two parts: part II*, p. 490.

[144] Symonds, *The fine arts*, pp. 35–6; Symonds, *The Catholic Reaction: in 2 parts: part II*, pp. 422–3.

[145] Symonds, *Renaissance in Italy: the revival of learning* (London, 1877) [volume 2], p. 23.

[146] J.A. Symonds to A. Galton, 5 April 1887, in Schueller and Peters, *Letters of John Addington Symonds*, iii, 220; cf. A. Galton, 'Matthew Arnold; his practice, teaching, and example: an essay in criticism', *CGHH*, 3:11 (1888), pp. 83–108, esp. p. 106: Galton had sent Symonds a copy of the essay. For identification of Galton, see M. Arnold, *The letters of Matthew Arnold*, ed. C.Y. Lang (6 vols, Charlottesville, VA, and London, 1996–2001), v, 427 n.

[147] Quoted in Grosskurth, *John Addington Symonds*, at p. 104.

[148] A. Vincent, 'Green, Thomas Hill (1836–1882)', *ODNB*.

He also received instruction in Hegel from Jowett, who became a lifelong friend.[149] While Symonds cast around for some satisfying alternative to law in the 1860s, Jowett imposed on him the ungrateful task of translating a part of Eduard Zeller's *Philosophie der Griechen*, in which he persevered for several years.[150] Zeller's post-Hegelian treatment of Greek philosophy as forming an evolving organic unity which anticipated Christian theology, together with Green's influence, helped to implant loosely idealist assumptions into Symonds' mind in the 1860s.[151] As he explained to a correspondent shortly afterwards, 'it is the immense amount of culture'—which Symonds distinguished from 'what M. Arnold calls culture'—'contained in solution in the German theories of the Universe that gives them a value superior to the systems of the empirical schools.'[152] Idealist intimations continued to surface in the *Renaissance in Italy*, where his literary flourishes invoked 'the Divine Mind' and 'the eternal sunrise of God's presence'.[153] No part of history, he assumed, was sufficient in itself. Symonds accordingly found it difficult to think of history in terms of radical ruptures, or that one side of a world-historical development—the Renaissance—could truly be complete without its religious counterpart. 'The strife of Protestantism and Catholicism was needed for preserving moral and religious elements which might have been too lightly dropped, and for working these into the staple of the modern consciousness.'[154]

Symonds' ambivalent view of the relationship between religious and secular forces in shaping progressive humanity gave way to an effulgent emphasis on their deeper affinities in the hands of liberal Protestant historians who wrote with a more assured sense of apologetic purpose. As early as the 1850s, these historians had tried to link the Reformation to a preceding change in cultural sensibility, in a sense that was more conceptually charged than simply pointing to the discovery of textual criticism or the invention of the printing press as technical preconditions for the restoration of the Bible. Henry Hart Milman, hopeful of spiritualizing Protestantism by freeing it from scholastic doctrinalism, had sketched the foothills of the Reformation anew in the last volume of his *Latin Christianity*. The freeing of Christian art from the trammels of

---

[149] Grosskurth, *John Addington Symonds*, pp. 48–53, 100.
[150] Tübingen Universitätsbibliothek, Md. 747.757: J.A. Symonds to E. Zeller, 31 August 1867. The missive is omitted from Schueller's and Peters' edition of Symonds' *Letters*.
[151] Hartung, 'Ein Schatzkammer des Wissens'; On Zeller in Britain, see chapter two of this volume at p. 85.
[152] J.A. Symonds to H.G. Dakyns, 29 October 1873, in Symonds, *Letters of John Addington Symonds*, ii, 318.
[153] Symonds, *The Catholic Reaction: in 2 parts: part II*, pp. 432, 438.
[154] Ibid., pp. 411–12.

Byzantine tradition and formalism, especially through the softer and humanizing brushstrokes of 'the great deliverer', Giotto, was for Milman 'prophetic, at least, if not presentient of a wider Catholicism'.[155] Drawing on earlier reappraisals of Christian art history, Milman came close to giving voice to the idea of a unified 'Renaissance' by proposing that a generalised transformation of the human spirit had taken place in the later Middle Ages, of which Protestantism was the religious expression.[156]

Similar assessments became more common, and more directly present-minded, as the Renaissance took more definite shape in the minds of religious progressives. Those of an advanced disposition, especially, posited that the common origins of the Renaissance and the Reformation in an underlying spiritual and critical revolution both vindicated the rationality of religion and demanded that the atmosphere of the Renaissance should now be let in afresh to clear away the obscurantism of the Reformation's misshapen heirs. The Unitarian historian Charles Beard, editor of his denomination's *Theological Review* between 1864 and 1879, went so far as to define the progressive features of the Reformation in terms of the Renaissance, in order to encourage modern Protestants to align themselves with earthly fulfilment and scientific advance.[157] In the Hibbert Lectures he gave in Oxford and London in 1883, the published version of which he couched as a contribution to the Luther commemoration then underway, Beard declared that the Reformation 'was not, primarily, a theological, religious, or ecclesiastical movement at all'. Instead 'it was part of a general awakening of the human intellect', originating in the fourteenth century and urged on by the revival of classical learning and the discovery of the printing press. 'It was the life of the Renaissance infused into religion, under the influence of men of the grave and earnest Teutonic race.' The return wrought by the Reformation was properly to Hellenism, not Judaic Christianity.[158] The fact that Protestantism, down to Beard's time, had not been true to its nature was responsible for the difficulties in which theology now found itself. Historical reassessment, to Beard, was a precondition for righting the wrong.

Beard accepted that the initial impulse of the Reformation, through Luther, was religious.[159] But the early Reformers 'understood neither the

[155] *HLC*, vi, 612.

[156] Ibid., vi, 603 n.; cf. C. Lindsay, *Sketches of the history of Christian art* (3 vols, London, 1847), i, [xi]–xvii; A.F. Rio, *De la poésie Chrétienne dans son principe, dans sa matière et dans ses formes: forme de l'art, seconde partie* (Paris, 1836).

[157] A. Gordon, rev. R.K. Webb, 'Beard, Charles (1827–1888)', *ODNB*.

[158] C. Beard, *The Reformation of the sixteenth century in its relation to modern thought and knowledge* (London and Edinburgh, 1883), p. 2.

[159] Ibid., p. 80.

system which they attacked nor that which they founded, in its full relation to the long progress of the human mind'.[160] Luther's magical views of the sacraments; his belief in the devil; and the antinomian and anti-intellectual aspects of the doctrine of justification by faith alone, not to mention Calvin's reversion to scholasticism, were among those forces that conspired to make the Reformation 'a failure' when judged 'only by its theological and ecclesiastical development'.[161] But the principles of Protestantism, which might themselves be turned to criticize stale Protestant orthodoxism, were worth more than the use their pioneers had made of them. Luther's rejection of the scholastics' four-fold sense enabled the Bible, in course of time, to be read historically.[162] The liberty the Reformers claimed for themselves could not forever be denied to yet bolder spirits.[163] Beard traced how the tide unleashed by the Reformers overcame the barriers they vainly tried to erect in the subsequent development of philosophy, philology, higher criticism, geology, and evolutionary theory.[164] As part of the growth of philosophy, Beard included the emergence of historical sensibility. As societies advanced, and became conscious that they were advancing, forms of belief that belonged to earlier stages of society, such as the vengeful God implied in the penal theory of the atonement, became perceptibly irrational.[165]

Beard stopped short of treating the significance of the Reformation as lying exclusively in the impetus it gave to science and criticism. Luther's liberation of subjectivity, and the power of conscience, enabled 'changed individuality' by incorporating the human soul with the saviour's.[166] Negatively alluding to Arnold, Beard criticized those who valued religion 'as the supreme agent in the softening, the sweetening, the elevating of human life', and yet who imagined that its emotional benefits could exist independently of positive theology or the historical Jesus. 'Absolute Religion', purified of extinct forces through science and the continuing application of the Reformation principle, must crystallize around the fatherhood of God, the brotherhood of man, the kingdom of God, and the future state.[167] This new theology was, nevertheless, to owe very little to that of the Reformers. 'The Reformation that has been, is Luther's monument: perhaps the Reformation that is to be, will trace itself back to Erasmus.'[168] Karl Pearson pooh-poohed Beard's hopeful anticipation in

---

[160] Ibid., pp. 113–14.
[161] Ibid., pp. 137–9, 145–82, 263–99.
[162] Ibid., pp. 114–26.
[163] Ibid., p. 172. [164] Ibid., pp. 337–400.
[165] Ibid., esp. pp. 374–9.
[166] Ibid., pp. 130–1, 141–4.
[167] Ibid., pp. 404–30.
[168] Ibid., p. 73.

the *Westminster Review*: but for Luther, would not the Reformation have been Erasmian in the first place?[169]

The claim that the Protestant revolution ultimately could not live unless it reintegrated the critical and intellectual developments it had temporarily blocked nevertheless became argumentative staples for Protestants who hoped to impart an Erasmian spirit to their co-religionists. The Quaker activist, financier, and historian, Frederic Seebohm, favourably contrasted the poetical and critical temperaments of Erasmus, John Colet, and Thomas More with the regrettably Augustinan character of the Reformation in *The Oxford Reformers of 1498*.[170] Similarly, John Owen, a late-century Devonshire rector and Renaissance historian, saw the promising paths in nineteenth-century religion as leading back to the humanist movement rather than to the Reformation. In a series of studies published during the 1880s and 1890s, Owen argued that the Renaissance had been marked by a high-minded form of scepticism, which encouraged the intelligent exploration of the limits of knowledge without straying into irreligion. He supposed that the revivification of the spirit of Renaissance inquiry would teach humility to Darwinians, Hegelians, and religious dogmatists alike.[171] A friend of Charles Beard's, and a contributor to his *Theological Review*, Owen addressed the new Unitarian foundation at Manchester College, Oxford, in 1891 to express the hope that the society would invigorate the work of returning Christianity to its original simplicity which the Renaissance had begun.[172] Motifs with which Symonds had eclectically toyed gained systematic depth and polemical edge in the public moralism of *avant-garde* liberal Protestants.

The belief that the Renaissance was an important context for the Reformation, articulated in a swelling stream of polemical lectures and essays, quietly settled into the bedrock of a wider spectrum of historians' working assumptions. Writers whom an earlier generation of anti-Protestants had taught to be critical of the Reformation sometimes found their astringency softening under the influence of a changing climate. Mandell Creighton was too much of a high churchman and

---

[169] [Pearson], 'Martin Luther', p. 11.

[170] F. Seebohm, *The Oxford reformers of 1498: being a history of the fellow-work of John Colet, Erasmus, and Thomas More* (London, 1867), pp. 412–16; P.D.A. Harvey, 'Seebohm, Frederic (1833–1912)', *ODNB*.

[171] J. Owen, *The religious aspects of scepticism: a lecture delivered at the South Place Institute, London, April 19th, 1891* (London, 1891), pp. [5]–7; Owen, *The skeptics of the Italian Renaissance* (London, 1893), ix–xv, pp. 7–11, 416–17.

[172] Owen, *The modification of dogma regarded as a condition of human progress* (London, Edinburgh, and Manchester, 1891), pp. [3], 28–33. Owen even composed an elegy set at Beard's graveside: 'At Dr. C. Beard's grave', in his *Verse-musings on nature, faith, and freedom* (London, 1894), p. 312.

scrupulous scholar to be drawn into advocating visionary schemes of religious regeneration. But the former pupil of Edward Caird showed a certain idealizing sensibility when it came to identifying the spiritual undercurrents at work beneath the surface of history. His 1882–1894 *History of the Papacy*, in the midst of the publication of which he accepted the Dixie Chair, voiced regrets for the destructive and avoidable nature of the Lutheran Reformation in terms which registered his ecclesiological sympathies.[173] His temperamental gaiety and aesthetic refinement led him to criticize the hardened form of Reformation religion, puritanism, for having 'stamped upon English life the somewhat hard and joyless aspect which it still wears'.[174] Yet when he placed the main culpability for the severance of Christendom on the papacy, for refusing to adjust itself to the new reality of emergent European nationalities, Creighton was not reiterating the standard opinions of more sequacious high church historians.[175] Rather, he tended to characterize this movement towards nationality at the end of the Middle Ages as part of a general recovery of spiritual individuality, occurring through successive reformations in the life-stream of European history, encompassing politics, religion, and culture.

Creighton was especially given to expressing himself in these terms in his public addresses and occasional pamphlets, where the impartial self-repression evident in his *History* was less pronounced. 'To me it seems that the differentiation of nations is part of that continuous revelation of God's purposes which is contained in history', he remarked in a pamphlet entitled *The Idea of a National Church*, published by the Society for Promoting Christian Knowledge in 1898, while he was bishop of London. 'God bestows on mankind "diversities of gifts, but the same spirit."'[176] In a course of lectures which he delivered as bishop of Peterborough at St Paul's in 1892, and edited for posthumous publication by his widow, Louise, Creighton argued that the unity of the church might have survived the Reformation had it internalized the spirit of Francis of Assisi. Francis's authentically religious love of individual liberty, Christ's humanity, and God's presence in nature, and his indifference to the details of ecclesiastical systems, spurred on the Renaissance. But the rigidified church authorities vainly struggled to contain, instead of adopting, the historical forces which ultimately judged them and swept them away.[177] Creighton's

---

[173] M. Creighton, *History of the papacy from the great schism to the sack of Rome*, new edn (6 vols, London, 1907–1911), vi, 152–62. On Creighton's views of Luther, see O. Chadwick, *Creighton on Luther: an inaugural lecture* (Cambridge, 1959).
[174] M. Creighton, *The age of Elizabeth* (London, 1876), p. 197.
[175] Creighton, *Papacy*, i, 36; cf. Robertson, *Christian church*, iv, 649.
[176] Creighton, *The idea of a national church* (London, 1898), pp. 7–8.
[177] Creighton, 'The influence of the friars', in his *Historical lectures*, pp. 98–115.

ascription of a cross-fertilizing balance to the secular and spiritual forces that fed the Reformation expressed the partial supersession of ecclesiastical partisanship in his mind by a broader desire to trace the spiritual unity of history.

The integration of the Renaissance and the Reformation in historical explanation, while it hinted at the divine aspects of the world process to many, could seem to others to risk subsuming Protestantism into a bland idea of culture. That James Anthony Froude should have repeatedly drawn attention to the past and present tensions between those forces testified to his wish to challenge what he perceived to be the creeping popularity of such an assimilation. Escaping the youthful theological struggles that precipitated his resignation from Exeter College, Oxford, in 1849, to settle into life as an independent and independent-minded man of letters, Froude came to see historical study, especially that of the sixteenth century, as a way of shaking his contemporaries out of different kinds of complacency and falsehood.[178] Froude did not see history as a smooth evolution, or a balanced dialectic. Rather it was a story of gains won, and losses accrued, by means of a semi-Carlylean oscillation between living and dead forms, which it was the function of criticism to interrogate and character to forge. Protestantism, on Froude's reading, was foundational to England's historical and present identity.[179] History had now worn out its dogmatic content—the once-great doctrine of justification by faith had become as 'barren as the soil of a trodden footpath'—but Protestantism possessed abiding relevance as a kind of perennial anti-theology that could, if viewed rightly, reproach cant, externalism, and conventional opinion.[180]

Froude's lectures on the 'Times of Erasmus and Luther' at Newcastle in 1867 witnessed to his tendency to treat historical characters as significant for how they represented religious or cultural principles that straddled past and present. He detected that literary wisdom was now turning against the Reformers. Anglo-Catholics denounced Luther as a heretic; more worryingly, 'advanced thinkers'—he instanced Matthew Arnold, Thomas Babington Macaulay, Henry Thomas Buckle, and Goethe—deprecated him as narrow-minded and intolerant. The latter would have preferred that Europe had trusted in the course set by Erasmus towards gradual

---

[178] Garnett, 'Protestant histories'; A.F. Pollard, rev. W. Thomas, 'Froude, James Anthony (1818–1894)', *ODNB*.

[179] J.A. Froude, *History of England from the fall of Wolsey to the death of Elizabeth* (12 vols, London, 1856–1870); J.A. Froude, 'On progress', in his *Short studies on great subjects*, new edn (4 vols, London, 1895–1897), ii, 366–7.

[180] J.A. Froude, 'Times of Erasmus and Luther: three lectures delivered at Newcastle, 1867', in his *Short studies on great subjects*, new edn (4 vols, London, 1895–1897), i, 139.

religious reform by means of the expansion of knowledge.[181] Erasmian scepticism, Froude accepted, had helped to prepare the ground for an honest successor to the Roman system. But the world was ultimately moved, in the sixteenth century as at all times, by 'men of faith' rather than 'large-minded latitudinarian philosophers', of which Luther and Erasmus were respectively the ideal types. Toleration and cultivation only yielded benefits once mind and conscience were already roused.[182] Froude returned to Luther and Erasmus in a lecture series which he delivered after his return to the reformed Oxford as Regius Professor of Modern History in 1892. The exclusive self-certainty of Rome, latterly represented by Cardinal Newman, demanded Luther's sword, Froude said. Displaying greater sympathy for the Dutch scholar then he had previously shown, he acknowledged that the conflict came at the price of the 'purity and justice and mercy' which, for Erasmus, were the gospel's ideals. These were, however, simply not obtainable from the sixteenth-century papacy.[183] If history were to remain open to God, Froude's hearers had to listen for reorientations of value which the mere intellect could quicken, but not supply.

Froude's attempts to revitalize Protestantism in order to regenerate culture and politics more generally, a unifying theme in his wide-ranging authorial career, were given a highly idiosyncratic character by his preference for an open, even Erasmian, moral theism over the particular tenets of the theology that had first made the Reformation. Evangelicals, for whom Protestant doctrines were stems in need of cultivation rather than a Froudean uprooting, treated the new fashion for the Renaissance as a spur to emphasize more confidently what Europe distinctively owed to the Reformation, both religiously and as a civilization. R. W. Dale reassured intending preachers that the modern-day challenge presented by scientific intellectualism to religious belief amounted to a less comprehensive one than the church had faced from 'the new learning of the Renaissance', for the latter's literary and philosophical character had 'appealed to those very elements of our nature which are shaped by religious faith'. Casting the succession of the Renaissance by the Reformation as one of those church-historical cycles in which worldliness had given way to revival, Dale considered that effective preaching was no less capable of awaking the sense of guilt in his own, prideful age than it had been during the sixteenth century.[184] He went on to preach against secular understandings of the

---

[181] Ibid., i, 47–8.   [182] Ibid., I, 87, 114, 135.

[183] J.A. Froude, *Life and letters of Erasmus: lectures delivered at Oxford 1893–4* (London, 1894), pp. 360–1. On Froude's lectures, see Brady, *James Anthony Froude*, pp. 442–8.

[184] Dale, 'Evangelistic preaching', in his *Nine lectures*, pp. 186–211.

Reformation's origins during the Luther commemoration of 1883. It was not a sound 'philosophy of history', he told his Birmingham congregation, that turned the Reformation into a mere impersonal product of intellectual forces. Such a movement was inconceivable without the religious genius of Luther, whose God-given strength changed the course of European history.[185] Henry Wace offered a similar analysis in his introduction to the commemorative translation of Luther's works which he co-edited while principal of King's College, London. 'Erasmus lacked alike the moral energy necessary to rouse the action of the laity, and the spiritual insight necessary to justify that action', he judged, whereas 'Luther possessed both'.[186]

Such authors increasingly connected their defence of the theological heritage of the Reformation to an insistence that the purification of doctrine had given birth to social achievements, which advanced critics often preferred to ascribe to the Renaissance's reclamation of the truth that man was the measure of all things. In his Religious Tract Society pamphlet on Christian evidences, Principal Cairns declared that the Reformation had added an inner light to the work of 'the greatest humanists'. He pointed to Britain, Germany, and America, to support his claim that 'wherever there is a Bible, a Sabbath, a regulated liberty, a national education, a pure and manly literature, the Reformation is its fountain-head.'[187] 'The principles of liberty', Wace remarked in conclusion to one of his Bampton Lectures, were only secure in that part of the world that had let in the Reformation. Half of Europe, and much of the globe, remained chained to superstitions, idolatries, and delusions. 'The power which originally emancipated men from that servitude may safely be relied on to effect a similar deliverance', and to assuage that pessimism as to the prospects of civilization which Wace saw drifting from Germany to England. Although evangelicals resisted the secularization of late-Victorian Protestantism, they often humanized it as they did so.[188]

The main lineaments of later-Victorian evangelicals' defences of the Reformation connected the sermons and pamphlets in which they were controversially evolved to Thomas Martin Lindsay's weightier 1906–1907 *History of the Reformation*. Published in T. & T. Clark's *International Theological Library*, this was the most scholarly and substantial treatment of the Reformation as a European movement to come from any of its Victorian British students. In the attention he gave to socio-economic

---

[185] [Anon.], 'Carr's Lane Chapel', *Birmingham Daily Post*, 12 November 1883, p. 5.

[186] Wace, 'Primary principles', xxix–xxx.

[187] Cairns, *Christ the central evidence of Christianity*, pp. 19–20.

[188] Wace, *Foundations*, pp. 185–6.

dislocation in Germany as a context for the spread of the Reformation, Lindsay was a British pioneer.[189] At the same time, his insistence that 'the central thing about the Reformation was that it meant a rediscovery of religion as *faith*' located the work within the longer-term debates about the Reformation's authority in which Lindsay had participated as an active Free Churchman.[190] William Robertson Smith's former defender explained that the religion restored by the Reformation, centring on the allied doctrines of the universal priesthood of believers and justification by faith, was 'no philosophical abstraction, to be described in definitions'. Rather, it represented the 'personal experience of the believing Christian'; Lindsay's conceptual vocabulary now registered definite traces of contact with Ritschl and Harnack.[191] He accordingly affirmed that the Reformers read the Bible in 'the simple historical sense' as 'a new home for a new life within which they could have intimate fellowship with God'.[192] To insist that the Reformers' religious imaginations had centred upon the Bible's verbal inerrancy, rather than the living word the text disclosed to its prayerful readers, was fundamentally to misunderstand the Reformation doctrine of scripture. Lindsay's decision to devote substantially more space to Luther than to Calvin reflected the separation he made between the undergirding truths of the Reformation and subsequent attempts to define them systematically. Calvin's theology, he remarked, was leavened by neither 'poetry nor art'.[193]

The counterpart to Lindsay's positive case was his resistance to recent and continuing attempts either to lessen the Reformation's spiritual achievement, or to secularize its historical significance. Lindsay accepted that the origins of the Reformation stretched back into the Middle Ages; but some contexts were more pertinent than others. Citing Symonds and Burckhardt, Lindsay agreed that the Renaissance embodied the 'transition from the mediaeval to the modern world'. Its faith was chiefly placed in man rather than in God, however, and so its role in preparing the way for the Reformation was limited to the dissemination of printing and the critical spirit.[194] Socinianism, much more than Lutheranism, was the child of humanism.[195] The Reformation's deeper background was instead to be found in the popular religious life of late-medieval Germany, evident in pious households and the spread of popular preaching and

---

[189] T.M. Lindsay, *A history of the Reformation*, 2nd edn (2 vols, Edinburgh, 1907–1908), i, 79–113.
[190] Ibid., ii, 473.   [191] Ibid., i, 426, 430–2, 447.
[192] Ibid., i, 453, 455, 459.   [193] Ibid., i, 189–399, ii, 61–135, 154.
[194] Ibid., i, 42–78.   [195] Ibid., ii, 473–4.

'fireside teaching'.[196] Lindsay's ascription of a proto-Protestant character to medieval Christian domesticity may have informed his belief, expressed in correspondence with the Anglo-Florentine author, Janet Ross, that the Reformation represented a masculine principle, ever-necessary to prevent religion from becoming overly feminized.[197] The new evangelical openness to the constructive aspects of medieval religion buttressed Lindsay's restatement of the Reformation's historical uniqueness.

The convictions which led Lindsay to distance the Reformation from the Renaissance, also caused him to chafe against a newer, sociopolitical appraisal of its significance. Albert Frederick Pollard, a graduate of Oxford's relatively young history school and, from 1903, professor of constitutional history at University College, London, made marked conceptual breaks in the study of the English Reformation that matched his institutional innovations as a strong-armed organizer of England's emergent historical profession.[198] Pollard sought to wrest the period from theological ructions by treating religious issues as subordinate to, or as code for, imperatives that were, at root, political. The English Reformation lent itself especially well to an interpretation which he extended to sixteenth-century Europe more generally. 'The Reformers set up the divine right of the state against the divine right of the Church', he declared in his 1907 *Factors in Modern History*; 'and the king was their Great High Priest'.[199] Where his Methodist forebears might have condemned the English Reformers for such Erastianism, Pollard, a thoroughly secularized New Liberal, celebrated them for aiding the work of the New Monarchy in ushering on the modern national state.[200] Though he linked the English Reformation to the political realism and secular learning of the European Renaissance, symbolized for Pollard more by Machiavelli than Signorelli, he distanced it from the extremism of the Continental theological movements led by Luther and Zwingli.[201] Instead he emphasized

---

[196] Ibid., i, 114–57, here at 126; cf. Lindsay's 'Family and popular religion in Germany on the eve of the Reformation', *LQR*, 10:2 (1903), pp. 209–38.

[197] T.M. Lindsay to J. Ross, 19 October 1907, in his *Letters of Principal T.M. Lindsay to Janet Ross* (London, Bombay, and Sydney, 1923), p. 27.

[198] Pollard went on to found the Institute of Historical Research in 1921. On his significance in the history of historiography, see P. Collinson, 'Pollard, Albert Frederick (1869–1948)', *ODNB*; Bentley, *Modernizing England's past*, pp. 204–5 and *passim*; Blaas, *Continuity and anachronism*, pp. [274]–344.

[199] A.F. Pollard, *Factors in modern history* (London, 1907), pp. 76–7, 159.

[200] Pollard, *Henry VIII*, new edn (London, 1905), pp. 439–40 (first edition 1902); Blaas, *Continuity and anachronism*, p. 293.

[201] Pollard, *Factors*, pp. 69–70, 158–9; Pollard, *Thomas Cranmer and the English Reformation 1489–1556* (New York and London, 1904), p. [303]; Pollard, 'The Reformation under Edward VI', in A.W. Ward, G.W. Prothero, and S. Leathes (eds), *The Cambridge Modern History: volume II: The Reformation* (Cambridge, 1904), p. 478.

the debts of Cranmer and other commonsensical Reformers to the indigenous anti-clericalism of John Wycliffe, which looked to the state to restrain church abuses.[202]

Pollard's affirmation of the Reformation, and contempt for the decayed state of the late-medieval church, belonged in one respect to a venerable English Protestant tradition; but his unsentimentally political assessment of the sixteenth century, heralding a break from cherished Victorian pieties, made Lindsay uncomfortable. He respectfully drew on Pollard's studies, whilst adding corrective notes to preserve the English Reformation's links to a universal epiphany. 'Mr. Pollard', he wrote, did not sufficiently allow for the fact that 'the theological question which separated every medieval Reformer from the thinkers of the Reformation was, How the benefits won by the atoning work of Christ were to be appropriated by men?'[203] Where earlier Free Church historians did not shy away from opportunities to deprecate the Church of England's Erastian origins, Lindsay deemed it more important to secure the Reformation's common spiritual legacy from those who would marginalize or ignore it.[204]

The non-metaphysical and Protestant ecumenical strains of Lindsay's *History of the Reformation* epitomized one important strand of the wider Victorian response to Protestant history. By reclaiming the transformational importance of the sixteenth-century religious revolution from the temporarily necessary but now superseded doctrinal forms which had developed after it, evangelical Protestants were able to reinvigorate the atonement-centred religion which the Reformation had restored. By situating the Reformation in the context of general history, they were able to emphasize its particularity, whilst integrating it within a continuous spiritual history that bound nations and denominations into a larger providential scheme. Liberal Protestants such as Tulloch and Beard advanced a partly overlapping argument, to rather different ends. They too regretted the intrusion of the scholastic spirit into Protestant theology, but identified its contaminating effects from an earlier date, and sometimes in doctrines that evangelicals regarded as fundamental, such as justification by faith alone. At the same time, they often stressed the Reformation's affinities to the Renaissance, in order to produce an historic precedent for a reasonable religion of the progressive intelligence such as they hoped to forge in the present day. Although secularist writers denied that such a reconciliation was possible, the idea that the Reformation and the Renaissance might be held together in a kind of solution, by a loosely

---

[202] Pollard, *Cranmer*, pp. 90–1.
[203] Lindsay, *History of the Reformation*, ii, 318, 358 n.–359 n.
[204] Cf. Cunningham, *Historical theology*, i, 401.

idealist and consciously sacralized vision of human time, exerted a wider appeal. It touched high churchmen such as Creighton and, in Symonds, a critic at the outermost edges of religiosity. Thus the Reformation, which together with the early church and the Middle Ages had once been isolated and made absolute by certain kinds of religious actor, came to seem part of a progressively evolving spiritual order to a broad spectrum of later-Victorian moralists. The projection of sectarian disputes onto history lost something of its former urgency, as the specifically Protestant or more loosely spiritual roots of progress within history demanded more deliberate vindication.

5

Reason and Religion in Modern History

POSITIVISM AND HISTORY

As history came to acquire intellectual authority over theological questions, different phases of the religious past became significant for what they revealed about Christianity's normative state. Confessional identities that were at first reinforced by static idealizations or deprecations of particular periods, thereafter underwent redefinition or erosion as interest grew in the ways in which progressive development had shaped and connected different epochs of ecclesiastical history. This changing emphasis, as has been indicated, did not solely arise from a dialogue internal to theological culture. It also represented an adaptive response to the external sting and stimulus of secular understandings of time and value. The history of human moral and religious consciousness became a new kind of divine evidence, now that non-theological accounts of history and science intruded into ethical and philosophical provinces which theologians had once regarded as securely their own. In this environment, religious and irreligious critics began to clash over the origins of modernity, and the forms of knowledge appropriate to it. As well as interacting in Victorian conceptions of the early church, the Middle Ages, and the Reformation, religious and relatedly secular ideas of history came to structure conceptions of progress in this more general sense.

This debate is the focus of the present chapter. 'Modernity' was not a term Victorians much used; but it fairly denotes their own sense that they inhabited what John Stuart Mill called an 'age of transition in opinions' between an old and a new world.[1] The intellectual task of that age, in Mill's view and that of many others, was to mend the broken lights of the present so as to illuminate the bases of knowledge and value on which the future might stably rest. Mill's famous division of philosophy into the

---

[1] J.S. Mill, *Autobiography*, ed. J.M. Robson (London, 1989), p. [1] (first edition 1873).

school of 'Intuition' on the one hand, which treated received or supposedly innate ideas as the voice of God and nature, and his own, more
radical school of 'Experience' which denied the authority of intuition on
the other, was one tendentious intervention in a wider debate over the
proper relationship between mind, spirit, and knowledge.[2] At the heart of
this chapter is the problem of how the competing epistemologies associated with that division drove debate over the history of mind. Differing
accounts of the origins and essence of modern thought involved contrasting assessments of its ultimate direction.

In Victorian conditions, critics who provocatively dismissed or fore-
closed metaphysical and theological argument often simultaneously laid
claim to modernizing intellectual ancestries in the post-Reformation
period. The spread of anti-metaphysical conceptions of knowledge
expressed itself in the coining of neologisms which worked their way
into a common critical vocabulary. 'Positivism', a word that entered
widespread English usage in the 1850s in specific reference to the philosophy of Auguste Comte, soon acquired overlapping, looser implications
(and often a lower case 'p') as it came to be associated with phrases such as
'agnosticism', coined by Thomas Huxley in 1869, and 'scientific materialism'. Whilst these terms possessed different conceptual ancestries, contemporaries often came to employ them and their cognates broadly and
interchangeably to describe conceptions of mind which limited the sphere
of knowledge to the world of observable phenomena.[3] This is the sense in
which they are used here. Nineteenth-century epistemological phenomenalism was often inflected by Kant's insistence that the necessary conditions of perception separated the knowing subject from things in

---

[2] Ibid., pp. 202–3.

[3] On the wider importance of scientific and epistemological neologisms in nineteenth-
century intellectual culture, see Turner, *Between science and religion*; C.D. Cashdollar, *The
transformation of theology 1830–1890: positivism and Protestant thought in Britain and
America* (Princeton, NJ, 1989); B. Lightman and G. Dawson (eds), *Victorian scientific
naturalism: community, identity, continuity* (Chicago, IL, 2014); Lightman, *Origins of
agnosticism*; J. Bennett, 'A history of "rationalism" in Victorian Britain', *Modern Intellectual
History*, 15:1 (2018), pp. 63–91. Turner and Lightman stress that many freethinkers
distanced themselves from Positivism on the grounds of its pseudo-religious character:
Turner, *Between science and religion*, p. 11; Lightman, *Origins of agnosticism*, p. 23. But it
was common for contemporaries implicitly to align Positivism with other intellectual
categories, insofar as they involved an anti-metaphysical epistemology. Writing in 1887,
the Positivist James Cotter Morison claimed that whilst the sceptics of the 1850s had been
'pantheists' or 'deists', today they were 'agnostics': J. Cotter Morison, *The service of man: an
essay towards the religion of the future* (London, 1887), pp. 42–3. Robert Flint, in an essay
published in 1905, claimed that the most powerful movement of the day was 'the one
variously designated empiricism, positivism, phenomenalism': 'Tendencies of the age with
reference to the Church and Clergy', in his *On theological, biblical, and other subjects*
(Edinburgh and London, 1905), p. 95.

themselves, and by Hume's earlier suggestion that thought was merely a cerebral agitation with no necessary connection to the reality of the external world. It came to be strongly linked both to the scientific method, and to particular readings of that method's historical origins and projected triumph. In particular, Auguste Comte's and Henry Thomas Buckle's attempts to unearth the laws governing social progress quintessentially represented that synthetic tendency.[4] Though often stereotyped as materialists by their opponents, both conceived of the motor of historical progress in intellectual terms, as consisting essentially in the ever-greater understanding of the reign of discoverable law in the natural and human worlds. That understanding had been expanding rapidly in the period connecting the early glimmers of the scientific revolution in the sixteenth century to the present day. A relatively agnostic view of mind—though more physiological in Comte's case, and associationist in Buckle's—expressed itself in a correspondingly empiricist and provocatively secular conception of where progressive intellectual transition began.

Buckle and Comte were immensely if diffusely influential writers; but they helped to call alternative, theologically rooted understandings of historical progress into self-conscious existence. William Lecky's researches into the dynamics of 'rationalism', somewhat preceding his *European Morals*, heralded the first of two significant directions taken by this reaction.[5] The clubbable Anglo-Irish politician showed himself to have been closer than either Buckle or Comte to the conventional centre of Victorian thought, by integrating elements of Comte's and Buckle's sociological approaches to history with the supposition that the historical operation of rationalism purified and strengthened the free Protestant conscience. Lecky was concerned to differentiate the decay of dogmatic theology, substantially rooted in the progressive effects of the Reformation denied by Comte and Buckle, from the timeless, partly intuitive kernel of the Christian religion. This marked him out, not as an ambivalently external observer of Christianity, but as practising a radical form of what

---

[4] A. Comte, *Cours de philosophie positive* (6 vols, Paris, 1830–1842), trans. H. Martineau as *The positive philosophy of Auguste Comte* (2 vols, London, 1853); A.,Comte, *Système de politique positive; ou, traité de sociologie instituant le religion de l'humanité* (4 vols, Paris, 1851–1854), trans. J.H. Bridges et al. as *System of positive polity* (4 vols, London, 1875–1877); *HCE*. Important secondary studies of these writers and their influence include E. Fuchs, *Henry Thomas Buckle: Geschichtsschreibung und Positivismus in England und Deutschland* (Leipzig, 1994); M. Pickering, *Auguste Comte: an intellectual biography* (3 vols, Cambridge, 1999–2009); T.R. Wright, *The Religion of Humanity: the impact of Comtean Positivism on Victorian Britain* (Cambridge, 1986); Cashdollar, *Transformation of theology*.

[5] *HRE*; McCartney, *Lecky*; B. Stuchtey, *W.E.H. Lecky (1838–1903): historisches Denken und politisches Urteilen eines anglo-irischen Gelehrten* (Göttingen and Zurich, 1997).

was a widespread Victorian apologetic procedure.[6] After 1870, an increasing number of historians became concerned to make a comparable case. John Tulloch in the Church of Scotland, and John Hunt in the Church of England, argued that post-Reformation intellectual history witnessed not to the supersession of religious thought, but to its purification. The history of seventeenth-century theology acquired a new significance in this context, whilst that of the eighteenth century—which revivalists often deprecated—underwent notable rehabilitation.[7] The argument that the modern history of theology manifested its progressive energy, able constructively to interact with and even to shape scientific and political improvement, did not persuade everyone. Leslie Stephen, especially, presented a less roseate construal of eighteenth-century theology. But the history of rational theology came to offer a powerful authorization to those who believed that religious ideas could retain their place at the foundations of intellectual culture in the present.

In constructing alternative intellectual ancestries of modernity, Victorian rational theologians began to broaden the notion of induction and experience beyond the phenomenal limits which Comte and Buckle had affixed to them. Religious thought, in their hands, ceased to be a quantity of dogma eroded by advancing empiricism, and became instead a dynamic current of experience in its own right, whose self-renovating power witnessed to the mind's contact with the divine. This assumption, which also reinvigorated contemporary understandings of Catholic and Protestant orthodoxy, lay at the basis of the second main component of anti-agnostic interpretations of history. In an historical parallel to the more familiar late-Victorian reaction against scientific naturalism in favour of non-physiological understandings of the self and a new emphasis on the autonomy of the reasoning consciousness, a conception of experience expanded to incorporate religious experience in time became a means of vindicating the mind's capacity for transcendental intuition.[8] For secularizing historians concerned to disperse metaphysics, Comte and Mill had acted as invaluable philosophical helpmeets. A mixture of 'common sense' and Idealist philosophy in the cases of John Tulloch and Robert Flint, and purer Idealism in that of Edward Caird, offered anti-agnostic historians alternative conceptual resources as they sought to formulate objectively theistic philosophies of history from an examination of the contents of

---

[6] Arx misreads Lecky in this respect: *Progress*, pp. 64–123.

[7] On the complex Victorian response to this period, see B. Young, *The Victorian eighteenth century: an intellectual history* (Oxford, 2007).

[8] Turner, *Between science and religion*; R. Rylance, *Victorian psychology and British culture, 1850–1880* (Oxford, 2000); S.M. den Otter, *British Idealism and social explanation: a study in late Victorian thought* (Oxford, 1996).

subjective religious consciousness. The latter became a basic datum of experience, which secular readings of intellectual modernization could not touch. History, in such treatments, began to pass into psychology. An examination of the early writings of William Inge, a future dean of St Paul's, suggests that widespread and growing interest in the history of religious experience paved the way for the more systematic development of the psychology of religion as a field of apologetic inquiry around 1900. It was not a simple transition; these ways of thinking overlapped. But as a figure who illustrates how the authority of history might be eroded both by the internal dynamics of the arguments it fostered, and by the external shock ineluctably administered to progressivist assumptions by the First World War, Inge provides an appropriate end point for this study.

SOCIOLOGY, RELIGION, AND THE MODERN MIND

Religious and metaphysical questions lay at the heart of the excitement and antagonism generated by the high-Victorian development of sociological understandings of history.[9] At a period when it was common to strive unabashedly for comprehensive synthesis across different fields of knowledge, intellectuals' search for the causes of historical advance in time, as a means of unearthing the laws of social progress, was never a self-contained exercise. For the ways they understood those causes were founded on particular ideas of what it was possible—and desirable—for the human mind to know. Auguste Comte and Henry Thomas Buckle, especially, pursued an historical method that rested on an anti-intuitive epistemology. To them deduction made in dialogue with empirical induction was the activity through which general laws were discovered. The same process lay at the foundation of a progressive science of society. Placing that science at the spearhead of European modernity, they accordingly sought the origins of modern intellectual progress, in no small part, in the history of the inductive sciences, and the corresponding decline of theological authority over intellect and politics. Certain assumptions about the normative foundations of knowledge, therefore, invited a pointedly secular appraisal of the course history had taken in the past, and would pursue in the future. Theological claims, whether on the part of the

---

[9] O.Chadwick, *The secularization of the European mind in the nineteenth century* (Cambridge, 1975), pp. 229–49; G. Hawthorn, *Enlightenment and despair: a history of sociology* (Cambridge, 1976), p. 112; L. Goldman, *Science, reform, and politics in Victorian Britain: the Social Science Association 1857–1886* (Cambridge, 2002), pp. 313–15.

present-day historian or that of the historical subjects he studied, became either an irrelevance or an active impediment both to historical truth, and to the progressive advance of reason in time. Widespread unease over this position formed the backdrop to a large part of William Lecky's popularity, and thereafter to the growth of apologetic interest in the history of religious thought.

Whether by conscious discipleship, selective adaptation, or misrepresentation by hostile critics, it was difficult for British practitioners of the emergent science of 'sociology' to escape from the shadow of Comte, who had first publicly applied that term to the scientific study of social 'statics' and 'dynamics'.[10] Comte, who developed his interest in the reconstructive potential of a post-Revolutionary social science as a follower of Saint-Simon, went far beyond his French predecessors in his systematic importation of models and concepts borrowed from the natural sciences into social theory. Unlike many of the British historians who used scientific comparisons to understand religious development, Comte's historical science wholly excluded the explanatory invocation of spiritual forces. His writings were first systematically translated into English in the 1850s, disseminating his vastly influential elaboration of the 'law of three stages'.[11] From 1822, the year in which he claimed to have discovered that principle during a nocturnal epiphany, Comte maintained that all branches of human knowledge passed through a tripartite progress: a process which, though susceptible to disturbing influences, was as natural and inevitable as biological development.[12]

As Comte explained in his *Course in Positive Philosophy* (1830–1842), a primary theological stage of history, in which relatively primitive humans invoked supernatural ideas to explain the limited range of facts they observed, gave way to a second, metaphysical stage as experience widened. In this transitional period, vivid supernaturalism gave way to personified abstractions, such as the ideas of will and causation, which seemed capable of explaining an apparently more extensive and interconnected conception of nature. Yet the disintegration of theological authority accompanying this dynamism gave it a critical, even anarchic, character. This could only be overcome by the achievement of a new synthesis at the third, 'positive' stage. For it was only then that the search for metaphysical causes gave way to the full apprehension of the reign of discoverable law in the natural and human worlds, and the recognition of social unity.[13] Comte believed that European society had been inching towards the positive stage of social

---

[10] Pickering, *Auguste Comte*, i, 615.
[11] On Comte's British reception, see Wright, *Religion of Humanity*.
[12] Pickering, *Comte*, i, 60–8, 195–213.   [13] Comte, *Positive philosophy*, i, [1]–3.

organization since the first emergence of modern industry and science during the fourteenth century. The advance of positive philosophy, he held, had first accelerated rapidly from the time of Bacon, Descartes, and Galileo.[14] But it was only at the present day—and especially with Comte's development of the most sophisticated and all-comprehending science of them all, sociology—that the positive philosophy had grown to the point of self-consciousness, and might now claim the future.[15]

Comte's totalizing historical philosophy, in which theological claims were dismissed by virtue of their belonging to a pre-modern mental stage, developed from and reinforced a remarkably relative conception of knowledge. A student of Hume, Comte recognized the futility of searching for divine wills or ultimate causes underlying phenomena. Modern science must instead seek to identify discoverable sequences, behind whose veil the mind could not penetrate.[16] Knowledge was not obtained by reasoning outwardly from the human consciousness to the phenomena of nature—an essentially theological approach—but from the positive recognition of the subjection of consciousness to external law.[17] Reason alone, however, was insufficient to place social practice on the basis of discoverable law. Social solidarity had also to engage the religious affections. In his *System of Positive Polity* (1851–1854), Comte applied his imagination to the structure of a ritualistic 'Religion of Humanity', preserving the benevolent and integrative effects of superseded Catholicism which, he supposed, the destructiveness of the Reformation had threatened. Supported by a meritocratic industrial administration, the new religion would enable his synthesis to be subjectively internalized and propagated in the society of the future.[18] Comte's sociological system bore crucial characteristics in common with subsequent forms of British social theory formed or touched by it, which presented a challenge to Christian apologists, and often to sociologists themselves. First, it took its methodological point of departure from a rigidly anti-metaphysical epistemology that was itself made the inexorable outcome of the historical process. Second, it left the individual—and the individual's claims to historical importance or religious insight—subordinate to historical law. Comte's primarily intellectual account of the foundations of progress, excluding theology though not religious institutions from a creative role in the positive stage which mind had now attained, became an important

[14] Ibid., i, 6–7, ii, 363–4.   [15] Pickering, *Comte*, i, 655–87.
[16] Pickering, *Comte*, i, 311–12.   [17] Comte, *Positive philosophy*, i, 356.
[18] Comte, *Positive polity*, i, 257–321, [325]–368; Pickering, *Comte*, iii, 159–183, 223–40; Wright, *Religion of Humanity*, pp. 18–39.

and often radically secularizing resource for British sociologists and sociologically minded historians.

Few were more provocative than Henry Thomas Buckle, who saluted
Comte for having 'done more than any other to raise the standard of
history', although he agreed with him more in his explanation of past
development than in his technocratic and pseudo-Catholic prescriptions
for the future.[19] Buckle's *History of Civilization in England* (1857–1861)
offered an account of the origins of modern civilization which, as Comte
had done, located progress as consisting essentially in mental tendencies
which gradually dethroned and replaced theological claims, but without
endorsing the high value Comte reposed on the preservation of religious
sentiment in humanity's future. In some respects a specimen of the
Enlightenment tradition of conjectural history that never entirely perished
in nineteenth-century Britain, Buckle's work joined Comte's in encouraging the genesis of alternative conceptions of modern intellectual history
that were to be more consonant with the demands of religious apology.

Buckle's *History* also proceeded from a particular and, in some ways,
agnostic conception of cognition. More wholehearted than Buckle's
admiration for Comte's writings was his endorsement of John Stuart
Mill's *System of Logic*, a work which, he wrote, had procured 'a vast and
permanent fame' for its author.[20] Mill's treatment of general propositions
as deductions derived by inference from induction involved a purely
phenomenal approach to knowledge, resembling Comte's, which informed
Buckle's own conception of historical science. Mill's was a reasoning process
equally applicable to the human and the natural worlds, trenchantly
detached from reliance on metaphysical a priori ideas.[21] In order for history
to be raised to the level of the natural sciences, Buckle declared in the
opening pages of his *History*, it must accordingly become properly inductive.
By attending to 'almost innumerable facts', and excluding all metaphysical or
theological hypotheses, it would be possible to determine the laws governing the relationship between human motives and their mental or
external antecedents. If history rose to the level of enabling deductions
to be made from inductions, the forces conducing to 'virtuous' or 'vicious'
behaviour in a species whose minds were *tabulae rasae*—an associationist

[19] *HCE*, i, 5 n; H.T. Buckle, 'Mill on liberty', *FM*, 59:353 (1859), p. 511. On Buckle's
relationship with Positivism, see B. Young, 'History', in Bevir, *Historicism*, pp. 154–85.
[20] J.S. Mill, *A system of logic, ratiocinative and inductive: being a connected view of the
principles of evidence and the methods of scientific investigation* (2 vols, London, 1843). For a
concise assessment of this text, see Harris, 'Mill, John Stuart'; Buckle, 'Mill on liberty',
pp. [509]–42, here at 519.
[21] Mill formed his view of induction independently of Comte, but thereafter recognized
the affinity between them: Mill, *Autobiography*, pp. 161–2.

idea essential to Buckle, even if he did not use the phrase—would become clear.[22]

Buckle's utilitarian historical procedure possessed a twofold secularity. First, it made religious commitment irrelevant and even harmful to historical inquiry. Scientific history, he believed, was incompatible with the ancient and, to his mind, reviving belief in 'the moral government of the world', in which God became 'some clumsy mechanic' interfering in temporal processes.[23] Buckle's deist sympathies, and interest in Kant's relegation of religious reasoning to a purely transcendental plane, buttressed his confidence that religious and historical analysis were essentially separate exercises.[24] His pungently irreligious understanding of science, secondly, structured in turn his understanding of the origins and motors of progressive civilization. What marked out European history over the histories of other continents, Buckle argued, was the relative primacy of mental over natural forces in swaying human destiny.[25] Within the active mental sphere which distinguished European civilization, progress was intellectual rather than moral in nature, driven chiefly by the growth of the inductive sciences: a history which, to Buckle's own isolated mind, had reached a high-point in his own effort at synthesis. Buckle's historical prioritization of inductivism echoed Comte's. But whereas Comte regarded moral progress as characteristic of the human race, reaching its apotheosis in a Religion of Humanity, Buckle held ethical doctrines to be stationary, capable of achieving little by themselves. The New Testament, he thought, often reprised pagan philosophy.[26] Theology, in short, played no constructive role either in the historical origins or in the progressive practices of intellectual modernity. Even Comte, by contrast, had accepted that theology and metaphysics had at least contributed to the process by which the positive stage emerged, even as they were ushered aside by it.

Buckle's view of knowledge, and concomitant understanding of the laws of European intellectual development, led him constantly to depict dogmatic theology and the institutional church as barriers to progress. Buckle advanced the point both in reference to the broader development of European society from the Middle Ages to the present day, and in relation to his especial focus on post-Reformation English and Scottish history. Though hostile to medieval Catholicism—whose clergy had first been able to impress their petrifying influence on southern European societies

---

[22] *HCE*, i, 2–32; for citations of Mill, see ibid., i, 139 n.–140 n., 224 n.–225 n.

[23] Ibid., ii, 598–9.

[24] Ibid., i, 342 n.–343 n.; G. St Aubyn, *A Victorian eminence: the life and works of Henry Thomas Buckle* (London, 1958), p. 86.

[25] *HCE*, i, [36]-137.   [26] Comte, *Positive polity*, i, 84–5; *HCE*, i, 163-4 and n.

because of the superstitions produced by natural disasters—Buckle refused to ascribe subsequent European advance to the positive effects of Protestantism.[27] The Reformation arose less from a theological desire to purify the church than from the wishes of the secular classes to restrict its influence, Buckle argued.[28] Yet Protestantism had often not fulfilled this early promise, for it joined its predecessor religion in making alliances with interventionist governments to arrest intellectual development.[29] The rise of toleration and scientific experimentation in seventeenth-century England demonstrated that progress did not arise from theological change, but from the application of scepticism to received ideas. The fact that a similar process operated in Catholic France, Buckle insisted, underscored the absurdity of invoking confessional determinism to explain progress.[30]

The deleterious results of dogmatic Protestantism were, for Buckle, amply illustrated by the history of Scotland since the sixteenth century. Aside from the socially cramping effects of the Calvinist clergy's gloomy fanaticism, the latter's theological and thus deductive habits of thought had passed into wider culture. This chained Scotland's eighteenth-century political economists to axiomatic reasoning, and her philosophers to stolid doctrines of innate ideas, instead of trusting in comprehensive induction.[31] The religious history of England in the same period afforded a pleasing contrast. For English clerics had succumbed to the progress of opinion, instead of distending it. Where later historians of a kind liable to feel antipathy for Buckle saw the tolerance and reasonableness of England's rational theologians—Richard Hooker, Jeremy Taylor, and William Chillingworth—as expressing Christian renewal, Buckle attributed these qualities, rather summarily, to a combination of scepticism and pressure from the secular classes. In a trajectory that led from these writers down to the nineteenth century, ecclesiastical power had become marginal to English political and intellectual life; Buckle's footnotes drew attention to the haplessness of the Oxford Movement as a case in point. Scotland, unfortunately, had not yet followed suit.[32] Buckle's ideal future for religion lay in its passing into a wholly transcendental and privatized form, whilst progress, deriving from other sources, rolled on unencumbered by its protective historical effects.

Buckle's antipathy to the role of spirit in the history of civilization released an unnerving spectre into the Victorian historical imagination. The implications of Buckle's work for theology and Protestantism drew

---

[27] Ibid., i, 108–23, ii, [1]–155.   [28] Ibid., i, 463.   [29] Ibid., i, 240–4.
[30] Ibid., i, 317–18, 473–505.   [31] Ibid., ii, [410]–601.
[32] Ibid., i, 310–20 and 320 n., 324–5, ii, 589–95.

more attention than the questions he raised about historical method, except where the latter related to religious or metaphysical problems. Radical secularists welcomed Buckle's iconoclasm; but they were in a minority.[33] Writers in the conservative *Quarterly Review* and the high church *Christian Remembrancer* unflatteringly regarded him as a follower of Comte, made still more objectionable than Comte by his contemptuous refusal to recognize the services of religion to civilization.[34] Henry Reeve, a long-serving editor of the *Edinburgh Review*, of Unitarian extraction, faulted Buckle for denying the reality of moral progress and underestimating the historic power of Christianity in advancing political and social freedom. Buckle was, in this sense, akin to the flippant *philosophes* of the previous century.[35] The Unitarian leader James Martineau, speaking to intending ministers at Manchester New College in London in 1860, criticized him as he had previously disparaged Comte for asserting that progress was henceforth to be separated from theological commitment: a view that flew in the face of the evident vitality of nineteenth-century churches.[36]

Fundamentally different assumptions about the relationship between historical interpretation and religious commitment, and the nature of human knowledge, underlay such criticisms. Richard Holt Hutton, a critic Gladstone admired who subsequently became an Anglican theologian, replied to Buckle in the Unitarian *National Review*. There he presented civilization as a state of becoming, not as self-sufficient being. It was moved by its trust in and openness to God, which laws of intellect facilitated but could not supplant.[37] The Free Church minister, Walter Smith, linked Buckle to Comte in the Free Church–aligned *North British Review*. He traced the former's rejection of the moral force of Christianity to his dismissal of the spirituality of mind, for Buckle allegedly held that 'man may be regarded, not as a *person*, but simply as a *thing* whose individual consciousness is of no moment.'[38] Buckle, and behind him Comte, appeared to many British readers to brush metaphysical questions

---

[33] A. Besant, *The fruits of Christianity* (London, [1878?]).

[34] For example [W. Frederick Pollock], 'Buckle's *History of Civilization in England*', *QR*, 104:207 (1858), pp. 71–2; [Anon.], 'Buckle's Civilisation in England', *CHR*, 35:100 (1858), pp. 331–2.

[35] [H. Reeve], 'Buckle's *Civilization in Spain and Scotland*', *ER*, 114:231 (1861), p. 184.

[36] J. Martineau, 'Comte's life and philosophy', in his *Essays, reviews, and addresses* (4 vols, London, 1890–1891), i, 355 (repr. from the *NR* for 1858); Martineau, 'Factors of spiritual growth in modern society', in his *Essays*, iv, 77.

[37] [R.H. Hutton], 'Civilisation and faith', *NR*, 11 (1858), pp. 198–228; H. Orel, 'Hutton, Richard Holt (1826–1897)', *ODNB*.

[38] [W. Smith], 'Mr Buckle on the civilisation of Scotland', *NBR*, 35:69 (1861), pp. 254–7.

aside in favour of a peculiarly cramped form of empiricism, which seemed unjustifiably to exclude the full range of human aspirations from its notion of what experience involved. Even Buckle's hero, Mill, criticized him in the *Westminster Review* for 'regarding the intellectual as the only progressive element in man', a mistake Comte avoided.[39]

For many British readers, William Lecky's *History of Rationalism* offered an alternative and more reassuring way of understanding the modern history of mind. It was one that, in important respects, pointed forwards to a new phase of discussion in which the evidence of the mind itself, and the analogy between the individual mind and a transcendent mind within or beyond the universe, gradually worked their way to the centre of religious historians' apologetic preoccupations. Lecky's *History* avowedly separated historical from theological analysis. But it also sought to leave scope for the historical importance, and ultimate truthfulness, of religious insight within a sociological framework which examined the implications of the triumph of 'rationalism' over supernaturalism and dogmatism in modern European history.

Together with Comte and Buckle, whom he admired without straightforwardly replicating, Lecky prioritized 'the history of opinions' as an agent in the development of civilization.[40] In common with these precursors, he aimed to recover the 'law of orderly and progressive transformation to which our speculative opinions are subject'.[41] For Lecky that law consisted in rationalism's ever-greater permeation of all social spheres. He defined this process not as the spread of 'any class of definite doctrines or criticisms, but rather a certain cast of thought, or bias of reasoning, which has during the last three centuries gained a marked ascendancy in Europe'.[42] Lecky insisted that the historian's duty was to understand the changing habits of mind upon which opinion rested: a responsibility that distinguished him from the theologian, who was instead concerned to adjudicate upon the truth or otherwise of the doctrines thus historicized.[43] In this way, Lecky distanced himself from positive commitment to rationalism. His belief that its ascendancy relied not so much on its intrinsic truth as on changes in opinion, at root somewhat mysterious, reflected an ambivalent view of progress which distinguished him from Comte, Buckle, and several of the rational theologians who followed him.[44] He nevertheless conceded that 'it is impossible to reveal the causes that called

[39] J.S. Mill, 'Auguste Comte and Positivism', in his *Essays on ethics, religion and society*, pp. 322–3 (repr. from the *WR* for 1865).

[40] *HRE*, i, ix, 87–8; McCartney, *Lecky*, pp. 12, [26]–32; Stuchtey, *Lecky*, pp. 67–9.

[41] *HRE*, i, 317–18.   [42] Ibid., i, xviii–xix.   [43] Ibid., i, [v]–ix.

[44] Ibid., i, vii.

an opinion into being without throwing light upon its intrinsic value.'[45] The result was a history that, whilst admittedly corrosive of 'received theological doctrines', affirmed the basically theistic conception of knowledge and value from which Lecky took rationalism to have arisen.[46]

In accordance with Lecky's notably capacious definition of rationalism, his *History* examined how changes in one department of opinion had wrought connected changes in others. Since the sixteenth century, the increasing complexity of civilization, the growing systematization of scientific conceptions, and, above all, the decay of dogmatic theology, interacted to produce the decline of belief in witchcraft and the miraculous, the end of persecution, the 'secularization of politics', and the spread of industrial rationality as distilled in modern political economy. Lecky's description of the growth of 'a secular atmosphere' in intellectual history, deriving from and further reinforcing the decline of the appeal and influence of theology, brought his own master-narrative of modern time into partial alignment with those of Buckle and Comte.[47]

Lecky's conception of mind, however, provided him with markedly different analytical premises from either of those figures, and led him to reach correspondingly divergent conclusions as to the overall significance of the historical process. The 'central conception' of rationalism, Lecky argued, was 'the elevation of conscience into a position of supreme authority as the religious organ, a verifying faculty distinguishing between truth and error.'[48] Unlike Comte or Buckle, therefore, Lecky held to an intuitive theory of ethics. Lecky's later *History of European Morals* distinguished this approach from that of utilitarians, including Mill, who conflated the process of framing ethical theories with the ultimate basis of ethical action. The latter rested in an original moral faculty capable of distinguishing humanity from cruelty: a position akin to that which Henry Sidgwick, whose doubting mind never quite gave up attempting to rescue some fragment of spirit from the wreckage of orthodoxy, adopted in his *Methods of Ethics*. The principle of humanity, Lecky acknowledged, may have been applied imperfectly or perversely in the early ages of society. But he insisted, against Buckle, that morals possessed a progressive history, in which Christianity—although not dogmatic theology—acted together with advancing civilization and intellectual sophistication to refine the innate moral sense and its practical implications.[49] The same conception of ethics was at work in his *History of Rationalism*, where he

---

[45] Ibid., i, xvi–xvii.   [46] Ibid., ii, 403.   [47] Ibid., i, 200–1.
[48] Ibid., i, 182.
[49] *HEM*, i, [1]–158, esp. pp. 105–6, 142, 156–7; cf. H. Sidgwick, *The methods of ethics* (London, 1874), pp. 472–3; S. Collini, 'Sidgwick, Henry (1838–1900)', *ODNB*.

gave it a theistic gloss, if not obviously an orthodox one. 'The great characteristic of Christianity, and the great moral proof of its divinity, is that it has been the main source of the moral developement of Europe', he claimed: an office it had discharged not so much by inculcating an ethical system as by 'the assimilating and attractive influence of a perfect ideal'.[50] Lecky buttressed this stance with criticisms of contemporary unbelief. Though in places he echoed elements of Comte's tripartite theory of religious development, Lecky faulted him as a materialist.[51] At the same time as he treated 'the declining sense of the miraculous' in modern Europe as an expression of the rationalist spirit, Lecky argued that the claim that an 'Infinite mind' was capable of modifying the laws of nature in the ways recorded in the New Testament, was no more absurd than the belief that such a being had created the world at all.[52] Lecky's was the historical vision of one who identified with the Christian rationalism of Richard Whately and Joseph Butler, the argument of whose 1736 *Analogy of Religion* concerning New Testament miracles Lecky here implicitly endorsed.[53]

It was in accordance with Lecky's broader intellectual dispositions, therefore, that his *History of Rationalism* should have ascribed a more creative and continuing role to spirit in the history of the modern intellect than either Buckle or Comte had done. Lecky's account was as much a history of ethics as it was a history of ideas. He welcomed how the growth of reasonable conscience into the awareness of its own powers had undermined the terrifying conception of divine forces that lay at the root of belief in witchcraft, and the doctrine of exclusive salvation that underpinned persecution.[54] Unlike Buckle, Lecky credited Protestantism, more than the growth of the inductive sciences, with the responsibility for having wrought that transition towards 'the general secularisation of the European intellect'. 'There certainly has never been a movement which, in its ultimate results,' he wrote, 'has contributed so largely to the emancipation of the human mind from all superstitious terrors as the Reformation.'[55] He was no confessional determinist, seeing scepticism at work in undermining exclusive ecclesiastical claims in Catholic countries; and he recognized that the short-term effect of the Reformation was to

---

[50] *HRE*, i, 337.   [51] *HEM*, i, 142; *HRE*, i, 407–8.

[52] Ibid., i, [1]-205, here at 198 n.–199 n.

[53] Lecky, 'Formative influences', [90]–103; cf. J. Garnett, 'Bishop Butler and the *Zeitgeist*: Butler and the development of Christian moral philosophy in Victorian Britain', in C. Cunliffe (ed.), *Joseph Butler's moral and religious thought: tercentenary essays* (Oxford, 1992), pp. [63]–96.

[54] *HRE* i, 13–14, 336, ii, 11–12.   [55] Ibid., i, 62.

intensify dogmatic disputes.[56] Protestantism, nevertheless, offered a positive rather than a purely negative principle of criticism which ultimately tended to elevate the individual conscience over ecclesiastical claims.[57] The Reformation, Lecky considered, rested on the right to interpret particular creeds by 'the principles of universal religion'.[58] He diverged from Buckle when he allowed that the growth of rationalism within theology represented something more than a fatal compromise with an antagonistic principle. Protestantism encouraged the rise of reverent scepticism, whereby rational theologians such as William Chillingworth and Jeremy Taylor had begun to distinguish between opinions that were certain and those that were only probable. These writers, 'earnestly attached to positive religion', established the principle of toleration in England by uniting 'the spirit of scepticism with the spirit of Christianity'. In a manner pregnant with significance for the future, they showed how 'the boldest speculations... may find elements of assimilation in a Protestant creed.'[59] Lecky's interest in how the history of religious thought recorded, in some respects, its integration with advancing knowledge, instead of their disseveration, would soon find a wider echo.

For all the favourable results he ascribed to it, the professedly impartial historian's account of rationalism was neither wholly celebratory nor completely consistent. The decay of loyalty, the destruction of asceticism, and the restriction of the sphere of charity that followed from advancing rationalism had 'given our age a mercenary, venal, and unheroic character'. With greater ambivalence about progress than Buckle or Comte ever showed, Lecky regretted that the advance of utilitarianism on the basis of sensationalist psychology had restricted the powers of human nature.[60] Implicitly distinguishing rationalism from 'the moral or religious faculty' with which he elsewhere linked it, he declared in the conclusion of his *History* that it was really the latter that yielded the 'the impress of the divine image, the principle of every heroism'. It seemed to Lecky, as it had to Mill, that the scope for great individualities to sway the course of social development had dwindled as history progressed.[61] The tensions between these regretful ruminations, and his confidence that rationalism regarded Christianity 'as designed to preside over the moral development of mankind' as an ever-more 'sublimated and spiritualised' idea, were ones that Lecky never quite resolved.[62]

---

[56] Ibid., i, 62–3, 155–60.   [57] Ibid., ii, 62–3.   [58] Ibid., i, 400–2.
[59] Ibid., ii, 89–93.   [60] Ibid., ii, 406.
[61] Ibid., ii, 403–6; cf. J. S. Mill, 'On Liberty', in his, *On Liberty and other essays*, ed. J. Gray (Oxford, 1991), pp. [62]–82.
[62] *HRE*, i, 182.

As an essay in compromise, Lecky's *History of Rationalism* attracted antipathy from the opposing intellectual tendencies between which it had aimed to pass. The *Christian Remembrancer*, which had previously warned its readers against Buckle, surmised that Lecky had derived his views of theology and metaphysics from Comte; but the reviewer consoled himself that in time 'Rationalism will reveal the cloven foot, and from that how its doom is sealed'.[63] The Congregationalist *British Quarterly Review* objected to Lecky's reduction of all human phenomena into 'one grand process' governed by a law under which dogmatism inexorably decayed.[64] 'Men tell you that Leckie's [*sic*] work on "The Influence of Rationalism throughout Europe," [*sic*] is the book of the day', encouraging them to form their own views on religious history without clerical guidance, one anonymous layman was reported to have said in an 1867 pamphlet, published by fretful Anglican clergy, concerning problems facing contemporary preachers.[65] Where elements of the religious press found that Lecky had conceded too much to secular approaches to history, authors who instead vibrated to the strains of Comte and Mill found his mediating position muddled. Writing in the *Fortnightly Review*, a liberal periodical recently launched under the editorship of G. H. Lewes, George Eliot complained of the 'fatiguing use of vague or shifting phrases' such as 'modern civilisation', 'spirit of the age', and 'tone of thought' which carried much of Lecky's argument. He seemed to ascribe primary importance in developments in these phenomena to changes in religious conceptions. The weightier factor, in Eliot's view, was in fact 'the gradual reduction of all phenomena within the sphere of established law'. Lecky's failure to see this, she suggested, was of a piece with his ignorant view of 'philosophers of the sensational school'.[66]

Lecky's argument nevertheless resonated strongly with critics who likewise conceived of modern intellectual progress as involving the refinement rather than the retirement of Protestantism. William Kirkus in the *Journal of Sacred Literature*, an important medium in familiarizing British clerics with the results of German biblical criticism, praised Lecky for offering a Christianized antidote to Newman's theory of development.[67]

[63] [Anon.], 'Lecky's History of Rationalism', *CHR*, 51:131 (1866), pp. 216, 225.

[64] [Anon.], 'Lecky's History of Rationalism', *BQR*, 84 (1865), p. 403.

[65] [Anon.], *Lay suggestions on modern preaching and preachers* (London, Oxford, and Cambridge, 1867), p. 55.

[66] G. Eliot, 'The influence of rationalism', *FR*, 1 (15 May, 1865), pp. 54–5. On Comte, Mill, and Eliot, see A. Fleishman, *George Eliot's intellectual life* (Cambridge, 2010), pp. 58–69.

[67] W. Kirkus, 'Rationalism in Europe', *JSL*, 8:15 (1865), p. 185; on Newman's theory of development, see chapter two of this volume at pp. 66–80.

Henry Reeve held him up as a model over Buckle, for Lecky saw 'in the great principles of religion an indispensable element of civilization' and the enlightened application of Christian precepts as 'the consummation of all that the human race can hope to attain to'.[68] The Unitarian minister and historian, Charles Beard, similarly saw a welcome contrast in Lecky's high view of mind and conscience to 'the ignoble theory of the materialist and the statistician'.[69] Beard nevertheless criticized Lecky's inclination to view rationalism as an unconscious tendency, and so to distance himself from more forthright endorsement of it. Theology and history were, as Lecky himself appeared to see, not wholly separable. Conscious rationalism was needed in the present, as in the past, to arrive at clearer statements of updated 'dogmas' than Lecky himself made.[70] If Lecky represented an improvement on Comte or Buckle, modern-day rational theologians made it their concern to improve on Lecky by developing a less ambiguous conception of the history of reason than the one he offered to them.

RATIONAL THEOLOGY?

The debate over the origins of intellectual progress stimulated by socio-logical conceptions of history focused attention on the theological and anti-theological innovations of the post-Reformation period. Ideas of intellectual history which made scientific inductivism the motor of mental progress in the period between the sixteenth century and the nineteenth, and the demolition of metaphysics its outcome, helped to call a very different sense of the nineteenth century's intellectual lineage into exist-ence. This prioritized instead the history and promise of rational theology. Something of that divergence was latent in the difference between Buckle and his critics. For Buckle, theologians' concessions to reason really amounted to their uncomprehending defeat by secular forces. Seeking to distinguish strands of past thought from one another that were at that time less well-known than they would subsequently become, R. H. Hutton criticized Buckle for lumping together the scepticism of Hume and Montaigne, which denied the possibility of knowing absolute truth, with that of Chillingworth and Locke, which did the reverse.[71] Lecky's 1869 essay on the origin of the moral sense interestingly noticed that on the fundamental question of whether morals arose from external sanction, or from the mind itself, the seventeenth-century Cambridge Platonists

---

[68] [H. Reeve], 'Lecky's *Influence of Rationalism*', *ER*, 121:248 (1865), pp. 426–7.
[69] [C. Beard], 'Lecky's History of Rationalism', *TR*, 2:9 (1865), p. 436.
[70] Ibid., pp. 443–4. [71] [Hutton], 'Civilisation and faith', p. 225.

had opted for a doctrine of innate ideas which, in the meantime, 'has almost disappeared'.[72] These gravid observations, made often but at first incidentally so, were the premonitory signs of what in the later 1860s and 1870s would become a striking growth of interest in the history of seventeenth- and eighteenth-century religious thought in clerical and even anticlerical circles.

John Tulloch's *Rational Theology and Christian Philosophy in England in the Seventeenth Century* (1872), and John Hunt's *Religious thought in England from the Reformation* (1870–1873), expressed most substantially the increasingly widespread and pan-denominational clerical desire to assert theology's progressiveness, and so present-day legitimacy, by means of the exploration of the relatively recent intellectual past.[73] Tulloch's energies were concentrated in the century of the civil wars, and Hunt's theologically more radical inclinations told in his focus on the age of deism. But their works alike reflected the maturation of an interest, in both cases developing for some years, which was common to liberal theologians across Britain. This was a concern to find an historical mode of steering between those whom they regarded as theological reactionaries on the one hand, and advocates of secular ideas of progress on the other, along with the phenomenal conceptions of knowledge the latter so often assumed. In a procedure common to religiously committed critics in the latter part of the century, they expanded the scope of experience and induction beyond the evidence of outward data to which anti-metaphysical critics tried to restrict it, so as to include the historical workings of the religious mind. Religious thought, understood as religious experience, became a substrate from which the practitioners of a Chris-tianized historical science might develop the theology of the future. In the periods under discussion, it was argued that theology had kept pace with, and even constructively shaped, political and scientific improvement, whilst it had also learned the difference between the great principles of faith and subsidiary dogmatisms. The experience of history, therefore, showed how theology might fruitfully develop in the nineteenth century and afterwards, so as to enable it to maintain its historic place as the foundation of intellectual and moral culture. Perhaps still more import-antly, history also witnessed to the self-renewing dynamism of religious thought, in a way that suggested the divine origin of religious reason.

---

[72] *HEM*, i, 127–8.
[73] Reference here is to Tulloch's second edition: J. Tulloch, *Rational theology and Christian philosophy in England in the seventeenth century*, 2nd edn (2 vols, Edinburgh and London, 1874); J. Hunt, *Religious thought in England from the Reformation to the end of the last century: a contribution to the history of theology* (3 vols, London, 1870–1873).

Although Leslie Stephen drew rather different lessons from the kind of movement he discovered in eighteenth-century theology, this was a notion that was to be replete with broader anti-agnostic possibility.

It has been seen how Tulloch, full of admiration for August Neander, had first elaborated his progressive conception of the development of Protestant truth in opposition both to negative rationalism and Calvinist traditionalism in a post-Disruption situation.[74] Tulloch's criticisms of Protestant sectarianism had evinced his wish to subordinate internal Protestant debates to vindicating the reality of objective religious truth against external assailants. As early as 1854, Tulloch had ended his inaugural lecture at St Andrews by warning against the tendency to abandon the historical authority of scripture in favour of what he called '*subjective arbitrariness*' of any kind.[75] Over time, he became increasingly inclined to see that 'subjective arbitrariness', synonymous in his mind with any kind of religious or irreligious exclusive dogmatism—more than specifically denominational dangers—as the greatest threat to common religion.

In a lecture on 'Dogmatic Extremes' he delivered to the opening of the 1873 session of his St Andrews college, and subsequently published in the *Contemporary Review*, Tulloch complained that the advance of free discussion in religious questions had corroded the restrained humility necessary to rational argument. He likened contemporary Roman Catholicism to 'Straussism', and evangelicalism to Darwinism, in the sense that all showed an unwelcome tendency to abandon reasonable intercommunication in favour of a sectarian proclamation of the all-absorbing truth of their own fetishized principles.[76] Newman presented a connected danger. Reviewing his 1870 *Grammar of Assent*, Tulloch joined those Protestant critics examined in the second chapter who objected to Newman for the way he allegedly refused to see the foundations of belief as a matter for reasoned debate, instead treating religious philosophy—as he had already used history—as a means of accounting for a complex of assumed dogmas. Newman's 'mind, while intensely dogmatic and authoritative in expression, is yet in spirit and essence really sceptical, seeing difficulties although refusing to own them, and from the depths of its very restlessness casting itself forcibly into the arms of authority', wrote Tulloch.[77] 'What the world needs is a *Rationale* of Belief in the face alike of scepticism and superstition', he insisted.[78]

---

[74] See chapters one and four of this volume.
[75] Tulloch, *Theological tendencies*, pp. 13, 27.
[76] Tulloch, 'Dogmatic extremes', *CR*, 23 (1873), pp. [182]–96.
[77] [Tulloch], 'Dr. Newman's *Grammar of Assent*', *ER*, 132:270 (1870), p. 392.
[78] Ibid., p. 412.

Tulloch lamented that 'the *Whig*—the genuine type of the older liberalism—is heard of no more.'[79] Together with all good Whigs, Tulloch held that the antidote to extremism lay in historical study, correctly approached. History, he came to believe, supported the claims of the subjective conscience to be a window into the progressively self-manifesting spiritual world. Interpreted in this way, history simultaneously became an objective guiding authority in religious questions. It freed theology from the subjective thoughts of any given individual theologian or speculator as to the normative form religion should take, by locating particular religious expressions in relation to the broader kind of religious experience that history recorded.

The other sources of Tulloch's developing conception of the larger significance of historical inquiry will be considered in the next section; but here it is important to note that his ideas partly took shape in response to the subjective and arbitrary approaches to that question which he encountered in Buckle, Comte, and to a significantly lesser extent, Lecky. In an essay appraising two comparatively blameless clerical historians of the Scottish Church in the *Edinburgh Review* for 1861, Buckle's remorseless treatment of that subject functioned as an anti-type to Tulloch's conception of sound history. 'Under pretence of dealing peculiarly with facts and the great laws by which they are marshalled into history', wrote Tulloch, Buckle showed himself 'arbitrarily devoted to theory' and capable of only those 'loose and mechanical' generalizations made available to him by 'sceptical Positivism'. Despite his own objections to classically Calvinist Scottish theology, Tulloch insisted that Buckle had no conception of its real historical significance.[80] As he made clear in an 1868 *Edinburgh Review* essay on Comte, Tulloch did not object to the idea that social phenomena should be regarded as subject to law. Rather, he objected to the exclusion of a superintending intelligence from active work in law-governed history. Comte's law of three supposititious stages, which ruled out the truth value of theology and metaphysics altogether, begged the whole question of how mankind could have real knowledge, Tulloch argued. The Positivist was merely negative, in that he regarded divine will as incompatible with historical order. The theist claimed instead that there was 'Will *plus* Order, Intelligence *plus* Law'. To attain to the idea of law, Tulloch continued, we use 'Mind'. Mind relied on

---

[79] Tulloch, 'Dogmatic extremes', p. 183.
[80] [J. Tulloch], 'Cunningham's *Church History of Scotland*', *ER*, 114:232 (1861), pp. 394–424, here at 404, 415.

human self-consciousness, which itself, Tulloch supposed, bore the impress of the divine.[81]

Tulloch's belief that mind was animated by larger, providential forces led him to form a more favourable view of Lecky's *History of Rationalism* than he took of either Comte or Buckle. Unlike Buckle, he argued in his review of the *History*, Lecky was open to a just conception of the province of theology, as was evident in his treatment of the rational divines of seventeenth-century England. But he did not distinguish with sufficient clarity between the rationalism of the natural intellect, out of which the 'partial' Positivist philosophy had grown in recent times, and true rationalism. True rationalism started within the church, and recognized Christian knowledge as a progressively growing insight based on the truth revealed in scripture and the spiritual consciousness; Neander was its model.[82] Real rationalism presented a truer, or at least a clearer, conception of the reign of law than Lecky offered. Lecky's view of the causes of intellectual or moral change left open the possibility that these occurred accidentally or unaccountably. But Tulloch did not believe this could be so. 'The "spirit of the age" is a mere expression, and has no power, save in so far as it represents some real growth of enlightenment, some expansion of man's powers of comprehension of the world around him, or of the world of thought within him.'[83] Rather as Charles Beard had argued, Tulloch considered it to be the historian's duty to depict the transcendent reason at work within reason's human history.

Tulloch's *Rational Theology and Christian Philosophy*, which he thought of as his greatest work, recorded just such a process of divine growth and spiritual expansion.[84] The two volumes began to take shape at the same time as Tulloch developed his criticisms of alternative modes of approaching intellectual history; earlier versions of several chapters had started to appear in Dean Alford's *Contemporary Review* shortly after the journal published his review of Lecky.[85] Tulloch's *dramatis personae* were the 'rational theologians' of seventeenth-century England, among whom he traced distinctive lines of development running from Richard Hooker, through early advocates of ecclesiastical latitude such as Jeremy Taylor and William Chillingworth, to the Cambridge Platonists. In his preface, Tulloch drew out the underlying unity connecting his individual subjects

---

[81] Tulloch, 'Auguste Comte and Positivism', repr. in his *Modern theories in philosophy and religion* (Edinburgh and London, 1884), pp. 56–65.

[82] Tulloch, 'Rationalism', pp. [361]–84.   [83] Ibid., p. 364.

[84] Oliphant, *Memoir*, pp. 270–7.

[85] Beginning with J. Tulloch, 'Studies in the history of religious thought in England. I.-: John Hales', *CR*, 5 (1867), pp. 190–221; and ending with Tulloch, 'John Smith and his Select Discourses', *CR*, 19 (1871), pp. [789]–811.

to one another in terms reminiscent of Coleridge. 'The "Rational" element in all Churches is truly the ideal element', Tulloch wrote, 'which raises the Church above its own little world, and connects it with the movements of thought, the course of philosophy, or the course of science—with all, in fact, that is most powerful in ordinary human civilisation.' 'Rationalism', therefore, should not be denounced as evil, but deserved to be acknowledged as possessing 'high and true Christian uses'.[86]

In the seventeenth century, those uses had been to mitigate and finally overcome the different kinds of extremism which were now reasserting themselves, in new forms, in the nineteenth. Here Tulloch identified two interrelated trajectories. In his first volume, he concentrated on how a group of English divines, taking up a torch passed to them by Hooker and the Dutch Arminians, applied reason anew to religious questions at a time when Lutheran and Calvinist theology had become stereotyped and sectarian.[87] Lord Falkland, John Hales, Taylor, Chillingworth, and Edward Stillingfleet elevated the authority of individual faith and the plain word of scripture over the claims of competing dogmatic systems, so as to argue for a distinction between essentials and inessentials in matters of faith.[88] In the century of wars between Puritan and Anglo-Catholic theories of the church, conflicts which had resurfaced in Tulloch's own day, it had been progressive theology, rather than negative scepticism, that had fostered rational religion and doctrinal toleration.

Tulloch's second volume focused on the distinctive, and in some ways more fundamental work of the later 'Cambridge Platonists'. This group comprised those mid- to late-century theologians such as Benjamin Whichcote, John Smith, and Ralph Cudworth who, though no opponents of Baconian science, resisted its tendency to run on to 'atomistic materialism', chiefly in the form of the philosophy of Thomas Hobbes.[89] Rather as their Victorian successors were learning to argue, they did so by separating the study of the natural world from philosophical exploration of an inner one. Drawing above all on the resources of Platonic philosophy, the Cambridge divines held that moral aspirations, and reason itself, sprang from a divine source. In their analysis, the fact that the individual mind was able to make moral judgements, and to think, proved that there was a soul apart from the world of sense, able by its use of those faculties to discern the purposes of the divine mind which illuminated it.[90] Characteristically,

---

[86] Tulloch, *Rational theology*, i, ix–x.   [87] Ibid., i, 1–75.
[88] Ibid., i, 167–9, 259–60, 307–43, 377–463.
[89] Ibid., ii, [1]–44, here at 30; cf. J. Harris, 'Victorian interpretations of Thomas Hobbes', in Goldman and Ghosh, *Politics and culture*, pp. [237]–60.
[90] Tulloch, *Rational Theology*, ii, 281–282, 416–417, 468–469.

Tulloch pointed out that the full promise of the Cambridge Platonists' approach was stymied, to an extent, by the superstition and literary traditionalism of their day. Their lack of an historical sense meant that that they struggled to distinguish between Neo-Platonist phantasmagoria, and the purer idealism of Plato himself; and they regrettably believed in witchcraft.[91] But Tulloch was convinced that their chief legacy was to have exploded Hobbesian philosophy in its fundamentals, and to have delineated a core of rational religion that lay beneath denominational divisions.[92] Considering both phases of the rational movement together, Tulloch drew a pleasing moral. It had not been dogmatic or atheist extremes that had shaped the tolerant terms of Britain's 1688–1689 religious settlement, he reasoned, but the silently spreading precepts of rational theology, which fed the living waters of the moderate nineteenth-century liberalism that lay downstream.[93] 'I believe I have shown beyond all dispute', Tulloch ended his lecture on 'Dogmatic Extremes' by maintaining with reference to his recent book, that all higher progress was driven 'not by antagonism, but by tolerance, charity, and mutual co-operation.'[94]

This exploration of the achievements, as well as the limitations, of seventeenth-century rational theology constituted, to Tulloch's mind, an example of how historical criticism might function as a kind of induction, whereby progressive principles could be extracted from past experience and applied to present-day problems. 'The law of all true progress is continuous and not revolutionary.'[95] Now that the days of 'Augustinian dominance' in theology were at an end, the future for theology lay in 'the slow elaboration of the Christian reason', which must build on what the same reason had already achieved in the past.[96] A rational theology capable of meeting the needs of the nineteenth century, starting not from principles of private interpretation but working to understand the common experience of humanity in history, would not succeed merely by replicating the ideas of the seventeenth century. But it must draw on the historic sense, witnessing as it did to divine reason:

> The vast volume of religious experience will slowly unfold its characters to inductive and patient thinkers, as other volumes of experience have done. And as this volume is steadily read—its pages compared, and their facts co-ordinated and explained—the divine meaning will become clearer. A Religious Philosophy will at last become possible when it is sought in this way,—not in any favourite speculation of this or that thinker, however great—but in the

---

[91] Ibid., ii, 449, 478–82.   [92] Ibid., ii, 471.   [93] Ibid., i, [vii]-xvii, ii, 473–5.
[94] Tulloch, 'Dogmatic extremes', p. 196.   [95] Ibid., p. 191.
[96] Tulloch, *Rational theology*, i, xii–xiii.

comprehensive interpretation of the religious consciousness working through all history, and gathering light and force as it works onward.[97]

A. P. Stanley, to whom Tulloch dedicated the volumes, saluted them as 'the first systematic account of the long series of divines who, whether under the name of Rational, Platonist, Latitudinarian, or Liberal, have never ceased out of the Church of England from the days of Colet to the days of Milman'.[98]

Tulloch's account of seventeenth-century intellectual history, relating how mental progress rendered the reasonable religion that fed it more rather than less influential over time, also resonated with an audience notably more extensive than his more conspicuous liberal Anglican sympathizers. In his preface to the second edition of *Rational Theology*, Tulloch expressed his gratification at the high church *Guardian*'s favourable review of the work.[99] Although the paper's reviewer had adopted a cool view of the undogmatic and latitudinarian tendencies of the 'rational theologians' discussed in Tulloch's first volume, he had hailed the Cambridge Platonists for their qualities as 'religious philosophers'. The latter vindicated the reality of divine intelligence, the eternity of moral ideas, and the existence of freedom: which was to say, the province of religion itself. These great principles were precisely the same as those which in the present day had to be upheld against the usurpations of physical science, pantheism, and utilitarianism, the writer contended.[100] Nonconformists, too, saw unrealized potential in the ideas of the philosophers Tulloch had integrated into an anti-materialist account of intellectual progress. James Martineau, in an essay expanding on the themes of an 1874 address to theological students, quoted John Smith, as Tulloch had reported his words, in support of his position that inward consciousness was the ultimate proof of religious claims against 'modern materialism'. 'Only by converse with our own minds can we ... "steal from them their secrets," and "climb up to the contemplation of the Deity"', Martineau reflected.[101] As the development of mind became increasingly interesting for the ways it witnessed against the claims of modern empiricism to sit at its summit, not only did previously unfamiliar philosophers become more attractive; but traditional heroes appeared under new aspects. In his

[97] Ibid., ii, 487–8.

[98] [A.P. Stanley], 'The church and dissent', *ER*, 137:279 (1873), p. 198.

[99] Tulloch, *Rational theology*, i, xv.

[100] [Anon.], 'Rational Theology and Christian Philosophy in England', *Guardian*, 29 October 1873, pp. 1404–5; cf. S. Cheetham, *A history of the Christian church since the Reformation* (London, 1907), pp. 63–4, 63 n.

[101] J. Martineau, *Modern materialism: its attitude towards theology: a critique and defence* (London, 1876), pp. 9–10, 78 and n.

contribution to an 1877 cross-party series of lectures on *Masters in English Theology*, Richard Church presented Lancelot Andrewes, a fondly remembered predecessor of Archbishop Laud, as the sounding board for Bacon's inductive study of nature.[102] Tulloch's *Rational Theology* was a powerful, but by no means isolated instance of a growing inclination among the learned clergy and their sympathizers to find an ancestry in recent history for the kind of reconciliation between theology and progressive knowledge which they hoped to effect in the present.

The rehabilitation of eighteenth-century theology, often associated with mechanical reasoning, unspiritual practitioners, and deistic spectres, inherently presented greater obstacles than renewing interest in the religious literature of the more earnest century of Milton and Cromwell. The high churchman G. H. Curteis, preaching before the University of Oxford in 1871, spoke for many Victorian clergy when he declared that 'there is no one, probably, now living who does not congratulate himself that his lot was not cast in the Eighteenth Century.'[103] The fact that the first scholarly treatment of English deism was written in Germany, by the *evangelisch* Tübingen scholar Gotthard Lechler, reflected the strength of such attitudes.[104] Yet even in this sensitive department of learning, many clerical historians and their sympathizers became committed to integrating Enlightenment era theology into a continuous story of religious purification at the same time, and for largely the same reasons, as Tulloch and others were looking to seventeenth-century rational theologians for the origins of progressive theological culture.

John Hunt's *Religious Thought in England* was a major example of that attempt. The fruit of a gathering apologetic agenda rather more radical than Tulloch's, Hunt's work represented an Anglican analogue to the former's confidence in the historical reality of rational progress in human understanding of the divine. For Hunt, as for Tulloch, the history of theology amounted to a form of induction from which the religious philosophy of the future might durably emerge. Hunt, a broad church cleric who devoted his spare hours to the history of religious thought while he served in parish ministry in Cambridgeshire, London, and Kent, conceived of his three-volume *magnum opus* as a history of theology 'on the rigid principles of natural science'.[105] It took its theme, Hunt later remembered, from Mark Pattison's more sceptical essay on eighteenth-century

---

[102] R.W. Church, 'Lancelot Andrewes', in A. Barry (ed.), *Masters in English theology; being the King's College lectures for 1877* (London, 1877), pp. 64–5.
[103] Quoted in K. Hillebrand, 'England in the eighteenth century', *CR*, 37 (1880), p. [1].
[104] G.V. Lechler, *Geschichte des englischen Deismus* (Stuttgart and Tübingen, 1841).
[105] Hunt, *Religious thought*, iii, [vii].

theology in *Essays and Reviews*. Pattison's treatise, starting from the principle that 'the laws of thought' must be regarded as applying to 'the course of English theology', argued that reason had at that time come practically to overmaster revelation in the hands of orthodox and heterodox writers alike.[106] Reiterating Pattison's call for a scientific approach to the history of religious thought, Hunt declared that—unlike high church or nonconformist ecclesiastical histories—his was constrained by no peculiarities of party, country, or creed. It aimed to accord with John Stuart Mill's wise maxim that 'a doctrine is not judged at all till it is judged in its best form'.[107] At the same time, however, Hunt broke with the precedent Pattison had set by investing his researches with an affirmative theological significance. For he intended the work to be 'a record of progress', showing how 'the naturally conservative English mind has been working out its own religious position'.[108] It was becoming ever clearer, Hunt considered, that religion must decide either to throw itself upon the presumed infallibility of external oracles, in the manner of the Roman hierarchy; or else to recognize, with Bishop Temple in *Essays and Reviews*, that the work of the church was the education of the human race. 'Observation of the actual history of revelation' evinced such an education at work. Revelation, in the sense in which Hunt here deployed it, consisted in the wider history of religious mind, in relation to which the Bible was a participative stage rather than an overriding authority.[109] 'The mere history' he recorded in his pages 'will itself refute many arguments which are vehemently urged in party controversies.'[110]

Hunt's essay in neutral description was thus really a form of broad church prescription. His antecedent interest in the history of religious thought, developing since 1859 under the influence of F. D. Maurice, had already issued in an *Essay on Pantheism* arguing that all higher theology, from Plato down to Schleiermacher, amounted to 'spiritual pantheism', in that it assumed a God active in creation and so knowable by human reason rather than by supernatural historical revelation.[111] If this was a position that rendered Hunt distant from conservatives, and from Tulloch, it also made him hostile to Comtean Positivism's limitation of human intellect to that which was 'cognizable by the outward sense'.[112] The inward religious

---

[106] J. Hunt, 'Mr. Leslie Stephen on English thought in the eighteenth century', *CR*, 29 (1877), p. 415; M. Pattison, 'Tendencies of religious thought in England, 1688–1750', in Shea and Whitla, *Essays and reviews*, pp. [387]–430, here at 388.

[107] Hunt, *Religious thought*, iii, vii.   [108] Ibid., i, viii.

[109] Ibid., i, vi; J. Hunt, 'Christianity and modern evidences', *CR*, 18 (1871), pp. 163–6.

[110] Hunt, *Religious thought*, ii, vi–vii.

[111] J. Hunt, *An essay on pantheism* (London, 1866), pp. [1]–2, 375–9.

[112] Hunt, 'Christianity and modern evidences', p. 155.

reason to which Positivism denied rational status, at work beneath variable doctrinal forms, could for Hunt—as for Tulloch—be apprehended through historical analysis. Hunt's interest in German doctrinal historians, ranging from Neander to those he solicited to write for the *Contemporary Review*, betokened this confidence.[113] Hunt ended his *Essay on Pantheism* with the reflection, based on his survey of the history of theology, that religious philosophy ultimately turned on the question of whether human reason could know God as the infinite, or else, as philosophers such as H. L. Mansel held, was incapable of arriving at such knowledge.[114] Only the former position was consistent with the possibility of revelation, in Hunt's capacious understanding of the word.

Hence it was that the wider argument of Hunt's *Religious Thought in England* came to hinge on his treatment of eighteenth-century deists, on whom he had already written for Alford's *Contemporary Review*.[115] From the first, according to Hunt, England's Reformers appealed 'to reason, and to the Scriptures as interpreted by reason'; in the seventeenth century, the rational character of Anglican theology had been salvaged from Puritan and Anglo-Catholic aberrations by rational theologians such as Chillingworth, Cudworth, and—in a bold addition to the list—Thomas Hobbes.[116] But it was only in the eighteenth century, under the leadership of deists such as John Toland and Matthew Tindal, that the full implications of the Reformation's rejection of external authority in religion became clear. The deists pointed out the truth that ultimately it was by reason, and reason only, that the scriptures could be recognized and interpreted and God's nature known.[117] Hunt did not directly endorse the deists' arguments, but conveyed his views more subtly, by sympathetically portraying them as rational Christians, whilst gently satirizing their flustered opponents.[118] It was not only the deists, however, who confirmed the renewed ascendancy of 'the practical rational element . . . of the English Church' in the later seventeenth and eighteenth centuries.[119] Unlike Buckle, who had claimed erroneously that the clergy were deeply opposed to the foundation of the Royal Society, Hunt connected the reformed religion of the Church of England to the reformed philosophy of

---

[113] Ludwig-Maximilians-Universität, Munich, Universitätsbibliothek, 4⁰ Cod. ms. 917 m (181)/5: John Hunt to Jakob Frohschammer, 25 June 1870; Hunt, *Essay on pantheism*, p. 315.

[114] Ibid., pp. 372–5; cf. Hunt, *Pantheism and Christianity* (London, 1884).

[115] For example, J. Hunt, 'Henry St John Lord Bolingbroke', *CR*, 10 (1869), pp. [405]–21.

[116] Hunt, *Religious thought*, i, [1], 368–464.

[117] Ibid., ii, 238–9, 333–43, iii, 377.   [118] Ibid., ii, 243–5, 342–3.

[119] Ibid., iii, 373.

the early natural scientists.[120] Even the Methodist movement indirectly participated in the wider rationalism of the period, witnessing as it did to thenotion that 'Christianity did not depend on external evidences, but on inward feelings'.[121] The complete development of the rational character of English religion, Hunt concluded, 'may be the work of centuries to come'. Yet that development would necessarily advance from the positions attained to in the eighteenth century, for every age 'has a place to fill in the historic development of the education of the human race'.[122]

Hunt's revival of the deists' memory, he later recalled, attracted the hostility of fellow churchmen.[123] It nevertheless signified wider changes. The publication of Hunt's *magnum opus*, along with the other books and essays he wrote in a similar spirit, earned him the patronage and applause of liberal ecclesiastics. Tulloch probably played a role in Hunt's subsequent award of a doctorate of divinity from St Andrews, his undergraduate university; and Stanley nominated him to the agreeable Kentish living of Otford in 1877.[124] Pattison, welcoming Hunt's decision to focus on complex interactions of thought rather than a narrow history of theology, favourably likened him to Buckle.[125]

Other historians, of various ecclesiastical hues, soon followed Hunt in depicting eighteenth-century thought as involving the purification, rather than the erosion, of Christian theology, even if they did not share the radicalism of his conclusions. The moderate high churchmen Charles Abbey and John Overton, in their jointly authored history of *The English Church in the Eighteenth Century*, could not sympathize with deist criticism in the way that Hunt did.[126] But whilst they repeated the Oxford Movement's traditional criticisms of the practical listlessness of the eighteenth-century church, they were notably positive towards the orthodox theology it produced. According to Abbey and Overton, Reformation era controversies had worn themselves out. Questions 'far more profound and fundamental' concerning the possibility of revelation, and the future life, had now rightly taken their place.[127] The deist challenge called out, among other texts, 'the immortal work of Bishop Butler', whose *Analogy* often received pride of place in optimistic accounts of the eighteenth

---

[120] Ibid, ii, 177–9; cf. *HCE*, i, 340–1.   [121] Hunt, *Religious thought*, iii, 396.
[122] Ibid., iii, 373, 400.   [123] Hunt, 'Mr. Leslie Stephen', p. 414.
[124] Ludwig-Maximilians-Universität, Munich, Universitätsbibliothek: 4° Cod. ms. 917 m (181)/38–9: John Hunt to Jakob Frohschammer, 20 November 1877, 13 August 1878.
[125] Hunt, *Religious thought*, iii, [vii]; M. Pattison, 'Religious Thought in England from the Reformation to the End of the Last Century', *Academy*, 3:49 (1872), pp. 210–11.
[126] C.J. Abbey and J.H. Overton, *The English Church in the eighteenth century* (2 vols, London, 1878). On this text, see B. Young, 'Knock-kneed giants: Victorian representations of eighteenth-century thought', in Garnett and Matthew, *Revival and religion*, pp. 79–93.
[127] C.J. Abbey, 'Introductory', in Abbey and Overton, *English Church*, i, 2–4.

century's intellectual achievements written from an orthodox point of view.[128] The deists themselves, for all their errors, thereby played a constructive part in the history of thought. 'Toland failed to prove that there were no mysteries in Christianity', but showed the danger of theologians using scholastic 'words without knowledge'. If Tindal was not correct to say that Christianity was as old as the creation, 'there was an aspect in which it is undoubtedly true', given the religion's reasonable nature.[129] The authors nevertheless steered away from arguing, as Hunt had done, that deist assumptions had effectively won the field in the period: in fact they had disintegrated, successfully answered by orthodox apologists who knew their ground. Although no high churchman, William Lecky presented a comparable account of eighteenth-century religious philosophy in his *History of the Eighteenth Century*. He tellingly criticized Buckle for exaggerating clerical resistance to the earlier foundation of the Royal Society.[130] The deists, he argued, were intellectually marginalized and philosophically superficial.[131] By contrast, 'the evidences of Christianity were elaborated with a skill and power that had never before been equalled' by Berkeley, Butler, and other clergy inclined to place more emphasis on reason than on sacerdotal pretensions.[132] Amongst a broad spectrum of religiously apologetic historians writing in the final third of the century, therefore, the intellectual master-narrative of eighteenth-century religion, together with that of the century before it, became the rationalization of Christianity, rather than its dissolution.

Contemporary unbelievers, however, traced rather different ancestries in the thought of the preceding century, which emphasized its secularizing effects rather than downplaying them. The Comtean Positivist Frederic Harrison, reviewing the eighteenth century's legacy in an essay of 1883, counted its chief bequests to the nineteenth as lying in the idea of law; the 'genius for synthesis'; and the ideals of social reconstruction that had produced the American and French Revolutions and the reformed Parliament. In his accompanying list of proto-Positive worthies, consecrating the memories of Hume, Lamarck, Voltaire, Gibbon, and Burke, among others, theologians were conspicuously absent.[133] If dismissiveness was one possible response from anti-theological critics to the reasonable

---

[128] J.H. Overton, 'The Deists', in Abbey and Overton, *English Church*, i, 213; cf. J.R.T. Eaton, *Bishop Butler and his critics* (Oxford and Cambridge, 1877).
[129] Overton, 'The Deists', pp. 234–5.
[130] W.E.H. Lecky, *History of England in the eighteenth century* (8 vols, London, 1878–1890), ii, 528.
[131] Ibid., ii, 525 and n.   [132] Ibid., ii, 544–5.
[133] F. Harrison, 'A few words about the eighteenth century', repr. in his *The choice of books and other literary pieces* (London and New York, 1891), pp. 370–1.

theology of the eighteenth century, an anxious preoccupation with the historical reasons for its failure was another. Although he shared certain starting points with Harrison, Leslie Stephen's 1876 *History of English Thought in the Eighteenth Century* disclosed such a concern. In much the same way as religious liberals looked to the period to provide a conceptual ancestry and divine legitimation for rational theology, Stephen took the century to have been marked by the unconscious unwinding of theistic fallacies and the doctrines of innate ideas on which they relied. He shared the growing desire of his contemporaries properly to historicize an ignorantly maligned century. His wish was given a personal and familial poignancy by the final death, in Leslie and his brother James, of the evangelicalism ebulliently promoted by his grandfather and inherited, somewhat diminished, by his father.[134] Stephen treated the essential inadequacy of eighteenth-century religious thought, almost by prolepsis, as lying in its failure to realize that the rationalist premises adopted by deists and orthodox alike unavoidably ran on to the agnosticism into which the Stephen brothers eventually settled. History's bequest was not the ascent, but the death, of religious belief, which modern thought had no rational choice but to accept.[135]

The preface to the *History* announced the tone of the whole. The idea of the work, Stephen explained, was to give a fuller account of the movement of the 'tendencies of religious thought in England from 1688 to 1750' that had been 'so admirably characterised' in Pattison's essay.[136] Stephen thought Lechler's *Geschichte des Englischen Deismus* the best account of that subject; but he added that it neglected the telling relations between the deists and more orthodox writers, 'who in reality represent a superficial modification of the same general tendencies of thought.'[137] Though Hunt had shown 'candour and industry', Stephen regarded him as 'rather an annalist than a historian of thought'. Stephen confessed to differing 'widely from his estimate—so far as he has revealed it—of the true significance and relative importance of many of the writings concerned'. Given the differences between their starting principles, 'it would be strange, indeed, if I were in this respect quite satisfied with his performance.'[138]

Stephen's *History* proceeded from a countervailing conception of the history of reason to that which Tulloch or Hunt took as their respective points of departure. Far from representing the expansion of man's spiritual powers, or the education of the race, the history of religious thought was,

---

[134] Young, *Victorian eighteenth century*, pp. [103]–47.

[135] L. Stephen, *History of English thought in the eighteenth century* (2 vols, London, 1876).

[136] Ibid., i, [v].   [137] Ibid., i, [v]-vi.   [138] Ibid., i, vi.

to Stephen's mind, deeply irrational. For it exemplified the wider law of intellectual-historical growth that the historical development of thought often did not correspond to a logical process. Although thought, by Stephen's day, was at 'the scientific stage', there was never a neat outwards sweep from the known to the unknown. The lack of recognition accorded by eighteenth-century contemporaries to Hume's sceptical philosophy— in which Stephen invested the epochal significance others attached to Butler—showed that childlike conceptions dissolved only very slowly. The imagination was stronger than reason. The implications of an advance in one area for the sacred character of another became evident confusedly and hesitatingly, often following developments in society rather than the arguments of leading minds. Stephen's argumentative premises showed traces of Comte, whose reasoning powers Stephen admired, and whom a few years later Stephen was positively to contrast with Buckle's unhistorical 'English empiricism' and shallow Macaulayan complacency.[139] 'Actual decay may alternate with progress, and even true progress implies some admixture of decay.'[140]

So it was that the religious thought of the eighteenth century always trundled behind the critical avant-garde that had already undermined the paths which it drowsily followed. Theology was to Stephen one of those imaginative forces which had long outlived its underpinnings in philosophy; the Cambridge Platonists were the last expression of their unconscious and spontaneous union.[141] Stephen took eighteenth-century thought to have begun with Descartes, who resolved to doubt everything, elevating reason above tradition as the source of authoritative belief. Such a position might, Stephen thought, be most obviously turned against elaborate dogmatic systems; but there was no inherent reason why it might not also dissolve those innate ideas Descartes supposed to have discovered in his own mind: God, self, the opposition of soul and matter.[142]

Though Cartesian philosophy was never completely naturalized in England, Stephen explained, similar premises underpinned both ortho- dox and deist criticism in the following century. These writers had taken their stand upon assumptions which had already decayed. Hume's sev- erance of the chain of reasoning, particularly the idea of causation, on which deist and orthodox apologetics relied, passed unnoticed by those authors.[143] They made farragoes of credible religion by assuming that theology had some meaning, delimited according to personal predilection

---

[139] L. Stephen, 'An attempted philosophy of history', *FR*, 27:161 (1 May 1880), pp. [672]–95, at 680.
[140] Stephen, *English thought*, i, 17.   [141] Ibid., i, 79–80.   [142] Ibid., i, 21–9.
[143] Ibid., i, 34–54.

and subordinated to reason, but without probing its foundations too carefully. The debate between orthodox and deists over Christianity's internal evidences—the question of whether unaided reason was adequate to construct a religion—amounted to investing arbitrarily selected traditional conceptions such as God and immortality, whether derived from orthodoxy or natural religion, with an appearance of logical and practical necessity.[144] One side did not triumph over the other; rather, both wore each other out. Whereas Abbey, Overton, and Lecky supposed the orthodox to have defeated the deists, to Stephen all that had in fact happened was that the orthodox had met them 'more than half way.'[145] Hunt, reviewing Stephen's work for the *Contemporary Review*, supposed that the very fact that the ethical power of Christianity had outlived eighteenth-century philosophical disputes witnessed to its truth. For Stephen, however, that persistence simply witnessed to the sway tradition held over human minds.[146] In its fundamentals, eighteenth-century religious thought was over before it began.

The inadequacies of eighteenth-century thought, according to Stephen, did at least clear the ground for more lasting nineteenth-century solutions. Hume could not be undone; but absolute scepticism need not be the only result of the demolition of metaphysics. While Hume saw that his own mental operations proved nothing, he lacked the means of rising out of absolute scepticism to more positive conceptions. The nineteenth century, however, possessed two means through which a more durable approach to knowledge might emerge. The first was its comparative historical method. Whereas Tulloch and Hunt had lauded a conception of history understood as confirming the abiding force of innate ideas of God and spirit, Stephen thought history capable of explaining how religious ideas supposed to be universal and objective had arisen. A supposedly innate idea, in truth derived unconsciously from earliest childhood, 'might easily pass itself off as implied in the very structure of the mind'. It required the application of the comparative method to ideas, 'which enables us to trace their origin and development in minds different from our own', to indicate the limits of reasoning upon the contents of what a private philosopher's self-examination revealed.[147] The second starting point was Kant's recognition of the structuring power of subjectivity, in reply to Hume's insistence on its illusoriness. Kant showed that the idea of cause was no phantasm, but was instead implied in the perceiving faculty which corresponded to the perceived regularity of the external world. The conditions of mind, linking subject to object, moulded what was known

---

[144] Ibid., i, 91–191.   [145] Ibid., i, 169.
[146] Hunt, 'Mr. Leslie Stephen', pp. 423, 427.   [147] Stephen, *English thought*, i, 23.

about experience. The notion of experience, in short, had to be expanded beyond Humean limits, to incorporate history, sociology, and psychology.[148] Stephen's next major work, his 1882 *Science of Ethics*, cautiously sketched how such an expansion might enable students better to grasp the development of the social and moral affections.[149] Stephen's tentative essays in moving beyond the end points of eighteenth century thought reflected how agnostics and liberal theologians alike increasingly looked to wider conceptions of induction than Buckle had assumed in order to find the basis of knowledge. Experience was not something that happened to the mind understood as a unitary and passive receptacle, but was more a phenomenon within it. This was a notion which, just as it had informed spiritualized reappraisals of the history of rational theology, also stimulated the emergence and diffusion of anti-agnostic philosophies of history.

AGNOSTICISM AND THE HISTORY OF RELIGIOUS EXPERIENCE

Debate over the historical possibility of rational theology had proved inextricable from the fundamental epistemological question of whether mind participated in a reason that transcended the phenomenal world. By treating religious thought as a form of experience that was both inwardly illuminating and capable of offering an inductive contribution to the philosophy of the future, rationalizing historians of theology shared in a second, distinct mode of rebutting agnosticism and the conceptions of value that followed from it. This was the tendency, gathering especial strength after 1870, for critics to interpret personal religious experience as evidence of the ultimately rational and essentially spiritual historical process of which it was supposedly a part. This proceeded from alternative philosophical starting points to those which Comte and Buckle had assumed. Idealism—both in its purer form, and by its refreshment of the Scottish 'common sense' tradition as represented by John Tulloch and the more conservative figure of Robert Flint—helped to bind the believing subject to divine, historically immanent object. History, understood as a field where the points of connection between the human and divine minds might be vindicated, started to become a form of psychology. That transition, distilled in William Inge's reflections on mysticism, expressed something of the movement from nineteenth- to twentieth-century intellectual culture.

---

[148] Ibid., i, 48–60.
[149] L. Stephen, *The Science of Ethics* (London, 1882), pp. [1–39].

The way in which Scottish theologians came to treat the history of religious consciousness as evidence of the objective truth of its contents partly stemmed from their education in the indigenous tradition of common sense philosophy. Inaugurated by Thomas Reid in reply to Hume, this egalitarian, anti-intellectual, and intuitive philosophical approach proposed that the best answer to scepticism lay in accepting the conclusions of 'common sense'. In practice, it involved a critical appeal both to the common wisdom of the people, and especially to a descriptive psychology of the process of belief formation. These manoeuvres, it was held, revealed things in themselves and so proved traditional religious truth-claims.[150] Just as sensations revealed external stimuli, Reid supposed, reflection straightforwardly disclosed the reality of its objects, including the existence and attributes of the Supreme Being.[151] This tradition, which underwent significant modification as its practitioners came into contact with German intellectual currents and the early glimmers of agnosticism, figured prominently in the broad Scottish undergraduate curriculum until the Caird brothers' ascendancy at Glasgow began to dispel it from the 1860s.[152] Some representatives, chiefly Sir William Hamilton, defended religious orthodoxy by seeking, rather hazardously, to reconcile Reid's commitment to the possibility of absolute knowledge with Kant's insistence that it was impossible to know things in themselves. Anticipating Mansel, Hamilton concluded that it was simply necessary to accept the authority of revelation.[153] James Frederick Ferrier, professor of moral philosophy and political economy at St Andrews from 1845 to his death in 1864, pursued a more Idealist approach to the problem of knowledge. A student of Hegel, but one who saw his own system less as a German importation than as an attempt to solve problems bequeathed by earlier Scottish philosophers, Ferrier sought to defend the possibility of absolute knowledge by distinguishing consciousness, as a necessary element of all intelligence, from the mere description of mental operations.[154] Although he antagonized traditional Calvinists, Ferrier

---

[150] See Rylance, *Victorian psychology*, pp. [21]–39.

[151] T. Reid, *An inquiry into the human mind, on the principles of common sense*, 5th edn (Edinburgh, 1801), pp. 468–71.

[152] D. Macmillan, *The life of Robert Flint D.D., LL.D.* (London, New York, and Toronto, 1914), pp. 225–6.

[153] A. Ryan, 'Hamilton, Sir William Stirling (1788–1856)', *ODNB*; G. Graham, 'A re-examination of Sir William Hamilton's philosophy', in Graham, *Scottish philosophy*, pp. [47]–66.

[154] J.F. Ferrier, *Institutes of metaphysic: the theory of knowing and being* (Edinburgh and London, 1854). On Ferrier, see J. Keefe, 'James Frederick Ferrier: the return of Idealism and the rejection of common sense', in Graham, *Scottish philosophy*, pp. [67]–94;

presented fewer problems than Hamilton to self-consciously reasonable theologians.

Whether in the form presented by Ferrier, or in some more eclectic arrangement, a common sense approach to the philosophy of mind facilitated the emergence of a corresponding philosophy of history. It was not accidental that Tulloch made occasional journalistic forays into the philosophy of consciousness at the same time that he conducted his more extensive historical researches. He was a friend and admirer of Ferrier, in whose philosophy he recognized spiritual and anti-materialist qualities.[155] Common-sense principles, developed to take account of criticisms levelled by Ferrier and others against their early forms, provided central components of Tulloch's first book, a treatise vindicating *Theism*.[156] The spectre of agnosticism determined his appraisal of other, less amenable kinds of philosophy. In an essay on Kant first published in the *Edinburgh Review* for 1883, and subsequently reprinted in a volume of philosophical tracts targeted against 'the naturalistic or agnostic principle', Tulloch denounced his categories of understanding as 'a tangled mass of confusion', and their originator as 'an agnostic before the birth of Agnosticism' and 'a positive philosopher before Positivism'.[157] Although no Hegelian, Tulloch credited Hegel by comparison for at least picturing 'a *rational* world, of which "consciousness" was not an accident, but the essence'.[158]

The conclusions Tulloch drew from his study of mental and metaphysical philosophy fed his historical sensibility. *Rational Theology and Christian Philosophy* had ended by calling for, and predicting, the emergence of a compelling religious philosophy based on historical experience. Tulloch never systematically expounded what could be called a philosophical system, the constant indefiniteness of religious thought being for him both unavoidable, and a virtue rooted in intellectual humility.[159] But he did find something of an apologetic resting point, implicit in his preoccupation with theological transmutations, in the power of religious consciousness as his commitment to final credal formulations weakened. Tulloch never publicly wavered in his belief in the historicity of the

---

E.S. Haldane, *James Frederick Ferrier* (Edinburgh and London, 1899), pp. [27]–33, 74–5, 125, 90–100, 151.

[155] Tulloch, 'Professor Ferrier and the higher philosophy', in his *Modern theories*, pp. 337–74 (repr. from the *ER* for 1867).

[156] Tulloch, *Theism: the witness of reason and nature to an all-wise and beneficent creator* (Edinburgh, 1855), pp. 6–7, 12 n.–13 n., 204 n.

[157] Tulloch, *Modern Theories*, vi–vii, and 'Back to Kant; or, Immanuel Kant and the Kantian Revival', ibid., pp. 414–15, 423–4 (repr. from the *ER* for 1883).

[158] Tulloch, 'Pessimism: Leopardi, Schopenhauer, Hartmann', in his *Modern theories*, p. 196.

[159] Tulloch, 'Dogmatic extremes', pp. 193–5.

New Testament miracles.[160] But his early confidence that the Apostles' Creed differed from subsequent creeds in the fundamental nature of the truths it declared, evident in his early essay on Neander, gave way to the belief that even this amounted to a relative expression of the Christian mind at the period of its formation.[161] By 1879, Tulloch took 'the essentials of religion' to consist not in a form of sound words, but in a 'conscious relation to a Divine Personality' and 'the revelation of Eternal Life'.[162] He admitted that 'the mere satisfaction that a religion gives to its votaries could never be held as evidence of its divinity'.[163] There was nevertheless, as Pascal had perceived, 'a primitive endowment of spiritual instinct in man, which looks forth upon a higher world of reality'.[164]

When it came to the historical workings of that instinct, only a religion that imparted contact with a living character, and not the contemporary gospels of science or Arnoldian culture, could have inspired the action of personalities as religiously heroic as Francis Xavier, Reginald Heber, David Livingstone, or George Selwyn. Christian intuition could not be other than a real testament to that which was intuited.[165] Neander's studies of the outward realizations of inward spirit easily resonated with one socialized as Tulloch had been. 'The essential question betwixt the two schools' of Christianity and 'modern scientific materialism', Tulloch argued in his reply to the physicist John Tyndall's anti-theological if not especially materialist 1874 'Belfast Address', was 'What is Mind in man?' For Tulloch, this was a question to which religion—as 'a great fact in human life and history', and 'the highest of human experiences'—ultimately returned its own compelling answer.[166]

Tulloch's unsystematic transmutation of common-sense principles of knowledge into a Christianized philosophy of history found a parallel in the writings of Robert Flint. Flint succeeded Ferrier, whose philosophy he admired, at St Andrews in 1864, a candidature for which he had Tulloch's support. He thereafter became professor of divinity at Edinburgh from 1876 to 1903.[167] In that time, Flint established a popular reputation as a late and strong defender of Scottish common-sense philosophy, and

---

[160] Tulloch, *Beginning life*, pp. 66–123.
[161] [Tulloch], 'Augustus Neander', pp. 319–20; Tulloch, 'Dogmatic extremes', p. 189.
[162] Tulloch, 'The essentials of religion', *GW*, 20 (1879), p. 141.
[163] Tulloch, *Beginning life*, pp. 126–7.
[164] Tulloch, *Pascal* (Edinburgh, 1878), pp. 4, 187–8.
[165] Tulloch, 'The essentials of religion', pp. 139–44.
[166] [J. Tulloch], 'Modern scientific materialism', *BEM*, 96:529 (1874), pp. [519]–39, here at pp. 532, 520.
[167] Oliphant, *Memoir*, p. 199; S.R. Obitts, 'The thought of Robert Flint' (Edinburgh Univ. PhD thesis, 1962), p. 52.

a relatively conservative view of the Church of Scotland's traditional doctrine.[168] Flint's Baird Lectures on *Theism*, published in 1877, recorded his early period of relatively uncomplicated allegiance to common-sense assumptions. Against forms of contemporary unbelief including Positivism, which straightforwardly denied God, and Kantianism, which absurdly held that God 'cannot be *proved*, yet still *is*', Flint maintained the traditional common-sense position that the existence of God was implied by the essential role of causality, will, and intelligence—of which faculties God was the highest expression—in the human mental constitution.[169] Flint's confidence in the inferential attestation of divinity by and in consciousness did not diminish over time; but it had acquired an Idealist tinge by the time he published his major work on *Agnosticism* in 1903.[170] Flint now looked to a distinctly Christianized version of Hegel's and Schelling's philosophy of the Absolute as the 'unconditioned' implied in the necessary conditions of knowledge which Kant had delimited. In common with several of the critics considered in the second chapter, Flint now held that the mind's apprehension of that Absolute as a Trinitarian divinity, immanent in time, harmonized more and more with what was coming to be known about the evolving universe and the moral ends of human progress.[171] For Flint, as it had in a somewhat different way for Tulloch, the mind increasingly presented itself as a part of the history through which divinity moved.

The theistic inference Flint derived from his examination of the elements of human consciousness informed his pronounced interest in appraising history as a religiously significant whole. 'Historical analysis may supplement and correct, but can neither be severed from nor substituted for, psychological analysis', he observed in an 1874 study entitled *The Philosophy of History*, a study of previous critics' adventures in the subject which he intended to be preparatory to his own extended engagement with it.[172] Flint died before he could fulfil his hopes, but the implications of his belief that the meaning of history could not be ascertained apart from an assessment of the psychological, and especially spiritual capacities of historical actors found expression in his own apologetic writings. In a

[168] Ibid.; A.P.F. Sell, 'Flint, Robert (1838–1910)', *ODNB*; Sell, *Defending and declaring the faith: some Scottish examples 1860–1920* (Exeter, 1987), pp. 39–63.

[169] R. Flint, *Theism: being the Baird Lecture for 1876* (Edinburgh and London, 1877), pp. 52–3, 59–60, 64–8; cf. D. Stewart, 'The philosophy of the active and mental powers of man', in W. Hamilton (ed.), *The collected works of Dugald Steward, esq., F.R.SS.* (10 vols, Edinburgh and London, 1854–1858), vii, 17–33.

[170] Macmillan, *Robert Flint*, pp. 218–27.

[171] R. Flint, *Agnosticism* (Edinburgh and London, 1903), pp. 579–95.

[172] Flint, *The philosophy of history in France and Germany* (Edinburgh and London, 1874), pp. 174–175.

lecture to divinity students published in 1905, Flint argued that just as all science started from experience, so must theology begin from the history of religion. Flint recognized that Positivists studied that history; but they began from the polemical assumption that religion was false. The more the course of philosophy, art, and moral life were studied, however, the less likely it was that their spiritual roots could be viewed as illusory. Religion was verified by its psychological capacity to sustain piety, virtue, and purity. 'If the history of the world be, as has been said, the judgment of the world, it is incredible that that judgment should be the condemnation of a fact so permanent and universal as religion.' To believe the reverse was not empiricism but pessimism. It was a sign of the pressure Flint felt to be pressing in on revealed religion that such a defence of human spiritual powers should have come from one who, unlike Tulloch, counted himself an orthodox Calvinist.[173]

Flint was thus increasingly drawn from old-fashioned common sense into Idealist modes of thought, though not Idealism proper, as he worked out the implications of his position that there was an analogy between the individual consciousness and the divine mind animating the world process. From the point of view of one whose break with the common-sense tradition in favour of Idealism was complete, Edward Caird developed a comparable argument for a necessary connection between inward feeling and higher intelligence in a series of *Contemporary Review* essays, afterwards published as a book in 1885, which aimed to rebut the 'scientific Agnosticism' of Comte's mental and historical philosophy.[174] Comte's historical error, Caird argued, was to regard the intellect of the past three centuries as having been in conflict with the social and religious affections, and so in need of a new creed that would educate the intellect into altruism. This claim was rooted in his psychological mistake. Comte's error was to assume that the reason was merely a formal power of apprehending what was external to it, and so separate from the act of moral apprehension. In fact, the knowing subject was a unity. Religious and ethical feeling pointed towards their own completion in divine rationality. Neander and Tennyson, Caird noted, grounded religion in feeling; but feeling, in the very act of distinguishing itself from the reason, brought itself into relation with the conditions of its rational development. For Caird, that development consisted in the recognition that the primary doctrine of Christianity was its proclamation of the reconciliation between God and man. This was both a moral insight and a logical necessity, for the self—as both an ethical and a rational subject—could only ever find

---

[173] Flint, 'Tendencies of the age', pp. 95–105.
[174] E. Caird, *The social philosophy and religion of Comte* (Glasgow, 1885), xiii.

completion in the not-self. As Caird was to argue at greater length in his study of *The Evolution of Theology*, it was this primary truth that enabled historical Christianity to reconcile the antagonisms of spirit and nature, and the church and the world. 'Modern history is more than anything else the history of the long process whereby this logical necessity manifested itself in fact.'[175]

In the early years of his authorial career, William Inge's conception of the larger significance of the history of mysticism drew something of its shape and wider aspirations from the Idealism that suffused much of late-Victorian intellectual culture. Inge was a fellow of Hertford College, Oxford, from 1888 and, after a brief spell in parish ministry from 1905, Lady Margaret's Professor of Divinity at Cambridge between 1907 and his 1911 appointment to the deanery of St Paul's. A product of King's College, Cambridge, where he had taken firsts in both parts of the Classical Tripos, Inge's contact with Platonic philosophy—to the afterlife of which in Christian mysticism he was continually attentive—arguably predisposed him to appreciate the religious significance of mental activity in a manner comparable to the influence exerted by the common sense tradition on his Scottish precursors.[176] His widely influential research into mysticism as an autonomous form of the psychology of religion, which he later combined with well-paying journalistic assaults on democracy, socialism, and other forms of what he considered to be modish sentimentality, was essentially historical. In his 1899 Bampton Lectures on *Christian Mysticism*, he disparaged contemporary enthusiasts for psychical research as 'dabblers in occultism'.[177] The true type of mysticism, Inge argued, was to be drawn out of the inward and contemplative thinkers of Christian history.

Although not the first British student of his chosen subject, Inge was in an important respect a pioneer in it. Half a century previously, Robert Alfred Vaughan had published a history of mysticism in the form of a two-volume series of dialogues.[178] A Congregationalist minister whose investment in the strife between church and dissent waned as his wish to give expression to fundamental religious verities grew, Vaughan's early vocation as a Christian poet grew into that of an historian of mysticism under the dual influence of his father, Robert, and a period spent studying

---

[175] Ibid., pp. 177–249, here at 222–223. The allusions to Tennyson and Neander are at ibid., p. 190. Caird did not name the latter, but quoted his well-known maxim, 'the heart makes the theologian': Neander, *Allgemeine Geschichte*, i [pt. 1], dedication page.

[176] Inge, *Platonic tradition*; M. Grimley, 'Inge, William Ralph (1860–1954)', *ODNB*.

[177] W.R. Inge, *Christian mysticism: considered in eight lectures delivered before the University of Oxford* (London, 1899), ix.

[178] R.A. Vaughan, *Hours with the mystics: a contribution to the history of religious opinion* (2 vols, London, 1856).

German philosophy at Halle.[179] Inge recognized Vaughan's study in the notes to his own *Christian Mysticism* as 'the solitary work in English which attempts to give a history of Christian mysticism'. Yet he objected to Vaughan's criticism of mysticism, rooted in its lack of scriptural correctives, as implying a binary opposition between the subject of experience and the object of knowledge.[180] This division was also important to traditional high churchmen, who criticized mystics' enthusiastic indifference to external evidences, and, in a different way, to Positivists such as Frederic Harrison, for whom mysticism was a mode of obscuring scientific knowledge.[181] For Inge, however, the significance of mysticism lay precisely in how it showed that the human subject found its end in the divine object. Distinguishing the true, proto-Protestant mysticism of medieval northern Europe from the supernatural and authoritarian religion with which it was allegedly associated in Roman Catholicism, Inge related how Christian mysticism began in 'that dim consciousness of the *beyond*, which is part of our nature as human beings'.[182]

> Mysticism arises when we try to bring this higher consciousness into relation with the other contents of our minds. Religious Mysticism may be defined as the attempt to realise the presence of the living God in the soul and in nature, or, more generally, as *the attempt to realise, in thought and feeling, the immanence of the temporal in the eternal, and of the eternal in the temporal.*[183]

The mystical life, according to Inge, was a process of becoming, aspiring after movement from the lower to the higher self: an originally Platonic idea which Christianity had found fully consonant with its own purposes.[184] Contrition and amendment led on first to the 'illuminative life', where the faculties were concentrated on God, until the attainment of 'the unitive or contemplative life', in which the mystic beheld God face to face. True mysticism rested not on supernaturalism, but on the assumption that man partook of the divine nature, for he could only come to knowledge of that which was akin to himself. The real basis of mysticism, just as it was the basis of all true philosophy, was thus the Johannine doctrine of the Logos.[185] Mysticism, thought Inge, presumed

[179] Vaughan, *Essays and remains*, i, xxv, xxxiv–xxxv, lii–lviii.

[180] Inge, *Christian mysticism*, pp. 347–8; Vaughan, *Hours with the mystics*, i, [v]–xi,ii, [293]–312.

[181] Palmer, *Doctrine of development*, viii; F. Harrison, *The positive evolution of religion* (London, 1913), p. 66.

[182] Inge, *Christian mysticism*, viii–ix, pp. 4–5, 167–245.   [183] Ibid., p. 5.

[184] Ibid., p. 78; Inge, *Personal Idealism and mysticism: the Paddock Lectures for 1906 delivered at the General Seminary New York* (London, 1907), p. 104.

[185] On the doctrine of the Logos, see chapter two of this volume.

the unity of all existence and took the human mind to be the throne of the divine reason that permeated God, Christ, and the history of creation.[186]

Inge was fond of Plotinus' principle that man was a microcosm of the universe.[187] In his earlier books, sermons, and lectures, he tended to treat mysticism in the same way, as holding the key to a broadly Idealist metaphysical philosophy of historical and mental experience. To buttress his belief that mysticism disclosed how feeling passed into will, and will into intelligence, through the Logos, Inge often alluded to Idealist philosophers.[188] In *Christian Mysticism*, Inge quoted from a sermon of John Caird's as offering an admirable definition of the subject he treated: 'of all things good and fair and holy there is a spiritual cognisance which precedes and is independent of that knowledge which the understanding conveys.'[189] Inge correspondingly deprecated as 'empiricist' all philosophical and psychological attempts—multiplying in number around the turn of the twentieth century—radically to sever subject from object, and to restrict the mind from the possibility of discovering absolute truth. Preaching before Oxford University in 1904, he explained that indigenous agnosticism, as distilled by Leslie Stephen, proceeded from a shallow view of the data of experience.[190] His writings recurrently objected to how Kant and too many of those who had followed him in Germany—such as Neander and Harnack—had comparably separated the province of subjective experience from that of ultimate reason.[191] Although Inge sympathized with personal Idealism insofar as it recognized the claims of individuality which the older Idealism sometimes suppressed, he disparaged Hermann Lotze for allegedly separating the claims of personality from those of the higher reason that properly informed it.[192] Inge was pleased to remark in 1899 that 'while in Germany philosophy is falling more and more into the hands of the empirical school, our own thinkers are nearly all staunch idealists.'[193] Though he welcomed the fact that the psychology of religion was coming to attract wider attention as a field of scientific research, a curtailment of true philosophy occurred wherever it departed from the pursuit of truth as absolute, and instead took it to be

---

[186] Inge, *Christian mysticism*, pp. 28–9.   [187] Ibid., pp. 33–4.

[188] Inge, *Personal Idealism*, p. 145 and n.; Inge, *Christian mysticism*, p. 139 n.

[189] Ibid., pp. 322 n.–323 n.

[190] Inge, 'Wisdom', in his *Faith and knowledge: sermons* (Edinburgh, 1904), p. 33.

[191] Inge, *Personal Idealism*, pp. 97, 137; Inge, *Christian mysticism*, pp. 344–5. Inge evoked Neander in the same way as Caird had done: cf. note 175 of this chapter.

[192] Inge, *Faith and knowledge*, v–viii; Inge, *Light, life and love: selections from the German mystics of the middle ages* (London, 1904), lvi.

[193] Inge, *Christian mysticism*, xii and n.

relative to what gave satisfaction to believers: an objection he levelled against the emergent pragmatism of William James.[194]

As a route to absolute knowledge, harmonizing different aspects of experience, mysticism also offered a means of finding ultimate meaning in the movement of history. Inge's confidence in progress was never totalizing. He distinguished Johannine mysticism from pantheism's identification of God with the cosmic process, and thought Positivism's humanitarian millennium unattainable.[195] Yet there was a larger significance to Inge's sympathetic observation in *Christian Mysticism* that mystics typically regarded the life of the individual as a recapitulation of the history of the race.[196] In his earlier sermons and public lectures, he developed the idea that the spiritual future of mankind would involve the further spread of that rational apprehension of the divine, as a unifying centre to the entirety of experience, which past mystics had realized individually. In a sermon he delivered in Liverpool in 1912, he conceived of the religious history of Christendom as the authority of the inner light struggling against the efforts of false authorities to foreclose it.[197] Lecturing to an audience of London women in the same year, he insisted that to deny 'real progress' was to deprive 'history of all interest and the time-process of all rational meaning'. That progress consisted in the slow and often-interrupted teleological realization of the God-consciousness in man, 'casting its roots downward and bearing fruit upward'.[198]

Inge's Platonism, given shape by his study of past personalities who in important respects transcended the limits of their own ages, always inhibited him from placing too great a confidence in the general progressive movement of the world of sense. But it was his experience of the war and disruption of the twentieth century that led him to bring the mystical principle, affording a kind of illumination available to a relative few, and the actual course of human history into more self-conscious tension. 'The period of expansion is over, and we must adjust our view of earthly providence to a state of decline', he wrote soon after the end of the Great War.[199] Shortly before his death in 1954, in the wake of the next war, Inge wrote a new preface for his dyspeptic pen-portrait of *England*, first published twenty-eight years previously. There he explicitly opposed

---

[194] Inge, *Studies of English mystics: St Margaret's Lectures 1905* (London, 1906), pp. [1]–37; Inge, *Light, life and love*, xlviii–lx; cf. W. James, *The varieties of religious experience: a study in human nature*, ed. M. Bradley (Oxford, 2012), first edition 1902.
[195] Inge, *Christian mysticism*, p. 119, pp. 323n.–324n.   [196] Ibid., p. 35.
[197] W.R. Inge, *Authority and the inner light: delivered in St. Peter's Church, Liverpool, on June 3rd, 1912* (Liverpool, 1913), p. 23.
[198] Inge, *The church and the age* (London, 1912), pp. 28–30, 40–1.
[199] Inge, 'Our present discontents', in his *Outspoken essays* (London, 1919), p. 26.

the lamentable actual course of recent and more distant history to the solace and promise of mysticism. Inge recalled how 'the modern version of millenarianism was evolutionary optimism', which even the church had come to extol; he instanced Bishop Creighton as an example of this wrong turning. 'Kind-hearted humanitarians' had expelled the devil from the Christian system, 'and to their surprise God took His departure'. The churches were emptying; western civilization, as Spengler understood, had outlived its creative phase. But if history no longer could be said to correspond to what Christians had convinced themselves they ought to expect, this did not mean that religion was futile. 'Church history is not an edifying story', but it was not true, as Chesterton had said, that Christianity had never been tried. 'The real apostolic succession has been in the lives of the saints', although they numbered in the thousands rather than the millions. Revelation could only be of truths, not events. George Tyrrell, the Catholic modernist, 'once predicted that the time may come when nothing will be left of Christianity except mysticism and the law of love'.[200]

Insofar as that formulation described the religion of St Paul, the prospect did not leave Inge dejected. The larger hope had to be scaled down, its projection onto the history of the race slowly drawn back into the experience of the individual. The Idealist's dream of integrating all dimensions of reality within a Christian philosophical perspective, halt-ingly present in Inge's earlier thought, had slipped beyond his grasp. Inge's intellectual development, like that of any interesting thinker, was idiosyncratic; and other modes of defending religious belief circulated in the earlier twentieth century besides those he adopted.[201] But by coming to privilege individual consciousness over historical process—the sub-jective over the objective—as the route to truth, Inge's development expressed an important aspect of the transition from nineteenth- to twentieth-century intellectual conditions. As the revolt of Coleridge and Newman against putatively external and mechanical Enlightenment philosophy had been before him, it was also a new iteration of an ancient intellectual-historical cycle.

---

[200] Inge, *England*, rev. edn (New York and Toronto, 1953), viii–xviii; first edition 1926.
[201] On which, see Bowler, *Reconciling science and religion*.

6

Conclusion

At one of those symbolic turning points upon which autobiographies, perhaps more so than the lives they depict, often hinge, the Reverend Mark Pattison's 1885 *Memoirs of an Oxford Don* relate the moment at which their author resolved to take his leave of ecclesiastical history. It had been the reception accorded to his contribution to *Essays and Reviews* on 'Tendencies of Religious Thought in England, 1688–1750', he wrote, that finally drove him from the subject he had originally been induced to study by Newman. 'So wholly extinct is scientific theology in the Church of England' that 'our clergy knew only of pamphlets which must be either for or against one of the parties in the Church.' 'We were at cross purposes . . . I resolved to wash my hands of theology and even of Church history, seeing that there existed in England no proper public for either.'[1] Pattison's essay was offensive because, in common with his *Memoirs*, it was completely free from that highly wrought *pietas* which has placed such a formidable barrier between twenty-first century minds and the typical patterns of Victorian thought and prose.[2] Pattison's argument that religion, like all belief, could not exist apart from historical development was becoming a familiar, and not necessarily subversive assumption among his contemporaries. His further supposition that development had in fact rendered religious commitment less rather than more secure, however, made his argument unsettling. The way in which Pattison historicized historicism helps to encapsulate both the attraction, and the inherent limitations, of approaching the history of Christianity as though it were a vital raw material for the remodelling and fortification of Victorian religion.

'Tendencies of Religious Thought', suggestive for different reasons both to John Hunt and Leslie Stephen, offered a history of the rise and extinction of eighteenth-century deism. 'The genuine Anglican', Pattison noted, omitted the period between 1688 and 1833 from church history

---

[1] Pattison, *Memoirs*, pp. 157, 159. As we have seen, Pattison's claim was untrue.
[2] R.W. Church's daughter and biographer, Mary, criticized Pattison in this respect: *Dean Church*, pp. 230–1.

altogether.[3] But it had inescapably established the limits of modern thought. The belief of one period was, he continued, inevitably conditioned by that of the phase preceding it. Religious truth was not simply discerned by the application of some favoured principle of an individual—whether along Catholic or Protestant lines—but by what antecedent development had left thinkable.[4] The eighteenth century's prioritization of reason as the proper test for religious claims had, to his mind, settled nothing. But its dissipation of the old assumption that biblical and ecclesiastical authority was self-evident was an historical fact, from which, he hinted, the nineteenth century could not escape. Perhaps that is why the high church historian, Alfred Plummer, remarked in a letter to the dissentient Catholic Ignaz von Döllinger that Pattison's essay was 'one of the most sceptical, though apparently most innocent of the essays in "Essays and Reviews."'[5] Pattison's was a polemical move at the time. But he pointed to an important truth when he positioned the nineteenth century as the heir of the 'rationalist' eighteenth, however reluctant it may have been to bear this mantle. Kant, he said, merely gave formal definition and recognized position to a situation that was by Kant's time generally prevalent. In demolishing the traditional assumptions of theology and metaphysics, and declaring that credible religion had to be grounded in moral self-consciousness or 'practical reason', Kant distilled the religious implications of Enlightenment era epistemology.[6] However much Victorian religious thinkers resented this inheritance from their predecessor culture, they struggled to escape from it.

The history of religion, understood as the evolving record of mankind's collective moral experience, accordingly obtained a new interest for British authors. The filtration of post-Kantian German historical philosophy into British intellectual life often shaped the directions this took. But even those who disagreed with Kant and his successors implicitly recognized that logical deduction from self-authenticating scriptural texts, or the self-disclosing power of tradition, no longer provided authoritative bases for religious commitment. Different moralists looked to the conscience, or to the poetic, philosophical, or scientific faculties as ways of making historical experience religiously intelligible in an environment where, as Pattison ended his essay by saying, an accepted basis of religious authority—whether a text, an institution, an inward light, or reason—was unclear,

---

[3] Pattison, 'Tendencies', p. [387].   [4] Ibid., pp. 388–9.
[5] Bayerische Staatsbibliothek, Munich, Doellingeriana II: A. Plummer to I. v. Döllinger, 85/83, n.d.
[6] Cf. N. Smart, J. Clayton, P. Sherry, and S. Katz, 'Editorial introduction', to Smart et al., *Nineteenth century religious thought*, i, 5.

but widely sought-for.[7] 'Put not from you what you have here found', Newman wrote in conclusion to his *Essay on Development*. 'Regard it not as mere matter of present controversy; set not out resolved to refute it.'[8] What Newman thought of as his indefectible certitude appeared to others to amount to the wilful foreclosure of rational argument. But connections of the kind Newman drew between the historical interpretation of religion, the religious implications of history, and the province of the conscience became very widespread. Addressing the problem of religious persecution in church history in the series of Hulsean Lectures which he delivered before Cambridge University in 1893 and 1894, Mandell Creighton insisted that the deliberate moralization of past experience was inseparable from present-day determinations of value:

> It is not history which teaches conscience uprightness, it is conscience which teaches it to history. The accomplished fact is corrupting: it is for us to correct it by persisting in our ideal. The soul moralises the past that it may not be demoralised by it. Like the alchemists of the Middle Ages, it only finds in the crucible of experience the gold which itself has poured in before.[9]

Such statements make it difficult to suppose that Victorian historical thought represented merely the abstracted and passive register of cultural and intellectual changes that really took place elsewhere. History became inherent to how Victorians perceived, criticized, and tried to change lived experience, of which religion and its apparent power constituted integral parts. Historical interpretation, and the dissemination of historical types, became intrinsic to liberal and, increasingly, conservative attempts both to vindicate Christian truth, and to rearticulate it in terms which the newly authoritative knowing and judging subject might accept. 'The last was an objective age, at whose cool assumptions we have learned to smile; the present is a subjective and critical age, at whose rash denials the next will no less probably smile', John Tulloch wrote in his advice book for young men, *Beginning Life*.[10] The aim of religious philosophy was accordingly to unite the historical and objective with the inward and conscientious dimensions of Christianity; each must regulate the other. Tulloch made this observation in relation to the biblical record. In his own writings, however, he applied it much more often to the course of Christian history; and in his belief that post-apostolic history unignorably illuminated the true nature of religion, as to which Newman became for him a kind of

---

[7] Pattison, 'Tendencies', p. 430.   [8] Newman, *Essay*, p. 453.
[9] M. Creighton, *Persecution and tolerance: being the Hulsean Lectures preached before the University of Cambridge in 1893–4* (London and New York, 1895), pp. 29–30 and n.; he was quoting from the Swiss philosopher Henri-Frédéric Amiel's *Journal Intime*.
[10] Tulloch, *Beginning life*, pp. 47–8.

Caliban, he was far from unusual. As assumptions akin to Tulloch's took their place at the foundations of Victorian debate, conventional understandings of doctrinal orthodoxy, Roman Catholicism, and Protestantism became notably less severe, scholastic and politically embedded, and more ecumenical, idealist, and ethically personal, between the 1840s and the 1900s. If these trends amounted to a further stage in the slow dissolution of Christian authority in the West, beginning with Erasmus or Socinus and ending somewhere around 1968, most of those who promoted them during the Victorian period were unaware of and, indeed, directly opposed to such an ending. Positive reconstruction, more than internal secularization and steady intellectual retreat, best describes what Victorian religious historians believed they were accomplishing.

In this process there occurred a certain convergence between the ways in which late-Victorian religious critics discussed the different phases of the religious past. Early orthodoxy, medieval Catholicism, and Reformation Protestantism, once celebrated or disparaged as a function of reviving ecclesiastical partisanship, now became progressively evolving moments in the mind of God. Forming a continuum with the higher mental life of the seventeenth and eighteenth centuries, years which were newly opened to historical perspective, these periods took their significance from their place in the providential movement of history. The present and, it was hoped, the future of civilization, and of the nations which comprised it, thus rested secure in the nets first cast by the fishermen of Galilee. It became possible to accept, and even to celebrate, religious plurality, changing ethical sensibilities, and the growth of biblical criticism and scientific knowledge by interpreting them as belonging to the spiritual unfolding of time. In this way, religious kinds of historicism undergirded Victorian conceptions of progress more generally. By restoring to historical perspective the forgotten voices of those who once believed that the past and future of civilization were integrally founded upon the Christian religion, this book has in one respect considered the intellectual projection and anticipation of an historical path that was, in the end, not taken. In a more positive if also a more limited sense, however, the assumptions it has explored facilitated, for a time, Britain's distinctive experience of what it meant to become modern. It was a testament to religion's continuing power at the heart of Victorian culture that secular progressives found it necessary to argue with reference to models of historical development which assumed orthodoxy's past importance, whilst contesting its claims on the future.

Positivists and agnostics did not yet have the weight of intellectual opinion on their side. Deliberately idealist or experiential readings of the religious past offered moralists writing in the final third of the century, anxious about the creep of anti-metaphysical conceptions of knowledge and secularizing ideas of historical teleology, greater succour than Stanley, Milman, or Hatch had provided. 'It is now generally recognized that an idea is best understood when thus unfolded along the whole line of its history', Tulloch announced in his 1876 Croall Lectures, administered by the Edinburgh divinity professors and the Moderator of the General Assembly of the Church of Scotland for the purpose of expounding the evidences for natural and revealed religion. 'Nay', he continued, it was now clear 'that the best verification of the idea, or proof of its being true and not false, is just the manner in which it is seen from the beginning to cleave to the human mind and heart as a living possession'.[11]

Tulloch's confidence, as has been seen, was widely shared. Yet even among those most convinced of the power of the historical method to sift, dislodge, and reconfirm religious claims, doubts surfaced about the capacity of historical thought to yield positive propositions that would not themselves be overborne by history in their turn. 'The historian of ideas is no more bound to constitute himself the judge of their truth or falsity', wrote Robert Flint in a preface to a translation of the *evangelisch* Jena theologian Bernhard Pünjer's work on the *History of the Christian Philosophy of Religion*, 'than the historian of events is bound to pronounce on their wisdom or folly, rightness or wrongness'. The historian was not a critic, he wrote: the former's motto should be 'Darstellung, nicht Beurtheilung'—representation, not judgement. In Flint's work, as in that of many other professedly impartial critics, representation in practice invariably became a form of judgement: but his ideal of keeping them separate, by no means shared by all late Victorians, pointed to a certain instability in his and others' reliance on history to provide a form of spiritual epistemology.[12] Frederic William Farrar's *History of Interpretation* showed a similar duality. He simultaneously held that 'the History of Exegesis'—by tending towards the historical method—'leaves us with a Bible more precious than the old, because more comprehensible', and also that no correct theory of biblical interpretation emerged from that history, even though it disproved many false ones.[13] The idea that history could save and purify belief, though it exerted an immensely powerful hold over the Victorian mind, often had something of William James's 'ever not quite' in relation to the aspirations of its bolder advocates. As historical argument about religion came to focus late-Victorian

[11] Tulloch, *The Christian doctrine of sin* (Edinburgh and London, 1876), pp. 23–4.
[12] R. Flint, 'Preface', to B. Pünjer, *History of the Christian philosophy of religion from the Reformation to Kant*, trans. W. Hastie (Edinburgh, 1887), ix–x; the publisher was T. & T. Clark.
[13] Farrar, *History of Interpretation*, xi, xix–xx.

attention increasingly on the problem of mind, the ground was prepared for religious philosophers and their opponents to colonize and expand the psychology of religion in the first part of the twentieth century.

By 1914, the religious power with which the Victorians had invested history had not yet subsided; but its original impetus was receding into the past. Although many historical interpreters were sure that history undermined religious traditionalism, and could in principle replace it with something more durably rooted in human experience, they struggled to make history yield a positive and generally agreed religious programme. There was also something inherently hazardous about the grateful enthusiasm with which so many Victorians embraced the idea that the progress of the world vindicated Christian claims. The twentieth century was not to prove favourable to that hypothesis. It may be that, in future attempts to understand when and why secularization in the West has taken place, changing perceptions of humanity's moral past come to acquire a greater significance than they have so far held. But the idea that a fragmented society might find a kind of unity in a shared historical imagination has not altogether lost its relevance, even in a secular and forgetful age.

Select Bibliography

I. PRIMARY SOURCES

Bible

The Bible: Authorized King James Version, ed. R. Carroll and S. Prickett (Oxford, 1997)

MANUSCRIPT SOURCES

Berlin

Staatsbibliothek—Preussischer Kulturbesitz: Slg. Darmstaedter:
L. Creighton—T. Kolde, 2f 1880 (12)
M. Creighton—T. Kolde, 2d 1894 (24)
J. Hunt—E. Du Bois-Reymond, 2 m 1852 (6)

Bonn

Universität- und Landesbibliothek:
M. Pattison—J. Bernays, S 971, 155–166

Cambridge

Emmanuel College:
H. M. Gwatkin papers

Trinity College:
Bayne-Powell papers: J. Hare commonplace book, Add. MS c 205
C. Thirlwall—W. Whewell, Add. MS a 213/177–188
J. Hare diary, Add. MS c 206
J. Hare—W. Whewell, Add. MS a 206/154–189; Add. MS a 55 8; R 18 14/13–15; Add MS a 77/126–162

University Library:
J. Acton—M. Creighton,

Edinburgh

National Library of Scotland:
H. H. Milman—J. Murray, MS 40819–40823
J. G. Lockhart—H. H. Milman, MS 42443–42444
Correspondence relating to a memorial for H. H. Milman, MS 42483
H. M. Gwatkin and associates—T & T Clark, DEP 247: Box 8
J. Tulloch—J. Blackwood, MS 4113, 4121, 4144, 4154, 4165, 4175, 4205

New College:
R. Flint papers, FLI 1–3
R. Rainy papers, RAI 1–5

Glasgow
Glasgow University:
J. L. Steven, 'Notes of lectures on moral philosophy delivered by by Professor Edward Caird', DC 379/1/1 31355–31356

London
Lambeth Palace Library:
E. Hatch papers, MS 1467

University College:
K. Pearson papers, 2/1/4/1/5; 3/1/1/6; 3/1/2/12; 3/1/2/21–22; 3/1/3/17, 19

Marburg
Universitätsbibliothek:
A. Harnack—A. Jülicher, HS 695/371–411

Munich
Bayerische Staatsbibliothek:
Doellingeriana II: Plummer, Alfred (85); Stanley, Arthur Penrhyn (4); Hunt, John (1); Wordsworth, Christopher (2); Palmer, William (5)

Ludwig-Maximilians-Universität: Universitätsbibliothek:
J. Hunt—J. Frohschammer, 4° Cod. ms. 917 m (181)

Oxford
Bodleian Library:
MS Eng. lett. d. 166 (Milman letters 1841–1904)
MS Pattison 113–116, 128–134, 136–137
MS Phillipps-Robinson b. 153, c. 519, c. 549

Harris Manchester College:
'Manchester College Library chronological catalogue', MS Misc 25 XVI–XVIII

Oriel College:
E. Hatch papers, Orielensia H 50

St Andrews
St Andrews University:
J. M. Strachan notebooks, MS BT 19.T8–T86 (MS 4356–4358)

Tübingen
Universitätsbibliothek:
J. A. Symonds—E. Zeller, Md. 747.757
E. Caird—E. Zeller, Md. 747.100

ONLINE RESOURCES

Gale British Library Newspapers, Parts I and II: 1800–1900 [http://ezproxy-prd.bodleian.ox.ac.uk:2119/bncn/start.do?prodId=BNCN&userGroupName=oxford; last accessed 20 September 2018]

ProQuest British periodicals (1689–1939) [https://ezproxy-prd.bodleian.ox.ac.uk:7316/britishperiodicals/index?accountid=13042; last accessed 20 September 2018]

The Times Digital Archive 1785–2012 (Gale) [http://ezproxy-prd.bodleian.ox.ac.uk:2119/ttda/start.do?prodId=TTDA&userGroupName=oxford; last accessed 20 September 2018]

PRINTED PRIMARY SOURCES

Abbey, C. J., and Overton, J. H., *The English Church in the eighteenth century* (2 vols, London, 1878)

Ammon, C. F., *Die Fortbildung des Christenthums zur Weltreligion in kirchlicher Rücksicht* (4 vols, Leipzig, 1836–1840)

[Anon.], *Pamphlets in defence of the Oxford usage of subscription to the XXXIX Articles at matriculation* (Oxford, 1835)

[Anon.], 'Taylor's *Ancient Christianity*', *Eclectic Review*, 12 (1842), pp. 1–23

[Anon.], 'Newman's Essay on Development', *English Review*, 4:8 (1845), pp. 386–433

[Anon.], 'The literary examiner', *The Examiner*, 30 October 1852, pp. 691–2

[Anon.], 'Bunsen's Hippolytus', *Times*, 18 May 1853, p. 7

[Anon.], 'Bunsen's *Hippolytus and his Age*', *Edinburgh Review*, 97:197 (1853), pp. [1]–40

[Anon.], 'The fact and principle of Christianity', *Westminster Review*, 62:121 (1854), pp. [195]–221

[Anon.], 'History of Latin Christianity', *Morning Chronicle*, 19 April 1854, p. 7

[Anon.], 'History of Latin Christianity', *New Quarterly Review*, 3:11 (1854), pp. 315–9

[Anon.], 'Milman's history of Latin Christianity', *Journal of Sacred Literature*, 7:13 (1854), pp. [1]–24

[Anon.], 'Milman's Latin Christianity', *Dublin University Magazine*, 44:262 (1854), pp. 492–508

[Anon.], 'Milman's Latin Christianity', *Fraser's Magazine*, 50:298 (1854), p. 430–9

[Anon.], 'Bunsen's Christianity and Mankind', *Journal of Sacred Literature*, 1:1 (1855), pp. 1–16

[Anon.], 'Latin Christianity', *London Quarterly Review*, 4:7 (1855), pp. 142–78

[Anon.], 'Milman's Latin Christianity', *Saturday Review*, 1:15 (9 February 1856), pp. 277–8

[Anon.], 'Milman's Latin Christianity', *Saturday Review*, 1:17 (23 February 1856), pp. 324–5

[Anon.], 'Buckle's Civilisation in England', *Christian Remembrancer*, 35:100 (1858), pp. 330–60

[Anon.], 'Lectures on the History of the Eastern Church', *Saturday Review*, 11:289 (11 May 1861), p. 481–3

[Anon.], 'The Eastern Church: its past and future', *National Review*, 13:25 (1861), pp. 27–61

[Anon.], 'Handsome presentation to a clergyman', *Sheffield and Rotherham Independent*, 2 January 1862, p. 3

[Anon.], 'Lecky's History of Rationalism', *British Quarterly Review*, 84 (1865), pp. 401–33

[Anon.], 'Lecky's History of Rationalism', *Christian Remembrancer*, 51:131 (1866), pp. 214–41

[Anon.], *Lay suggestions on modern preaching and preachers* (London, Oxford, and Cambridge, 1867)

[Anon.], 'Longborough', *Jackson's Oxford Journal*, 2 March 1867, p. 7

[Anon.], 'The late Dean Milman', *Pall Mall Gazette*, 25 September 1868, p. 10

[Anon.], 'Funeral of the Dean of St Paul's', *Standard*, 2 October 1868, p. 6

[Anon.], 'The charge of heresy against a clergyman', *Reynolds's Newspaper*, 20 November 1870, p. 6

[Anon.], 'Rational Theology and Christian Philosophy in England', *Guardian*, 29 October 1873, pp. 1404–5

[Anon.], 'Carr's Lane Chapel', *Birmingham Daily Post*, 12 November 1883, p. 5

[Anon.], *A catalogue of the valuable theological library of the late Very Revd. Henry Wace, D.D., Dean of Canterbury* (London, [1924])

Arnold, M., *On the study of Celtic literature* (1867)

Arnold, M., *St. Paul and Protestantism; with an introduction on puritanism and the Church of England* (London, 1870)

Arnold, M., *Essays religious and mixed*, ed. Super, R. H. (Ann Arbor, MI, 1972)

Arnold, M., *The letters of Matthew Arnold*, ed. Lang, C. Y. (6 vols, Charlottesville, VA, and London, 1996–2001)

Arnold, M., *Culture and anarchy*, ed. Garnett, J. (Oxford, 2006)

Arnold, T., *Principles of church reform* (London, 1833)

Baeumker, C., *Das Problem der Materie in der griechischen Philosophie* (Münster, 1890)

Baur, F. C., *Die Epochen der kirchlichen Geschichtschreibung* (Tübingen, 1852)

[Beard, C.], 'Lecky's History of Rationalism', *Theological Review*, 2:9 (1865), pp. 429–53

[Beard, C.], 'Bishop Thirlwall's Remains', *Theological Review*, 15:61 (1878), pp. 216–35

Beard, C., *The Reformation of the sixteenth century in its relation to modern thought and knowledge* (London and Edinburgh, 1883)

Beard, C., *Martin Luther and the Reformation in Germany until the close of the Diet of Worms*, ed. Smith, J. F. (London, 1889)

Bedford, A. M., 'Introduction', to Benson, E. W., *Addresses on the Acts of the Apostles*, ed. M. Benson (London, 1901), [ix]–xiv

Besant, A., *The fruits of Christianity* (London, [1878?])

Bickersteth, E., *The Christian student designed to assist Christians in general in acquiring religious knowledge: with lists of books, adapted to the various classes of society*, 3rd edn (London, 1832)

Bickersteth, E., *A brief practical view of the Evangelical Alliance; in regard to its character, principles, objects, organization, and Christian spirit* (London, 1846)

Bigg, C., *The Christian Platonists of Alexandria: eight lectures preached before the University of Oxford in the year 1886* (Oxford, 1886)

Bigg, C., *Neoplatonism* (London, 1895)

Bigg, C., *A critical and exegetical commentary on the epistles of St. Peter and St. Jude* (Edinburgh, 1901)

Bigg, C., *The origins of Christianity*, ed. Strong, T. B. (Oxford, 1909)

Bigg, C., *The spirit of Christ in common life*, ed. Strong, T. B. (London, 1909)

Blunt, J. H., *The Reformation of the Church of England: its history, principles and results [A.D. 1514–1547]*, 2nd edn (London, Oxford, and Cambridge, 1869)

Blunt, J. J., *An introduction to a course of lectures on the early fathers, now in delivery in the University of Cambridge* (Cambridge, 1840)

Blunt, J. J., *On the right use of the early fathers: two series of lectures, delivered in the University of Cambridge* (London, 1857)

Bradley, G. G., *Recollections of Arthur Penrhyn Stanley, late Dean of Westminster: three lectures delivered in Edinburgh in November, 1882* (London, 1883)

Brodrick, G. C., *A history of the University of Oxford* (London, 1886)

Buckle, H. T., *History of civilization in England* (2 vols, London, 1857–1861)

Buckle, H. T., 'Mill on liberty', *Fraser's Magazine*, 59:353 (1859), pp. [509]–42

Bunsen, C. C. J., *Hippolytus and his age; or, the doctrine and practice of the church of Rome under Commodus and Alexander Severus: and ancient and modern Christianity and divinity compared* (4 vols, London, 1852)

Bunsen, C. C. J., *Hippolytus und seine Zeit: Anfänge und Ansichten des Christenthums und der Menschheit* (2 vols, Leipzig, 1852–1853)

Bunsen, C. C. J., *Christianity and mankind, their beginnings and prospects* (7 vols, London, 1854)

Bunsen, C. C. J., *Hippolytus and his age; or, the beginnings and prospects of Christianity*, 2nd edn (2 vols, London, 1854)

Bunsen, C. C. J., *God in history or the progress of man's faith in the moral order of the world*, trans. Winkworth, S. (3 vols, London, 1868–1870)

Bunsen, F., *A memoir of Baron Bunsen* (2 vols, London, 1868)

Burckhardt, J., *Die Kultur der Renaissance in Italien: ein Versuch* (Basel, 1860)

Burckhardt, J., *The civilisation of the period of the Renaissance in Italy*, trans. Middlemore, S. G. C. (2 vols, London, 1878)

Burton, E., *Testimonies of the ante-Nicene fathers to the divinity of Christ*, 2nd edn (Oxford, 1829)

Burton, E., *Sermons, preached before the University of Oxford* (London, 1832)

Burton, E., *History of the Christian church; from the ascension of Jesus Christ, to the conversion of Constantine* (London, 1836)

Burton, E., *Sermons, doctrinal and practical*, ed. Woodward, T., 2nd edn (Dublin, 1852)

Butler, W. A., *Letters on the development of Christian doctrine in reply to Mr. Newman's Essay*, ed. Woodward, T., (Dublin, 1850)

Caird., E., *The social philosophy and religion of Comte* (Glasgow, 1885)

Caird., E., *The evolution of theology in the Greek philosophers: the Gifford Lectures delivered in the University of Glasgow in sessions 1900–1901 and 1901–1902* (2 vols, Glasgow, 1904)

Caird, E., *Miscellaneous pamphlets, lay sermons and addresses, 1866–1907*, ed. Tyler, C. (Bristol, 1999)

Caird, J., *University addresses: being addresses on subjects of academic study delivered at the University of Glasgow* (Glasgow, 1898)

Caird, J., *The fundamental ideas of Christianity* (2 vols, Glasgow, 1899)

Cairns, J., *Christ the central evidence of Christianity and other present day tracts* (London, 1893)

Candlish, R. S., *The fatherhood of God: being the first course of the Cunningham Lectures delivered before the New College, Edinburgh, in March 1864* (Edinburgh, 1864)

Carlyle, T., *Oliver Cromwell's letters and speeches, with elucidations*, 2nd edn (3 vols, London, 1846)

Carlyle, T., *Critical and miscellaneous essays* (4 vols, London, 1893)

Carlyle, T., *On heroes, hero-worship, and the heroic in history* (London, 1893)

Carlyle, T., *Past and Present* (London, 1893)

Cattley, S. R., and Townsend, G. (eds), *The acts and monuments of John Foxe* (8 vols, London, 1837–1841)

Chalmers, T., *Christian union: address of the Rev. Dr. Chalmers at the bicentenary commemoration of the Westminster Assembly, July 13, 1843* (London, 1843)

Cheetham, S., *A history of the Christian church since the Reformation* (London, 1907)

Church, M. C., *Life and letters of Dean Church* (London, 1894)

Church, R. W., *Civilization and religion: a sermon preached before the University of Oxford, at St. Mary's Church, on the fifth Sunday in Lent, March 29, 1868* (Oxford and London, 1868)

Church, R. W., 'Lecky's "History of European Morals"', *Macmillan's Magazine*, 20:115 (1869), pp. 76–88

Church, R. W., 'Lancelot Andrewes', in Barry, A. (ed.), *Masters in English theology; being the King's College lectures for 1877* (London, 1877), pp. [61]–112

Church, R. W., *The gifts of civilisation and other sermons and lectures delivered at Oxford and at St Paul's*, new edn (London, 1880)

Church, R. W., *The Oxford Movement: twelve years 1833–1845* (London, 1891)

Church, R. W., *The beginning of the middle ages* (London, 1895)

Church, R. W., *Occasional papers selected from the Guardian, the Times, and the Saturday Review 1846–1890*, ed. Church, M. C. (London, 1897)

Coleridge, S. T., *Aids to reflection and the confessions of an inquiring spirit* (London, 1893)

Comte, A., *Cours de philosophie positive* (6 vols, Paris, 1830–1842)

Comte, A., *Système de politique positive; ou, traité de sociologie instituant le religion de l'humanité* (4 vols, Paris, 1851–1854)

Comte, A., *The positive philosophy of Auguste Comte*, trans. Martineau, H. (2 vols, London, 1853)

Comte, A., *System of positive polity, or, treatise on sociology, instituting the Religion of Humanity*, trans. Bridges, J. H., et al. (4 vols, London, 1875–1877)

Conybeare, W. D., *An analytical examination into the character, value, and just application of the writings of the Christian Fathers during the ante-Nicene period: being the Bampton Lectures for the year MDCCCXXXIX* (Oxford, 1839)

Coulton, G. G., *From Francis to Dante: a translation of all that is of primary interest in the chronicle of the Franciscan Salimbene; (1221–1288) together with notes and illustrations from other medieval sources* (London, 1906)

Coulton, G. G., *Pearl: a fourteenth-century poem* (London, 1906)

Coulton, G. G., *Fourscore years: an autobiography* (Cambridge, 1944)

[Cox, G. W.], 'Milman's *History of Latin Christianity*', *Edinburgh Review*, 107:217 (1858), pp. 51–87

Cox, G. W., *Latin and Teutonic Christendom: an historical sketch* (London, 1870)

[Craufurd, J.], the Hon. Lord Ardmillan, 'Introduction', to Wylie, J. A. (ed.), *Disruption worthies: a memorial of 1843* (Edinburgh, 1881), xiii–xxiv

Creighton, L., *Life and Letters of Mandell Creighton, D.D. Oxon. and Cam., sometime bishop of London* (2 vols, London, 1904)

Creighton, M., *The age of Elizabeth* (London, 1876)

Creighton, M., *Persecution and tolerance: being the Hulsean Lectures preached before the University of Cambridge in 1893–4* (London and New York, 1895)

Creighton, M., *The idea of a national church* (London, 1898)

Creighton, M., *Historical lectures and addresses*, ed. Creighton, L. (London, New York, and Bombay, 1903)

Creighton, M., *History of the papacy from the great schism to the sack of Rome*, new edn (6 vols, London, 1907–1911)

Cruttwell, C. T., *A literary history of early Christianity, including the fathers and the chief heretical writers of the Ante-Nicene period* (2 vols, London, 1893)

Cunningham, W., *The Reformers and theology of the Reformation* (Edinburgh, 1862)

Cunningham, W., *Discussions on church principles: popish, Erastian and Presbyterian* (Edinburgh, 1863)

Cunningham, W., *Historical theology: a review of the principal doctrinal discussions in the Christian church since the apostolic age* (2 vols, London, 1960)

Dale, A. W. W., *The life of R. W. Dale of Birmingham* (London, 1899)

[Dale, R. W.], 'The expiatory theory of the atonement', *British Quarterly Review*, 92 (1867), pp. 463–504

Dale, R. W., *The evangelical revival and other sermons: with an address on the work of the Christian ministry in a period of theological decay and transition* (London, 1880)

Dale, R. W., *Christian doctrine: a series of discourses* (London, 1894)

Dale, R. W., *Nine lectures on preaching: delivered at Yale, New Haven, Connecticut*, 9th edn (London, 1896)

Dale, R. W., *Protestantism: its ultimate principle* (London, 1928)

Donaldson, A. B., *Five great Oxford leaders: Keble, Newman, Pusey, Liddon and Church*, 3rd edn (London, 1902)

Dorner, I., *History of Protestant theology: particularly in Germany*, trans. Robson, G., and Taylor, S. (2 vols, Edinburgh, 1871)

Dunoyer, C., *De la liberté du travail ou simple exposé des conditions dans lesquelles les forces humaines s'exercent avec le plus de puissance* (3 vols, Paris, 1845)

Eaton, J. R. T., *Bishop Butler and his critics* (Oxford and London, 1877)

Elfe Tayler, W., *Hippolytus, and the Christian church of the third century: with a copious analysis of the newly-discovered MS.; and a translation of all its important parts, from the original Greek* (London, 1853)

Eliot, G., 'The influence of rationalism', *Fortnightly Review*, 1 (15 May 1865), pp. 43–55

Eliot, G., *Romola*, ed. Barrett, D. (London, 1996)

Eliot, G., *Middlemarch*, ed. Carroll, D. (Oxford, 1997)

Farrar, F. W., 'Calvin as an expositor', *The Expositor*, 7 (1884), pp. 426–44

Farrar, F. W., 'The reformers as expositors. II. Luther', *The Expositor*, 7 (1884), pp. 214–29

Farrar, F. W., *History of interpretation: eight lectures preached before the University of Oxford in the year MDCCCLXXXV* (London, 1886)

Farrar, F. W., *Lives of the fathers: sketches of church history in biography* (2 vols, Edinburgh, 1889)

Ferrier, J. F., *Institutes of metaphysic: the theory of knowing and being* (Edinburgh and London, 1854)

Flint, R., *The philosophy of history in France and Germany* (2 vols, Edinburgh and London, 1874)

Flint, R., *Theism: being the Baird Lecture for 1876* (Edinburgh and London, 1877)

Flint, R., 'Preface', to B. Pünjer, *History of the Christian philosophy of religion from the Reformation to Kant*, trans. Hastie, W. (Edinburgh, 1887), v–xiv

Flint, R., *Historical philosophy in France and French Belgium and Switzerland* (Edinburgh and London, 1893)

Flint, R., *Agnosticism* (Edinburgh and London, 1903)

Flint, R., *On Theological, Biblical, and other Subjects* (Edinburgh and London, 1905)

Forde, G. M., *A goodly heritage: a simple church history* (London, 1902)

[Frederick Pollock, W.], 'Buckle's *History of Civilization in England*', *Quarterly Review*, 104:207 (1858), pp. 38–74

Froude, J. A., *History of England from the fall of Wolsey to the death of Elizabeth* (12 vols, London, 1856–1870)

Froude, J. A., *Life and letters of Erasmus: lectures delivered at Oxford 1893–4* (London, 1894)

Froude, J. A., *Short studies on great subjects*, new edn (4 vols, London, 1895–1897)

Froude, R. H., *Remains of the late reverend Richard Hurrell Froude, M.A.*, ed. [Newman, J. H., and Keble, J.] (4 vols, London, 1838–1839)

Galton, A., 'Matthew Arnold; his practice, teaching, and example: an essay in criticism', in *The Century Guild Hobby Horse*, 3:11 (1888), pp. 83–108

Gibbon, E., *The history of the decline and fall of the Roman Empire*, ed. Milman, H. H. (12 vols, London, 1838–1839)

Gibbon, E., *The life of Edward Gibbon [by himself], with selections from his correspondence*, ed. Milman, H. H. (London, 1839)

Gladstone, W. E., *The Gladstone Diaries*, ed. Foot, M. R. D., and Matthew, H. C. G. (14 vols, Oxford, 1968–1994)

Goode, W., *The divine rule of faith and practice* (2 vols, London, 1842)

Gore, C., *Leo the Great* (London, 1881)

Gore, C., *The church and the ministry: a review of the Rev. E. Hatch's Bampton Lectures* (London and Oxford, 1882)

Gore, C., *The clergy and the creeds: a sermon preached before the University of Oxford on Trinity Sunday, 1887* (London, 1887)

Gore, C. (ed.), *Lux mundi: a series of studies in the religion of the incarnation* (London, 1889)

Gore, C., *The Incarnation of the Son of God, being the Bampton Lectures for the year 1891* (London, 1891)

Gough, H., *A general index to the publications of the Parker Society* (Cambridge, 1855)

Gould, F. J., *The pioneers of Johnson's court: a history of the Rationalist Press Association*, rev. edn (London, 1935)

Green, S. G., *The story of the Religious Tract Society for one hundred years* (London, 1899)

Greenwood, T., *Cathedra Petri: a political history of the great Latin patriarchate* (6 vols, London, 1856–1872)

Gregory, I., *Morals on the book of Job*, trans. Marriott, C., and Bliss, J. (3 vols, Oxford, 1844–1850)

Grimm, J., *Deutsche Mythologie* (Göttingen, 1835)

Grindal, E., *The Remains of Edmund Grindal, D.D. successively bishop of London, and archbishop of York and Canterbury*, ed. Nicholson, W. (Cambridge, 1843)

Guizot, M., *Histoire générale de la civilisation en Europe depuis la chute de l'empire romain jusqu'à la révolution française*, 4th edn (Paris, 1840)

Guizot, M., *Histoire de la civilisation en Europe depuis la chute de l'empire romain jusqu'à la révolution française*, 8th edn (Paris, 1866)

Günther, A., *Vorschule zur speculativen Theologie des positiven Christenthums: in Briefen*, 2nd edn (2 vols, Vienna, 1846–1848)

Gurney, A., *King Charles the First: a dramatic poem*, 2nd edn (London, 1852)

Gwatkin, H. M., *Studies of Arianism, chiefly referring to the character and chronology of the reaction which followed the Council of Nicaea* (Cambridge and London, 1882)

Gwatkin, H. M., *The meaning of ecclesiastical history: an inaugural lecture* (Cambridge, 1891)

Gwatkin, H. M., *The unrest of our time: a paper read at the Church Congress, Bradford, September, 1898* (Derby, 1898)

Gwatkin, H. M., *The knowledge of God and its historical development* (2 vols, Edinburgh, 1906)

Haldane, E. S., *James Frederick Ferrier* (Edinburgh and London, 1899)

Hallam, H., *View of the state of Europe during the middle ages*, 4th edn (3 vols, London, 1826)

Hampden, R. D., *The scholastic philosophy considered in its relation to Christian theology* (Oxford, 1833)

Hampden, R. D., *The work of Christ, and the work of the spirit, considered in two sermons* (London, 1847)

Hardwick, C., *A history of the Christian church: Middle Age* (Cambridge, 1853)

[Hare, A., and Hare, J. C.], *Guesses at truth by two brothers*, new edn (London and New York, 1871)

Hare, A. J. C., *Memorials of a quiet life*, 12th edn (2 vols, London, 1875)

Hare, J. C., *The victory of faith, and other sermons* (Cambridge, 1840)

Hare, J. C., *The mission of the comforter and other sermons with notes* (2 vols, London, 1846)

Hare, J. C., *Vindication of Luther against his recent English assailants*, 2nd edn (London, 1855)

Harnack, A., *Lehrbuch der Dogmengeschichte* (3 vols, Freiburg im Breisgau, 1886–1890)

Harnack, A., 'Nachwort', to Hatch, E., *Griechentum und Christentum: zwölf Hibbertvorlesungen über den Einfluss griechischer Ideen und Gebräuche auf die christliche Kirche*, trans. Preuschen, E. (Freiburg im Breisgau, 1892), pp. 263–68

Harnack, A., *Reden und Aufsätze* (2 vols, Giessen, 1904)

Harrison, F., *The choice of books and other literary pieces* (London and New York, 1891)

Harrison, F., *The positive evolution of religion: its moral and social reaction* (London, 1913)

Hatch, E., 'A Free Anglican Church', *Macmillan's Magazine*, 18 (1868), pp. [449]–60

Hatch, E., *The organization of the early Christian churches: eight lectures delivered before the University of Oxford, in the year 1880* (London, Oxford and Cambridge, 1881)

Hatch, E., *Die Gesellschaftsverfassung der christlichen Kirche im Alterthum: acht Vorlesungen*, trans. Harnack, A. (Giessen, 1883)

Hatch, E., 'From metaphysics to history', *Contemporary Review*, 55 (1889), pp. [864]–72

Hatch, E., *The influence of Greek ideas and usages upon the Christian church*, ed. Fairbairn, A. M. (London, 1890)

Hatch, E., 'Diversity in unity the law of spiritual life', in S. Hatch (ed.), *Memorials of Edwin Hatch, D.D. sometime reader in ecclesiastical history in the University of Oxford, and Rector of Purleigh* (London, 1890), pp. [163]–77

Hatch, E., *Towards fields of light, sacred poems* (London, 1890)

[Hatch, S.], 'Biographical notices', in Hatch, S. (ed.), *Memorials of Edwin Hatch, D.D. sometime reader in ecclesiastical history in the University of Oxford, and Rector of Purleigh* (London, 1890), [xv]–xliii

Hauréau, B., *De la philosophie scolastique* (2 vols, Paris, 1850)

Hetherington, W. M., *History of the Westminster Assembly of Divines* (Edinburgh, 1843)

Hetherington, W. M., 'Introductory essay', to R. Shaw, *An exposition of the Confession of Faith of the Westminster Assembly of Divines* (Edinburgh, 1845), [ix]–xxxvi

Heurtley, C. A., *Wholesome words: sermons on some important points of Christian doctrine preached before the University of Oxford*, ed. W. Ince (London, 1896)

Hillebrand, K., 'England in the eighteenth century', *Contemporary Review*, 37 (1880), pp. [1]–30

Holland, H. S., *The fathers for English readers: the apostolic fathers* (London, 1878)

Hook, W. F., *The three Reformations: Lutheran-Roman-Anglican* (London, 1847)

Hort, A. F., *Life and letters of Fenton John Anthony Hort D.D., D.C.L., LL.D., sometime Hulsean Professor and Lady Margaret's Reader in Divinity in the University of Cambridge* (2 vols, London, 1896)

Hort, F. J. A., *Two dissertations* (Cambridge and London, 1876)

[Hunt, E. M.], *The wards of Plotinus* (3 vols, London, [1881])

Hunt, J., *An Essay on Pantheism* (London, 1866)

Hunt, J., 'Henry St John Lord Bolingbroke', *Contemporary Review*, 10 (1869), pp. [405]–21

Hunt, J., *Religious thought in England from the Reformation to the end of the last century: a contribution to the history of theology* (3 vols, London, 1870–1873)

Hunt, J., 'Christianity and modern evidences', *Contemporary Review*, 18 (1871), pp. [152]–73

Hunt, J., 'Mr. Leslie Stephen on English thought in the eighteenth century', *Contemporary Review*, 29 (1877), pp. [410]–30

Hunt, J., *Pantheism and Christianity* (London, 1884)

Hussey, R., *Sermons mostly academical* (Oxford, 1849)

Hussey, R., *The rise of the papal power traced in three lectures* (Oxford, 1851)

[Hutton, R. H.], 'Civilisation and faith', *National Review*, 11 (1858), pp. 198–228

Illingworth, J. R., *The doctrine of the Trinity apologetically considered* (London, 1907)

Illingworth, J. R., *Divine transcendence and its reflection in religious authority* (London, 1911)

Inge, W. R., *Christian mysticism: considered in eight lectures delivered before the University of Oxford* (London, 1899)

Inge, W. R., *Faith and knowledge: sermons* (Edinburgh, 1904)

Inge, W. R., *Light, life and love: selections from the German mystics of the middle ages* (London, 1904)

Inge, W. R., *Studies of English mystics: St Margaret's Lectures 1905* (London, 1906)

Inge, W. R., *Personal Idealism and mysticism: the Paddock Lectures for 1906 delivered at the General Seminary New York* (London, 1907)

Inge, W. R., 'Charles Bigg', *Journal of Theological Studies*, 10 (1908), pp. [1]–2

Inge, W. R., *The church and the age* (London, 1912)

Inge, W. R., *Authority and the inner light: delivered in St. Peter's Church, Liverpool, on June 3rd, 1912* (Liverpool, 1913)

Inge, W. R., *Outspoken essays* (London, 1919)

Inge, W. R., *The Platonic tradition in English religious thought: the Hulsean Lectures at Cambridge 1925–1926* (London, 1926)

Inge, W. R., *England*, rev. edn (New York and Toronto, 1953)

James, W., *Pragmatism, a new name for some old ways of thinking: popular lectures on philosophy* (London, 1907)

James, W., *The varieties of religious experience: a study in human nature*, ed. Bradley, M. (Oxford, 2012)

Janssen, J., *Geschichte des deutschen Volkes seit dem Ausgang des Mittelalters* (8 vols, Freiburg im Breisgau, 1876–1894)

Jewel, J., *The works of John Jewel, Bishop of Salisbury*, ed. Ayre, J. (4 vols, Cambridge, 1845–1850)

Jones, H., and Muirhead, J. H. (eds), *The life and philosophy of Edward Caird LL. D., D.C.L., F.B.A.* (Glasgow, 1921)

Jowett, B., *Letters of Benjamin Jowett, M.A.: Master of Balliol College, Oxford*, ed. Abbott, E., and Campbell, L. (London, 1899)

Jowett, B., 'On the interpretation of Scripture', in Shea, V., and Whitla, W. (eds), *Essays and Reviews: the 1860 text and its reading* (Charlottesville, VA, and London, 2000), pp. [477]–536

Kaye, J., *The ecclesiastical history of the second and third centuries: illustrated from the writings of Tertullian* (Cambridge, 1826)

Kidd, B. J., *The Thirty-nine Articles: their History and Explanation* (2 vols, London, 1899)

Killen, W. D., *The Old Catholic Church: or the history, doctrine, worship, and polity of the Christians traced from the apostolic age to the establishment of the Pope as temporal sovereign, A.D. 755* (Edinburgh, 1871)

Kirkus, W. 'Rationalism in Europe', *Journal of Sacred Literature*, 8:15 (1865), pp. 157–85

Krabbe, O., *August Neander: ein Beitrag zu seiner Charakteristik* (Hamburg, 1852)

Lechler, G. V., *Geschichte des englischen Deismus* (Stuttgart and Tübingen, 1841)

Lecky, E., *A memoir of the Right Hon. William Edward Hartpole Lecky* (London, 1909)

Lecky, W. E. H., *The leaders of public opinion in Ireland* (London, 1861)

Lecky, W. E. H., *History of the rise and influence of the spirit of rationalism in Europe* (2 vols, London, 1865)

Lecky, W. E. H., *History of European morals from Augustus to Charlemagne* (2 vols, London, 1869)

Lecky, W. E. H., *History of England in the eighteenth century* (8 vols, London, 1878–1890)

[Lecky, W. E. H.], 'Dean Milman', *Edinburgh Review*, 191:392 (1900), pp. 510–27

Lecky, W. E. H., *Historical and political Essays*, ed. Lecky, E. (London, 1908)

Lindsay, C., *Sketches of the history of Christian art* (3 vols, London, 1847)

Lindsay, J., *The progressiveness of modern Christian thought* (Edinburgh and London, 1892)

Lindsay, T. M., 'The critical movement in the Free Church of Scotland', *Contemporary Review*, 33 (1878), pp. [22]–34

Lindsay, T. M., *The Reformation*, 2nd edn (Edinburgh, 1883)

Lindsay, T. M., 'Family and popular religion in Germany on the eve of the Reformation', *London Quarterly Review*, 10:2 (1903), pp. 209–38

Lindsay, T. M., *A history of the Reformation*, 2nd edn (2 vols, Edinburgh, 1907–1908)

Lindsay, T. M., *College addresses: and sermons preached on various occasions* (Glasgow, 1915)

Lindsay, T. M., *Letters of Principal T.M. Lindsay to Janet Ross* (London, Bombay, and Sydney, 1923)

Lotze, H., *Mikrokosmus: Ideen zur Naturgeschichte und Geschichte der Menschheit* (3 vols, Leipzig, 1856–1864)

Lotze, H., *Microcosmus: an essay concerning man and his relation to the world*, trans. Hamilton, E., and Constance Jones, E. E. (2 vols, Edinburgh, 1885)

Macaulay, T. B., *The letters of Thomas Babington Macaulay*, ed. Pinney, T. (6 vols, Cambridge, 1974–1981)

Macewen, A. R., *Life and letters of John Cairns D.D., LL.D.* (London, 1895)

Mackintosh, R., *The obsoleteness of the Westminster Confession of Faith* (Glasgow, 1888)

Mackintosh, R., *Essays towards a new theology* (Glasgow, 1889)

Macmillan, D., *The life of George Matheson D.D., LL.D., F.R.S.E.* (London, 1907)

Macmillan, D., *The life of Robert Flint D.D., LL.D.* (London, New York, and Toronto, 1914)

[Maitland, B.], 'Thomas Aquinas and the Vatican', *Quarterly Review*, 152:303 (1881), pp. 105–40

Mansel, H. L., *The limits of religious thought examined: in eight lectures, preached before the University of Oxford, in the year M.DCCC.LVIII* (Oxford, 1858)

Mansel, H. L., *The Gnostic heresies of the first and second centuries*, ed. Lightfoot, J. B. (London, 1875)

Martineau, J., *A word for scientific theology in appeal from the men of science and the theologians* (London, 1868)

Martineau, J., *Modern materialism: its attitude towards theology: a critique and defence* (London, 1876)

Martineau, J., 'Preface', to Müller, F. M., *Lectures on the origin and growth of religion as illustrated by the religions of India: deliveredin the Chapter House, Westminster Abbey, in April, May, and June, 1878* (London, 1878), [vii]–viii

Martineau, J., *Essays, reviews, and addresses* (4 vols, London, 1890–1891)

Matheson, G., *Aids to the study of German theology* (Edinburgh, 1874)

Matheson, G., *Growth of the spirit of Christianity from the first century to the dawn of the Lutheran era* (2 vols, Edinburgh, 1877)

Maurice, F. (ed.), *The life of Frederick Denison Maurice chiefly told in his own letters* (2 vols, London, 1884)

Maurice, F. D., *The kingdom of Christ: or hints on the principles, ordinances, and constitution of the Catholic Church* (3 vols, London, [1838])

Maurice, F. D., *The Epistle to the Hebrews; being the substance of three lectures delivered in the chapel of the honourable society of Lincoln's nn, on the foundation of Bishop Warburton* (London, 1846)

Maurice, F. D., *Lectures on the ecclesiastical history of the first and second centuries* (Cambridge, 1854)

McCrie, T., et al., *Communications on the principles of the Free Church of Scotland: issued by the Committee of the General Assembly* (Edinburgh, 1855)

McCrie, T., *The life of John Knox with biographical notices of the principal Reformers, and sketches of the progress of literature in Scotland, during a great part of the 16th century* (London, Edinburgh, and New York, 1889)

Merivale, C., *The conversion of the Roman Empire: the Boyle Lectures for the year 1864 delivered at the Chapel Royal, Whitehall* (London, 1864)

Merivale, C., *The conversion of the northern nations: the Boyle Lectures for the year 1865 delivered at the Chapel Royal, Whitehall* (London, 1866)

[Merivale, C.], 'History of European Morals', *North British Review*, 50:100 (1869), pp. 381–405

Merivale, C., *Conversion of the west: the continental Teutons* (London, 1878)

Merivale, C., *Autobiography and letters of Charles Merivale Dean of Ely*, ed. Merivale, J. A. (Oxford, 1898)

Merle d'Aubigné, J. H., *Histoire de la Réformation du seizième siècle* (5 vols, Paris and Geneva, 1835–1853)

Merle d'Aubigné, *History of the Reformation of the sixteenth century*, trans. White, H. (5 vols, Edinburgh, 1846–1853)

Mill, J. S., *A system of logic, ratiocinative and inductive: being a connected view of the principles of evidence and the methods of scientific investigation* (2 vols, London, 1843)

Mill, J. S., *Inaugural address delivered to the University of St Andrews Feb. 1st 1867*, 2nd edn (London, 1867)

Mill, J. S., *Essays on ethics, religion and society*, ed. J. M. Robson (Toronto, 1969)

Mill, J. S., *Autobiography*, ed. J.M. Robson (London, 1989)

Milman, A., *Henry Hart Milman, D.D. Dean of St. Paul's: a biographical sketch* (London, 1900)

[Milman, H. H.], *The history of the Jews* (3 vols, London, 1829)

[Milman, H. H.], 'Guizot's *Edition of Gibbon*', *Quarterly Review*, 50:100 (1834), pp. [273]–307

[Milman, H. H.], 'The popes of the sixteenth and seventeenth centuries', *Quarterly Review*, 55:110 (1836), pp. [287]–323

Milman, H. H., *Address delivered at the opening of the City of Westminster literary, scientific, and mechanics' institute*, 2nd edn (London, 1837)

[Milman, H. H.], 'Ranke *on the popes of Rome in the sixteenth and seventeenth centuries*', *Quarterly Review*, 58:116 (1837), pp. 371–406

Milman, H. H., *The history of Christianity, from the birth of Christ to the abolition of paganism in the Roman Empire* (3 vols, London, 1840)

Milman, H. H., *The poetical works* (London, 1840)

[Milman, H. H.], 'Newman *on the Development of Christian Doctrine*', *Quarterly Review*, 77:154 (1846), pp. 404–65

Milman, H. H., *History of Latin Christianity: including that of the popes to the pontificate of Nicolas V* (6 vols, London, 1854–1855)

Milman, H. H., *War and peace: a sermon* (London, 1856)

Milman, H. H., *A memoir of Lord Macaulay*, 2nd edn (London, 1862)

Milman, H. H., *The history of the Jews: from the earliest period down to modern times*, 3rd edn (3 vols, London, 1863)

Milman, H. H., *Hebrew prophecy: a sermon preached before the University of Oxford, March 26, 1865* (Oxford and London, 1865)

Milman, H. H., 'Preface to the fourth edition', in Ranke, L., *The popes of Rome: their ecclesiastical and political history during the sixteenth and seventeenth centuries*, trans. Austin, S., 4th edn (3 vols, London, 1866), i, [v]–viii

Milman, H. H., *History of Latin Christianity; including that of the popes to the Pontificate of Nicolas V*, 4th edn (9 vols, London, 1867)

Milman, H. H., *Savonarola, Erasmus, and other essays* (London, 1870)

Milman, H. H., *History of Latin Christianity: including that of the Popes to the pontificate of Nicolas V*, 4th edn (9 vols, London, 1883)

Milner, J., *The History of the Church of Christ*, ed. Milner, I., and Grantham, T. (4 vols, London, 1847)

Möhler, J. A., *Die Einheit in der Kirche oder das Prinzip des Katholicismus dargestellt im Geiste der Kirchenväter der drei ersten Jahrhunderte* (Mainz and Wiesbaden, 1925)

Morison, J. C., *The service of man: an essay towards the religion of the future* (London, 1887)

[Mozley, J. B.], 'Newman on development', *Christian Remembrancer*, 13:55 (1847), pp. [117]–265

Mozley, J. B., *Essays historical and theological* (2 vols, London, 1878)

Mozley, T., *Reminiscences chiefly of Oriel College and the Oxford Movement*, 2nd edn (2 vols, London, 1882)

Müller, F. M., *Lectures on the origin and growth of religion as illustrated by the religions of India: delivered in the Chapter House, Westminster Abbey, in April, May, and June, 1878* (London, 1878)

Müller, J. (ed.), *Dr. A. Neander's theologische Vorlesungen* (5 vols, Berlin, 1857–1864)

Mullinger, J. B., *A history of the University of Cambridge* (London, 1888)

Neale, J. M., *A history of the Holy Eastern Church* (5 vols, London, 1847–1873)

Neander, J. A. W., *Allgemeine Geschichte der christlichen Religion und Kirche* (6 vols, Hamburg, 1825–1852)

Neander, J. A. W., *The history of the Christian religion and church during the first three centuries*, trans. Rose, H. J. (2 vols, London, 1831–1841)

Neander, J. A. W., *Das Leben Jesu in seinem geschichtlichen Zusammenhange und seiner geschichtlichen Entwickelung* (Hamburg, 1837)

Neander, J. A. W., *General history of the Christian religion and church: from the German of Dr Augustus Neander*, trans. Torrey, J. (9 vols, Edinburgh, 1847–1855)

[Newman, F.], 'Hallam's Supplemental Notes', *Prospective Review*, 16 (1848), pp. 503–23

Newman, J. H., *The Arians of the fourth century, their doctrine, temper, and conduct, chiefly as exhibited in the councils of the church between A.D. 325, & A.D. 381* (London, 1833)

[Newman, J. H.], 'Remarks on certain passages in the Thirty-Nine Articles', *Tracts for the Times*, vol. 6 (London, 1841), no. 90

[Newman, J. H.], 'Milman's *History of Christianity*', *British Critic*, 29 (1841), pp. 71–114

[Newman, J. H.], *The Cistercian saints of England: S. Stephen Harding* (London, 1844)

Newman, J. H., *An essay on the development of Christian doctrine* (London, 1845)

Newman, J. H., *Apologia pro vita sua: being a reply to a pamphlet entitled 'What, then, does Dr. Newman mean?'* (London, 1864)

Newman, J. H., *An essay in aid of a grammar of assent* (London, 1870)

Newman, J. H., *The letters and diaries of John Henry Newman*, ed. Ker, I., et al. (32 vols, Oxford, 1978–2008)

Niebuhr, B. G., *History of Rome*, trans. Hare, J. C., Thirlwall, C., Smith, W., and Schmitz, L. (Cambridge, 1828–1832; London 1842)

Oliphant, M., *A memoir of the life of John Tulloch, D.D., LL.D.*, 3rd edn (Edinburgh and London, 1889)

Owen, J., *The modification of dogma regarded as a condition of human progress* (London, Edinburgh, and Manchester, 1891)

Owen, J., *The religious aspects of scepticism: a lecture delivered at the South Place Institute, London, April 19th, 1891* (London, 1891)

Owen, J., *The skeptics of the Italian Renaissance* (London, 1893)

Owen, J., *Verse-musings on nature, faith, and freedom* (London, 1894)

Oxford University Examination Papers: Second Public Examination: Honour School of Modern History: Trinity Term, 1898 (Oxford, 1898)

Oxford University Examination Papers: Second Public Examination: Honour School of Theology: Trinity Term, 1895 (Oxford, 1895)

Page Roberts, W., *Liberalism in religion and other sermons* (London, 1886)

Palmer, W., *A compendious ecclesiastical history, from the earliest period to the present time*, new edn (London, 1840)

Palmer, W., *A treatise on the church of Christ: designed chiefly for the use of students in theology*, 3rd edn (2 vols, London, 1842)

Palmer, W., *The doctrine of development and conscience considered in relation to the evidences of Christianity and of the Catholic system* (London, 1846)

Palmer, W. [of Magdalen], *A letter to the Rev. Dr. Hampden, Regius Professor of Divinity in the University of Oxford* (Oxford, 1842)

Parkinson, R., *The moderation of the Church of England, a sermon, preached in the Collegiate Church of Christ, in Manchester, on Sunday the 27th of April, 1834* (London, 1834)

Pater, W. H., *Studies in the history of the Renaissance* (London, 1873)

Pattison, M., 'Religious Thought in England from the Reformation to the End of the Last Century', *Academy*, 3:49 (1872), pp. 210–11

Pattison, M., *Isaac Casaubon 1559–1614* (London, 1875)

Pattison, M., *Sermons* (London, 1885)

Pattison, M., *Milton* (London, 1913)

Pattison, M., *Memoirs of an Oxford don*, ed. Green, V. H. H. (London, 1988)

Pattison, M., 'Tendencies of religious thought in England, 1688–1750', in Shea, V., and Whitla, W. (eds), *Essays and reviews: the 1860 text and its reading* (Charlottesville, VA, and London, 2000), pp. [387]–430

[Pearson, K.], 'Humanism in Germany', *Westminster Review*, 119:236 (1883), pp. [315]– 33

[Pearson, K.], 'Martin Luther: his influence on the material and intellectual welfare of Germany', *Westminster Review*, 121:241 (1884), p. [1]–41

Pollard, A. F., 'The Reformation under Edward VI', in Ward, A. W., Prothero, G. W., and Leathes, S. (eds), *The Cambridge modern history: volume II: the Reformation* (Cambridge, 1904), pp. 474–511

Pollard, A. F., *Thomas Cranmer and the English Reformation 1489–1556* (New York and London, 1904)

Pollard, A. F., *Henry VIII*, new edn (London, 1905)

Pollard, A. F., *Factors in modern history* (London, 1907)

Prothero, R. E., and Bradley, G. G., *The life and correspondence of Arthur Penrhyn Stanley, D.D.* (2 vols, London, 1893)

Pusey, E. B., Newman, J. H., and Keble, J. (eds), *A library of fathers of the Holy Catholic Church anterior to the division of the east and west* (47 vols, Oxford and London, 1838–1881)

Pusey, E. B., *The rule of faith, as maintained by the fathers, and the Church of England* (Oxford, 1851)

[Pusey, E. B.], 'Scriptural views of Holy Baptism, as established by the consent of the Ancient Church, and contrasted with the systems of modern schools', *Tracts for the Times*, vol. 2, 3rd edn (London and Oxford, 1840), no. 67

Rainy, R., *Delivery and development of Christian doctrine* (Edinburgh, 1874)

Ranke, L., *Geschichten der romanischen und germanischen Völker von 1494 bis 1535*, vol. 1 (Leipzig and Berlin, 1824)

Ranke, L., *Die römischen Päpste: ihre Kirche und ihr Staat im sechszehnten und siebzehnten Jahrhundert*, 2nd edn (3 vols, 1838–1839)

Ranke, L., *The ecclesiastical and political history of the popes of Rome during the sixteenth and seventeenth centuries*, trans. Austin, S. (3 vols, London, 1840)

Ranke, L., *History of the Reformation in Germany*, trans. Austin, S., 2nd edn (3 vols, London, 1845–1847)

[Rawstorne, W. E.], 'Milman's *History of Latin Christianity*', *North British Review*, 22:43 (1854), pp. 84–112

[Reeve, H.], 'Buckle's *Civilization in Spain and Scotland*', *Edinburgh Review*, 114:231 (1861), pp. 183–211

[Reeve, H.], 'Lecky's *Influence of Rationalism*', *Edinburgh Review*, 121:248 (1865), pp. 426–55

Reid, T., *An inquiry into the human mind, on the principles of common sense*, 5th edn (Edinburgh, 1801)

Ridley, N., *The Works of Nicholas Ridley, D.D. sometime Lord Bishop of London, Martyr, 1555*, ed. Christmas, H. (Cambridge, 1841)

Rio, A. F., *De la poésie Chrétienne dans son principe, dans sa matière et dans ses forms: forme de l'art, seconde partie* (Paris, 1836)

Ritter, H., *Geschichte der christlichen Philosophie* (8 vols, Hamburg, 1841–1853)

Rivington, S., *The publishing house of Rivington* (London, 1894)

Roberts, A., and Donaldson, J. (eds), *Ante-Nicene Christian library: translations of the writings of the fathers down to A. D. 325* (24 vols, Edinburgh, 1867–1872)

Robertson, J. C., *History of the Christian church* (4 vols, London, 1854–1873)

Rose, H. J., *The study of church history recommended* (London, 1834)

[Russell, C. W.], 'Milman's History of Latin Christianity', *Dublin Review*, 37:74 (1854), pp. 404–49

[Russell, C. W.], 'Pope Callistus on the Trinity', *Dublin Review*, 39:78 (1855), pp. 384–412

[Russell, C. W.], 'Milman's Latin Christianity', *Dublin Review*, 40:80 (1856), pp. [281]–99

Russell, J., *Essays on the rise and progress of the Christian religion from the reign of Tiberius to the end of the Council of Trent* (London, 1873)

Ryle, J. C., *Church principles and church comprehensiveness* (London, 1879)

Schaff, P. (ed.), *A select library of the Nicene and post-Nicene fathers of the Christian church*, first series (14 vols, Buffalo, NY, and New York, 1886–1890)

Schelling, F. W. J., *System der transcendentalen Idealismus* (Tübingen, 1800)

Schelling, F. W. J., *Vorlesungen über die Methode des akademischen Studium* (Tübingen, 1803)

Shaw, R., *An exposition of the Confession of Faith of the Westminster Assembly of Divines* (Edinburgh, 1845)

Schleiermacher, F. D. E., *A critical essay on the Gospel of St Luke*, [trans. Thirlwall, C.] (London, 1825)

Schleiermacher, F. D. E., 'Der christliche Glaube nach den Grundsätzen der evangelischen Kirche im Zusammenhang dargestellt', in his *Werke: Auswahl in vier Bänden*, ed. Braun, O., and Bauer, J. (4 vols, Leipzig, 1910–1913), iii, [633]–729

Schleiermacher, F. D. E., 'Über die Religion: Reden an die Gebildeten unter ihren Verächtern', in his *Werke: Auswahl in vier Bänden*, ed. Braun, O., and Bauer, J. (4 vols, Leipzig, 1910–1913), iv, [211]–399

Seebohm, F., *The Oxford reformers of 1498: being a history of the fellow-work of John Colet, Erasmus, and Thomas More* (London, 1867)

[Seeley, R. B.], *Essays on the church, by a layman*, new edn (London, 1838)

[Seeley, R. B.], *The church of Christ in the middle ages: an historical sketch compiled from various authors* (London, 1845)

Shepherd, E. J., *The history of the Church of Rome, to the episcopate of Damasus, A.D. 384* (London, 1851)

[Sidgwick, H.], 'The prophet of culture', *Macmillan's Magazine*, 16:94 (1867), pp. 271–80

Sidgwick, H., *The methods of ethics* (London, 1874)

[Smith, W.], 'Mr Buckle on the civilisation of Scotland', *North British Review*, 35:69 (1861), pp. 253–87

Stanley, A. P., *Life and correspondence of Thomas Arnold* (2 vols, London, 1844)

Stanley, A. P., *Sermons and essays on the apostolical age* (Oxford, 1847)

[Stanley, A. P.], 'Latin Christianity', *Quarterly Review*, 95:189 (1854), pp. 38–70

[Stanley, A. P.], 'Archdeacon Hare', *Quarterly Review*, 97:193 (1855), pp. 1–28

Stanley, A. P., *Lectures on the history of the Eastern Church: with an introduction on the study of ecclesiastical history*, 2nd edn (London, 1862)

Stanley, A. P., *A letter to the lord bishop of London on the state of subscription in the Church of England and in the University of Oxford* (Oxford and London, 1863)

Stanley, A. P., 'Preface', to Bunsen, C. C. J., *God in history or the progress of man's faith in the moral order of the world*, trans. Winkworth, S. (3 vols, London, 1868–1870), i, [v]–x

Stanley, A. P., *Essays chiefly on questions of church and state from 1850 to 1870* (London, 1870)

Stanley, A. P., *Lectures on the history of the Church of Scotland: deliveredin Edinburgh in 1872* (London, 1872)

[Stanley, A. P.], 'The church and dissent', *Edinburgh Review*, 137:279 (1873), p. 196–224

Stephen, J., *Essays in ecclesiastical biography* (2 vols, London, 1849)

Stephen, L., *Essays on freethinking and plainspeaking* (London, 1873)

Stephen, L., *History of English thought in the eighteenth century* (2 vols, London, 1876)

Stephen, L., 'An attempted philosophy of history', *Fortnightly Review*, 27:161 (1 May 1880), pp. [672]–95

Stephen, L., *The science of ethics* (London, 1882)

Stephen, T., *The spirit of the Church of Rome, its principles and practices, as exhibited in history* (London, 1840)

Stewart, D., *The collected works of Dugald Stewart, esq., F.R.SS.*, ed. Hamilton, W. (10 vols, Edinburgh and London, 1854–1858)

Stoughton, J., *Lectures on Tractarian theology* (London, 1843)

Stoughton, J., *Ages of Christendom: before the Reformation* (London, 1857)

Stoughton, J., *An introduction to historical theology: being a sketch of doctrinal progress from the apostolic era to the Reformation* (London, 1880)

Stoughton, J., *Religion in England from 1800 to 1850: a history with a postscript on subsequent events* (2 vols, London, 1884)

Stoughton, J., *Golden legends of the olden time* (London, 1885)

Stoughton, J., *Lights and shadows of primitive Christendom* ([n.p.], 1891)

Stoughton, J., *Recollections of a long life*, 2nd edn (London, 1894)

Stoughton, J., *Lights and shadows of church life* (London, 1895)

Strauss, D. F., *Das Leben Jesu, kritisch bearbeitet* (2 vols, Tübingen, 1835–1836)

Stubbs, W., *The constitutional history of England in its origin and development*, library edn (3 vols, Oxford, 1880)

Symonds, J. A., *Renaissance in Italy* (7 vols, London, 1875–1886)

Symonds, J. A., *Renaissance in Italy: the age of the despots*, 2nd edn (London, 1880) [volume 1]

Symonds, J. A., *Letters and papers of John Addington Symonds*, ed. Brown, H. F. (London, 1923)

Symonds, J. A., *The letters of John Addington Symonds*, ed. Schueller, H. M., and Peters, R. L. (3 vols, Detroit, MI, 1967–1969)

'T.', 'Hippolytus and his age', *Journal of Sacred Literature*, 3:6 (1853), pp. 461–77

[Tayler, J. J.], 'History of Latin Christianity', *Prospective Review*, 39 (1854), pp. [305]–25

Taylor, I., *Ancient Christianity and the doctrines of the Oxford Tracts for the Times* (2 vols, London, 1839–1842)

Temple, F., 'The education of the world', in Shea, V., and Whitla, W. (eds), *Essays and reviews: the1860 text and its reading* (Charlottesville and London, 2000), pp. [137]–64

Temple, R., 'The evangelical movement in the Church of England', in Wace, H., et al., *Church and faith: being essays on the teaching of the Church of England* (Edinburgh and London, 1910), pp. [365]–98

Tennyson, A., *Tennyson: a selected edition*, ed. Ricks., C., revised edn (London and New York, 2007)

Thirlwall, C., *The spirit of truth the Holy Spirit: a sermon, preached before the University of Cambridge, on Whitsunday, May 16, 1869* (London, Oxford, and Cambridge, 1869)

Thirlwall, C., *Essays, speeches and sermons*, ed. Perowne, J. J. S. (London, 1880)

Thirlwall, C., *Letters literary and theological of Connop Thirlwall, late Lord Bishop of St. David's*, ed. Perowne, J. J. S. and Stokes, L. (London, 1881)

Thirlwall, C., *Letters to a friend*, ed. Stanley, A. P. (London, 1881)

Townsend, W. B., Eayrs, G., and Workman, H. B. (eds), *A new history of Methodism* (2 vols, London, 1909)

Trench, R. C., *Sacred Latin poetry, chiefly lyrical, selected and arranged for use; with notes and introduction* (London, 1849)

Tuckniss, W., 'The agencies at present in operation within the metropolis, for the suppression of vice and crime', in Mayhew, H. (ed.), *London labour and the London poor* (4 vols, London, 1861–1862), iv, [xi]–xvi

[Tulloch, J.], 'Augustus Neander', *British Quarterly Review*, 24 (1850), pp. [297]–337

[Tulloch, J.], 'German Protestantism', *British Quarterly Review*, 26 (1851), pp. 432–76

[Tulloch, J.], 'Carlyle's *Life of Sterling*', *North British Review*, 16:32 (1852), pp. 359–89

[Tulloch, J.], 'The Life and Letters of Niebuhr', *North British Review*, 17:34 (1852), 422–58

[Tulloch, J.], 'Hippolytus and his Age', *North British Review*, 19:37 (1853), pp. 85–128

Tulloch, J., *Theism: the witness of reason and nature to an all-wise and beneficent creator* (Edinburgh, 1855)

Tulloch, J., *Theological tendencies of the age: an inaugural lecture, delivered at the opening of St. Mary's College on Tuesday, the 28th November 1854* (Edinburgh, 1855)

Tulloch, J., 'Alexandria and its Christian school', *Good Words*, 2 (1861), pp. 613–16

Tulloch, J., 'Cunningham's *Church history of Scotland*', *Edinburgh Review*, 114:232 (1861), pp. 394–424

Tulloch, J., *English puritanism and its leaders: Cromwell, Milton, Baxter, Bunyan* (Edinburgh and London, 1861)

[Tulloch, J.], 'Stanley's *Eastern Church*', *North British Review*, 35:69 (1861), pp. 82–106

Tulloch, J., *The Christ of the gospels and the Christ of modern criticism: lectures on M. Renan's 'Vie de Jésus'* (London, 1864)

[Tulloch, J.], 'Tübingen in 1864', *Macmillan's Magazine*, 10 (1864), pp. 433–42

Tulloch, J., 'Rationalism', *Contemporary Review*, 1 (1866), pp. [361]–84

Tulloch, J., *Theological controversy; or, the function of debate in theology : an address to the members of the Theological Society of the University of Edinburgh*, 4th edn (Edinburgh and London, 1866)

Tulloch, J., 'Studies in the history of religious thought in England. I. –: John Hales', *Contemporary Review*, 5 (1867), pp. 190–221

[Tulloch, J.], 'The positive philosophy of M. Auguste Comte', *Edinburgh Review*, 127:260 (1868), pp. 303–57

[Tulloch, J.], 'Dr. Newman's *Grammar of Assent*', *Edinburgh Review*, 132:270 (1870), pp. 382–414

Tulloch, J., 'The English and Scotch churches', *Contemporary Review*, 19 (1871), pp. 223–37

Tulloch, J., 'John Smith and his Select Discourses', *Contemporary Review*, 19 (1871), pp. [789]–811

Tulloch, J., 'Dean Stanley and the Scotch "Moderates"', *Contemporary Review*, 20 (1872), pp. [698]–717

Tulloch, J., 'Dogmatic extremes', *Contemporary Review*, 23 (1873), pp. [182]–96

Tulloch, J., 'On dogma and dogmatic Christianity', *Contemporary Review*, 23 (1873), pp. [919]–33

[Tulloch, J.], 'Modern scientific materialism', *Blackwood's Edinburgh Magazine*, 116:709 (1874), pp. [519]–39

Tulloch, J., *Rational theology and Christian philosophy in England in the seventeenth century*, 2nd edn (2 vols, Edinburgh and London, 1874)

Tulloch, J., *Religion and theology: a sermon for the times*, 2nd edn (Edinburgh and London, 1875)

Tulloch, J., *The Christian doctrine of sin* (Edinburgh and London, 1876)

Tulloch, J., 'Progress of religious thought in Scotland', *Contemporary Review*, 29 (1877), pp. [535]–51

Tulloch, J., 'St Dominic and his age', *Good Words*, 18 (1877), pp. 161–8

Tulloch, J., 'St. Francis: partI.', *Good Words*, 18 (1877), pp. 418–23

Tulloch, J., *Pascal* (Edinburgh, 1878)

Tulloch, J., *Position and prospects of the Church of Scotland: address delivered at the close of the General Assembly of the Church of Scotland: June 3, 1878* (Edinburgh and London, 1878)

Tulloch, J., 'The essentials of religion', *Good Words*, 20 (1879), p. 139–44

[Tulloch, J.], 'Dean Stanley as a spiritual teacher and theologian', *Nineteenth century*, 10:58 (1881), pp. 869–85

Tulloch, J., *Beginning life: a book for young men*, revised edn (London, 1882)

Tulloch, J., *Luther and other leaders of the Reformation*, 3rd edn (Edinburgh and London, 1883)

Tulloch, J., *The theological faculties of the Scottish universities in connection with university reform* (Edinburgh and London, 1883)

Tulloch, J., 'Luther and recent criticism', *Nineteenth Century*, 15:86 (1884), 652–668

Tulloch, J., *Modern theories in philosophy and religion* (Edinburgh and London, 1884)

Tulloch, J., 'Coleridge as spiritual thinker', *Fortnightly Review*, 37:217 (1885), pp. [11]–25

Tulloch, J., *Sundays at Balmoral: sermons preached before her majesty the Queen in Scotland*, ed. Tulloch, W. W. (London, 1887)

Tulloch, J., *Movements of religious thought in Britain during the nineteenth century* (Leicester, 1971)

Ueberweg, F., *System of logic and history of logical doctrines*, trans. Lindsay, T. M. (London, 1871)

Van Mildert, W., *An historical view of the rise and progress of infidelity, with a refutation of its principles and reasonings: in a series of sermons preached for the lecture founded by the Hon. Mr. Boyle, in the parish church of St. Mary le Bow, from the year 1802 to 1805* (2 vols, London, 1806)

[Vaughan, R.], 'Buckle on civilization—destiny and intellect', *British Quarterly Review*, 28:55 (1858), pp. [3]–43

Vaughan, R. A., *Hours with the mystics: a contribution to the history of religious opinion* (2 vols, London, 1856)

Vaughan, R. A., *Essays and remains of the rev. Robert Alfred Vaughan*, ed. Vaughan, R. (2 vols, London, 1858)

Wace, H., *Christianity and morality or the correspondence of the Gospel with the moral nature of man: the Boyle Lectures for 1874 and 1875* (London, 1876)

Wace, H., *The foundations of faith considered in eight sermons preached before the University of Oxford in the year M.DCCC.LXXIX* (London, 1880)

Wace, H., and Buchheim, C. A. (trans.), *First principles of the Reformation or the Ninety-Five Theses and the three primary works of Dr. Martin Luther* (London, 1883)

Wace, H., and Schaff, P. (eds), *A select library of Nicene and post-Nicene fathers of the Christian church*, second series (14 vols, Oxford and Buffalo, NY, 1890–1900)

Wace, H., *Principles of the Reformation practical and historical* (London, 1910)

Wace, H., *Prophecy Jewish and Christian considered in a series of Warburton Lectures at Lincoln's Inn* (London, 1911)

Wedgwood, J., 'Arthur Penrhyn Stanley', *Contemporary Review*, 40 (1881), pp. 490–506

Welsh, D., *Elements of church history: vol. I: comprising the external history of the church during the first three centuries* (Edinburgh, 1844)

Westcott, A., *Life and letters of Brooke Foss Westcott D.D., D.C.L., sometime bishop of Durham* (2 vols, London, 1903)

Westcott, B. F., *The spiritual office of the Universities: a sermon preached in the chapel of Trinity College, Cambridge, at the Commemoration of Benefactors, December 15, 1868* (London and Cambridge, 1869)

Westcott, B. F., *The gospel according to St John: the authorized version with introduction and notes* (London, 1882)

Westcott, B. F., *The historic faith: short lectures on the Apostles' Creed* (London and Cambridge, 1883)

Westcott, B. F., *Essays in the history of religious thought in the west* (London, 1891)

Westcott, B. F., *The Gospel of Life: thoughts introductory to the study of Christian doctrine* (London and Cambridge, 1892)

Whittaker, T., *The Neo-Platonists: a study in the history of Hellenism* (Cambridge, 1901)

Wordsworth, C., *St. Hippolytus and the Church of Rome in the earlier part of the third century: from the newly-discovered Philosophumena* (London, 1853)

Wordsworth, C., *The two tercentenaries: the thirty-nine Articles and the Council of Trent: a sermon, preached in Westminister Abbey, on Sunday, December 13, 1863* (London, 1863)

Wordsworth, C., *A church history to the council of Nicaea A.D. 325* (London, 1881)

Workman, H. B., *The church of the west in the middle ages* (2 vols, London, 1898)

Workman, H. B., *The place of Methodism in the catholic church*, new edn (London, 1921)

[Worthington, S. D.], 'Neander's Werke', *British Quarterly Review*, 96 (1868), pp. [305]–50

Wylie, J. A., *The papacy: its history, dogmas, genius, and prospects: being the Evangelical Alliance first prize essay on popery* (Edinburgh, 1851)

Wylie, J. A., *The history of Protestantism* (3 vols, London, Paris and New York, 1874–1877)

Wylie, J. A., *Luther; or the Reformation worked out in the person of Luther before being worked out on the stage of Christendom* (London and Edinburgh, 1883)

Zeller, E., *Die Philosophie der Griechen in ihrer geschichtlichen Entwicklung*, 2nd edn (3 vols, Tübingen, 1856–1865)

II. SECONDARY SOURCES

Reference Works

Houghton, W. E. (ed.), *The Wellesley Index to Victorian Periodicals, 1824–1900* (5 vols, Toronto and London, 1966–1989). [online edition: http://ezproxy-prd.bodleian.ox.ac.uk:3520/home.do; last accessed 20 September 2018]

Matthew, H. C. G., Harrison, B., Goldman, L., and Cannadine, D. (eds), *Oxford Dictionary of National Biography* (2004–) [online edition: http://ezproxy-prd.bodleian.ox.ac.uk:2167; last accessed 20 September 2018]

Neue Deutsche Biographie (1953–) [online edition: http://www.deutsche-biographie.de; last accessed 20 September 2018]

Oxford English Dictionary [online edition: http://ezproxy-prd.bodleian.ox.ac.uk:2355; last accessed 20 September 2018]

Unpublished Secondary Sources

Boylan, C., 'Ireland, religion and reform: Archbishop Richard Whately, 1831–63' (Oxford Univ. DPhil thesis, 2008)

Kennedy, A., 'John Kenrick and the transformation of Unitarian thought' (Stirling Univ. PhD, 2006)

Lloyd, M. J., 'The historical thought of S. T. Coleridge: the later prose works' (Oxford Univ. DPhil thesis, 1998)

Obitts, S. R., 'The thought of Robert Flint' (Edinburgh Univ. PhD thesis, 1962)

Walsh, J. D. 'Joseph Milner's evangelical church history: a biography' [MS, forthcoming]

Other Secondary Sources

Altholz, J., *The religious press in Britain, 1760–1900* (New York and London, 1989)

Andrew Penny, D., 'John Foxe's Victorian reception', *Historical Journal*, 40:1 (1997), pp. 111–42

Annan, N., et al., *Ideas and beliefs of the Victorians: an historic revaluation of the Victorian age* (London, 1949)

[Anon.], 'Hunt', *Meyers Grosses Konversations-lexikon*, 6th edn, vol. 9 (Leipzig and Vienna, 1905), pp. 659–60

Arx, J. P. von, *Progress and pessimism: religion, politics, and history in late nineteenth century Britain* (Cambridge, MA, 1985)

Ashton, R., *The German idea: four English writers and the reception of German thought 1800–1860* (Cambridge, 1980)

Ashton, R., *142 Strand: a radical address in Victorian London* (London, 2006)

Atkins, G., 'Truth at stake? The posthumous reputation of Archbishop Cranmer', in Nockles, P. B., and Westbrook, V. (eds), *Reinventing the Reformation in the nineteenth century: a cultural history, Bulletin of the John Rylands Library*, 90:1 (2014), pp. [257]–286

Atkins, G. (ed.), *Making and remaking saints in nineteenth-century Britain* (Manchester, 2016)

Aubert, A. G., *The German roots of nineteenth-century American theology* (Oxford, 2013)

Bahners, P., ' "A place among the English classics": Ranke's *History of the Popes* and its British readers', in Stuchtey, B., and Wende, P. (eds), *British and German historiography, 1750–1950: traditions, perceptions, and transfers* (Oxford, 2000), pp. [123]– 57

Basse, M., *Die dogmengeschichtliche Konzeptionen Adolf von Harnacks und Reinhold Seebergs* (Göttingen, 2001)

Bauspiess, M., Landmesser, C., and Lincicum, D. (eds), *Ferdinand Christian Baur und die Geschichte des frühen Christentums* (Tübingen, 2014)

Bayly, C. A., *The birth of the modern world 1780–1914: global connections and comparisons* (Oxford, 2004)

Beard, M., *The invention of Jane Harrison* (Cambridge, MA, and London, 2000)

Bebbington, D. W., *The nonconformist conscience: chapel and politics, 1870–1914* (London, 1982)

Bebbington, D. W., *Evangelicalism in modern Britain: a history from the 1730s to the 1980s* (London, 1989)

Bebbington, D. W., 'Revival and Enlightenment in eighteenth-century England', in Waller, A., and Aune, K. (eds), *On revival: a critical examination* (Carlisle, 2003), pp. [71]–85

Bebbington, D. W., *The mind of Gladstone: religion, Homer, and politics* (Oxford, 2004)

Bebbington, D. W., *The dominance of evangelicalism: the age of Spurgeon and Moody* (Leicester, 2005)

Bebbington, D. W., 'The growth of voluntary religion', in Gilley, S., and Stanley, B. (eds), *The Cambridge History of Christianity: volume 8: world Christianities c. 1815–c. 1914* (Cambridge, 2006), pp. 53–69

Bebbington, D. W., 'Calvin and British evangelicalism in the nineteenth and twentieth centuries', in Backus, I., and Benedict, P. (eds), *Calvin and his influence, 1509–2009* (Oxford, 2011), pp. 282–305

Beer, G., *Open fields: science in cultural encounter* (Oxford, 1996)

Beiser, F., *The German historicist tradition* (Oxford, 2011)

Bell, D., *The idea of greater Britain: empire and the future of world order, 1860–1900* (Princeton, NJ, 2007)

Bendall, S., Brooke, C., and Collinson, P., *A history of Emmanuel College, Cambridge* (Woodbrige, 1999)

Bennett, J., *The Victorian high church and the era of the Great Rebellion* (Oxford, 2011)

Bennett, J., 'The British Luther commemoration of 1883–1884 in European context', *Historical Journal*, 58:2 (2015), pp. 543–64

Bennett, J., 'The age of Athanasius: the Church of England and the Athanasian Creed, 1870–1873', *Church History and Religious Culture*, 97:2 (2017), pp. 220–47

Bennett, J., 'A history of "rationalism" in Victorian Britain", *Modern Intellectual History*, 15:1 (2018), pp. 63–91

Benrath, G. A., 'Evangelische und katholische Kirchenhistorie im Zeichen der Aufklärung und der Romantik', *Zeitschrift für Kirchengeschichte*, 82 (1971), pp. 203–17

Bentley, J., *Ritualism and politics in Victorian Britain: the attempt to legislate for belief* (Oxford, 1978)

Bentley, M., *Lord Salisbury's world: Conservative environments in late-Victorian Britain* (Cambridge, 2001)

Bentley, M., *Modernizing England's past: English historiography in the age of modernism, 1870–1970* (Cambridge, 2005)

Bentley, M., 'Shape and pattern in British historical writing, 1815–1945', in Macintyre, S., Maiguashca, J., and Pók, A. (eds), *The Oxford history of historical writing: volume 4: 1800–1945* (Oxford, 2011), pp. [204]–24

Berchman, R. M., 'Neoplatonism', in Ferguson, E. (ed.), *Encyclopedia of early Christianity*, 2nd edn (New York and London, 1998), pp. 801–4

Berger, S., and Lorenz, C. (eds), Nationalizing the past: historians as nation builders in modern Europe (Basingstoke, 2010)

Bevir, M., 'Historicism and the human sciences in Victorian Britain', in Bevir, M. (ed.), *Historicism and the human sciences in Victorian Britain* (Cambridge, 2017), pp. 1–20

Binfield, C., *So down to prayers: studies in English nonconformity 1780–1920* (London, 1977)

Binfield, C. (ed.), *The cross and the city: essays in commemoration of Robert William Dale 1829–1895*, supplement to the *Journal of the United Reformed Church History Society*, vol. 6 (Cambridge, 1999)

Blaas, P. B. M., *Continuity and anachronism: Parliamentary and constitutional development in Whig historiography and in the anti-Whig reaction between 1890 and 1930* (The Hague, Boston, MA, and London, 1975)

Blackbourn, D., *Marpingen: apparitions of the Virgin Mary in Bismarckian Germany* (Oxford, 1993)

Blair, K., *Form and faith in Victorian poetry and religion* (Oxford, 2012)

Borutta, M., *Antikatholizismus: Deutschland und Italien im Zeitalter der europäischen Kulturkämpfe* (Göttingen, 2010)

Bowden, H. W. (ed.), *A century of church* history: the *legacy of Philip Schaff* (Carbondale and Edwardsville, IL, 1988)

Bowler, P. J., *Reconciling science and religion: the debate in early-twentieth-century Britain* (Chicago, IL, and London, 2001)

Boylan, T. A., and Foley, T. P., *Political economy and colonial Ireland: the propagation and ideological function of economic discourse in the nineteenth century* (London, 1992)

Brady, C., *James Anthony Froude: an intellectual biography of a Victorian prophet* (Oxford, 2013)

Brent, R., *Liberal Anglican politics: whiggery, religion, and reform 1830–1841* (Oxford, 1987)

Brooke, J. H., *Science and religion: some historical perspectives* (Cambridge, 1991)

Brown, C. G., *The death of Christian Britain: understanding secularization 1800–2000*, 2nd edn (London and New York, 2009)

Brown, S. J., *The national churches of England, Ireland, and Scotland 1801–1846* (Oxford, 2001)

Brown, S. J., and Nockles, P. B. (eds), *The Oxford Movement: Europe and the wider world 1830–1930* (Cambridge, 2012)

Burns, A. (ed.) 'W. J. Conybeare: "church parties"', in Taylor, S. (ed.), *From Cranmer to Davidson: a Church of England miscellany* (Woodbridge, 1999), pp. [215]–385

Burrow, J. W., *Evolution and society: a study in Victorian social theory* (London, 1966)

Burrow, J. W., *A liberal descent: Victorian historians and the English past* (Cambridge, 1981)

Bury, J. B., *The idea of progress: an inquiry into its origin and growth* (London, 1920)

Cameron, E., *Interpreting Christian history: the challenge of the churches' past* (Malden, MA, and Oxford, 2005)

Cashdollar, C., *The transformation of theology, 1830–1890: positivism and Protestant thought in Britain and America* (Princeton, NJ, 1989)

Chadwick, O., *Creighton on Luther: an inaugural lecture* (Cambridge, 1959)

Chadwick, O., *The Victorian Church* (2 vols, London, 1966–1970)

Chadwick, O., *The secularization of the European mind in the nineteenth century* (Cambridge, 1975)

Chadwick, O., *From Bossuet to Newman*, 2nd edn (Cambridge, 1987)

Chandler, A., *A dream of order: the medieval ideal in nineteenth-century English literature* (London, 1971)

Clark, C., and Kaiser, W. (eds), *Culture wars: secular-Catholic conflict in nineteenth-century Europe* (Cambridge, 2003)

Colley, L., *Britons: forging the nation, 1707–1837* (New Haven, CT, and London, 1992)

Collini, S., *Public moralists: political thought and intellectual life in Britain 1850–1930* (Oxford, 1991)

Corsi, P., *Science and religion: Baden Powell and the Anglican debate, 1800–1860* (Cambridge, 1988)

Cowling, M., *Religion and public doctrine in modern England* (3 vols, Cambridge, 1980–2001)

Curtis, A. W., 'The faculty of divinity', in Logan Turner, A. (ed.), *A history of the University of Edinburgh 1883–1933* (Edinburgh, 1933), pp. 56–82

Dahm, J. J., 'Science and apologetics in the early Boyle Lectures', *Church History*, 39:2 (1970), pp. 172–86

Davie, G. E., *The democratic intellect: Scotland and her universities in the nineteenth century*, 3rd edn (Edinburgh, 2013)

Davis, J. R., *The Victorians and Germany* (Oxford and Bern, 2007)

DeLaura, D., *Hebrew and Hellene in Victorian England* (Austin, TX, 1969)

Dellheim, C., *The face of the past: the preservation of the medieval inheritance in Victorian England* (Cambridge, 1982)

Dempster, J. A. H., *The T&T Clark story: a Victorian publisher and the new theology with an epilogue covering the twentieth-century history of the firm* (Durham, 1992)

den Otter, S. M., *British Idealism and social explanation: a study in late-Victorian thought* (Oxford, 1996)

Dickens, A. G., and Tonkin, J., *The Reformation in historical thought* (Oxford, 1985)

Dixon, T., *The invention of altruism: making moral meanings in Victorian Britain* (Oxford, 2008)

Dockhorn, K., *Der deutsche Historismus in England: ein Beitrag zur englischen Geistesgeschichte des 19. Jahrhunderts* (Göttingen, 1950)

Dowling, L., *Hellenism and homosexuality in Victorian Oxford* (Ithaca, NY, and London, 1994)

Drobner, H. R., *The fathers of the church: a comprehensive introduction*, trans. Schatzmann, S. S. (Peabody, MA, 2007)

Drummond, A. L., and Bulloch, J., *The Scottish church 1688–1843: the age of the moderates* (Edinburgh, 1973)

Drummond, A. L., and Bulloch, J., *The church in Victorian Scotland, 1843–1874* (Edinburgh, 1975)

Drummond, A. L., and Bulloch, J., *The church in late Victorian Scotland, 1874–1900* (Edinburgh, 1978)

Dwight Culler, A., *The Victorian mirror of history* (New Haven, CT, and London, 1985)

Eliot, S., *Some patterns and trends in British publishing 1800–1919* (London, 1994)

Ellens, J. P., *Religious routes to Gladstonian Liberalism: the church rate conflict in England and Wales, 1832–1868* (University Park, PA, 1994)

Ellis, H., and Kirchberger, U. (eds), *Anglo-German scholarly networks in the long nineteenth century* (Leiden and Boston, MA, 2014)

Engel, A. J., *From clergyman to don: the rise of the academic profession in nineteenth-century Oxford* (Oxford, 1983)

Evangelista, S.-M., *British aestheticism and ancient Greece: Hellenism, reception, Gods in exile* (Basingstoke, 2009)

Fisher, D., *Roman Catholic saints and early Victorian literature: conservatism, liberalism, and the emergence of secular culture* (Farnham and Burlington, VT, 2012)

Fleischer, D., *Zwischen Tradition und Fortschritt: der Strukturwandel der protestantischen Kirchengeschichtsschreibung im deutschsprachigen Diskurs der Aufklärung* (2 pts, Waltrop, 2006)

Fleishman, A., *George Eliot's intellectual life* (Cambridge, 2010)

Flint, K., *The woman reader 1837–1914* (Oxford, 1993)

Foerster, F., *Christian Carl Josias von Bunsen: Diplomat, Mäzen und Vordenker in Wissenschaft, Kirche und Politik* (Bad Arolsen, 2001)

Forbes, D., *The liberal Anglican idea of history* (Cambridge, 1952)

Frappell, L., '"Science" in the service of orthodoxy: the early intellectual development of E.B. Pusey', in Butler, P. (ed.), *Pusey rediscovered* (London, 1983), pp. 1–33

Frei, H.W., *The eclipse of biblical narrative: a study in eighteenth and nineteenth century hermeneutics* (New Haven, CT, and London, 1974)

Fritzsche, P., *Stranded in the present: modern time and the melancholy of history* (Cambridge, MA, and London, 2004)

Fuchs, E., *Henry Thomas Buckle: Geschichtsschreibung und Positivismus in England und Deutschland* (Leipzig, 1994)

Fueter, E., *Geschichte der neueren Historiographie*, 3rd edn (Munich and Berlin, 1936)

Gagnier, R., *Subjectivities: a history of self-representation in Britain 1832–1920* (New York and Oxford, 1991)

Gange, D., and Ledger-Lomas, M. (eds), *Cities of God: the Bible and archaeology in nineteenth-century Britain* (Cambridge, 2013)

Garnett, J., 'Bishop Butler and the *Zeitgeist*: Butler and the development of Christian moral philosophy in Victorian Britain', in Cunliffe, C. (ed.), *Joseph Butler's moral and religious thought: tercentenary essays* (Oxford, 1992), pp. [63]–96

Garnett, J., 'Hastings Rashdall and the renewal of Christian social ethics, c. 1890–1920', in Garnett, J., and Matthew, H. C. G. (eds), *Revival and religion since 1700: essays for John Walsh* (London and Rio Grande, TX, 1993), pp. 297–316

Garnett, J., 'Protestant histories: James Anthony Froude, partisanship and national identity', in Ghosh, P., and Goldman, L. (eds), *Politics and culture in Victorian Britain: essays in memory of Colin Matthew* (Oxford, 2006), pp. [171]–91

Garnett, J., Grimley, M., Whyte, W., Harris, A., and Williams, S. (eds), *Redefining Christian Britain: post-1945 perspectives* (London, 2007)

Geiselmann, J. R., *Lebendiger Glaube aus geheiligter Überlieferung: der Grundgedanke der Theologie Johann Adam Möhlers und der katholischen Tübinger Schule*, 2nd edn (Freiburg im Breisgau, 1966)

Gerrish, B. A., 'Friedrich Schleiermacher', in Smart, N., Clayton, J., Sherry, P., and Katz, S. T. (eds), *Nineteenth-century religious thought in the west* (3 vols, Cambridge, 1985), i, 123–56

Ghosh, P., and Goldman, L. (eds), *Politics and culture in Victorian Britain: essays in memory of Colin Matthew* (Oxford, 2006)

Ghosh, P., *Max Weber and* The Protestant Ethic: *twin histories* (Oxford, 2014)

Gilley, S., 'The papacy', in Gilley, S., and Stanley, B. (eds), *The Cambridge history of Christianity: volume 8: world Christianities, c. 1815–c. 1914* (Cambridge, 2006), pp. 13–29

Girouard, M., *The return to Camelot: chivalry and the English gentleman* (New Haven, CT, and London, 1981)

Goldhill, S., *Who needs Greek? Contests in the cultural history of Hellenism* (Cambridge, 2002)

Goldhill, S., *Victorian culture and classical antiquity: art, opera, fiction, and the proclamation of modernity* (Princeton, NJ, 2011)

Goldhill, S., 'What has Alexandria to do with Jerusalem? Writing the history of the Jews in the nineteenth century', *Historical Journal*, 59:1 (2016), pp. 125–51

Goldman, L., *Science, reform, and politics in Victorian Britain: the Social Science Association 1857–1886* (Cambridge, 2002)

Goldstein, D. S., 'The professionalization of history in Britain in the late nineteenth and early twentieth centuries', *Storia della storiografia*, 3 (1983), pp. 3–27

Gossman, L., *Basel in the age of Burckhardt: a study in unseasonable ideas* (Chicago, IL, 2000)

Graf, W. G. (ed.), *Profile des neuzeitlichen Protestantismus* (2 vols, Gütersloh, 1990–1992)

Graham, G., 'A re-examination of Sir William Hamilton's philosophy', in Graham, G. (ed.), *Scottish philosophy in the nineteenth and twentieth centuries* (Oxford, 2015), pp. [47]–66

Green, A., and Viaene, V. (eds), *Religious internationals in the modern world: globalization and faith communities since 1750* (Basingstoke, 2012)

Green, S. J. D., *Religion in the age of decline: organization and experience in industrial Yorkshire, 1870–1920* (Cambridge, 1996)

Green, S. J. D., 'As if religion mattered: an alternative reading of English intellectual history since c. 1840', in Cowcroft, R., Green, S. J. D., and Whiting, R. (eds), *The philosophy, politics and religion of British democracy: Maurice Cowling and conservatism* (London, 2010)

Green, S. J. D., *The passing of Protestant England: secularization and social change, c. 1920–1960* (Cambridge, 2011)

Grimley, M., *Citizenship, community, and the Church of England: liberal Anglican theories of the state between the wars* (Oxford, 2004)

Grimley, M., 'The religion of Englishness: Puritanism, providentialism and "national character," 1918–1945', *Journal of British Studies*, 46:4 (2007), pp. 884–906

Gross, M. B., *The war against Catholicism: liberalism and the anti-Catholic imagination in nineteenth-century Europe* (Ann Arbor, MI, 2004)

Grosskurth, P., *John Addington Symonds: a biography* (London and Southampton, 1964)

Haig, A. G. L., 'The church, the universities and learning in later Victorian England', *Historical Journal*, 29:1 (1986), pp. 187–201

Harris, H., *The Tübingen School: an historical and theological investigation of the school of F.C. Baur*, new edn (Leicester, 1990)

Harris, J., 'Victorian interpretations of Thomas Hobbes', in Goldman, L., and Ghosh, P. (eds), *Politics and culture in Victorian Britain: essays in memory of Colin Matthew* (Oxford, 2006), pp. [237]–260

Harris, R., *Lourdes: body and spirit in the secular age* (London, 1999)

Hartung, G., 'Eine Schatzkammer des Wissens: Leben und Werk des Gelehrten Eduard Zeller', in Hartung, G. (ed.), *Eduard Zeller: Philosophie- und Wissenschaftsgeschichte im 19. Jahrhundert* (Berlin and New York, 2010), pp. [1]–18

Hawthorn, G., *Enlightenment and despair: a history of sociology* (Cambridge, 1976)

Heimann, M., 'Catholic revivalism in worship and devotion', in Gilley, S., and Stanley, B. (eds), *The Cambridge History of Christianity: volume 8: world Christianities c. 1815–c. 1914* (Cambridge, 2006), pp. 70–83

Hellemans, S., 'How modern is religion in modernity?', in Frishman, J., Otten, W., and Rouwhorst, G. (eds), *Religious identity and the problem of historical foundation: the foundational character of authoritative sources in the history of Christianity and Judaism* (Leiden and Boston, MA, 2004), pp. 76–94

Hesketh, I., *The science of history in Victorian Britain: making the past speak* (London, 2011)

Hesketh, I., *Victorian Jesus: J.R. Seeley, religion, and the cultural significance of anonymity* (Toronto, Buffalo, NY, and London, 2017)

Heyck, T. W., *The transformation of intellectual life in Victorian England* (London, Sydney, and New York, 1982)

Hill, R., *God's architect: Pugin and the building of Romantic Britain* (London, 2007)

Hilton, B., *The age of atonement: the influence of evangelicalism on social and economic thought, 1795–1865* (Oxford, 1988)

Hinchliff, P., *Benjamin Jowett and the Christian religion* (Oxford, 1987)

Hinchliff, P., *God and history: aspects of British theology 1875–1914* (Oxford, 1992)

Hinchliff, P., 'Religious issues, 1870–1914', in Brock, M. G., and Curthoys, M. C. (eds), *The history of the University of Oxford: volume VII: nineteenth-century Oxford, part 2* (Oxford, 2000), pp. [97]–112

Höcker, W., *Der Gesandte Bunsen als Vermittler zwischen Deutschland und England* (Göttingen, 1951)

Holloway, J., *The Victorian sage: studies in argument* (London, 1953)

Holmes, A. R., 'The Scottish reformations and the origin of religious and civil liberty in Britain and Ireland: Presbyterian interpretations, c. 1800–60', in Nockles, P. B., and Westbrook, V. (eds), *Reinventing the Reformation in the nineteenth century: a cultural history, Bulletin of the John Rylands Library*, 90:1 (2014), pp. [135]–53

Hopkins, M., *Nonconformity's romantic generation: evangelical and liberal theologies in Victorian England* (Carlisle, 2004)

Houghton, W. E., *The Victorian frame of mind, 1830–1870* (New Haven, CT, and London, 1957)

Howard, T. A., *Religion and the rise of historicism: W.M.L. de Wette, Jacob Burckhardt, and the theological origins of nineteenth-century historical consciousness* (Cambridge, 2000)

Howard, T. A., *Protestant theology and the making of the modern German university* (Oxford, 2006)

Howsam, L., *Kegan Paul: a Victorian imprint: publishers, books and cultural history* (London and Toronto, 1998)

Howsam, L., *Past into print: the publishing of history in Britain 1850–1950* (London, 2009)

Iggers, G. G., *The German conception of history: the national tradition of historical thought from Herder to the present*, rev. edn (Middletown, CT, 1983)

Iggers, G. G., 'Historicism: the history and meaning of the term', *Journal of the History of Ideas*, 56:1 (1995), pp. 129–52

Inman, D., *The making of modern English theology: God and the academy at Oxford, 1833–1945* (Minneapolis, MN, 2014)

Jann, R., *The art and the science of Victorian history* (Columbus, OH, 1985)

Jenkyns, R., *The Victorians and ancient Greece* (Oxford, 1980)

Johnson, D. A., *The changing shape of English nonconformity 1825–1925* (Oxford, 1999)

Jones, E., *Edmund Burke and the invention of modern Conservatism, 1830–1914: an intellectual history* (Oxford, 2017)

Jones, H. S., *Intellect and character in Victorian England: Mark Pattison and the invention of the don* (Cambridge, 2007)

Josaitis, N. F., *Edwin Hatch and early church order* (Gembloux, 1971)

Kaye, E., *Mansfield College, Oxford: its origin, history, and significance* (Oxford, 1996)

Keefe, J., 'James Frederick Ferrier: the return of Idealism and the rejection of common sense', in Graham, G. (ed.), *Scottish philosophy in the nineteenth and twentieth centuries* (Oxford, 2015), pp. [67]–94

Kelley, D. R., *The descent of ideas: the history of intellectual history* (Aldershot, 2002)

Kenyon, J. P., *The history men: the historical profession in England since the Renaissance* (London, 1983)

Ker, I., *John Henry Newman: a biography* (Oxford, 1988)

Kidd, C., *The forging of races: race and scripture in the Protestant Atlantic world, 1600–2000* (Cambridge, 2006)

Kidd, C., *Union and unionisms: political thought in Scotland, 1500–2000* (Cambridge, 2008)

Kidd, C., *The world of Mr Casaubon: Britain's wars of mythography, 1700–1870* (Cambridge, 2016)

King, B. J., *Newman and the Alexandrian fathers: shaping doctrine in nineteenth-century England* (Oxford, 2009)

Kirby, J., 'An ecclesiastical descent: religion and history in the work of William Stubbs', *Journal of Ecclesiastical History*, 65:1 (2014), pp. 84–110

Kirby, J., *Historians and the Church of England: religion and historical scholarship, 1870–1920* (Oxford, 2016)

Lang, T., *The Victorians and the Stuart heritage: interpretations of a discordant past* (Cambridge, 1995)

Larsen, T., *Friends of religious equality: nonconformist politics in mid-Victorian England* (Woodbridge, 1999)

Larsen, T., *Contested Christianity: the political and social context of Victorian theology* (Waco, TX, 2004)

Larsen, T., *Crisis of doubt: honest faith in nineteenth-century England* (Oxford, 2006)

Larsen, T., *A people of one book: the Bible and the Victorians* (Oxford, 2011)

Larsen, T., and Ledger-Lomas, M. (eds), *The Oxford history of Protestant dissenting traditions: volume III: the nineteenth century* (Oxford, 2017)

Ledger-Lomas, M., '*Lyra Germanica*: German sacred music in mid-Victorian England', *German Historical Institute London Bulletin*, 29:2 (2007), pp. 8–42

Ledger-Lomas, M., 'Mass markets: religion', in McKitterick, D. (ed.), *The Cambridge history of the book in Britain: volume VI: 1830–1914* (Cambridge, 2009), pp. 324–58

Lightman, B., *The origins of agnosticism: Victorian unbelief and the limits of knowledge* (Baltimore, MD, 1987)

Lightman, B., and Dawson, G. (eds), *Victorian scientific naturalism: community, identity, continuity* (Chicago, IL, 2014)

Loewenstein, B., *Der Fortschrittsglaube: Europäisches Geschichtsdenken zwischen Utopie und Ideologie*, 2nd edn (Darmstadt, 2015)

Lossky, N., 'The Oxford Movement and the revival of patristic theology', in Vaiss, P. (ed.), *From Oxford to the people: reconsidering Newman and the Oxford Movement* (Leominster, 1996), pp. 76–82

Macintyre, S., Maiguashca, J., and Pók, A. (eds), *The Oxford history of historical writing: Volume 4: 1800–1945* (Oxford, 2011)

Mander, W., *British Idealism: a history* (Oxford, 2011)

Mandler, P., ' "Race" and "nation" in mid-Victorian thought', in Collini, S., Whatmore, R., and Young, B. (eds), *History, religion, and culture: British intellectual history 1750–1950* (Cambridge, 2000), pp. 224–44

Matthew, H. C. G., 'Noetics, Tractarians, and the reform of the University of Oxford in the nineteenth century', *History of Universities*, 9 (1990), pp. 195–225

Matthew, H. C. G., *Gladstone 1809–1898* (Oxford, 1997)

Matthew, H. C. G., 'Introduction: the United Kingdom and the Victorian century, 1815–1901', in Matthew, H. C. G. (ed.), *The nineteenth century: the British Isles: 1815–1901* (Oxford, 2000), pp. [1]–38

McCartney, D., *W. E. H. Lecky: historian and politician 1838–1903* (Dublin, 1994)

McLeod, H. (ed.), *European religion in the age of great cities 1830–1930* (London and New York, 1995)

McLeod, H. *Religion and the people of Western Europe 1789–1989*, 2nd edn (Oxford, 1997)

McLeod, H. *Secularization in western Europe, 1848–1914* (Basingstoke and London, 2000)

Meijering, E. P., *Theologische Urteile über die Dogmengeschichte: Ritschls Einfluss auf von Harnack* (Leiden, 1978)

Merrill Distad, N., *Guessing at truth: the life of Julius Charles Hare (1795–1855)* (Shepherdstown, WV, 1979)

Mommsen, W. J. (ed.), *Leopold von Ranke und die moderne Geschichtswissenschaft* (Stuttgart, 1988)

Mordaunt Crook, J., *The dilemma of style: architectural ideas from the picturesque to the post-modern* (London, 1987)

Morris, J., 'A social doctrine of the Trinity? A reappraisal of F. D. Maurice on eternal life', *Anglican and Episcopal History*, 69:1 (2000), pp. 73–100

Morris, J., *F. D. Maurice and the crisis of Christian authority* (Oxford, 2005)

Morris, J., 'The spirit of comprehension: examining the Broad Church synthesis in England', *Anglican and Episcopal History*, 75:3 (2006), pp. 423–43

Morris, J., 'Afterword', in Nockles, P. B., and Westbrook, V. (eds), *Reinventing the Reformation in the nineteenth century: a cultural history, Bulletin of the John Rylands Library*, 90:1 (2014), pp. [377]–82

Morris, J., 'Liberalism Protestant and Catholic', in Brown, S. J., Nockles, P. B., and Pereiro, J. (eds), *The Oxford handbook of the Oxford Movement* (Oxford, 2017), pp. [585]–604

Mulsow, M., Häfner, R., Neumann, F. and Zedelmaier, H., *Johann Lorenz Mosheim (1693–1755): Theologie im Spannungsfeld von Philosophie, Philologie, und Geschichte* (Wiesbaden, 1997)

Neill, S., and Wright, T., *The interpretation of the New Testament 1861–1986*, 2nd edn (Oxford, 1988)

Newsome, D., *The parting of friends: the Wilberforces and Henry Manning* (London, 1966)

Newsome, D., *Two classes of men: Platonism and English romantic thought* (London, 1972)

Nimmo, D., 'Learning against religion, learning as religion: Mark Pattison and the "Victorian crisis of faith"', in Robbins, K. (ed.), *Religion and humanism: papers read at the eighteenth summer meeting and the nineteenth winter meeting of the Ecclesiastical History Society* (Oxford, 1981), pp. 311–24

Nisbet, R., *History of the idea of progress* (London, 1980)

Nixon, M., *Samuel Rawson Gardiner and the idea of history* (London, 2011)

Nockles, P. B., *The Oxford Movement in context: Anglican high churchmanship 1760–1857* (Cambridge, 1994)

Nockles, P. B., 'The Reformation revised? The contested reception of the English Reformation in nineteenth-century Protestantism', in Nockles, P. B., and

Westbrook, V. (eds), *Reinventing the Reformation in the nineteenth century: a cultural history, Bulletin of the John Rylands Library*, 90:1 (2014), pp. [231]–56

Nottmeier, C., *Adolf von Harnack und die deutsche Politik 1890–1930: eine biographische Studie zum Verhältnis von Protestantismus, Wissenschaft und Politik* (Tübingen, 2004)

Nowak, K., 'Theologie, Philologie und Geschichte: Adolf von Harnack als Kirchenhistoriker', in Nowak, K., and Oexle, O. G. (eds), *Adolf von Harnack: Theologe, Historiker, Wissenschaftspolitiker* (Göttingen, 2001), pp. 189–228

O'Day, R., *The debate on the English Reformation*, 2nd edn (Manchester and New York, 2014)

Paget, J. C., 'The reception of Baur in Britain', in Bauspiess, M., Landmesser, C., and Lincicum, D. (eds), *Ferdinand Christian Baur und die Geschichte des frühen Christentums* (Tübingen, 2014), pp. [335]–86

Pals, D. L., *The Victorian 'lives' of Jesus* (San Antonio, TX, 1982)

Parker, K. L., 'Tractarian visions of history', in Brown, S. J., Nockles, P. B., and Pereiro, J. (eds), *The Oxford handbook of the Oxford Movement* (Oxford, 2017), pp. [151]–65

Parry, J. P., *The rise and fall of liberal government in Victorian Britain* (New Haven, CT, and London, 1993)

Parry, J. P., 'Nonconformity, clericalism and "Englishness": the United Kingdom', in Clark, C., and Kaiser, W. (eds), *Culture wars: secular-Catholic conflict in nineteenth-century Europe* (Cambridge, 2003), pp. 152–80

Parsons, G., 'Biblical criticism in Victorian Britain: from controversy to acceptance?', in Parsons, G. (ed.), *Religion in Victorian Britain: volume II: controversies* (Manchester and New York, 1988), pp. [238]–57

Patrick, G. A., *F. J. A. Hort, eminent Victorian* (Sheffield, 1988)

Patrick, G. A., *The miners' bishop: Brooke Foss Westcott*, 2nd edn (Peterborough, 2004)

Paz, D. G., *Popular anti-Catholicism in mid-Victorian England* (Stanford, CA, 1992)

Paz, D. G., *Dickens and Barnaby Rudge: anti-Catholicism and Chartism* (Monmouth, 2006)

Penzel, K., (ed.), *Philip Schaff: historian and ambassador of the universal church: selected writings* (Macon, GA, 1991)

Pereiro, J., 'Tradition and development', in Brown, S. J., Nockles, P. B., and Pereiro, J. (eds), *The Oxford handbook of the Oxford Movement* (Oxford, 2017), pp. [201]–15

Pickering, M., *Auguste Comte: an intellectual biography* (3 vols, Cambridge, 1999–2009)

Pocock, J. G. A., *Barbarism and religion* (6 vols, Cambridge, 1999–2016)

Pocock, J. G. A., *Political thought and history: essays on theory and method* (Cambridge, 2009)

Porter, T. M., *Karl Pearson: the scientific life in a statistical age* (Princeton, NJ, and Oxford, 2004)

Preyer, R., 'Bunsen and the Anglo-American community in Rome', in Geldbach, E. (ed.), *Der Gelehrte Diplomat: zum Wirken Christian Carl Josias Bunsens* (Leiden, 1980), pp. 35–44

Purvis, Z., *Theology and the university in nineteenth-century Germany* (Oxford, 2016)

Quantin, J.-L., *The Church of England and Christian antiquity: the construction of a confessional identity in the 17th century* (Oxford, 2009)

Railton, N. M., *No North Sea: the Anglo-German evangelical network in the middle of the nineteenth century* (Leiden, 2000)

Rasmussen, J. D. S., 'The transformation of metaphysics', in Rasmussen, J. D. S., Wolfe, J., and Zachhuber, J. (eds), *The Oxford handbook of nineteenth-century Christian thought* (Oxford, 2017), pp. [11]–34

Reardon, B. M. G., *Religious thought in the Victorian age: a survey from Coleridge to Gore*, 2nd edn (London, 1995)

Rex, R., 'Introduction: the morning star or the sunset of the Reformation?', in Nockles, P. B., and Westbrook, V. (eds), *Reinventing the Reformation in the nineteenth century: a cultural history, Bulletin of the John Rylands Library*, 90:1 (2014), pp. [7]–23

Robbins, K., *Protestant Germany through British eyes: a complex Victorian encounter* (London, 1993)

Rogerson, J. W., *Old Testament criticism in the nineteenth century: England and Germany* (London, 1984)

Roney, J. B., *The inside of history: Jean Henri Merle d'Aubigné and romantic historiography* (Westport, CT, and London, 1996)

Rose, J., *The intellectual life of the British working classes* (New Haven, CT, and London, 2001)

Rowell, G., *Hell and the Victorians: a study of the nineteenth-century controversies concerning eternal punishment and the future life* (Oxford, 1974)

Rössler, M., *Schleiermachers Programm der philosophischen Theologie* (Berlin and New York, 1994)

Rüsen, J., *Konfigurationen des Historismus: Studien zur deutschen Wissenschaftskultur* (Frankfurt am Main, 1993)

Rylance, R., *Victorian psychology and British culture, 1850–1880* (Oxford, 2000)

St Aubyn, G., *A Victorian eminence: the life and works of Henry Thomas Buckle* (London, 1958)

Samuel, R., 'The discovery of Puritanism, 1820–1914: a preliminary sketch', in Garnett, J., and Matthew, H. C. G. (eds), *Revival and religion since 1700: essays for John Walsh* (London and Rio Grande, TX, 1993), pp. 201–47

Schwartz, L., *Infidel feminism: secularism, religion and women's emancipation, England 1830–1914* (Manchester and New York, 2013)

Secord, J. A., *Victorian sensation: the extraordinary publication, reception, and secret authorship of* Vestiges of the Natural History of Creation (Chicago, IL, and London, 2000)

Selge, K.-V., 'August Neander – ein getaufter Hamburger Jude der Emanzipations- und Restaurationszeit als erster Berlin Kirchenhistoriker', in Beiser, G., and Gestrich, C. (eds), *450 Jahre evangelische Theologie in Berlin* (Göttingen, 1989), pp. [233]–76

Sell, A. P. F., *Defending and declaring the faith: some Scottish examples 1860–1920* (Exeter, 1987)

Skinner, S. A., *Tractarians and the 'Condition of England': the social and political thought of the Oxford Movement* (Oxford, 2004)

Skinner, S. A., '"A triumph of the rich": Tractarians and the Reformation', in Nockles, P. B., and Westbrook, V. (eds), *Reinventing the Reformation in the nineteenth century: a cultural history, Bulletin of the John Rylands Library*, 90:1 (2014), pp. [69]–91

Slee, P. R. H., *Learning and a liberal education: the study of modern history in the universities of Oxford, Cambridge and Manchester, 1800–1914* (Manchester, 1986)

Smart, N., Clayton, J., Sherry, P., and Katz, S., 'Editorial introduction', to Smart, N., Clayton, J., Sherry, P., and Katz, S. (eds), *Nineteenth-century religious thought in the west* (3 vols, Cambridge, 1985), i, 1–15

Smith, R. J., *The Gothic bequest: medieval institutions in British thought, 1688–1863* (Cambridge, 1987)

Smyth, C., *Dean Milman (1791–1868): the first rector of St Margaret's, Westminster, afterwards Dean of St Paul's* (London, 1949)

Spence, M., 'The renewal of time and space: the missing element of discussions about nineteenth-century premillennialism', *Journal of Ecclesiastical History*, 63:1 (2012), pp. 81–101

Spence, M., Heaven on earth: reimagining time and eternity in nineteenth-century British evangelicalism (Eugene, OR, 2015)

Stephan, H., and Schmidt, M., *Geschichte der evangelischen Theologie in Deutschland seit dem Idealismus*, 3rd edn (Berlin and New York, 1973)

Strachey, L., *Portraits in miniature and other essays* (London, 1931)

Stray, C. (ed.), *Classics in 19th and 20th-century Cambridge: curriculum, culture and community* (Cambridge, 1999)

Strong, R. (ed.), *The Oxford history of Anglicanism: volume III: partisan Anglicanism and its global expansion, 1829–c.1914* (Oxford, 2017)

Stuchtey, B., and Wende, P. (eds), *British and German historiography, 1750–1950: traditions, perceptions, and transfers* (Oxford, 2000)

Stuchtey, B., *W.E.H. Lecky (1838–1903): historisches Denken und politisches Urteilen eines anglo-irischen Gelehrten* (Göttingen and Zurich, 1997)

Symondson, A. (ed.), *The Victorian crisis of faith* (London, 1970)

Tessitore, F., 'Rankes "Lutherfragment" und die Idee der Universalgeschichte', in Mommsen, W. J. (ed.), *Leopold von Ranke und die moderne Geschichtswissenschaft* (Stuttgart, 1988), pp. 7–36

Thompson, D. M., *Cambridge theology in the nineteenth century: enquiry, controversy and truth* (Aldershot, 2008)

Thomson, M., *Psychological subjects: identity, culture, and health in twentieth-century Britain* (Oxford, 2006)

Toews, J. E., *Becoming historical: cultural Reformation and public memory in early nineteenth-century Berlin* (Cambridge, 2004)

Toon, P., *Evangelical theology 1833–1856: a response to Tractarianism* (London, 1979)

Treloar, G. R., *Lightfoot the historian: the nature and role of history in the life and thought of J.B. Lightfoot (1828–1889) as churchman and scholar* (Tübingen, 1998)

Trevor-Roper, H. R., 'From deism to history: Conyers Middleton', in his *History and the Enlightenment*, ed. Robertson, J. (New Haven, CT, and London, 2010), pp. [71]–119

Trevor-Roper, H. R., 'Jacob Burckhardt', in his *History and the Enlightenment*, ed. Robertson, J. (New Haven, CT, and London, 2010), pp. [246]–65

Turner, F. M., *Between science and religion: the reaction to scientific naturalism in late Victorian England* (New Haven, CT, and London, 1974)

Turner, F. M., *John Henry Newman: the challenge to evangelical religion* (New Haven, CT, and London, 2002)

Vance, N., *The Victorians and ancient Rome* (Oxford and Cambridge, MA, 1997)

Vogeler, M. S., *Frederic Harrison: the vocations of a Positivist* (Oxford, 1994)

Waller, R., 'James Martineau: the development of his religious thought', in Smith, B. (ed.), *Truth, liberty, religion: essays celebrating two hundred years of Manchester College* (Oxford, 1986), pp. 227–64

Walsh, J. D., 'Joseph Milner's Evangelical Church History', *Journal of Ecclesiastical History*, 10 (1959), pp. 174–87

Watt, H., *New College Edinburgh: a centenary history* (Edinburgh and London, 1946)

Wellings, M., *Evangelicals embattled: responses of evangelicals in the Church of England to ritualism, Darwinism and theological liberalism 1890–1930* (Carlisle, 2003)

Wheeler, M., *The old enemies: Catholic and Protestant in nineteenth-century English culture* (Cambridge, 2006)

Wheeler, M., *St John and the Victorians* (Cambridge, 2012)

Whyte, W., *Redbrick: a social and architectural history of Britain's civic universities* (Oxford, 2015)

Whyte, W., *Unlocking the church: the lost secrets of Victorian sacred space* (Oxford, 2017)

Wiles, M., *Archetypal heresy: Arianism through the centuries* (Oxford, 1996)

Winch, D., *Wealth and life: essays on the intellectual history of political economy in Britain, 1848–1914* (Cambridge, 2009)

Winkler, J., *Der Kirchenhistoriker Jean Henri Merle d'Aubigné* (Zurich, 1968)

Witheridge, J., *Excellent Dr Stanley: the life of Dean Stanley of Westminster* (Norwich, 2013)

Wittkau-Horgby, A., *Historismus: zur Geschichte des Begriffs und des Problems* (Göttingen, 1992)

Wolf, H., Burkard, D., and Muhlack, U., *Rankes 'Päpste' auf dem Index: Dogma und Historie im Widerstreit* (Paderborn, 2003)

Wolffe, J., *The Protestant crusade in Great Britain 1829–1860* (Oxford, 1991)

Wolffe, J., 'Anglicanism, Presbyterianism and the religious identities of the United Kingdom', in Gilley, S. and Stanley, B. (eds), *The Cambridge History of Christianity: volume 8: world Christianities c. 1815–c. 1914* (Cambridge, 2006), pp. 301–22

Wolffe, J., 'The commemoration of the Reformation and mid-nineteenth-century evangelical identity', in Nockles, P. B., and Westbrook, V. (eds), *Reinventing the Reformation in the nineteenth century: a cultural history*, *Bulletin of the John Rylands Library*, 90:1 (2014), pp. [49]–68

Wood, I., *The modern origins of the early middle ages* (Oxford, 2013)

Woodward, W. R., *Hermann Lotze: an intellectual biography* (Cambridge, 2015)

Worden, B., 'Thomas Carlyle and Oliver Cromwell', *Proceedings of the British Academy*, 105 (2000), pp. 131–70

Worden, B., 'The Victorians and Oliver Cromwell', in Collini, S., Whatmore, R., and Young, B. (eds), *History, religion and culture: British intellectual history 1750–1950* (Cambridge, 2000), pp. 112–35

Wright, D. F., ' "From a quarter so totally unexpected": translation of the Early Church Fathers in Victorian Scotland', *Records of the Scottish Church History Society*, 30 (2000), pp. 124–69

Wright, T. R., *The religion of humanity: the impact of Comtean Positivism on Victorian Britain* (Cambridge, 1986)

Young, B., 'Knock-kneed giants: Victorian representations of eighteenth-century thought', in Garnett, J., and Matthew, H. C. G. (eds), *Revival and religion since 1700: essays for John Walsh* (London and Rio Grande, TX,1993), pp. 79–93

Young, B., *Religion and Enlightenment in eighteenth-century England: theological debate from Locke to Burke* (Oxford, 1998)

Young, B., *The Victorian eighteenth century: an intellectual history* (Oxford, 2007)

Young, B., 'History', in Bevir, M. (ed.), *Historicism and the human sciences in Victorian Britain* (Cambridge, 2017), pp. 154–185

Young, G. M., *Victorian England: portrait of an age* (London, 1936)

Young, R. M., *Darwin's metaphor: nature's place in Victorian culture* (Cambridge, 1985)

Zachhuber, J., *Theology as science in nineteenth-century Germany: from F. C. Baur to Ernst Troeltsch* (Oxford, 2013)

Zachhuber, J., 'The historical turn', in Rasmussen, J. D. S., Wolfe, J., and Zachhuber, J. (eds), *The Oxford handbook of nineteenth-century Christian thought* (Oxford, 2017), pp. [53]–71

Zahl, S., 'Experience', in Rasmussen, J. D. S., Wolfe, J., and Zachhuber, J. (eds), *The Oxford handbook of nineteenth-century Christian thought* (Oxford, 2017), pp. [177]–95

Index